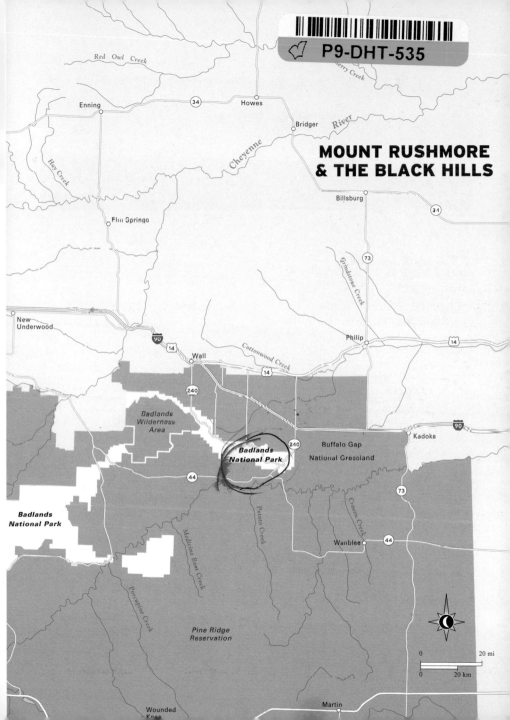

MOUNT RUSHMORE
& THE BLACK HILLS

Contents

Discover Mount Rushmore & the Black Hills

Carved into the side of a mountain, four U.S. presidents gaze placidly over the hills, over the pine forest and into the distance of the vast plains to the south. This is Mount Rushmore, one of America's most recognizable monuments. Admire its scope, scale, and artistry of the monument; then turn around and discover the breathtaking beauty of the Black Hills.

I am a road warrior by nature and it was on such a journey, drifting east across the plains of Colorado and north through the sandhills of Nebraska, that I crossed the state line into South Dakota for the first time. I was looking to visit a place I'd never been. I was looking for gas. What I found was a landscape that captured my heart.

The change from plains to hills is a subtle one. Miles of flatland transform into rolling swells of sparsely covered sand. One sharp incline and the view to the south is suddenly vast, empty, and as calming as staring out to sea. To the north, the soft hills are covered in dark ponderosa pine, the canyons are red, and the sky is an azure blue. This edge – this meeting of two worlds, the best of everything – is what the hills are all about. Farmland turns into ranchland here. Warm springs flow into cold rivers. Eastern birds and western birds mingle. Just 100 miles from north to south, and 65 miles from east to west, this "Island in the Plains" offers a remarkable diversity of landscape, wildlife, history, and recreation.

The broad western horizons and plains vistas create a space where storms are visible for miles before they arrive. Lightning streaks sideways across the sky and rain falls but never reaches the earth. Electric summer afternoon clouds crack open and pour white beads of hail over the grasslands, striking with just enough power to release the prairie scent of sage.

This is not a harsh country, though. The Black Hills are old and round and soft. Home to the American bison, this is a land sacred to Native Americans. Its history is steeped in gold, greed, gambling, gunfights, and broken treaties. It is a land of homesteading and healing waters.

Bestowed with great natural beauty, it has always been a beloved road trip destination. Remnants of the 1950s' love affair with the automobile remain. Look for old hotels and diners that sport neon signs with names like the Rocket Motel. Roadside attractions abound. Pan for gold, visit a vineyard, pet wild burros, or watch a rodeo. Bike, boat, ride a horse, or explore a cave. Hike the highest peak in North America east of the Rockies, or relax in the warm springs of a spa town. It's all here.

Planning Your Trip

▶ WHERE TO GO

Mount Rushmore and the Central Hills

Mount Rushmore is a symbol of American exploration and expansion, a testimony to the visionary dreams of our founding fathers, and a tribute to individual effort and collective achievement. It's also at the heart of local tourism. Served by urban and transportation center Rapid City and supported by the old mining communities of Hill City and Keystone, this mountainous region is the hub of a Black Hills visit.

The Southern Hills

It's all about wildlife, warm water, and history in the soft rolling landscape of the Southern Hills. Custer State Park provides the best wildlife-viewing opportunities in the state, with accommodations that range from rustic to luxurious. Hot Springs originated as a place to travel to "take the cure" in the warm mineral springs that gave the town its name. It's also home to beautiful sandstone buildings and the Mammoth Site. Wind Cave and Jewel Cave are both in this region, and Custer,

IF YOU HAVE . . .

Harney Peak Tower is at the highest point in the Black Hills.

- **THREE DAYS:** Spend a day visiting Mount Rushmore, the Needles Highway, and Sylvan Lake. Add a day to hike Harney Peak, followed by a trip to Hill City to enjoy the boardwalk shops and art galleries. The best attractions include Reptile Gardens and Bear Country U.S.A. On the third day, Prairie Edge is a must see in Rapid City, and the Journey Museum provides the best overall introduction to Native American culture and to the history and geology of the region.

- **FIVE DAYS:** Add a visit to Crazy Horse Mountain and Custer State Park. Drive the Wildlife Loop, traveling from the State Game Lodge south. Continue south to Wind Cave for a cave tour, and visit the Mammoth Site in Hot Springs.

- **SEVEN DAYS:** Add a day trip to Badlands National Park and a day trip to Deadwood.

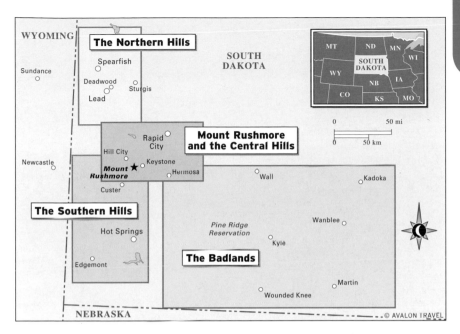

where gold was first discovered in the hills, provides easy access to all of the Southern Hills attractions, including the ongoing mountain carving of Crazy Horse, which honors the famous chief and the Lakota people who hold the Black Hills sacred.

The Northern Hills

Outdoor beauty and recreational opportunities grace every corner of the hills, and the northern region is no exception. Waterfalls, hiking, and biking trails abound in the Spearfish Canyon Scenic Byway, which connects the old mining communities of Spearfish and Lead. But the definition of wildlife is a little more expansive here. Once the stomping grounds of the likes of Wild Bill Hickok and Calamity Jane, this is a place where the raucous spirit of the Wild West flourishes. Gambling, gunfights, and rodeos set the ever active stage in Deadwood, and the roaring bikes of the

Sturgis Motorcycle Rally guarantee that the lights are always on in the Northern Hills.

The Badlands

Set in the midst of the vast plains, a wall of tall spires, flat-topped grassy buttes, and craggy eroding cliffs present an otherworldly landscape to visitors. Some 70 million years of environmental change are exposed to the eye, a product of the relentless and creative forces of wind and water. Each layer of time is different in color. When the sun is just right, the landscape of Badlands National Park turns into a wonderland of pastel yellow, dusty pink, burgundy, grey, green, and black. The town of Wall is the northern gateway to the park and home to Wall Drug, the ultimate roadside attraction. The South Unit of the park is located on the Pine Ridge Reservation, home to the Oglala Lakota people. The reservation offers recreational opportunities, art galleries, and historic sites for visitors interested in Lakota culture.

Sturgis Motorcycle Rally

▶ WHEN TO GO

National monuments and national parks (including Mount Rushmore) are open year-round. In old-fashioned vacation style, the Black Hills of South Dakota are fully open and ready for business between Memorial Day and Labor Day, which constitutes the high season for tourism. In the "shoulder season" (May 1–Memorial Day and Labor Day–mid-Oct.), most attractions are open and there is still plenty to do. If the purpose of your visit is primarily scenic and recreational in nature, there are hotels open year-round in every region.

The weather in the hills is unpredictable, but spring is the season during which cooler temperatures and rain are most likely. It is also the season when the region is at its greenest. Early summer tends to be warm and dry, and brief afternoon thundershowers are not uncommon. Mid- and late summer can be anywhere from comfortable to extremely hot,

and temperatures vary greatly between the warmer Southern Hills and the cooler mountain towns. For travelers not tied to a school schedule, early fall can be the best season to travel, with warm days and cool nights. It is my favorite season here.

The Sturgis Motorcycle Rally begins on the first Saturday in August, and lasts a week. During the rally, hundreds of thousands of bikers flock to the hills and fill the campgrounds and hotels. Traffic congestion in the parks and on the roads is common during the rally and room rates are at their highest. For some, it's the perfect week to come, but if the constant roar of motorcycles is not for you, it might be a week to avoid. If you've come to the hills inadvertently during the rally, rooms are generally available and the environment is a little quieter in the Southern Hills, particularly in Hot Springs.

► BEFORE YOU GO

It is always possible to find rooms in the hills, with the probable exception of the Northern Hills during the Sturgis Motorcycle Rally. If you desire to stay in the Custer State Park cabins or lodges during peak summer season, however, reservations are recommended—particularly if your heart is set on a specific lodge.

Reservations are also recommended if you are traveling with children who might be interested in digging for mammoth bones. The programs at the Mammoth Site in Hot Springs are very popular.

It's a good idea to check the websites of the governmental agencies that manage the public lands in the Black Hills. The National Park Service, the U.S. Forest Service, and the South Dakota Department of Game, Fish and Parks each sponsor summer activities and generally post information on summer happenings beginning in late spring. If you happen to be here during a full moon, for example, you won't want to miss a midnight hike in the Badlands.

Getting around the hills is not difficult, but if you didn't arrive by car, and don't mind driving, plan on renting one. There are many tour companies that provide day trips into each region of the hills, but more options are available if you drive. There are many small airports in the region, but the only commercial airport is in Rapid City.

What to Take

Be prepared for unpredictable weather in the Black Hills. While summers are generally pleasant and dry, temperatures can soar to over 100°F by afternoon and fall to 50°F in the evening. Caves maintain a temperature hovering in the mid-50s no matter the outside temperature. Wind on the plains can be brisk and strong. Given these weather possibilities, be sure to think in layers when you pack. Cotton T-shirts work well on hot afternoons, and can be layered with a long-sleeved shirt in the evening. Bring a windbreaker and pack a sweatshirt for cave tours and cool evenings. Layers are also key to comfortable hiking. Be prepared for afternoon thundershowers and bring raingear. Even the shortest of hikes can be hard on the feet, and this is especially true in the Badlands. Bring sturdy, ankle-supporting footgear. Another must is sunscreen and sunglasses. And don't forget binoculars. While a bathing suit might seem out of place in this landlocked region, many lodgings feature outdoor hot tubs, a very relaxing way to end a day, and there are many small lakes for swimming.

Dress is casual everywhere in the hills. You can dress up if you like, particularly in the finer restaurants, but jeans are welcome most everywhere.

Pactola Reservoir

Explore Mount Rushmore & the Black Hills

► THE BEST OF THE BLACK HILLS

The area of the Black Hills is small, but the variety of experiences offered to visitors in this compact region is outstanding: stunning scenic beauty, a fascinating Native American and Western history, and fabulous family roadside attractions. From the longest caves to the largest mountain carvings, from wildlife-viewing in Custer State Park to the wildlife of historic Deadwood, there really is something for everyone.

Day 1: Mount Rushmore

Rapid City makes a good starting point for your exploration of the region. Start your day with breakfast at Tally's Silver Spoon downtown and then head for the hills. The most scenic way to approach Mount Rushmore is Iron Mountain Road (U.S. 16A). Head south on Highway 79 and take a right on Highway 36, just past Hermosa. About nine miles in, take a right and head north on Iron Mountain Road just as you enter Custer State Park. Bring carrots or apples to feed the wild burros on the way, and wind through the narrow tunnels that frame the monument.

Spend the morning and early afternoon at Mount Rushmore and then head down the mountain toward Hill City. Stroll the compact boardwalk of downtown Hill City, visit the art galleries and The Museum at Black Hills Institute, and then head back to Rapid City.

Spend your evening enjoying Rapid City. Start at Prairie Edge Trading Company and

Main Street Square in Rapid City

Sylvan Lake

Galleries, then enjoy an evening micro-brew and dinner next door at the Firehouse Brewing Company. If a quiet dinner is your preference, stop in at the Wine Cellar. Stay at the Hotel Alex Johnson or the Adoba Eco Hotel in downtown Rapid.

Day 2: Badlands National Park

Today is a day of contrasts with a trip to Badlands National Park and Wall Drug. Head west on I-90 and take exit 110 at the town of Wall. Stop in for a quick visit to Wall Drug to pick up some of its freshly made cake donuts. (If it is off-season, stop by Subway to pack a picnic lunch.) Drive south to the main entrance of Badlands National Park. Meander the Loop Road, take the short Fossil Exhibit Trail, and stop at the Ben Reifel Visitor Center at the southern end of the park. If you didn't bring food, lunch is available at the Cedar Pass Lodge. Just north of the visitor center are two easy hiking trails, the Door Trail and the Window Trail, which are great for stretching the legs. The Notch Trail is a more strenuous alternative. Continue north on Highway 240, to return to I-90 and head east back to Wall. (You will pass the Minuteman Missile National Historic Site, home of the Launch Facility Delta-09, a good stop for military history enthusiasts.) Spend a little more time at Wall Drug. The kids will love the backyard and you will love the bookstore, the artwork, and the hot roast beef sandwich. Head back to Rapid City on I-90.

Day 3: Hot Springs

It's time to shift your base camp into the hills. Head south on Highway 79 to historic Hot Springs. If you love horses, take a tour of the Black Hills Wild Horse Sanctuary. Visit the Mammoth Site, and then have lunch at Wooly's Mammoth Grill. Walk the Freedom Trail beside Fall River and enjoy the town's beautiful sandstone architecture. Visit the Pioneer Museum, treat yourself to a spa experience at the Red Rock River Resort, or bring your swimsuits and take a plunge into the warm mineral waters at Evans Plunge. Head north on U.S. 385 to Wind Cave National Park for a cave tour. Return to Hot Springs for the evening. Plan to stay at the Historic Log Cabin Inn for a rustic experience, or stay at the FlatIron Historic Sandstone Inn for elegance. For dinner, join the local crowd at Dale's Family Restaurant.

Day 4: Custer State Park

Head out as early as you can today and plan to eat breakfast at the Bluebell Lodge in Custer State Park. To get there, drive north on U.S. 385 and take a right (north) on Highway 87. This will bring you right to Bluebell Lodge. After breakfast, backtrack on Highway 87 for a couple of miles to the park's ranger station entrance and enjoy the scenic Wildlife Loop. Bring your binoculars, because you're likely to see bison, prairie dogs, pronghorns, and another herd of wild burros. (Stock up on carrots and apples again.)

At the end of the loop, head west on U.S. 16A and stop at the State Game Lodge for a light snack or lunch. Continue west on U.S. 16A through Custer, stopping at Jewel Cave, named for the sparkling calcite crystal walls. This is the prettiest cave in the hills.

Return to Custer for the night. Plan to stay at the hillside cabins of the Shady Rest Motel or at the 1950s' themed Rocket Motel downtown. Have dinner at the Sage Creek Grille.

Day 5: Scenic Drive to Crazy Horse Memorial

After breakfast at Baker's Bakery, pack up the car and head back into Custer State Park for the most beautiful drive in the Black Hills. Heading east on U.S. 16A, turn north on Highway 87. (Be careful as it is easy to get turned around in the park.) This will become the Needles Highway. This scenic byway loops around towering granite spires and formations, through a very tight tunnel, and finishes at Sylvan Lake. Avid hikers

Needles Highway in the Black Hills

THE GREAT OUTDOORS

rock climbing on granite spires

The Black Hills offers inspiring experiences for both the quietly contemplative and the wildly adventuresome. Here are some of the best:

SURVIVAL OF THE FITTEST

- **Take the Wild Cave Tour at Wind Cave National Park:** This four-hour tour will have you crawling through narrow passages as you learn the basics of safe caving and see the deeper sections of one of the longest caves in the world. Hard hats, kneepads, and lights are provided by the park. Heavy gloves and study boots are required, and old clothes are recommended.

- **Go rock climbing in Custer State Park:** Call Sylvan Rocks Climbing School & Guide Service and have the adventure of your life. Learn to climb in the Needles of Custer State Park or take the best routes with the most knowledgeable climbers in the hills.

- **Bike the Mickelson Trail:** The Mickelson Trail offers over 100 miles of rails-to-trails riding from Edgemont to Deadwood. There are several companies that will shuttle you to and from any trailhead along the way.

- **Backpack the Sage Creek Wilderness Area:** Bring plenty of water and sunscreen

and spend a few days in the remote and otherworldly Badlands National Park. Camping is free but facilities are primitive.

- **Hike the Centennial Trail:** This 111-mile trail highlights the diversity of the Black Hills and runs from Bear Butte in the north through Wind Cave in the south. (Many, but not all, sections of the trail are bike accessible, as well.)

- **Run the Lean Horse Marathon:** Come to the hills in late August and test your endurance. Originating in Hot Springs, this 100-mile, half-hundred, or 50K race skirts Fall River in Hot Springs and then heads out to the Mickelson Trail. Experience the exhilaration of accomplishment and, after you recover, enjoy a runner's high for months.

QUIET PLACES

- **Balloon the Black Hills:** Drift over Custer State Park in the open-air basket of a colorful balloon. Bring a new perspective to your sightseeing as you view herds of bison and pronghorns roaming the park from a bird's-eye view.

- **Go fly-fishing:** Get out of the car and take some time to fish Spearfish Canyon or Rapid Creek south of Pactola Reservoir. You can rent equipment and explore on your own, or take a guided tour. Streams are stocked with brown, rainbow, and brook trout.

- **Golf:** Play the Southern Hills Municipal Golf Course just west of Hot Springs. There are stunning views from every tee of the award-winning front nine.

- **Hike up Crow Peak:** Just south of Spearfish, a hike to the top of Crow Peak will reward you with a gorgeous 360-degree view of the Black Hills of South Dakota and Wyoming.

- **Kayak, canoe, or pontoon:** Get away from the crowds at one of the most remote lakes in the hills. Check out Angostura Recreation Area in the south, or rent a pontoon boat on Pactola Reservoir in the Central Hills and dive into the water when the sun gets too warm.

Mammoth Site, Hot Springs

should note that the best trailhead to Harney Peak is located here. For everyone else, a walk around the lake is a nice alternative. Have a casual poolside lunch or, better yet, walk up to Sylvan Lake Lodge for lunch on the deck overlooking the lake and the granite spires of the Needles formation.

After leaving the lake area, continue north on Highway 87 to the junction with U.S. 385. Head south a short distance to Crazy Horse Memorial. This is the only large, on-going mountain carving project in the world. Watch the video history there and shop for Native American arts and jewelry. After your visit, turn north on U.S. 385 and head to Hill City. Enjoy the downtown boardwalk, dine at Desperados Cowboy Restaurant, and stay at the Lantern Inn.

Day 6: Keystone, Hill City, and Bear Country U.S.A.

Today will be a little easier with a little less driving. Have breakfast at the Slate Creek Grille this morning and take the early 1880 Train to Keystone. Walk the boardwalk in Keystone, buy some taffy, and enjoy some shopping, but plan on lunch at the Alpine Inn back in Hill City. After lunch, take U.S. 385 north and stop at the Prairie Berry Winery for some wine tasting. As you head back toward Rapid City, be sure to stop at Bear Country U.S.A. on your way. Plan to stay at the Big Sky Lodge and have dinner at The Colonial House Restaurant & Bar.

Day 7: Spearfish, Lead, and Deadwood

Today, we visit the Northern Hills. Have breakfast at the Colonial House and then continue north to I-90. Head west on I-90 to Spearfish. Take the 14A exit and travel the Spearfish Canyon Scenic Byway. Stretch your legs and enjoy the short hike to Roughlock Falls (near the Spearfish Canyon Lodge) and to Spearfish Falls. Save lunch for Cheyenne Crossing. Head into Lead for a surface tour of the Homestake Mine, then continue on to Deadwood. Take the trolley around town, then visit the Mount Moriah Cemetery, where the graves of Wild Bill Hickok and Calamity Jane are located. Try a hand of blackjack, then enjoy a casual dinner at one of the buffets—or fine dining at the Deadwood Social Club at Saloon No. 10 or at Jake's at the Midnight Star. Stay the night or return to Rapid City via the interstate.

▶ FAMILY FUN

The Black Hills are extremely family-friendly with attractions like Bear Country U.S.A., Reptile Gardens, Evans Plunge, Wall Drug, and the Mammoth Site.

Traveling with children can add a lot of fun to a vacation. With energy to burn, kids encourage us all to take a few more hikes, play mini golf, power a paddleboat, or slide down a mountainside.

Day 1: Bear Country U.S.A., Mount Rushmore, and Keystone

Leave Rapid City heading south on U.S. 16, also known as Mount Rushmore Road. This is road trip heaven for families with children. Stop first at Bear Country U.S.A. Do the driving tour around the park-like setting and be sure to visit babyland there. Younger children will also enjoy a stop at Old MacDonald's Petting Farm, just down the road from Bear Country.

Continue on to Mount Rushmore National Memorial. Visit the Lincoln Borglum Visitor Center, check out the Sculptor's Studio and enjoy the ranger talk, and then hike The Presidential Trail to the base of the mountain.

Head to Keystone for some creamy gourmet saltwater taffy from the Rushmore Mountain Taffy Shop, take a ride on the Rushmore Tramway, and zoom down the

a resident of Bear Country U.S.A.

bison

PAHA SAPA: SACRED LAND

Native American heritage is celebrated at powwows and other events throughout South Dakota.

For thousands of years, before mountain men, before Custer, before gold, and before Europeans made their way west, Native Americans called Paha Sapa (the Black Hills) their sacred land. Celebrate the history, culture, and ongoing achievement of the people who first called this region home.

- **Sioux History Collection at the Journey Museum:** Interactive exhibits and recordings provide an oral history and storytelling approach to the last 200 years of Lakota history.

- **Prairie Edge Trading Company and Galleries:** Find the best in Native American art, crafts, beadwork, and music in this stunning facility.

- **Tatanka: Story of the Bison:** A dramatic sculpture of 14 life-sized bison, cascading over a cliff, pursued by three Native American hunters, marks the entrance of Tatanka. Interactive displays and Native American interpreters demonstrate how the Lakota people depended upon the bison for food, clothing, and shelter. Learn the history of this magnificent plains animal and explore its relationship to Native American culture.

- **Crazy Horse Memorial:** Lakota Chief Henry Standing Bear and sculptor Korczak Ziolkowski reached an agreement in June 1948 to carve a monument in the sacred Black Hills to show white people that Native Americans had great leaders, too. Crazy Horse, a Lakota leader who never signed a treaty with Washington DC, was selected for the honor and the Memorial began. Today the complex includes a museum and a cultural center that hosts native artisans during the summer.

- **Art Galleries:** Look for Native American art at galleries throughout the hills. Visit the Warrior's Work & Ben West Gallery and the Sandy Swallow Gallery in Hill City, and the Heritage Center at Red Cloud Indian School on the Pine Ridge Reservation.

- **Powwows:** Native American tribes gather from across the country to celebrate their cultural traditions at powwows, held throughout the region all summer long. Enjoy the flash of color and movement that is the grand entry. Listen to the drums and watch the fancy, jingle, grass, and traditional dances. Taste the best Indian tacos (Indian fry bread with taco toppings).

President's Slide. Have a nice dinner at the Ruby House and spend the night at the Powder House Lodge.

Spend the night at the Bavarian Inn, just north of Custer, where a great dinner awaits and a pool is available for the kids.

Day 2: Needles Highway and Sylvan Lake

Pack your bags and head back in the direction of Mount Rushmore, but take a left before you get to the monument on U.S. 16A, also known as Iron Mountain Road, a twisting, turning, tunnel-filled scenic drive that heads toward Custer State Park. (Stay on U.S. 16A; do not head toward Mount Rushmore on Highway 244.) Keep an eye out for County Road 753 (Black Hills Playhouse Rd.). This road will enter Custer State Park and join up with Highway 87, which is Needles Highway. These are two of the most scenic byways in the state.

Head north on Needles Highway to Sylvan Lake. Hike around the lake and send the kids out in paddleboats. Have a picnic lunch at the lake or treat yourself to lunch at Sylvan Lake Lodge. Take Highway 89 south to Custer.

Day 3: Custer State Park and Hot Springs

Get an early breakfast at the Cattlemen's and head into Custer State Park via Mount Rushmore Road. Aim for the Wildlife Loop road just past the Game Lodge off of U.S. 16A. Traveling this road is most rewarding early in the day. Stop to let the kids feed the wild burros (keeping a watchful eye on their fingers!). At the end of the loop, drive south on Highway 87 to Wind Cave National Park for a cave tour. After the tour, continue on to Hot Springs on U.S. 385 south and stop at Evans Plunge. Kids will enjoy the spring-fed pool, as well as the water slide and the rings. Stay at the Budget Host Hills Inn, and play mini golf at the Putt-4-Fun next door. In the evening, take a walk down the Freedom Trail and look for ducks.

Black Hills Wild Horse Sanctuary, near Hot Springs

Day 4: Mammoth Site, Jewel Cave, and Crazy Horse

Start the day with a visit to the Mammoth Site. (If the kids are interested in digging for mammoth bones, make reservations in advance for the Junior Paleontology program.) Drive north to Custer on U.S. 385 and plan on visiting Jewel Cave National Monument. Have lunch in town and then continue north on U.S. 385 to enjoy a horseback ride with the Rockin' R outfit. Crazy Horse Memorial is just a couple of miles up the highway from there. Make sure to see the video and take a piece of the rock that was blasted off the mountain home for a souvenir. Continue on, and plan to spend the night in Hill City at the Lantern Inn.

Day 5: 1880 Train to Keystone

It's train time! Enjoy breakfast on the deck of the Slate Creek Grill and then head to the 1880 Train for a round-trip ride to Keystone and back. There's plenty of time to relax and enjoy the scenery as the steam train huffs up the hills and through the canyons. Little ones enjoy waving at the folks at the many train crossings. After the ride, it's time to head back to Rapid City. Head north on U.S. 385 and then follow the signs to Rapid City on U.S. 16. Once on U.S. 16, stop at the Cosmos Mystery Area, a quick but fun roadside attraction. Spend the rest of the afternoon at the fabulous Reptile Gardens, where kids can meet 100-year-old giant tortoises. Interactive demonstrations about raptors, crocodiles, and snakes are offered all day. Continue your journey back to Rapid City and spend the night at Big Sky Lodge.

Day 6: Badlands National Park and Wall Drug

Now is the time to visit an entirely different ecological niche. Travel east on Highway 44 from Rapid City until you come to the southern entrance of Badlands National Park. Stop at the Ben Reifel Visitor Center to get oriented and to check the daily activities. Note times and locations for ranger-guided tours and the Junior Ranger program. Hike the Door Trail and the Window Trail, and then head north on the Badlands Loop Road. Try to time it so that you can participate in a ranger-guided tour at the Fossil Exhibit Trail. Head out of the park into the town of Wall and visit Wall Drug—a must for the kids. Take pictures of them as one of the Mount Rushmore heads or saddled on top of a jackalope. Head back to Rapid City on I-90.

Day 7: Rapid City

Take it relatively easy today. Choose either the Journey Museum; Storybook Island, a charming free attraction; or Dinosaur Park, where gigantic dinosaurs overlook the city. Spend some time at Prairie Edge Trading Company and Galleries downtown and enjoy the dancing waters at Main Street Square across the street.

GETTING AWAY FROM IT ALL

Cascade Falls, south of Hot Springs

Looking for the road less traveled? Enjoy wilderness and solitude? There are hidden places and great campgrounds in every region of the hills.

THE CENTRAL HILLS

- **Horsethief Lake Campground:** The closest campground to Mount Rushmore, this primitive campground is not off the beaten path, but feels like it. Run by the Black Hills National Forest, it surrounds a 10-acre lake stocked with rainbow trout and perch.

THE SOUTHERN HILLS

- **French Creek Natural Area:** This area of Custer State Park has trails marked only by the creek and the boots of other hikers. Expect to see a lot of wildlife. Primitive camping is allowed, but there are no services.

- **Cascade Falls:** Eight miles south of Hot Springs, a parking lot with a small sign on the right side of the road marks the spot of this lovely local swimming hole and picnic area. Cross the lot and take the short path down to Cascade Creek. This nearly hidden, warm-water, spring-fed pool is a lush spot in the middle of the arid plains.

- **Cold Brook Lake Campground:** Located in Hot Springs, this small primitive campground is tucked up next to red sandstone canyon walls. The nearby lake is great for fishing and swimming. There are picnic tables, and just past the campground is a dog-friendly wilderness area.

- **Backcountry Camping, Wind Cave National Park:** Since Wind Cave is most famous for what is underground, the above-ground backcountry of the park is rarely visited. Camping is free; all that's required is a permit. Look for the huge elk herd in the park and avoid run-ins with bison!

THE NORTHERN HILLS

- **Spirit of the Hills Wildlife Sanctuary:** The animals in this sanctuary are, for the most part, not native to the region. Lions and camels and bears who have been discarded or abandoned find refuge for life in this donation-run safe haven.

- **Rimrock Lodge Cabins:** These six cabins tucked just inside the Spearfish Canyon Scenic Byway have no Internet, no televisions, gorgeous views, and lots of rustic charm.

stained-glass windows at Holy Rosary Church at the Red Cloud Heritage Center

▶ HIGH LIFE IN THE HIGH COUNTRY

As you explore the sublime landscape of South Dakota, take the time to immerse yourself in culture, steep yourself in history, discover contemporary art, and enjoy fine dining along the way.

Rapid City

Main Street Square: On a beautiful day stop by the square, let the kids splash about in the fountain, take your pick of fabulous shops and restaurants, and enjoy a milkshake at one of the outside tables. Visit with the on-site sculptor who is carving granite spires into representations of the Black Hills, Rapid City, and the Badlands.

Prairie Edge Trading Company and Galleries: With artwork that is beautiful, eclectic, and fabulously displayed, Prairie Edge is the most attractive gallery and gift shop and in the Black Hills. The best Native American artwork, jewelry and crafts, asre featured, and artists are frequently available on-site.

Reflections of South Dakota Gallery: Photographer (and former Director of Wildland Fire Suppression for the State of South Dakota) Joe Lowe and his wife Wendy, a painter, display their work at their gallery, which also features the work of other jewelymakers, woodworkers, and potters.

James Van Nuys Gallery: Artist James Van Nuys has mastered the prairie sky. If the size and scope of the beautiful plains landscape has captured your imagination, stop by this gallery and admire his work. He can frequently be found painting a canvas on-site.

Corn Exchange: Enjoy a relaxing dinner made from the freshest foods available at the finest—and coziest—restaurants in town. Chef

M.J. Adams trained at the French Culinary Institute, volunteered at the James Beard Foundation, and then transferred all of her know-how back to the Midwest.

Adoba Eco Hotel: Combine an excellent organic based restaurant (Enigma's) with an environmentally friendly hotel and you have the Adoba Eco Hotel. The wildly creative rooms feature recycled materials, including wall coverings, lamp shades, and serving trays (made from old street signs!).

Spearfish

Termesphere Gallery: Named after internationally acclaimed artist Dick Termes, this gallery isn't the easiest place to find, but it's worth the search. Termes three-dimensional paintings on spheres are gorgeous, fascinating, and one of a kind.

Latchstring Inn: Location, Location, Location! Within walking distance of two

of the three waterfalls in Spearfish Canyon, this log cabin restaurant has an outdoor patio with unbeatable views. It's perfect for warm summer afternoons. After a short hike to the falls, relax out on the deck with glass of wine.

Deadwood

Adams Museum: The oldest museum in the Black Hills (built in 1930) includes a display of the first steam train in the hills, artifacts of Wild Bill Hickok and Calamity Jane, and a superb collection of historic photos.

Deadwood Social Club: Handcrafted meals, an extensive wine list, and a rooftop patio overlooking the main street of historic Deadwood combine for a most memorable dining experience.

Bullock Hotel: When gambling breathed new life into the community, new owners completely restored this historic hotel (built by Seth Bullock between1894–1896), once the finest

Deadwood's Bullock Hotel

Deadwood's Adams Museum

in the West, to its original Victorian splendor. Fans of paranormal phenomena will be happy to know that Seth Bullock's ghost reportedly continues to supervise the kitchen staff.

Hill City

Jon Crane Gallery: Famous for his beautiful and detailed watercolor depictions of historic places and outdoor landscapes, Jon Crane has been perfecting his craft in South Dakota for over 35 years.

Sandy Swallow Gallery: Born on the Pine Ridge Reservation, Sandy Swallow Morgan is an enrolled member of the Oglala Lakota Nation. Her gallery features the works of other Oglala Lakota artists in the region. Sandy was invited to the White House for her painting of Devil's Tower on the White House Christmas ornament.

Warrior's Work & Ben West Gallery: There two large galleries in one location (focused on contemporary fine arts and Native American

arts) features some of the most striking paintings in the hills. It's also notable for the handcrafted leather frames, created by owner Randy Berger.

Prairie Berry Winery: Some of the friendliest and most knowledgeable staff in the hills offer samples of wines created from the fruits, grapes, and honey of the plains. To top it off, the winery features a gourmet restaurant with a lovely outdoor patio. It's just plain fun.

Custer State Park

State Game Lodge: All of the lodges in Custer State Park are exceptional, but none beats the State Game Lodge for history and elegance. Built in 1920, this wood and stone lodge was the "Summer White House" for President Calvin Coolidge in 1927. The dining room features the best in South Dakota game including pheasant, trout and buffalo. Step back in time and watch as herds of bison roam the grounds at will.

MOUNT RUSHMORE AND THE CENTRAL HILLS

Mount Rushmore is an enduring testimony to American exploration, expansion, unity, and preservation. Started in 1927 and completed in 1941, these faces of four presidents—George Washington, Thomas Jefferson, Abraham Lincoln, and Theodore Roosevelt—were created by 400 workers, who toiled to carve them into the hard granite mountain. The creators of the monument picked the location well. Gorgeous lakes, spires, and pine-covered peaks surround Mount Rushmore, offering numerous outdoor activities and winding mountain drives.

Hill City and Keystone are a few miles from Mount Rushmore, to the west and east, respectively. Each has seen its share of boom and bust cycles; first it was gold, then mica, then tin,

and then a long period of economic recession. When it was time to find a location for the monument, the fact that Keystone had a road, electricity, and a rail line in place clearly made a positive impression. Mount Rushmore brought life back to both communities, but each has evolved in its own direction. Keystone, closest to the monument, is action central, filled with gift shops, restaurants, and attractions. Hill City has evolved into a quaint, charming arts center in the hills.

As the biggest city in the area, Rapid City is the urban heart of the Black Hills. Initially created to serve as the commercial center for the mining towns of the Northern Hills, Rapid City made a concerted run to become

© NATIONAL PARK SERVICE

HIGHLIGHTS

◖ **Lincoln Borglum Visitor Center & Museum:** Everything you'd ever want to know about **Mount Rushmore,** its sculptor, the carving process, the wildlife at the park, and even Western American history can be found at the center. Did you know that Washington has the biggest nose of all the presidents on the mountain? This visitors center is full of fascinating facts (page 33).

◖ **The 1880 Train:** Created by rail enthusiasts who refused to allow steam trains to disappear from the landscape, the 1880 Train provides a leisurely trip between Hill City and Keystone (pages 38 and 50).

◖ **The Museum at Black Hills Institute:** The founders of the Black Hills Institute and subsequent museum were involved with the discovery of the infamous *Tyrannosaurus rex* Sue. There are dinosaur bones in South Dakota, and the Institute is known for excellent excavation and restoration work (page 51).

◖ **Prairie Edge Trading Company and Galleries:** This gallery of the best in contemporary and historic Native American arts includes exquisite beadwork, star quilts, powwow regalia, ledger art, and music (page 65).

◖ **Journey Museum:** The definitive museum of the Black Hills has great interactive exhibits on archaeology, Lakota culture, geology, pioneer history, and local ecology (page 66).

◖ **Storybook Island:** Fairy tales and nursery rhymes come to life at this children's theme park, where kids can meet the Three Little Pigs, the Cat in the Hat, Winnie the Pooh, and over 100 other characters (page 68).

◖ **Reptile Gardens:** At this delightful site for kids of all ages, daily shows feature live exhibits and talks about crocodiles, poisonous snakes, and raptors. Best of all are the free-roaming giant tortoises (page 68).

◖ **Bear Country U.S.A.:** Large animals roam this drive-through park, so you can view elk, bear, wolves, badgers, and wildlife babies from the safety of your car (page 70).

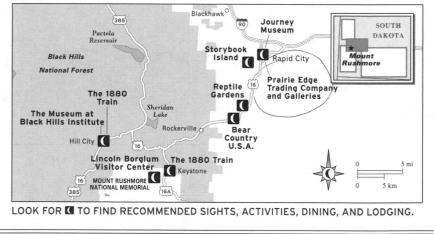

LOOK FOR ◖ TO FIND RECOMMENDED SIGHTS, ACTIVITIES, DINING, AND LODGING.

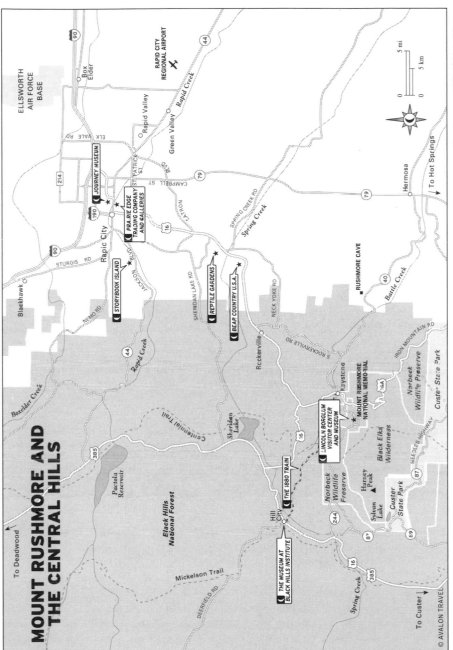

MOUNT RUSHMORE AND THE CENTRAL HILLS

the "Queen City of the Plains." It lost the title (and subsequent population growth) to Denver, but as a result of its efforts, the rich historic district has much to offer visitors. Cozy pubs, fine dining, art galleries, and boutique shopping are all within easy walking distance. Centrally located, and with the only commercial airport in the region, Rapid City frequently serves as the start and end point of a Black Hills vacation.

PLANNING YOUR TIME

Mount Rushmore and the small cities and tourist industries that grew up around it are filled with sights and activities to delight just about every kind of traveler. It is possible to spend as little as a day here, celebrating American history at Mount Rushmore, or a full two weeks or more, experiencing the outdoor recreation opportunities, museums, galleries, and attractions of the region. In order to experience the best the Central Hills region has to offer, plan to spend a minimum of three days in the area. The Black Hills region in its entirety is compact, but the winding mountain roads in the Central Hills can result in a lot of time behind the wheel, so you'll want to plan your time carefully.

There are two basic travel strategies for visiting the Black Hills. You can choose a location to use as a base camp and plot a series of day trips around it, or plan a meandering route through the hills, spending one night here, two nights there, as the route and attractions dictate. The ideal itinerary for you will depend on your overall travel plans and personal preference. If you plan to spend more than a day or two exploring the Central Hills, consider Hill City or Keystone as a base camp for your visit, as both are conveniently close to all of the attractions of the Central Hills. For a short visit, day trips from Rapid City, just 45 minutes from Mount Rushmore, can also be a successful approach.

If you are starting your journey into the hills from Rapid City, the fastest road to Mount Rushmore is U.S. 16, also known as **Mount Rushmore Road.** But if you have the time and would enjoy a dramatic approach, go a little out of your way to approach the carving from **Iron Mountain Road** (U.S. 16A). Iron Mountain Road begins in the south in Custer State Park and then heads north to Mount Rushmore. To drive to Mount Rushmore on this scenic byway, travel south on Highway 79, and then head west (take a right) on Highway 36. Continue on for nine miles. Just as you enter Custer State Park, go north (take a right) on Iron Mountain Road. Enjoy the scenery and watch for the faces of Mount Rushmore to appear, framed by one of the tunnels through which the road is carved. Bring carrots for the wild burro herd you are likely to encounter.

Exploring Mount Rushmore

Mount Rushmore National Memorial (13000 Hwy. 244, Bldg. 31, Ste. 1, 605/574-2523, www.nps.gov/moru) is nationally and internationally recognized as a symbol of American freedom and democracy. The park is open 364 days of the year, closed only on Christmas Day; hours vary seasonally. During the summer season, late May–mid-August, the park buildings, including the information center and the Lincoln Borglum Visitor Center,

are open daily 8 A.M.–10 P.M. Mid-August–September 30, hours are daily 8 A.M.–9 P.M. Winter hours, which take effect on October 1, are daily 8 A.M.–5 P.M.

Admission to Mount Rushmore is free, but there is an $11 per car parking fee. The parking permit is good from its date of purchase though December 31 of the same year. Since this is a use fee and not an admission fee, park passes (including the America the Beautiful

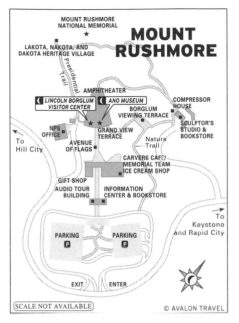

MOUNT RUSHMORE
NATIONAL MEMORIAL

MOUNT RUSHMORE

LAKOTA, NAKOTA, AND
DAKOTA HERITAGE VILLAGE

Presidential
Trail

AMPHITHEATER

LINCOLN BORGLUM
VISITOR CENTER

ANO MUSEUM

COMPRESSOR
HOUSE

BORGLUM
VIEWING TERRACE

NPS
OFFICE

GRAND VIEW
TERRACE

SCULPTOR'S
STUDIO &
BOOKSTORE

To
Hill City

AVENUE
OF FLAGS

Nature
Trail

CARVERS CAFE/
MEMORIAL TEAM
ICE CREAM SHOP

GIFT SHOP

AUDIO TOUR
BUILDING

INFORMATION
CENTER & BOOKSTORE

To
Keystone
and Rapid City

PARKING
P

PARKING
P

EXIT

ENTER

SCALE NOT AVAILABLE

© AVALON TRAVEL

Pass; National Park Passes; Golden Age, Access, and Eagle Passports) do not waive the parking fee. Walk-ins and bicyclists can visit the monument for free. There are bike racks near the entryway and bicyclists are welcome to wheel in their bikes with them.

The park is wheelchair accessible, and there is a zone in front of the entryway for unloading passengers and wheelchairs before parking in the lot. Wheelchairs are also available for loan at the Information Center on a first-come, first-served basis. The Presidential Trail is wheelchair accessible from the Lincoln Borglum Visitor Center to the base of the mountain, but not from the base to the Sculptor's Studio. The Sculptor's Studio is accessible to travelers in wheelchairs and other mobility-impaired visitors only through the remote parking lot, which must be arranged with a park ranger at the Information Center inside the park. All other buildings and sites on the grounds are fully wheelchair accessible. Service animals are

allowed on the grounds of the park, and there are two pet exercise areas near the upper levels of the parking garage. Other than service animals, pets are not allowed.

HISTORY

Mount Rushmore is the physical manifestation of the imaginations of two men: Doane Robinson and Gutzon Borglum. Doane Robinson moved to South Dakota to practice law and fell in love with the state. A Renaissance man of sorts, Robinson wrote poetry and fiction. He was also fascinated with South Dakota's history. This interest eventually led to his career as the South Dakota state historian. In this capacity, he wrote many historical and biographical papers on South Dakota and its citizens, and collected and archived artifacts for the state historical society. An ardent supporter of the state, Robinson believed that South Dakota could boost its tourism income by creating an attraction that would draw visitors from across the country. It was the dawn of the age of the automobile, and Robinson wanted South Dakota to cash in on this new method of traveling America. After reading about the Stone Mountain project in Georgia, a mountain-carving project under the direction of sculptor Gutzon Borglum, he became inspired. A huge mountain carving seemed the perfect project, and Robinson contacted sculptor Gutzon Borglum in 1924 to see if he would be interested in such an endeavor. Borglum accepted the challenge and the Mount Rushmore project began. While Robinson was the man behind the idea of a mountain carving, it was the vision of Gutzon Borglum that brought the presidential theme to the table, and finally to fruition.

Gutzon Borglum, born in Idaho in 1867, spent many of his formative years moving with his family. In addition to Idaho, the family lived in Utah, Nebraska, Kansas, and California, where Gutzon began his artistic career. Early success allowed him to pursue his studies overseas. He spent two years in Paris, where he was befriended by the famous French sculptor Auguste Rodin. He spent another year in Spain and five years in England, where he continued to experience a level of success most artists only dream of, including an exhibition of some of his pieces for Queen Victoria at Windsor Castle. Borglum finally returned to the United States in 1901 and brought with him a desire to create a distinctly American art form. Drawn to large surfaces, one of his first projects was a bust of Abraham Lincoln that stood nearly 40 inches tall and weighed about 375 pounds. Lauded by Abraham Lincoln's son, the piece received a lot of media attention. (Today, Abraham Lincoln's bust resides in the rotunda of the Capitol building in Washington DC.) The Lincoln sculpture inspired the United Daughters of the Confederacy to contact Borglum about creating a bust of Robert E. Lee on Stone Mountain in Georgia. Borglum proposed a much more ambitious project, believing that a single bust would be lost on the large mountainside, and his proposal was accepted.

The Stone Mountain project that Borglum envisioned included Robert E. Lee, Stonewall Jackson, and Jefferson Davis, all on horseback, leading a column of confederate soldiers. Initially, the carving was done with jackhammers and chisels. Later, a visiting engineer showed Borglum how to use dynamite with precision, and Borglum incorporated this into his work. Gutzon Borglum was a controversial character. Larger than life, highly opinionated, and reputedly short-tempered, he was a man not given to compromise and not easy to work with. By the time that Robinson contacted him about working at Mount Rushmore, there was trouble brewing at the Stone Mountain project and, shortly thereafter, Borglum was dismissed. This freed him to accept the Mount Rushmore project. After his departure from Stone Mountain, all evidence of Borglum's work on the mountain was erased with dynamite. While

no trace of Borglum's work on Stone Mountain remains, his experience there provided him with the knowledge he needed to tackle the colossal Mount Rushmore project. Work began on Mount Rushmore on October 4, 1927, when Borglum was 60 years old.

Originally, it was Doane Robinson's thought that Borglum could create a veritable parade of sculptures of American heroes, both white and Native American, on the many spires of the Needles formation near Sylvan Lake. After his first visit to the Black Hills, however, Borglum rejected that plan, as he felt that the Needles would be too fragile to withstand the carving process. He began his own search for a good location for the monument and selected the granite face of Mount Rushmore. The granite wall faced south, which would provide sunshine in the winter months and allow for a longer carving season. Also, granite is extremely hard and would guarantee that the countenances of Mount Rushmore would gaze over the plains for eons to come. In this, Borglum was correct. It is estimated that erosion on the granite face of Mount Rushmore will total one inch every 10,000 years.

Once Borglum found the appropriate location for his monumental project, he began to contemplate the form it should take. He wanted the monument to be national and not regional in nature, so he rejected Robinson's idea of carving local heroes. Instead, Borglum opted for a close look at the country's founding fathers and early leaders, and made his choice for the carving from former presidents of the United States.

The presidents were chosen, the models were made, and the carving commenced. Four hundred people toiled for 14 years to create the monument we see today. Mount Rushmore is huge. It is hard to get a feel for the sheer size of the monument from the various viewing platforms available at the base of the mountain. George Washington's head is six stories tall; the distance from his forehead to his chin is 60 feet. His eye alone is 11 feet wide and his

IMMORTALIZED IN STONE

Gutzon Borglum believed that for a project as monumental as a mountain carving, it would be best to honor individuals with national recognition and respect. He was looking for visionary leaders, and he elected to make his selection from those who had held the position of President of the United States. His first choices were George Washington and Abraham Lincoln. Soon after, the size of the project increased to include Thomas Jefferson and Theodore Roosevelt. These were men known for great leadership and men who were key players in the growth of the United States. George Washington was chosen for his role in leading America to independence from Great Britain, and for being the first democratic president of the new country. The selection of Abraham Lincoln elicited some grumbling on the part of the Southern states, but Borglum maintained that Lincoln deserved recognition and the honor of being a part of this great endeavor. (Borglum admired Lincoln's dedication to the preservation of the Union, and his firm belief in equality and freedom.) Thomas Jefferson authored the Declaration of Independence, a document that inspires emerging democracies to this day. He also had an expansive vision of what America could be, engineering the Louisiana Purchase during his tenure. Theodore Roosevelt was the most contemporary of the presidents selected for placement on the mountain. He was also the closest to being a local as well as a national character. Roosevelt owned a ranch in Dakota Territory (in what is now North Dakota). Prior to his presidency, he was famous for his role with the Rough Riders in Cuba during the Spanish-American War. After the famous battle of San Juan Hill, Roosevelt returned a popular American hero. After President William McKinley was assassinated in 1901, Roosevelt became president. He was an active conservationist who used his position to protect wildlife and public lands. Under his tenure, Roosevelt protected over 230 million acres with the creation of national parks, national forests, game preserves, bird reservations, and national monuments. Roosevelt was also known for taking care of the common man. He spearheaded anti-trust legislation, created the Food and Drug Administration, and regulated railroads.

mouth is 18 feet wide. If his entire body were carved proportionately, he would be around 465 feet tall. Add to those dimensions another three heads, making the monument approximately 60 feet high and 185 feet wide, and you have some insight into the project's size. The tools used to carve the mountain included pneumatic drills, jackhammers, chisels, and dynamite. The workers would hike the 700 stairs to the top of the mountain every morning, climb into sling chairs (called bosun chairs), and be lowered down the face of the mountain to their carving position for the day. The chairs were affixed to the top of the mountain by 3/8-inch steel cable and workers were lowered with winches. This was not a job for someone afraid of heights. Dangerous as it was, there were no fatalities and only a few minor injuries incurred at the monument over the 14 years of the carving project.

Gutzon Borglum was the designer and director of the project, but he was not always on-site. While he was gone in search of additional funding for the project or working on other commissions, he left his assistants, including his son, Lincoln Borglum, in charge of the project. He would return on a regular basis to inspect the progress of the carving, making corrections and changes to the design as needed in order to work with the rock structure of the mountain.

In March 1941, Gutzon Borglum died in Chicago from complications following surgery. He was just a few days shy of his 74th birthday. With the death of the artist, and at a time when America was facing involvement in World War II, the decision was made to discontinue work on the monument. The faces of Mount Rushmore were virtually finished. Lincoln Borglum supervised the finishing touches and clean-up of the monument site, and in October 1941, the monument was declared complete.

SIGHTS

The Information Center

The first stop on your visit to Mount Rushmore is the Information Center, located immediately to the right as you walk onto the grounds of the monument. Park rangers provide maps and basic guidance to the grounds. Schedules for ranger-guided programs are posted, and a park newspaper is stocked at the center. An audio tour is available for a $5 rental fee at the Information Center during the winter months; in the summer, the audio tour is available at the **Audio Tour Building,** located directly across the walkway from the Information Center. The award-winning *Mount Rushmore Audio Tour: Living Memorial* is two hours long. You can listen to the whole recording or listen at only a few of the stops along the guided tour. The audio includes historic recordings of Gutzon Borglum, Lincoln Borglum, and Mary Borglum Vhay, as well as recordings of some of the original workers on the site. The audio includes an informative narration about the people who envisioned and created the monument. It also provides information about the presidents selected for the carving, and tells the story of the Lakota people and their history in the Black Hills region, including interviews with Native Americans regarding their feelings about the monument. The recording is punctuated by music and sound effects. The audio tour is available in English, German, Lakota, and Spanish.

The Avenue of Flags

The Avenue of Flags was added to the grounds of Mount Rushmore as part of the celebration of the United States' Bicentennial in 1976. It was a visitor to the monument who suggested

© WWW.TRAVELSD.COM

the Avenue of Flags

the addition. As you enter the park, the flags line the pedestrian walkway and form a colorful frame for the majestic presidential faces straight ahead. There are 56 flags on display, one for each state, district, commonwealth, and territory of the United States. Each flagpole also reveals the date that statehood was attained. Delaware was the first state of the Union, granted statehood in 1787. South Dakota was the 40th state to be admitted, over 100 years later, in 1889. The 50 states and the District of Columbia account for 51 of the flags on display. Search for the other five, and keep the kids on the lookout for your home-state flag. Hint: The flags are in alphabetical order, with the A's beginning on the Lincoln side of the walkway and ending with W's on the Washington side.

The Grand View Terrace

The pedestrian walkway that begins at the entrance to the monument and passes through the Avenue of Flags terminates at the Grand View Terrace. Appropriately named, the terrace looks straight across at Mount Rushmore and is one of the best locations in the park for photographs of the monument. Directly in front of the Grand View Terrace, but below the sight line to the monument, is the outdoor **Amphitheater,** which is used for the park's evening programs during the summer months.

◖ Lincoln Borglum Visitor Center & Museum

The Lincoln Borglum Visitor Center & Museum is the main visitors center in the park. It is located on the lower level of the Grand View Terrace and is accessible by staircases on either side of the terrace or by elevators located on the Washington side of the monument. Geared toward interactive education, the exhibits in the museum include a timeline of American history, including the Civil War, westward expansion, and the Indian Wars. Here you'll learn about Mount Rushmore's sculptor, Gutzon Borglum, and about the workers who carved a mountain while dangling off the cliff face.

Part of the fun of Mount Rushmore is gleaning the facts about what it takes to carve a mountain. Viewing the mountain and *knowing* that Washington's nose is 21 feet long (a foot longer than any other president's nose!), that all of the faces are 60 feet tall, and that it took 400 workers more than 14 years to create this icon adds to the experience.

There are two small theaters in the museum, and two short films are available for viewing continuously throughout the day. There is a 14-minute film about carving Mount Rushmore and the artist behind it, filled with historic photographs of the carving and the period in which the work was done. The second film is a 12-minute presentation about the wildlife and ecology of the park. A bookstore located in the visitor center is run by The Mount Rushmore History Association to

benefit the monument. The store offers many books about Mount Rushmore and the Black Hills region, as well as books by local writers.

Borglum Viewing Terrace

From the Grand View Terrace, follow the concrete pathway located on the Lincoln side of the monument to the Borglum Viewing Terrace, the site of Borglum's first temporary studio, where he worked before a more spacious studio was built closer to the mountain. This site is not wheelchair accessible.

Just yards away from the Grand View Terrace, the Borglum Viewing Terrace offers a completely different view of the monument. More natural in its overall feel, here the view of the presidents is framed by large ponderosa pines—and the faces of Washington and Roosevelt dominate.

Mount Rushmore has an artist-in-residence program through which sculpture classes are offered at the Borglum Viewing Terrace. The classes are held outside, so if classes are going on, you are free to watch budding sculptors in action. Registration for the weeklong classes is available online through the monument's website. Information is also provided at the information desks located at the Lincoln Borglum Visitor Center or at the Information Center. The classes are open to anyone over the age of 13 and are free. All tools are provided.

The Borglum Viewing Terrace is the only area in the park available for weddings. Couples wishing to use the terrace for their wedding may do so by permit only. With the exception of the period June 25–July 4 and Christmas Day, weddings are allowed year-round. The cost of using Mount Rushmore as a wedding site is based on the number of rangers assigned to the special event and on the length of the wedding.

Sculptor's Studio

The Sculptor's Studio (open seasonally, Memorial Day–mid-Aug. daily 8 A.M.–7 P.M.)

is located at the bottom of the hill just past the Borglum Viewing Terrace. This was Borglum's second studio on-site and it contains the working model for Mount Rushmore. The model displayed at the studio is, in fact, the second model for the mountain carving. The first model had Jefferson situated to the left of Washington when facing the monument. Much work was done on that initial plan until it was discovered that the rock face where Jefferson was originally going to be located was not stable. Jefferson was dynamited off the face of the mountain, a new model was created, and Jefferson was moved to his current location between Roosevelt and Lincoln.

In addition to the model for the monument, the Sculptor's Studio displays a collection of tools and narrative descriptions of how these tools were used in the carving. There are several early photographs of Mount Rushmore before and after the carving, as well as many photos of the carving in process.

Mountain goats dine at the Mount Rushmore National Memorial.

© WWW.TRAVELSD.COM

The model displayed at the Sculptor's Studio is markedly different from the final project. All of the presidents were originally to be carved from head to waist. When Gutzon Borglum died in March 1941, it was determined that with the artist gone and with the country facing World War II, funding shortages would not allow work on the monument to progress. It was decided to leave the monument as it was since the faces were complete. Additional carving was deemed unnecessary. Also, because it was Borglum's vision, declaring the monument finished upon his death honored the sculptor. Lincoln Borglum, Gutzon Borglum's son, spent a few months more on the monument after his father's death supervising the final work on the project and the clean-up of the site.

The Presidential Trail

The Presidential Trail is a very pleasant half-mile loop that brings visitors to the closest viewing points of the monument. The trail is wheelchair accessible from the Washington side of the Grand View Terrace to the base of the mountain. It is not accessible from that point on, as there are a total of 421 wooden stairs that climb partially up the mountain and then continue down to the Sculptor's Studio.

It is not uncommon to see mountain goats along this trail—particularly near the beginning of the trail at the Grand View Terrace and at higher locations of the staircase mountainside. These beautiful white animals with contrasting black noses and hooves are not native to the region. In 1924, Canada gave six Rocky Mountain goats to Custer State Park. The goats escaped from their pens and have adapted well to the environment of the hills. There are now estimated to be more than 200 goats in the hills, mainly around Harney Peak, Sylvan Lake, Crazy Horse Mountain, and Mount Rushmore.

Lakota, Nakota, and Dakota Heritage Village

Mount Rushmore has always been controversial among the Lakota people. The Black Hills are sacred to them, and the presence of a large sculpture honoring white leaders in the middle of the hills isn't exactly welcome.

The village began as one tipi erected to the left of the monument off of The Presidential Trail. In subsequent years, the program expanded and two additional tipis were added. One of the tipis is furnished in the traditional manner, and the other two are used for demonstrations. During the summer, interpreters are on-site to talk about the traditional lifestyle and customs of the Native Americans before the arrival of Europeans to the area. Visitors to the heritage village learn about Native American languages, traditional living, arts, and storytelling. The programs are presented by members of various South Dakota tribes.

The Nature Trail

Most visitors enter the park via the wide entryway above the parking lot. However, there is a quieter way to approach the monument. As you leave the parking lot, the first structure that you encounter is a covered hallway that stretches to the left and right. Continuing straight ahead will bring you to the main entryway. Instead, take a right, follow the hallway, and skirt the edge of the parking lot. (This would be the far right-hand side of the parking lot, closest to the monument as you face the presidents.) The trail is short, not more than a quarter of a mile. It is a concrete walkway, but it winds through the sweetly scented ponderosa pines and ends at the scenic Borglum Viewing Terrace. Before taking the trail, you might want to stop at the Information Center just inside the monument grounds to pick up a map to orient yourself. Alternatively, consider using the trail to return to the parking lot when it's time to leave.

ACTIVITIES
Ranger-Led Programs

Three ranger-led programs are offered at Mount Rushmore during the summer months. The programs begin near the end of May and

cease at the end of summer. (The closing date varies from year to year.) Check with the Information Center or at the Lincoln Borglum Visitor Center on arrival to determine which programs are offered during your visit.

The 30-minute **Ranger Walk** is a ranger-led tour that follows The Presidential Trail to the base of the mountain carving. The discussion includes information about the four presidents selected for the monument and information about the natural and cultural history of Mount Rushmore and the Black Hills. The second program is a fascinating 15-minute **Sculpture Studio Talk** presented at the Sculptor's Studio. This program includes a discussion about the tools used to carve the mountain, stories about some of the workers on the mountain, and information about the first model for the sculpture. Samples of the tools are on-hand at the studio, as is the model for the current sculpture. The **Evening Program** (mid-May–mid-Aug., daily 9 P.M. and mid-Aug.–Labor Day, daily 8 P.M.) is the most popular program in the park. Attended by upwards of 2,500 people a night during the summer months, it is an inspirational program about the presidents, patriotism, and our nation's history. A short film entitled *America's Lasting Legacy* is shown, and the program ends with the singing of the national anthem, a flag ceremony honoring military personnel past and present, and the lighting of the monument. The monument is lit for one hour in the evening during the off-season, but there is no program presentation to accompany the lighting.

Junior Ranger Programs

All of the informational areas in the park carry free Junior Ranger Program activity books. Three booklets are available. One program is designed for children aged 3–5, one for children aged 5–12, and a third program is designed to enhance the Mount Rushmore experience for adults and children aged 13 and older. On completion of the activities, which generally take 30–60 minutes, young participants will receive a Junior Ranger badge and a certificate of completion. Older children and adults receive a certificate of completion. The programs include activities designed to educate the participant on the monument's history and ecology.

Stone and Clay Sculpture Workshops

During the summer months, free sculpture workshops are taught by an artist in residence. The on-site sculpture class is held at Borglum Viewing Terrace. This was the first studio used by Borglum and it is just to the left of the Sculptor's Studio. The sessions are held only during the summer months and the hours vary depending on the scheduling preferences of the artist in residence. The classes are held outside, so even non-participants can enjoy checking out the work of budding sculptors as they learn the art of stone carving and clay portraiture. Advance registration is required for the stone sculpture classes. All tools are provided. Call to register or stop by the Information Center or the Lincoln Borglum Visitor Center to discuss the workshops with a park ranger. Bring a hat, some sunscreen, and some water if you take the class or sit outside just to watch the students at work.

FOOD AND SHOPPING

Carvers Café (open year-round, mid-May–mid-Aug. daily 8 A.M.–9 P.M., mid-Aug.–mid-Sept. daily 8 A.M.–8 P.M., mid-Sept.–Labor Day daily 8 A.M.–7 P.M., Oct.–mid-May daily 8 A.M.–4:30 P.M.; during early spring and fall, closing time varies from week to week) is located near the entrance to the monument grounds on the Lincoln side of the sculpture and provides the only dining facilities on-site. It is a food court–style venue, with selections including hamburgers, pizza, pot roast, chicken, and pre-made salads. Entrées run about $9.50.

In the high summer season, the café can be very busy. Keep in mind that it might be fun to pack a picnic or to enjoy a meal in Keystone or Hill City. Both communities are just minutes away.

Memorial Team Ice Cream Shop (mid-May–mid-Aug. daily 11 A.M.–9 P.M., mid-Aug.–Sept., daily 11 A.M.–8 P.M.; spring hours vary, closed in winter) is located in the same building as the Carvers Café, the first building on your right past the Information Center as you enter the memorial grounds. The ice cream is great and the gourmet coffee is well worth a small wait. When the ice cream shop is closed in the winter, you can still get ice cream in the café.

The **Gift Shop** (open year-round, summer hours daily 8 A.M.–10:30 P.M.; spring, fall, and winter the shop opens at 8 A.M. but closing hours vary) is located in the first building to your left after the Information Center at the entryway to the monument grounds. The shop is large and well stocked with every kind of branded item you could desire, including photos, T-shirts, sweatshirts, caps, books about the carving and the region, bells, spoons, sunscreen, and rain gear, among other items.

GETTING THERE AND AROUND

The grounds of Mount Rushmore are relatively small. Once there, moving from site to site is all by foot. The distances are not great and there are no shuttles available.

By Car

The best way to travel throughout the region is by car. If you fly into Rapid City, which has the only commercial airport in the Black Hills, there are several car rental agencies located at the airport, including **Avis** (605/393-0740), **Budget** (605/393-0488), **Hertz** (605/393-0160), and **Alamo/National** (605/393-2664). Mount Rushmore is located just 32 miles from the Rapid City airport. The city center of Keystone is just 2.5 miles east of Mount Rushmore. Hill City is located about 11 miles north and west of Mount Rushmore. Either city would serve as a good base location for travel throughout the Central Hills region.

Tour Companies

For those who fly into Rapid City and elect not to drive, there are several tour companies that provide service to Mount Rushmore. Each company has a slightly different offering. **ABS Travel Group** (945 Enchantment Rd., Rapid City, 605/791-2520 or 888/788-6777, www. abstravelgroup.com, $70–125) specializes in short-duration (4–5 hours), small-group tours. Generally, only two sites per day are included; for instance, Mount Rushmore and Crazy Horse, Rapid City and Mount Rushmore, or Wall Drug and the Badlands. **Affordable Adventures** (5542 Meteor St., Rapid City, 605/342-7691, www.affordableadventuresbh. com, $35–240) is another small-group tour company that offers a wide variety of narrated tours. One interesting offering of Affordable Adventures is a ride to Mount Rushmore for the **Evening Lighting Ceremony** ($35). **Mount**

Rushmore Tours (2255 Fort Hayes Dr., Rapid City, 605/343-3113 or 888/343-3113, www. rushmoretours.com, adult $57–74, child aged 5–12 $27–37, child under 5 free for tour only, $5 for tour with meals) offers two itineraries. One tour includes a cowboy breakfast and a chuck wagon dinner at Fort Hayes (where part of the movie *Dances with Wolves* was filmed), along with a nine-hour tour of the Black Hills. The other tour does not include meals. This is a narrated standard chartered bus tour.

Helicopter Tours

Black Hills Aerial Adventures (106 U.S. 16A, 605/666-4212, daily 9 A.M.–7 P.M., $49–229), located on the grounds of the President's View Motel in Keystone, is the only helicopter tour company in the area. The company has three locations in the hills. There are six different flight tours to choose from, including a short introductory ride; tours featuring Mount Rushmore, Crazy Horse, Harney Peak, and Custer State Park; or a longer, 35-mile flight covering most of the central Black Hills.

Keystone

Minutes from the grounds of Mount Rushmore National Monument, Keystone is a tourist shopping hot spot in the hills. It's a place with a lot of hustle and bustle—a change from the generally quiet pace of the hills—and it is *the* place to get souvenirs. The town is nestled into a narrow gorge and many of the shops and activities are along two sections of U.S. 16A, which passes right through the heart of town. The first cluster of shops and restaurants is centered near the intersection of Highway 40 and the 1880 Train depot. The second cluster of small shops and restaurants is located at the Keystone Mall, which is closer to Mount Rushmore, about one mile farther south on U.S. 16A. Since tourism is the mainstay of the

town's economy, there is plenty of lodging and the energy level of the community is high during the height of the season.

The history of Keystone, like that of most of the hills communities, is centered on mining. The historic center of town is off the beaten path, just east of the downtown area. Follow Highway 40 east a few blocks to find some of Keystone's more historic buildings. While gold, mica, feldspar, tin, and many rare minerals were a part of Keystone's past, Mount Rushmore ensures its future.

Mount Rushmore is open all year, but visitation drops dramatically in the autumn, and many shops, restaurants, and attractions in Keystone close by the end of October.

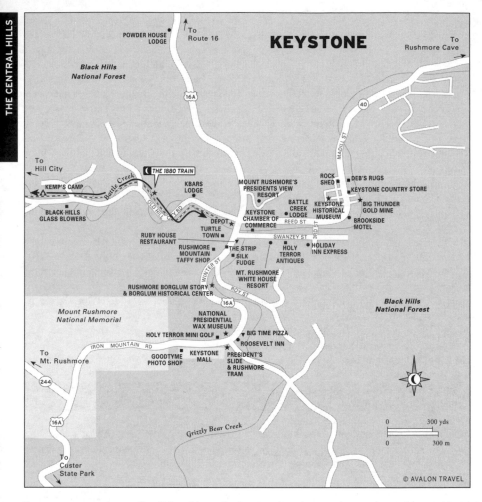

Late-season travelers will still be able to find lodging and a few intriguing shops open. Off-season pricing is always reasonable.

SIGHTS
◖ 1880 Train

The main terminal of the Hill City–Keystone 1880 Train (103 Winter St., 605/574-2222, www.1880train.com, mid-May–mid-Oct. round-trip: adult $24, child aged 3–12 $12; one way: adult $19, child $10) is located in Hill City, but the round-trip ride can be started and completed from either terminal. The round-trip narrated ride takes a little more than two hours.

Like many of the attractions in the hills, operating hours—and in this case, number of train departures—vary almost weekly as spring leads into the busy summer season and then back into the quieter schedules of fall. Be sure to verify departure times before you arrive. Reservations are recommended during the busy summer months and during Sturgis Motorcycle

© LAURAL BIDWELL

the 1880 Train station in Keystone

Rally week, held the first full week in August. Tickets are usually available on a walk-in basis the last week in May, the first week of June, and again in late August, as children return to school. Scheduled departures from the Keystone terminal are as follows: In May, two round-trip departures are available, one at 11:15 A.M. and one at 2:30 P.M. During the high summer season (beginning the second week in June and continuing through July), an additional round-trip departure is offered Monday–Saturday at 8:45 A.M. For most of August, the train returns to two departures daily. By September, the train provides a round-trip ticket only on the 11:15 A.M. departure, with a one-way ticket available on the 2:30 P.M. trip. In October, there is only a one-way ride to Hill City available, which departs at 2:30 P.M. A shuttle can be arranged to return you to Keystone.

Riding a stream train is an experience that many people never have the opportunity to enjoy. It's slow-paced and relaxing; it's a good time to sit back and wave at the folks that are waiting at the train crossing for the train to pass on by, and to enjoy a peaceful few hours gazing at the scenery with someone else at the wheel. Take the morning train from Keystone, shop the Hill City galleries, have lunch on the patio of the Alpine Inn, and return to Keystone for the evening—perhaps even for the evening lighting ceremony at Mount Rushmore.

Rushmore Borglum Story and Borglum Historical Center

The Rushmore Borglum Story and Borglum Historical Center (342 Winter St., 605/666-4448 or 800/888-4369, www.rushmoreborglum.com, mid-May–Aug. daily 8:30 A.M.–4:30 P.M., hours vary Sept.–Oct., closed Nov.–mid-May, adult $10, child $6) explores the story behind the carving of Mount Rushmore, particularly the life of Mount Rushmore sculptor Gutzon Borglum. The tour is self-guided, using audio wands that explain, point by point, a series of exhibits full of artifacts and information about Borglum, his son Lincoln, and the 14 years spent carving the monument. It's very well done and there are a lot of interesting artifacts on hand, including one of the earliest of the 12 models of the proposed carving. The model includes just three presidents (Washington, Jefferson, and Lincoln) in a line looking over each other's shoulders. The museum is large and there are a lot of exhibits, but be sure not to miss the film, located near the end of the tour, that is narrated by former South Dakota Senator Tom Daschle and includes historic film footage of workers carving Mount Rushmore.

National Presidential Wax Museum

The National Presidential Wax Museum (619 U.S. 16A, 605/666-4455, www.presidential-waxmuseum.com, Memorial Day–Labor Day daily 9 A.M.–8 P.M., Apr.–Memorial Day and Labor Day–Oct. daily 9 A.M.–5 P.M., closed in winter, adult $10, senior $8, child $7) is a favorite of history buffs. The wax figures of all of the presidents to date are included in the tour, portrayed in exhibits that illustrate the key events of the period each president was in office. There is a lot of information here about the history of the United States, and the timeline of the presidency is a unique way to follow the development of the country.

President's Slide and Rushmore Tramway

The President's Slide and Rushmore Tramway (203 Cemetery Rd., 605/666-4478, www.rush-morealpineslide.com, Memorial Day–Labor Day daily, weather permitting, closed in off-season; round-trip chairlift: adult $8, child $3; chairlift up and alpine slide down: adult $10, child $3) is a short but enjoyable ride. The lift is located right in Keystone and climbs the ridge of a nearby mountain. The chairlift ride to the top of the mountain is a relaxing and quiet ride.

On the way up, watch the faces of the folks enjoying the alpine slide down the hill. The alpine slide looks much like a sled on very small wheels. There are two tracks to choose from on the trip down. One is for the slowpokes, many of whom look terrified as they ride their brakes down the hill; the other is for the racers who zoom down the hill with a look of sheer manic bliss on their faces. This is a ride for all ages, but not necessarily for the timid at heart. At the top, there are several boardwalk viewing decks, from which there are distant views of Mount Rushmore and lofty views of the town of Keystone just below. The rock and flower gardens at the top are beautifully done, and a casual grill serves brats, burgers, and chicken sandwiches priced around $4.50–6. Beer is available also, though it would likely not be a good idea to imbibe heavily and then alpine slide down the hill. After enjoying the gardens and the views, slide or ride the chairlift down.

Rushmore Cave

The closest cave to Keystone and to Mount Rushmore is Rushmore Cave (13622 Hwy. 40, 605/255-4384, www.beautifulrushmorecave.com, June–Aug. daily 8 A.M.–8 P.M., May and Sept.–Oct. daily 9 A.M.–5 P.M., closed in off-season), located about five miles east of Keystone on Highway 40.

Discovered in 1876 by gold miners digging into the mountain to find a water source to bring to their mine below, the cave was opened to the public in 1927. Two cave tours are available. The standard one-hour tour runs continuously throughout the day (adult $14, child aged 5–12 $8) The 2.5-hour Adventure Tour (daily 10 A.M. and 3 P.M., $45) explores locations in the cave accessible only by crawling through tight passageways. Helmets, headlamps, knee pads, and elbow pads are provided. The tour is limited to five participants, all of whom must be at least 14 years of age and must sign a liability waiver.

Rushmore Cave contains a nice array of stalactites and stalagmites, and the path through the

© LAURAL BIDWELL

Beautiful gardens and a delightful lunch spot await at the top of the Rushmore Tramway.

cave is well maintained and well lit. There are several different cave rooms on the tour; the "Big Room" is impressively large and filled with interesting formations. It's a fun and interesting tour. Remember that caves remain very cool, generally around 58°F even in the hottest part of summer, so you'll want to bring a sweatshirt to keep warm.

In addition to the cave tours, the site has added some new attractions. The **Soaring Eagle Zipline** (June–Aug. daily 10 A.M.–6 P.M., May and Sept.–Oct. daily 10 A.M.–5 P.M., $9) is a short, quick (zippy, as it were) ride down and back up the side of the mountain. The chair zooms down the mountainside at a top rate of 23 mph, according to the staff. The **Gunslinger 7-D Interactive Theater** (Jun.–Aug. daily 9 A.M.–7 P.M., 9 A.M.–5 P.M. May and Sept.–Oct., $9) is an interactive three-dimensional gun fight which lasts a quick five minutes for those who find the experience exhilarating, and a long five minutes for those who feel the 3-D movement too intensely. Participants are provided with 3-D glasses and a gun, and are strapped into chairs that move with the action on the screen. (Folks who find the rushing trains, rivers, and canyon falls too dizzying can unplug themselves!) At the end of the adventure, your picture and score are flashed on the screen. Combination ticket packages are available (cave tour plus one additional attraction: adult $20, child $14; cave tour plus two additional attractions: adult $27, child $20).

Keystone Historical Museum

The Keystone Historical Museum (410 3rd St., 605/666-4847, www.keystonehistory.com, mid-May–mid-Aug. Mon.–Sat. 10 A.M.–3 P.M., closed Sun. and in off-season, voluntary donation) is housed in the old Keystone school, built in 1900. Two of the primary collections of the museum include a gem and mineral collection and memorabilia that once belonged to Carrie Ingalls Swanzey. Carrie Ingalls was the sister of Laura Ingalls Wilder, who was famous for

© LAURAL BIDWELL

Rushmore Cave, Keystone

authoring a series of books about life on the prairie, including *Little House on the Prairie,* which was made into a popular television series. Carrie Ingalls is an interesting example of an independent Western woman. She grew up in DeSmet, South Dakota, earned her teaching certificate, eventually ended up in the newspaper business, and at one time, homesteaded on her own land near Philip, South Dakota. In 1911, Carrie moved to Keystone, where she managed the *Keystone Register* newspaper until she married at the age of 42. History buffs and those interested in the history of women in the West will especially enjoy visiting the museum.

Big Thunder Gold Mine

The Big Thunder Gold Mine (604 Blair, Hwy. 40, 605/666-4847 or 800/314-3917, www.bigthundermine.com, June–Aug. daily 8 A.M.–8 P.M., May and Sept.–Oct. daily 9 A.M.–6 P.M., closed in off-season, adult $9.25, child $6.25) is located just a few blocks east of

U.S. 16A on Highway 40. The facility has a small but nice gift shop and a cafeteria on the grounds as well as the mine. The mine tour is somewhat short, but it does include some interesting facts about the history of mining in Keystone and there is a good collection of mining equipment inside the adjacent museum, which is included in the tour. Gold panning ($7.25 with the tour, $9.25 without the tour) seems to be the highlight of the mine. Staring raptly at the bottom of their gold pans, children and adults alike demonstrate how easy it is to catch gold fever.

RECREATION
Mini Golf

Playing at **Holy Terror Mini Golf** (609 U.S. 16A, 605/666-5170, www.presidentialwaxmuseum.com, May 15–Oct. 31 daily 9 A.M.–8 P.M., closed in off-season, adult $9, child aged 6–12 $7, child under 6 free) is a fun way to expend a little energy (especially for the

© LAURAL BIDWELL

Deb's Rugs in historic Keystone

kids) when visiting Keystone. The course is nestled into the side of the mountain and the views from some of the tees are quite pretty, with the lights and hustle-bustle of Keystone down below. Plan on getting a little exercise on this course, as there are more than a couple of steep climbs!

SHOPPING

Keystone has something for every visitor. There are kitschy souvenir shops right next door to shops featuring fine art and specialty gifts. As is common in most seasonal tourist areas, shops can change from year to year; sometimes the best way to find a treasure is to park the car and go walking. Off-season hours can be fairly whimsical, so it might not be a bad idea to call first if you are planning on visiting a specific shop. Look for funky specialty shops in the historic center of Keystone off of Highway 40 east of U.S. 16A. Along U.S. 16A (the main road to Mount Rushmore), there are two distinct

shopping districts. The first, called "the strip," is near the 1880 Train station at the junction of U.S. 16A and Highway 40. Farther south and closer to Mount Rushmore on U.S. 16A is the Keystone Mall.

Look for **The Rock Shed** (515 1st St., 605/666-4813 or 866/354-0894, www.therockshed.com, Apr.–Oct. Mon.–Sat. 8 a.m.–8 p.m., Sun. 10 a.m.–6 p.m.; off-season Mon.–Fri. 9 a.m.–5 p.m., closed Sat.–Sun.) in the historic Keystone area. It is one of the enduring shopping spots in town. In business since 1968, the store specializes in rocks, gemstones, fossils, and minerals. It's a beautiful little shop with bins and bins of sorted rocks and minerals for sale by the pound outside and a very clean and organized collection available inside. If you like rock-related products, there are some unique and exquisite items to be found here.

Across the street from The Rock Shed is **Deb's Rugs** (510 1st St., 605/666-4679, www.debsrugs.com, Memorial Day–Labor Day daily

10 A.M.–5 P.M., winter hours are weather depen-dent), a small shop selling woven rugs, scarves, placemats, and other products. If you enjoy the work of local artisans, check out this store. It's a tiny enterprise run by Deb Lervaag, who works on-site at one of the two looms set up in the middle of the shop floor. In Keystone since 2000, Deb is happy to provide custom work. In addition to the storefront, her work is available at the store website.

Holy Terror Antiques (221 Swanzey St., 605/666-5005, www.holyterrorantiques.com, May–Oct. daily 9 A.M.–5 P.M., Nov.–May Fri.–Sun. 10 A.M.–5 P.M.) is a fabulous shop. Owners Dennis Kling and Westly Parker have back-grounds in design and it shows: 6,000 square feet of furniture, advertising, glassware, pot-tery, old posters, wood carvings, and other col-lectibles are artfully arranged on the walls and in creative display pieces.

Located just one mile outside of town on the Old Hill City Road, **Black Hills Glass**

© LAURAL BIDWELL

Holy Terror Antiques

Blowers (909 Old Hill City Rd., 605/666-4542, www.blackhillsglassblowers.com, daily mid-May–mid-Sept. Mon.–Sat. 9 A.M.–5 P.M., Sun. 11 A.M.–5 P.M., off-season by appt.) is a unique studio and retail shop where beauti-ful wine glasses, water glasses, plates, vases, and glass figurines are created as you watch. Artisans Peter Hopkins and Gail Damin have been working together for decades and opened their studio and shop in Keystone in 1991. Each of them is proficient at creating both blown glass (off-hand work) and lamp-worked pieces. While there are no scheduled demon-strations of glass work, one of them is likely to be working any time the shop is open.

One of the most popular stops in town is the **Rushmore Mountain Taffy Shop** (203 Winter St., 605/666-4430, May–Sept. daily 8 A.M.–9 P.M., off-season daily 8 A.M.–4 P.M. or 6 P.M.)—no vacation-community boardwalk is complete without a taffy shop. I'm not sure what makes the sticky confection so irresistible, but it might be the many choices of exotic fla-vors. Strawberry cheesecake, peach, and choco-late cherry sound interesting, but jalapeño taffy sounds like something only a 10-year-old could love. The most popular flavors include cinna-mon and huckleberry.

If taffy isn't your brand of sweet, try **Turtle Town** (117 Winter St., 605/666-4675, www.turtletown.com, June–Aug. daily 7:30 A.M.–10 P.M., May and Sept.–Oct. daily 8 A.M.–7 P.M., closed in off-season), a fixture on the Keystone strip since 1977. The store owners have ex-panded the initial offerings from simple fudge to include handmade fine chocolates, ice cream, and a coffee bar. With nine different varieties of fudge alone, truffles, caramels, divinity, and toffee, there is something sweet for everyone.

Silk Fudge (234 Winter St., 605/666-5566, www.silkfudge.com, mid-Apr.–mid-Oct. Mon.–Sat. 9 A.M.–9 P.M., Sun. 12–9 P.M.) was launched when the family was disappointed with the fudge they purchased at a famous

© LAURAL BIDWELL

Keystone's boardwalk

California site and determined that following grandma's recipes resulted in the best fudge. There are 22 different flavors of fudge that compete for your attention here. This could be the creamiest fudge in town.

The **Goodtyme Photo Shop** (804 U.S. 16A, 605/666-4619, May–Sept. daily 9 A.M.–7 P.M., closed in off-season) is a great place to get something unusual for a souvenir. Take a family photo and bring the Old West home. The shop offers 11 different sets, including an Old West bar, a jailhouse, a sod house, a Victorian parlor, a buffalo scene, and a bathtub, all of which are Western or Victorian in nature. And then, just for something different, you can dress like Bonnie and Clyde and pose in front of a 1920s' car.

ACCOMMODATIONS

As with most hotels and motels in the Black Hills, Keystone hotel rates can vary from week to week, especially in the early spring and after

Labor Day. While Sturgis Motorcycle Rally week rates are the highest, rates are also high in Keystone during the first week of July due to the very popular Mount Rushmore Fourth of July programs. If making reservations in advance, check the Internet for pricing. Many hotels have Internet deals which could save you as much as $20 per night. Rates quoted here are for a standard room (generally two queens), double occupancy. Most include children for free.

$75-125

Keystone is the closest town to Mount Rushmore, so demand for rooms is high. Luckily there are many hotels available to choose from. Be forewarned that signs that advertise low-rate rooms in town generally refer to early- or late-season rates and are not applicable to the high summer season. On the other hand, there are quite a few charming places tucked away in the region.

The **C Powder House Lodge** (24125 U.S. 16A, 605-/666-4646, www.powderhouselodge.com, mid-May–mid-Oct., closed in off-season, $75–100) is just two miles north of Keystone on U.S. 16A, but it is far enough away to recapture the peaceful feel of the Black Hills. The lodge is family owned and operated and is beautifully maintained. There are a number of cabin and motel configurations available. There is a restaurant on the grounds and amenities include an outdoor pool and free Wi-Fi.

In the heart of Keystone, the **C Battle Creek Lodge** (404 Reed St./Hwy. 40, 605/666-4800 or 800/670-7914, www.battlecreeklodge.us, $90–110) is a family-run establishment that is a quaint and quiet alternative to the larger hotels. The lodge has nine rooms—most with double queen beds, free wireless, lovely decks to enjoy the cool evening air, and an outdoor fire pit—and is just a short walk to downtown Keystone shops and restaurants. The lodge serves a full continental breakfast, which includes one featured hot item every morning. For example, selections may include breakfast burritos, French toast, or sausage and scrambled eggs. The owners love the industry and are friendly and helpful to guests.

A little farther from the center of town, but still within walking distance, is the **Brookside Motel** (603 Reed St./Hwy. 40, 605/666-4496, open mid-May–mid-Sept., closed in off-season, $80–90). One of the older motels in town, it's a great non-chain alternative. Small, with just 28 rooms, the family-owned and -operated Brookside is tucked up close to the mountain. The owners are friendly and have the time to be attentive to their guests' needs. Don't be put off by the bright blue exterior, by the way. While chatting with the owner, I mentioned the color and she said with a sigh, "Yes, that is us and that was a mistake." Apparently, while they were off branding cattle, the painter came in with his spraying equipment and went wild. The owners were somewhat aghast at the result, but what was done, was done, and a complete repaint was out of the question. The rooms are nicely remodeled and have free Wi-Fi, and they are a good bargain in this somewhat pricey community.

$125-175

For beautiful seclusion, great decks, a gorgeous lobby, views of Mount Rushmore, and free breakfast featuring delicious waffles, choose the **(KbarS Lodge** (434 Old Hill City Rd., 605/666-4545 or 866/522-7724, www.kbarslodge.com, $150–170). Just minutes from Keystone, the lodge has 96 rooms and is located on 45 acres of forested land. The lobby has vaulted ceilings and a huge stone fireplace. Large wooden decks welcome guests in the evening. In the distance, you can see the lit profile of George Washington on Mount Rushmore. Deer and wild turkey are frequent trespassers on lodge grounds. The rooms are scattered in separate buildings throughout the property and are clean and spacious, though

the beauty of the facility is in the common areas. Breakfast is included in the room charge and is generous and tasty.

The **Roosevelt Inn** (206 Cemetery Rd., 605/666-4599 or 800/257-8923, www.rosyinn. com, open year-round, $120–140) is a small, family-run hotel. The inn prides itself on offering 32 reasonably priced, clean, basic rooms. The owners are friendly, knowledgeable, and humorous! Located near the Rushmore Tram, it is one of the closest hotels to Mount Rushmore.

If vacation means being on the go and enjoying evenings out on the town, consider the **Mount Rushmore White House Resort** (115 Swanzey St., 605/666-4917 or 866/996-6835, www.whitehouseresort.com, open year-round, $140), which is located just off the main boardwalk in town. The hotel has 94 rooms, of which a dozen or so remain open for use in the winter season. This is a great place for those who want to be in the center of Keystone's hustle and bustle. There is plenty of parking for guests, an indoor pool, a hot tub, an arcade, and free Wi-Fi. Pets are allowed at no extra charge, and the hotel is an easy walk to dining, the 1880 Train, and the gift shops along the strip.

$175 and up

The **Holiday Inn Express & Suites** (321 Swanzey St., 605/666-4925 or 888/465-4329, www.hiexpress.com, open year-round, $220–250) was built in 2000. The hotel has 62 rooms and is within easy walking distance of shops and restaurants in town. Amenities include free local phone calls, free wireless Internet, an indoor swimming pool, and a hot tub. The rooms are spacious and clean, if a bit plain. The lobby area is decorated in Western/Native American style and features a large, three-sided fireplace. A breakfast buffet with both hot and cold items is included in the room rate.

The **(Buffalo Rock Lodge** (24524 Playhouse Rd., 605/666-4781 or 888/564-5634, www.buffalorock.net, open year-round,

$145–200) is a gorgeous, log construction bed-and-breakfast with a massive stone fireplace. There are three rooms, each with a private bath and spa tubs. A pool table is available for billiards fans and the outdoor deck is superb. Hosts Art and Marilyn Oakes are extremely knowledgeable about the best activities and dining in the area, and both are also very well-versed in local history. (Marilyn's grandfather was the contractor for the State Game Lodge in Custer State Park!) A three-night minimum stay is required.

Cabins and Campgrounds

Kemp's Kamp (1022 Old Hill City Rd., 605/666-4654 or 888/466-6282, www.kempskamp.com, May–Sept., closed in off-season, sites $26–44, sleeping campers $49, cabins $69–175) is a quiet, well-maintained campground centrally located to all of the Black Hills attractions. Amenities include a good-sized heated pool, laundry facilities, free Wi-Fi, hot showers, elevated fire pits, and picnic tables covered by canopies. Old Hill City Road is the scenic route between Hill City and Keystone, and it is the route that the 1880 Train follows. It's a lovely location.

There is a Black Hills National Forest campground called **Grizzly** (605/574-4402 or 888/444-6777, Memorial Day–weekend after Labor Day, tents only, $20) for those who love to camp in the old-fashioned way. It is a primitive campground with no showers, though water and vault toilets are available on-site. From Keystone, head up U.S. 16A toward Mount Rushmore and stay on U.S. 16A when it veers left. Locally, U.S. 16A is known as Iron Mountain Road. (If you make it to Mount Rushmore, you missed the turn-off.) About a mile down the road, the campground is on the right. It's a nicely wooded site and Grizzly Creek runs through the property. Trying to save a little money? Alternate a night of camping with a night of motel life (for the hot showers!).

FOOD

One of the coziest spots in town, the ■**Powder House Lodge** (24125 U.S. 16A, 605/666-5214 or 800/321-0692, www.powderhouselodge.com, mid-May–mid-Oct. daily breakfast 7–11 A.M. and dinner 4–9 P.M., lunch mid-June–Labor Day only daily 11 A.M.–4 P.M., closed in off-season, breakfast $9, lunch $10, dinner $17–23) serves up the best breakfast in the area. It's a comfortable restaurant with wood-paneled walls and lots of booths, and it is lined with windows. Powder House Lodge serves all the breakfast standards, in addition to some great skillets and omelets. Lunch and dinner offerings are delicious as well. Lunch selections range from burgers and chicken sandwiches to paninis, wraps, and salads. The dinner menu includes the sandwiches offered at lunch, but also features some fish selections, including walleye and trout. Several varieties of beef cuts—including prime rib, buffalo, and elk—and pasta dishes round out the dinner options. For the curious, one of the house specialties is a game sampler that includes buffalo short rib, elk medallion, buffalo sausage, and a blended game sausage. There is also an excellent selection of wines available. The location of the restaurant is the inspiration for its name; it sits on the spot where one of the mining companies in town once stored explosives.

Prices for food in Keystone are a bit high, by South Dakota standards, and most of it is standard American fare, but there are some places that provide a uniquely Western feel, which makes even a hamburger taste better. One such place is the **Ruby House Restaurant** (124 Winter St., 605/666-4404, www.historicrubyhouse.com, Apr.–mid-Oct. daily 11 A.M.–9 P.M., closed in off-season, lunch $10, dinner $18), located on the strip in old Keystone across from the 1880 Train station. Dining is available in the restaurant or outside on the boardwalk deck, where people-watching is a favorite activity. Inside, the decor is classic

Victorian red velvet. Lunch features salads, wraps, burgers, chicken, and other sandwiches, and dinner features buffalo, prime rib, trout, walleye, and pasta dishes. Beverages are provided by the **Red Garter Saloon** (126 Winter St., 605/666-4274, www.redgartersaloon.com, open seasonally, Mon.–Sun. 11 A.M.–midnight). The Red Garter and the Ruby House were, at one time, a single establishment, but when it became too much for one family to run, the Ruby House was leased out to another family. This is why patrons receive two checks if both food and alcoholic beverages are consumed. The two venues flow together seamlessly, since you can eat at the bar and drink in the restaurant, but they are, in fact, two separate entities. The Red Garter also provides a comedy and gunfight show three times daily and live music in the evening.

There's nothing like a great pizza, and **Big Time Pizza** (206 Cemetery Rd., 605/666-4443, weekends in March, daily Memorial Day–Oct., 11:30 A.M.–9:30 P.M., $22) serves up a wide variety of delicious pizza, subs, salads, wine, and beer. The restaurant is located on the lower level of the Roosevelt Inn, but it is not affiliated with the inn. This family-owned and -operated place isn't fancy, but the food is so good that I suspect you'll dine here more than once. For the adults, there's beer. The owner insists that Big Time Pizza's Russian beer is the best beer she's ever tasted.

About five miles from town, a good place to relax and be hearty (in other words, not worry about making noise) is the **Gaslight Restaurant & Saloon** (13490 Main St., Rockerville, 605/343-9276, www.thegaslight-restaurant.com, open year-round, restaurant open daily 11 A.M.–9 P.M., saloon open until 2 A.M., $18). Take U.S. 16A north to U.S. 16 and head east toward Rapid City. Look for the Rockerville exits. Thanks to some interesting highway planning, the town ended up being wedged between U.S. 16 east and U.S. 16 west, which means traffic zooms by at a minimum of 55 miles per hour. The town has always been a boom-or-bust gold community, but this highway configuration returned the place to near ghost town status, with just the restaurant and bar open all year. Wood paneling and old movie posters adorn the restaurant walls. The adjacent full-service bar has added some 1950s' touches, including a 1953 Chevy Bel Air hanging from the wall and the front grill of a 1955 Cadillac protruding from the reception desk. Dinner includes beef standards, fajitas, seafood, and pasta dishes. It's a little on the noisy side, but for a casual night out, it works. There's live music on weekends.

INFORMATION AND SERVICES

The **Keystone Chamber of Commerce** (110 Swanzey Rd., 605/666-4896 or 800/456-3345, www.keystonechamber.com) is easy to find at the corner of Old Hill City Road and U.S. 16A at the traffic light. There are plenty of rack cards available with information about local events, lodging, and dining, and there is a chamber representative on hand to answer questions. Keep in mind that chamber representatives can't play favorites and represent all members. (If looking for opinions, ask shopkeepers.) For campers, basic supplies can be found at the **Keystone Country Store** (408 1st St., 605/666-4912). The Keystone **post office** (605/666-4830) is at 111 Winter Street.

Hill City

Hill City and its remarkable chamber and retail group have created a shopping experience geared toward quality and art. That doesn't mean you can't find inexpensive T-shirts here—there are plenty of those, too—but given its tiny size, with a year-round population of less than 800 people, there are more galleries here, per capita, than anywhere else in the hills. While business slows significantly in the off-season, Hill City, less than 30 miles from Rapid City, and with easy access via U.S. 385/16, remains an enjoyable place to visit throughout the year. Many of the art galleries in town are open year-round, and while dining and lodging options shrink, food and accommodations are still available.

Hill City's mining history was relatively short-lived and not particularly successful. In 1876, placer gold (panned from streams and creeks, instead of picked from underground mines) was detected in Spring Creek near town. It wasn't long, however, before reports of richer discoveries sent gold seekers to the Northern Hills. Miners headed back to Hill City when the Harney Peak Tin Mining, Milling, and Manufacturing Company set up headquarters in town in 1883. For about a decade, the Harney Tin Company, as it was called, paid good wages to many local miners and kept the community bustling. The company bought over 1,100 mining claims in the region. Many of the claims never yielded any tin. Financed mainly by English investors, the company eventually collapsed, apparently under a cloud of scandal. (As an interesting side note, in 1885, a young New York attorney was sent west on the company's behalf to investigate titles to some of the mining claims being purchased.

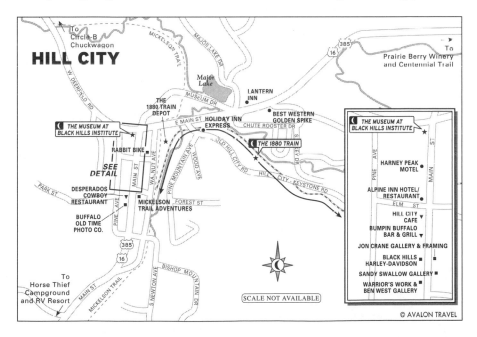

© AVALON TRAVEL

© WWW.TRAVELSD.COM

the 1880 train on the way to Keystone

At one point, he asked his guide what was the name of the mountain that they were passing. The mountain didn't have a name at the time. It does now. The young attorney's name was Charles E. Rushmore.) After the closing of the Harney Tin Company, it was quite some time before Hill City recovered economic ground.

Today, it's all about location and cooperation. Hill City is just three miles from the ongoing carving of Crazy Horse and 11 miles from Mount Rushmore, and it's the easiest town to reach from the Sylvan Lake area of Custer State Park—so it flourishes during the summer months. Harley-Davidson has set up shop in town and Hill City has become the second-favorite place for motorcycle enthusiasts to visit during the Sturgis Motorcycle Rally.

SIGHTS
◖ The 1880 Train
The original depot for the steam-powered 1880 Train (222 Railroad Ave., 605/574-2222,

www.1880train.com, round-trip adult $24, child aged 3–12 $12, one way: adult $19, child $10) is located in Hill City. In its earlier days, the train traveled only as far as the town of Oblivion and back—about half the distance it travels today. Oblivion, an abandoned town site, was once the home of Nelson Sawmill, which served lumber operations in the region. The train expanded its route and today it offers a two-hour round-trip rail ride between Hill City and Keystone.

The steam engine locomotive was first brought to the Black Hills in 1879 by the Homestake Mine in Lead. When the first narrow-gauge railroad line was completed in 1881, steam trains carried supplies and people between the mining camps. Most of the standard-gauge track used by the current 1880 Train was built by the Chicago, Burlington and Quincy Railroad during the gold rush and mining boom of the 1890s. By the 1940s, diesel engines were rapidly replacing steam engines. William B. Heckman, a local businessman and railroad fan, organized a group that was created for the sole purpose of ensuring that "there should be in operation at least one working steam railroad, for boys of all ages who share America's fondness for the rapidly vanishing steam locomotive." The Hill City train depot was built in 1890, but it wasn't until 1957 that the first 1880 Train left the station. All of the train cars and engines are historic, with most dating back to the early 1900s; the history of each car is available on the 1880 Train website.

The schedule of departures varies throughout the season. From mid-May–Labor Day, there are at least three daily departures (10 A.M., 1:15 P.M., and 3:45 P.M.). In mid-June, a morning departure at 7:30 A.M. is added to the schedule; late June–July, an evening departure at 6:45 P.M. is added, as well. In early May and after Labor Day, it's best to call the railroad or check the website for the schedule. The train also has a special "Fright Run" around Halloween, and

© LAURAL BIDWELL

Early advertising for the Black Hills was sponsored by the railroads.

has a Holiday Express Christmas trip for a couple of weekends in December.

On the grounds of the Hill City Train, the **South Dakota Railroad Museum** (222 Railroad Ave., 605/574-9000, www.sdsrm.org, mid-May–Oct. daily 10 A.M.–4:30 P.M., open seasonally in Nov. and Dec. for special events, closed Jan.–mid-May, adults $5, child aged 12 and under free) offers a fascinating look at the history of trains in South Dakota. One of the more interesting exhibits is a historical timeline mural painted on the wall outlining the historical growth of both freight and passenger travel in the state, with comparisons to the history of flight development and flight passenger statistics.

◖ The Museum at Black Hills Institute

The Museum at Black Hills Institute (117 Main St., 605/574-3919, www.bhigr.com, summer Mon.–Sat. 9 A.M.–7 P.M., Sun.

10 A.M.–6 P.M., winter (through Christmas) Mon.–Sat. 9:30 A.M.–5:30 P.M., Sun. noon–4 P.M., Jan.–May Mon.–Sat. 9:30 A.M.–5 P.M., closed Sun., adult $7.50, child aged 6–15 $4, child 5 and under free) was organized in 1991. Its mission was "to collect, conserve, curate, and display extraordinary geological and natural history specimens that have the power to educate, enlighten, and excite people about the wonders of the natural world." The story of the museum, and of the founders of the related Black Hills Institute of Geological Research, is fascinating, though somewhat tragic—and involves the infamous Sue, a *Tyrannosaurus rex* (T. rex) who was found in 1990. Since then, the Institute and the museum have been involved in the excavation and preservation of eight T. rex skeletons. Today, the most complete and the most-studied T. rex, Stan, is on display at the museum. Other displays include ammonites, minerals, and fossil remains of many other

dinosaurs, including duck-billed dinosaurs and triceratops.

The Institute has a large catalog of fossil replicas for sale. A replica of Stan costs around $100,000; his skull alone is $9,500. His toe, however, is a bargain at just $85. Many of the institute's replicas are purchased by universities to use in classrooms.

Prairie Berry Winery

The Prairie Berry Winery (23837 U.S. 385, 605/574-3898, www.prairieberry.com, summer daily 10 A.M.–7 P.M., winter Mon.–Sat. 10 A.M.–5 P.M., Sun. noon–4 P.M. shoulder season May and Sept.–Oct. 10 A.M.–6 P.M.) is located three miles north of Hill City on U.S. 385/16. The winery is not open for tours, but wines are available for tasting all day. While South Dakota seems an unlikely location for grape growing, Prairie Berry has won numerous awards for its wines. South Dakota–grown grapes and honey, as well as raspberries, rhubarb, chokecherries, cranberries, plums, and crabapples, are some of the ingredients used to create the winery's many lines. The wines, packaged with beautiful labels and creatively named, make fabulous gifts from South Dakota. Two favorites include Red Ass Rhubarb and Lawrence Elk. I have never visited the winery without being impressed with the friendly and outgoing staff. Customer service here is consistently excellent and all of the staff members are well educated about all of the various wines available for tasting. A tasting at this winery is just plain fun. While there, plan on having a snack at the **Prairie Berry Kitchen** which is open one hour after the winery opens and closes half an hour before the winery shuts down for the day. The kitchen serves gourmet cheeses, homemade soups, and local salamis, and provides a lovely outdoor deck for dining.

RECREATION
Hiking

Every region in the hills has something to offer

hikers. Located about eight miles north of Hill City, the **Flume Trail** follows the bed of a water channel built to divert water from Spring Creek and carry it to Rockerville. While most flumes are created to carry water for drinking to a growing community, this one was created to facilitate the processing of placer gold. The trail is open to foot traffic only and is a National Recreation Trail due to its historic significance.

FLUME TRAIL-CALUMET TRAILHEAD TO COON HOLLOW TRAILHEAD

- **Distance:** 11 miles, plus a 3-mile loop
- **Duration:** 6–7 hours
- **Elevation Gain:** 900 feet
- **Effort:** Easy
- **Trailhead:** Calumet Trailhead
- **Directions:** Drive north on U.S. 385 from Hill City. After the intersection with U.S. 16, stay on U.S. 385 for another 1.7 miles and take a right on Calumet Road. Follow the signs to the Sheridan Lake campground and then to the Calumet (or Flume) trailhead.

Even though the flume that gives this trail its name is no longer functional, water is still a presence on this hike. The trail starts at Sheridan Lake and crosses Spring Creek five separate times. Interesting features include two tunnels and visible remnants of the old wooden flume. The trail is well marked and there are interpretive signs posted along the way. It is one of the most popular hikes in the central hills outside of the Harney Peak area. About 6.5 miles into the hike, the trail has a spur to the left. This is the beginning of the 2.7-mile loop trail that starts and finishes at this point. If you elect to continue without the loop, follow the trail to the right for half a mile to the Boulder Hill trailhead. From there, the Boulder Hill overlook is about a mile. A fire tower was once located on the top of the hill,

© LAURAL BIDWELL

Horsethief Lake Campground

and this is the spot that will give the best views of the western Black Hills. Then return to the main trail. From here, it is another 3.8 miles to the Coon Hollow trailhead near Rockerville.

Biking

Hill City is a central hub for the **George S. Mickelson Trail** (www.gfp.sd.gov/state-parks/directory/mickelson-trail), a 109-mile biking/hiking trail that runs from Edgemont in the south to Deadwood in the north. This is a Rails-to-Trails project geared toward mountain biking and, as such, is a crushed gravel path. There is a $3 daily or $15 annual permit fee to use the trail. There are two shops in town that rent bicycles and provide shuttle service to any of the 14 trailheads. **Mickelson Trail Adventures** (412 E. Main St., 605/574-4094 or 605/391-4491, www.mickelsontrailadventures.com, daily 8 A.M.–4 P.M.) offers bike rentals for $29 per day, $19.50 per half-day, and $8.75 per hour. Shuttle rates are per person

and range from $33 to Deadwood to $45 to Edgemont. **Rabbit Bike** (175 Walnut St., 605/574-4302, www.rabbitbike.com, summer Mon.–Sat. 8 A.M.–5 P.M., Sun. 10 A.M.–4 P.M.) is the only full-service bike shop on the trail. With an extensive inventory of bikes in stock, there are comfort bikes and hardtail bikes as well as bikes for kids. Four-hour rentals are $25 for adults, $20 for kids, and 24-hour rentals are $35 for adults and $25 for children. Rentals include tire repair kits and helmets. Rabbit offers shuttle service to any trailhead on the Mickelson trail and will also shuttle to the Centennial trail. The shuttle is based on the trip, not the number of people. Six people fit in the shuttle van. Shuttle prices range from $50–150 for the van. Rabbit Bike offers package deals that include lodging. They really are a summer business, typically selling off their rental fleet at the end of the tourist season. But they sometimes open in the fall (Posted fall hours are "Open When We Want").

MICKELSON TRAIL-HILL CITY TO MYSTIC

- **Distance:** 14.6 miles
- **Duration:** 4 hours
- **Elevation Gain:** Negligible, and the grade never exceeds 4 percent
- **Effort:** Easy
- **Trailhead:** Tracey Park Trailhead
- **Directions:** Tracey Park is south of the Hill City Train near the intersection of Poplar and Railroad Avenues.

The Mickelson Trail was originally the Burlington Northern Railroad line that crossed western South Dakota from Edgemont to the gold mines in Deadwood. The line was abandoned in 1983 and, as part of the state centennial celebration, avid hikers began the project to convert the abandoned rails to trails. Completed in 1998, this 109-mile trail has 15 trailheads, one of which is the Tracey Park trailhead located in Hill City. From start to finish, the bed is packed gravel, wide, and well marked. This is a trail you will not get lost on. The segment from Hill City to Mystic is very rural. Highlights include riding along Crooked Creek, Newton Lake, Slate Creek dam, four railroad tunnels, and the historic gold mill town of Mystic.

CENTENNIAL TRAIL-DAKOTA POINT TRAILHEAD TO PILOT KNOB TRAILHEAD

- **Distance:** 19.6 miles one-way
- **Duration:** 5–6 hours
- **Elevation Gain:** 1,100 feet
- **Effort:** Moderate to strenuous
- **Trailhead:** From Hill City, drive north on U.S. 385 about 10 miles to Sheridan Lake Road. Take a right on Sheridan Lake Road and continue on for 1.6 miles. Take a right on Black Hills National Forest Road 434. The trailhead is 0.3 mile.

The Centennial Trail is not the easiest trail to navigate. Officially trail number 89, the markers are not always easy to find. Be sure to purchase trail maps at one of the forest service locations. (It wouldn't hurt to have GPS either!) Also be sure to carry plenty of water. That said, it's an exhilarating ride for those who want a nice long trip. This section of the trail is very hilly, but the hills aren't long. The trail winds through ponderosa pine forest and slate outcroppings and offers good views of Pactola Reservoir.

Boating

Fishing, swimming, and boat rentals are available at two beautiful lakes near Hill City. **Sheridan Lake** is a 380-acre lake located 10 miles north of Hill City off of U.S. 385. Kayaks, canoes, fishing boats, pedal boats, pontoons, and ski boats can be rented from **Sheridan Lake Marina** (16451 Sheridan Lake Rd., 605/574-2169, www.sheridanlakemarina. com, open year-round). Pontoons rent for $80 for two hours or $190 all day; fishing boats are $30 for two hours or $75 all day. Kayaks, canoes, and pedal boats are available for $10 an hour, $30 for a half-day, or $50 for all day. Life jackets are provided with all rentals. The marina store also sells bait, South Dakota fishing licenses (one-day resident $9, non-resident $16), rents fishing tackle, and provides camping supplies and basic groceries.

Pactola Reservoir, at 650 acres, is the largest body of water in the Central Hills. Located 14 miles from Hill City and just north of Sheridan Lake off of U.S. 385, it is a scenic location for boating or fishing. The marina there, **Pactola Pines** (U.S. 385, 605/343-4283 or 605/341-1286 off-season, www.pactolapines. com), has a variety of boats for rent, including several different sizes of pontoons which can accommodate 8–14 passengers, fishing boats, and canoes. Pontoons, based on size, range from $90–155 for two hours or $180–245 all day Monday–Friday, and $205–305 on weekends and summer holidays. Fishing boats rent for $40 for two hours, or $85 per day, and hold three or four people. Canoes are $20 for the

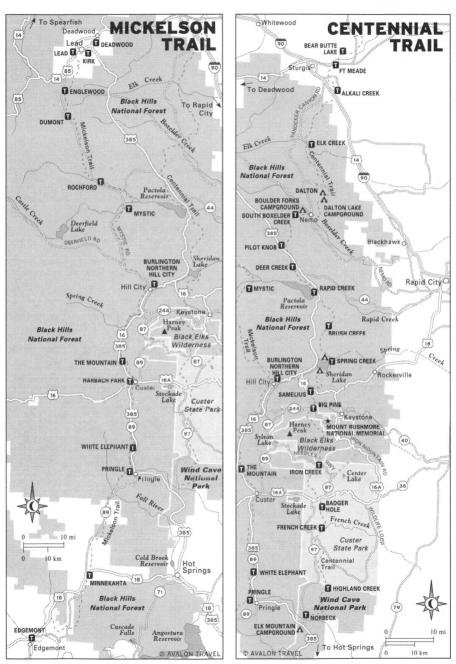

© AVALON TRAVEL

first hour, $10 for each additional hour, or $50 for the entire day.

Both Sheridan Lake and Pactola Reservoir (reservations 877/444-6777, 129 and 83 sites respectively) are part of the Black Hills National Forest and have day use fees of $6. Both also have camping facilities that include drinking water and toilets, but no electricity, hook-ups, or showers are available. Campsites are $21 per night.

ENTERTAINMENT

Enjoy a cowboy dinner and show at the **Circle-B Chuckwagon** (12138 Ray Smith Rd., 605/574-2129 or 800/403-7358, www.circle-b-ranch. com, Memorial Day–mid-Sept. Mon.–Sat., ticket office opens at 4:30 P.M., gunfight at 5:50 P.M., dinner at 6 P.M., adult $21–29, child $10–17). The Circle-B opened in 1976 and is the oldest chuck wagon dinner outfit in the hills. A traditional meal (chicken, beef, or buffalo served

with beans, a baked potato, applesauce, ginger cake, coffee, and lemonade) is followed by an evening performance of Western music—think "Sons of the Pioneers." Located four miles west of Hill City off of Deerfield Road, the facility also offers trail rides, gunfights, gold panning, a petting corral, and a gift shop.

SHOPPING

Hill City's main shopping district spans just a few blocks, but that small space packs in just about everything a shopping vacationer would want to bring home. The atmosphere is festive. Music is broadcast from outside speakers, there is a boardwalk, and there is always someone walking around with ice cream. Hill City looks and feels like summer. As with the lodging and restaurant establishments in town, many of the small shops operate seasonally; hours outside of the peak summer months of June, July, and August can vary with the weather and traffic.

© LAURAL BIDWELL

the Circle-B Chuckwagon show

Galleries

There are many fine galleries in Hill City. **Jon Crane Gallery & Framing** (256 Main St., 605/574-4440, www.joncranegallery.com, summer Mon.–Sat. 9:30 A.M.–7 P.M., Sun. noon–5 P.M., winter Mon.–Sat. 10 A.M.–6 P.M., closed Sun.) features the work of namesake artist Jon Crane, who is well known for his nostalgic and finely detailed watercolor rural landscapes. Jon's artwork is placed in galleries all over the country.

Sandy Swallow is an award-winning Lakota/Northern Cheyenne artist who is best known for her color-saturated block prints. Visit with her at the **Sandy Swallow Gallery** (280 Main St., 605/574-9505, www.sandyswallowgallery.com, June–Aug. daily 10 A.M.–7 P.M., May and Sept.–Oct. Mon.–Sat. 10 A.M.–6 P.M., closed Sun., closed Nov.–May.)

Stepping into **Warrior's Work & Ben West Gallery** (277 Main St., 605/574-4954, www.warriorswork-benwestgallery.com, open year-round, summer Mon.–Sat. 9 A.M.–8 P.M., Sun. 11 A.M.–4 P.M., spring and fall Mon.–Thurs. 10 A.M.–6 P.M., Fri.–Sat. 10 A.M.–7 P.M., closed Sun., winter Wed.–Sat. 11 A.M.–5 P.M., other hours by appt.) can be a little unsettling. The work on the walls is bold and emotionally powerful. Two galleries share the space. The Warrior's Work Gallery features powerful pieces by and about Native American people and culture. The Ben West Gallery specializes in contemporary art. Look for colorful pieces by Sarah Rogers. Between the two spaces, over 30 artists are represented. Owner Randy Berger also creates custom-designed leather frames that are works of art in themselves.

For those of you who wonder if the **Runs with Wolves Gallery** (253 Main St., 605/574-4700, open year-round, Apr. Tues.–Sat. 10 A.M.–5 P.M., closed Sun.–Mon., May open until 6 P.M., Jun.–Aug. Mon.–Sat. 10 A.M.–8 P.M., Sun. 10 A.M.–5 P.M., Sept. Mon.–Sat. 10 A.M.–6 P.M., closed Sun., winter hours vary) is a reference to the book of like title, it is. Owner Holly Kadis can be found behind the counter most days and is as direct, honest, and funny as they come. She stocks a great selection of local and regional books, in addition to a variety of creations by over 40 local artisans.

Across the street, **Artforms** (280 Main St., 605/574-4894, artforms.smugmug.com, Jun.–Aug. daily 9 A.M.–8 P.M., Sept.–mid-Oct. daily 9 A.M.–5 P.M., mid-Oct.–Dec. Thur.–Fri. and Sun 10 A.M.–4 P.M., Sat. 9 A.M.–5 PM., closed Jan.–Mar.) is in a quaint mall-like building that also includes an antiques gallery. Over 30 local and regional artists display their jewelry, painting, sculptures, and other pieces in the gallery. The store is an artist co-operative, which means that everyone behind the register is one of the artists whose work is represented in the store.

Gift and Specialty Shops

The best way to find great shops in Hill City is just to walk the downtown shopping district. There are many specialty gift shops up and down the boardwalk. Be sure to allow yourself a few hours to wander about.

If you've always dreamed of being a dance-hall girl, you can make your dream come true at **Buffalo Old Time Photo Co.** (309 Main St., 605/574-3314, www.buffalophoto.net, Memorial Day–Labor Day daily from 9 A.M., closing hours vary, closed in off-season). A photograph of the whole family in Western duds and waving firearms might become a favorite souvenir.

For a great collection of science-related and educational items (including dinosaur items), visit the **Everything Prehistoric Gift Shop** (117 Main St., 605/574-3919, www.everythingprehistoric.com, summer Mon.–Sat. 9 A.M.–7 P.M., Sun. 10 A.M.–6 P.M., winter through Christmas, Mon.–Sat. 9:30 A.M.–5:30 P.M., Sun. noon–4 P.M., Jan.–May Mon.–Sat. 9:30 A.M.–5 P.M., closed Sun.). The store has a great selection of books on archeology, mineralogy, paleontology, geology, and more, fossils and rocks, and rows and rows of fun and educational toys, as well as local jewelry. The gift shop serves as the entryway to the Museum at Black Hills Institute, so tickets for museum tours are sold here.

The Sturgis Motorcycle Rally is one of the biggest events in South Dakota, drawing several hundred thousand bikers to the state each year. That was enough to encourage Harley-Davidson to open a shop in downtown Hill City. Find branded leathers and other cool items at **Black Hills Harley-Davidson** (261 Main St., 605/574-3636, www.blackhillshd. com, Jun.–Aug. Mon.–Fri. 9 A.M.–7 P.M., Sat. 9 A.M.–6 P.M., Sun. 10 A.M.–6 P.M., May and Sept. Wed.–Sat. 9 A.M.–6 P.M., Sun. 10 A.M.–4 P.M., closed Mon.–Tues., closed Oct.–Apr.).

ACCOMMODATIONS

Room rates in the Black Hills vary widely from season to season. There are essentially three seasons in the hills: summer, shoulder season, and winter. Rates quoted are for the summer season, defined here as Memorial Day–Labor Day. (The shoulder season includes May, September, and October; winter, for tourism purposes, runs from November through April.) Rates also reflect the price of a standard room for two, or a single cabin or site for a single night. In many locations, discounted rates are available for longer stays, so be sure to ask about discounts. Shoulder season rates and winter rates are often significantly lower than rates in high summer (June–Aug.).

As is the case in every community in the hills, the chain hotels are well represented in Hill City. In Hill City, many of the chains are close to the town center and aren't a bad choice. If you are looking for a special experience, however, it's the cabins and small bed-and-breakfasts that provide the most charm and variety.

$50-100

The **Lantern Inn** (580 E. Main St., 605/574-2582, www.lanterninn.com, May–Sept., $100) has been a family-owned enterprise for many years in Hill City. It is an older, but extremely well maintained property with just 18 rooms. The rooms are spotlessly clean. Look for interesting touches—like shadow boxes built into the walls. Free wireless Internet, coffee in the office in the morning, a small pool, and a hot tub are available for guests.

The **Spring Creek Inn** (23900 U.S. 385, 605/574-2591 or 800/456-2755, www.spring-creekinn.com, motel rooms $89, cabins $169–199) is located just one mile north of Hill City off of U.S. 385, central to many of the hills attractions. Family owned and operated, the property is beautifully maintained. The inn is located on 3.5 acres and offers basketball and volleyball courts, playground equipment, a picnic shelter, and an outdoor grill on the grounds. A stream runs through the property. There are 12 motel rooms. They aren't big, but each has two beds and some have kitchenettes. Consider the motel rooms for a bargain stay. The cabins sleep 6–8 people and are extremely nice, light, and airy.

For location, the **Harney Peak Motel** (221 Main St., 605/574-2544, open seasonally, closed in winter, $80–95) can't be beat. It's an older property located in the heart of the downtown shopping and gallery district. Tucked away right off of Main Street, the non-smoking, pet-free rooms are very basic and clean, and come with air-conditioning, microwaves, and refrigerators. It's the downtown bargain.

$100-150

The Swiss are famous for their expertise in the field of hospitality, and Christine and Hanspeter Streich, owners of **Coyote Blues Village B&B** (23165 Horseman's Ranch Rd., Rapid City, 605/574-4477 or 888/253-4477, www.coyotebluesvillage.com, open year-round, $90–165), live up to the standards of their home country's reputation. Tucked away in the pines and surrounded by Black Hills beauty, Coyote Blues has a Rapid City address but is located just 14 miles (about 15 minutes) from Hill City. To get there, head north of town on U.S. 385 past Sheridan Lake and watch for the signs. There are 10 themed rooms, each decorated with art and furnishings from the country or era represented. Themes include Mediterranean, Turkish, African, Lakota, Antique, and Swiss decor and furnishings. Four of the 10 rooms have private decks or patios and private hot tubs. There are no phones, but free wireless Internet is available. The three Pine View rooms are smaller and share the public wraparound deck of the main house. These are the bargain rooms at $90 during the high summer season. This is a quiet location outside of town. If guests enjoy evening snacks, they will need to bring them since there are no restaurants close by. Breakfast is European style and includes meat and cheese plates, fresh fruit, breads, cereals, and eggs.

The nine-room **Black Forest Inn Bed & Breakfast** (23191 U.S. 385, Rapid City, 605/574-2000 or 800/888-1607, www.blackforestinn.net, open year-round, $85–160) has a Rapid City address but is much closer to Hill City. Located 12 miles north of town on U.S. 385, the inn is near Pactola Reservoir. Amenities include a game room with high-definition television, a pool table, and a video library. The inn is a dark brown and cream-trimmed frame building reminiscent of the style of National Park lodges. Inside, it's all light pine with elegant, spacious rooms. A massive stone fireplace is the center of the dining area. Breakfasts vary from day to day and include such items as pumpkin pancakes, stuffed French toast, and special egg bakes. Breakfast is served only to lodge guests and is included in the room rates, but dinner is open to the general public and is not included in room rates. During the summer months, light meals are available at the Bistro on the Terrace, located on the patio in front of the lodge.

$150 and up

The 87-room **Best Western Golden Spike** (601 E. Main St., 605/574-2577, www.bestwesterngoldenspike.com, Apr.–Oct., closed in off-season, $180) is family owned and operated and is a recipient of the South Dakota Governor's Great Service Award. Amenities include an indoor and an outdoor pool, a lovely garden area, free wireless Internet, bike rentals, and a guest laundry. There is a restaurant on-site, as well as a coffee bar serving pies, muffins, cookies, and cheesecake. The property is conveniently located at the southern edge of the downtown area. Packing for a picnic lunch is easy from this location, as groceries are available right across the street.

The **Holiday Inn Express** (12444 Old Hill City Rd., 605/574-4040 or 800/423-0908, www.ichotelsgroup.com, Apr.–Oct., $150–180) is located close to the 1880 Train depot. A handsome property set back from the main road, it is within walking distance of everything in town. There are 60 spacious, clean rooms; amenities include free local phone calls, free Wi-Fi, microwaves and mini-fridges, hot breakfast, an indoor swimming pool, a whirlpool tub, a small health and fitness center, and a guest laundry. No pets, though!

Cabins and Campgrounds

The closest campground to Mount Rushmore is on the Hill City side of the mountain and is a Black Hills National Forest Campground. The **Horsethief Lake Campground** (605/574-4402 or 877-444-6777, www.fs.usda.gov/recarea/blackhills, $23, plus $2 per pet per night) is four miles southeast of Hill City on Highway 244 and just two miles from Mount Rushmore. Sitting at 4,800 feet, this small, relatively primitive campground has a beautiful location nestled in the trees overlooking or near Horsethief

Lake. The campground does not have electricity or hook-ups, but vault toilets are available on-site. There are only 36 sites, of which 22 are suitable for either tents or RVs, and 14 sites are tent only. Reservations are suggested due to the campground's location near Mount Rushmore. The 10-acre Horsethief Lake is stocked with rainbow trout and perch, and boating is allowed (no powerboats, though). A nice 2.8-mile hiking trail skirts the lake.

With a similar name, but with entirely different amenities and facilities, there is the ◖ **Horse Thief Campground & RV Resort** (24391 Sylvan Lake Rd./Hwy. 87, 605/574-2668 or 800/657-5802, www.horsethief.com, open mid-May–Oct. 1, closed in winter, tent sites $21–27, RV sites $35–43, sleeping cabins $49–80, cottage $100). If there is a *most beautiful* region in the Black Hills, this mountainous, forested, granite-spired area near Sylvan Lake is it. The campground is located just three miles south of Sylvan Lake and sites are tucked into the pines. Services include wireless Internet, picnic tables, a heated pool, a playground, and a camp store with a small selection of groceries and gifts. Bring your own bedding and cooking utensils for the sleeping cabins and the cottage. To get there, head south from Hill City on U.S. 385, turn left on Highway 87, and go two miles to the campground.

FOOD
Family Fare
◖ **Desperados Cowboy Restaurant** (301 Main St., 605/574-2959, May 1–Labor Day daily lunch 11:30 A.M.–3 P.M., dinner 5–9 P.M., closed in off-season, lunch $9, dinner $9–22) is located in the oldest commercial building in town, a log cabin built in 1885. Don't let the rustic appearance of the outside of this building fool you. Inside the restaurant, the chinked log walls and cowboy decor make for a cozy dining experience. The upscale Western-themed restaurant features walleye, ribs, buffalo burgers,

sweet potato fries, and veggie wraps. A children's menu is available.

There are not many places open for breakfast in town, but check out the **Slate Creek Grille** (158 Museum Dr., 605/574-9422, www.slatecreekgrille.com, summer daily 7 A.M.–9 P.M., bar open nightly until 2 A.M., winter Sun.–Thurs. 7 A.M.–8 P.M., Fri.–Sat. 7 A.M.–9 P.M., breakfast $7, lunch $10, dinner $10–20). Located at the north edge of the downtown shopping district, the grill is not a fancy place—access to the restaurant is through the bar and pool room. However, there is a great deck outside with a pretty view of town. Serving breakfast, lunch, and dinner, the grill features traditional American fare from pancakes to burgers and steak.

The **Bumpin Buffalo Bar & Grill** (245 Main St., 605/574-4100, mid-Mar.–Oct. daily 11 A.M.–9 or 10 P.M., closed for winter, lunch $9, dinner $15–20) is a good family choice. There's a full menu of basic American fare, including steaks, pasta, chicken, and fish. Many of the booths are furnished with television sets that keep the kids from getting bored (or keep the adults up on the latest sports news) and allow for a leisurely meal. The decor is an interesting mix of beer signs and trains, including a train model that circles the room (when a buffalo isn't in the way). If you like views, head for the covered rooftop deck. Overall, with high tin ceilings, it can get a bit noisy inside, but this is still a great place for a beer and a sandwich.

The **Hill City Cafe** (209 Main St., 605/574-4582, summer daily 6 A.M.–9 P.M., winter daily 6 A.M.–2 P.M., $8–12) is the place most likely to be filled with locals. It has a bit of a dusty diner feel, but it's a friendly kind of place located right in the middle of the downtown boardwalk shopping district. Breakfast offerings are especially hearty, featuring more than a couple of steak and egg combos. Lunch features a wide variety of burgers and other sandwiches, and dinner options include grilled chicken, steak, and pork chops.

Located just two miles northeast of Hill City on U.S. 385, the **Big Horn Crossing & Sports Bar** (23855 U.S. 385, 605/574-9566, open year-round, summer daily 11 A.M.–9 P.M., $10) features burgers, tacos, pizza, and sandwiches. The bar and restaurant are in two different areas. The bar, while sporting a dozen or so televisions, is a slightly more intimate choice for dining. Just off the bar area, there is a spacious, covered outdoor deck. Try the broasted chicken, served piping hot—it's delicious.

Fine Dining

Alpine Inn (133 Main St., 605/574-2749, www.alpineinnhillcity.com, summer Mon.–Sat. 11 A.M.–2 P.M. and 5–10 P.M., closed Sun., winter Mon.–Thurs. 11 A.M.–2 P.M. and 5–9 P.M., Fri.–Sat. 11 A.M.–2 P.M. and 5–9 P.M., closed Sun., lunch $9, dinner $10–12) is always a great place to eat—and if you enjoy outdoor dining and people-watching, it's the best spot in town for lunch, with a spacious deck dining area. Inside, dining is scattered throughout various Victorian-style rooms. The lunch menu is extensive, offering a great selection of German plates, creative salad main courses, and a wide variety of sandwiches. In the evening, dinner is perfect for folks who have a hard time making decisions, since the only entrée on the menu is filet mignon: You can have a six-ounce filet mignon or a nine-ounce filet mignon. On the other hand, there are still over 30 delicious desserts on the menu—from tiramisu to crème brûlée to peanut butter chocolate ice cream pie and German white chocolate mousse—it's almost overwhelming! The inn was built in the late 1880s as the Harney Peak Hotel. The restaurant is located on the lower floor of the building and is richly decorated in the Victorian style of the era during which it was built. Have lunch at the Alpine Inn at least once during your time in the hills. It is a victim of its own success, though, so go early to avoid long waits.

The **(Prairie Berry Kitchen** (23837 U.S. 385, 605/574-3898, www.prairieberry.com, summer daily Mon.–Sat. 11 A.M.–6 P.M., shoulder season May and Sept.–Oct. daily 11 A.M.–5:30 P.M., winter Nov.–May 11 A.M.–4:30 P.M., Sun. noon–3:30 P.M., $8–22) is located at the Prairie Berry Winery just three miles north of Hill City on U.S. 385. For those looking for a healthy alternative, it's a wonderful choice for lunch. European in nature, appetizers, soups, and flat bread sandwiches are created daily to complement the wines. Everything is homemade and delicious. There are several tables set up on the winery's patio for summer dining. Prairie Berry wine is available with the meals. In winter, the homemade soups fly out of the kitchen.

The **Black Forest Inn** (23191 U.S. 385, Rapid City, 605/574-2000 or 800/888-1607, www.blackforestinn.net, open year-round, summer 5–9 P.M., winter hours vary, $10 sandwiches to $22 dinner entrées) is located about eight miles north of Hill City off of U.S. 385. This well-respected dining establishment features two restaurants. June–early September (weather permitting), dinner is served outdoors in front of the inn at the **Bistro on the Terrace.** The sandwiches include the standard hamburger or buffalo burger, but more creative options are available as well, including a Portobello mushroom sandwich and a chicken, avocado, cream cheese, and tarragon choice. Dinner specialties include light Mediterranean cuisine, as well as rib eye steaks, fish, and chicken dishes. In case of inclement weather, dining is inside. (In the winter, dining is always inside the inn.) The dining room at the inn is elegant and spacious with hardwood floors and a lovely stone fireplace. There's only one dinner seating and the time is set based on the first reservation made. So, if you are the first to make a reservation and would like to dine at 7 P.M., that's when dinner is scheduled. Dinner entrées average $20 and choices typically include rack of lamb, rib eye steak, duck, and various chicken and pasta dishes. The dining area is small and cozy, with candlelit tables and lots of lace. It's a very romantic setting.

INFORMATION AND SERVICES

For Hill City information, call the **Hill City Chamber of Commerce** (23935 U.S. 385, 605/574-2368 or 800/888-1798, www.hillcitysd.com). Campers can find groceries and basic supplies at **Krull's Market** (513 Main St., 605/574-2717). The **regional medical clinic** (557 East Main Street, 05/574-4470) and the **post office** (150 East Main Street) are both on Main Street.

Rapid City

Rapid City sits on the eastern edge of the Black Hills and is the only urban area in the region. While it has the second-largest population in the state after Sioux Falls, Rapid City is still a relatively small Midwestern community of about 70,000 residents. The city's history, like many of the Black Hills communities, dates back to the late 1800s and the discovery of gold by Custer's expedition in 1874. The original businesses were established to service the mining camps. The community was named after Rapid Creek, which flows through the center of town. Easily accessible from both the south and east, Rapid City also developed as the hub of railroad activity in the hills. As a result, it became a commercial center, not just for mining, but also for the ranching and timber industries that followed. The carving of Mount Rushmore firmly established Rapid City as the center of tourism for the Black Hills, and the construction of Ellsworth Air Force Base quickly increased the city's population and solidified it as the urban heart of the hills. Rapid City boasts the only commercial airport in the Black Hills region.

In more recent history, a natural disaster contributed to the landscape of Rapid City as it looks today. In June 1972, Rapid City and most of the eastern Black Hills experienced record rainfall. Rapid Creek rose 13 feet in five hours and sent a wall of water crashing through town. It was a frightening flood, made more so by its unexpected arrival in the middle of night.

Tragically, 238 people lost their lives in the flood. Some 1,265 families lost their homes and another 3,000 homes were damaged. Thirty-six businesses were destroyed, as were 5,000 vehicles. The cost of damage to homes and businesses was estimated to be over $165 million throughout the Black Hills. As devastating as it was, the flood resulted in some positive change for Rapid City. Research into the flood determined that it was likely that a flood of this magnitude could happen again. To prevent future loss of life and property damage, the city decided that rebuilding along Rapid Creek would not be allowed. Today, the Rapid Creek floodplain is lined with a series of city parks connected by a walking and biking path that parallels the creek all the way through town. It's one of the community's nicest outdoor assets.

While still a small city, by any standards, Rapid City has one of the fasted growing economies in the country and it shows in the energy and money being invested in the downtown area. Many restaurants and shops have opened in recent years and the charming heart of the city has expanded to encompass several more blocks of spruced up enterprises.

Rapid City is a fairly easy city to navigate, with four major traffic arteries. Highway 44 runs east–west and connects the Rapid City Regional Airport to the downtown and western sections of the city. Highway 79 South on the east side of town is a four-lane highway that makes travel between the Southern and Central

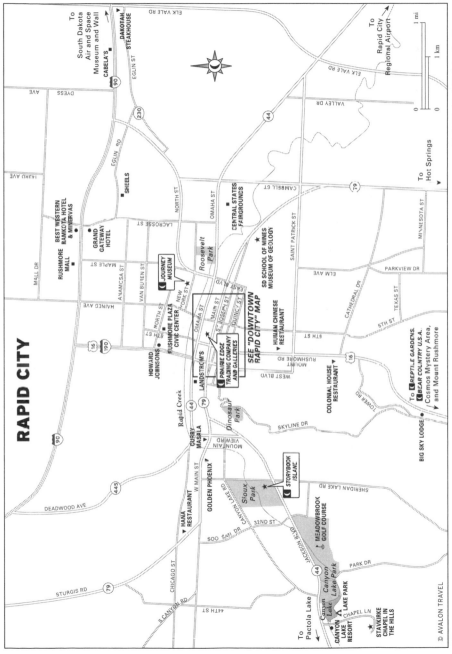

RAPID CITY

© AVALON TRAVEL

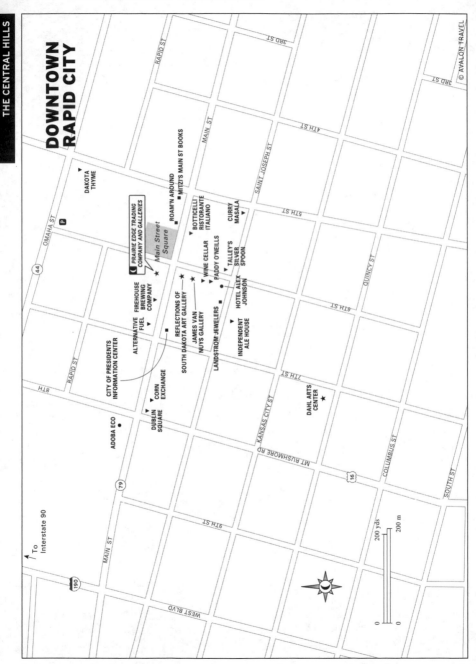

DOWNTOWN RAPID CITY

© AVALON TRAVEL

To Interstate 90

Hills fast and easy. The highway runs along the front range of the hills and as such doesn't involve the winding twisted roads you find within the hills themselves. Highway 79 North cuts through the heart of town and then heads north to Sturgis. I-90 runs right along the northern fringe of the city and is the primary route used by road-trippers heading to the Black Hills from the east and from the northwest. U.S. 16, otherwise known as Mount Rushmore Road, runs south from the downtown area and is the main artery that brings visitors from Rapid City to many of the region's best roadside attractions and to Mount Rushmore.

Lodging in and around the Rapid City region is concentrated in four separate areas of town. Most lodging options, not surprisingly, are along U.S. 16 (Mount Rushmore Rd.) because of its quick and direct access to Mount Rushmore and other attractions in the area. The historic district downtown has some nice choices, as well. It's fairly small, easily traversed on foot, and is dotted with galleries, restaurants, and unique shops. The western side of the city, near the Canyon Lake area, provides a more scenic (if slower) access route into the Black Hills. The winding roads west of Canyon Lake lead to Pactola Reservoir, to many hiking and biking trails, and to other outdoor recreation activities. There are more camping and cabin-type lodging options on this end of town. For road travelers arriving in Rapid City via I-90 from either the east or west, hotels—particularly the large chain hotels—are plentiful around exits 59 and 61. This location provides easy access to the Northern Hills for travelers headed west, and to the Badlands (and Wall) for those headed east. Exit 57 is the easiest exit off of I-90 to head south to the downtown district and to Mount Rushmore Road. There aren't many lodging choices available near the airport or on the eastern side of the city, but Highway 44 from the airport will bring travelers right downtown.

To get a feel for the city, its layout, and the location of many important sites, consider taking the one-hour narrated tour provided by **City View Trolley Tours** (333 6th St., 605/394-6631, www.rapidride.org, June 1–Aug. 31 Mon.–Sat. 10 A.M.–5 P.M., tickets $2 adult, $1 child). The trolley has 15 stops and can be picked up anywhere along the way. Hotel stops include the Rushmore Plaza Holiday Inn on the north end of town and the Adoba Eco and Alex Johnson Hotels located downtown. The fee for the tour can be paid to the operator. The trolley circulates at approximately 60-minute intervals.

SIGHTS
◖ Prairie Edge Trading Company and Galleries
In 1972, Ray and Rita Hillenbrand purchased the Triple Seven Ranch, a cattle ranch located between the Badlands of South Dakota and Rapid City. In 1985, the Hillenbrands decided to convert the ranch to a more environmentally friendly place and started ranching buffalo instead of cattle. Buffalo is much more suited to the plains weather and ecology than cattle. Today, there are over 1,500 head of buffalo on the ranch. The Hillenbrands expanded their interest in the plains and plains culture and decided that they would also like to preserve the heritage and culture of the Northern Plains tribes and to present that heritage to the general public. Equally important to them was a mission to create an outlet for the finest in Native American fine arts and crafts. The successful end result is the Prairie Edge Trading Company and Galleries (606 Main St., 605/342-3086 or 800/541-2388, www.prairieedge.com, open year-round Mon.–Sat. 9 A.M.–7 P.M., Sun. 10 A.M.–5 P.M.). The store presents the best in traditional and contemporary Native American art, as well as work by local and regional artists who are not native to the land. From drums to dresses and artifacts, to jewelry, beadwork, glassware, pottery, quilts, fine art, clothing, beads and other art supplies, and unique gift items, this store

MAIN STREET SQUARE SCULPTURE PROJECT

Ten granite stones border Rapid City's Main Street Square on the west side. Nine granite stones form a border along the south side. Two 35-foot granite clad spires sit between them. The stones, in and of themselves, are not all that attractive. But they will be. Over the course of 3-5 years, and in the eye of the public, one sculptor is going to carve these stones into representations of the flora, fauna, geology, and cultural and natural history of the Badlands, the Black Hills, and Rapid City. Beginning in the spring of 2013, if all goes as planned, visitors to downtown Rapid City will have the opportunity to watch the sculptor in action.

While the final project will be chosen from the artist's proposal, the original plan is for the nine stones on the south side of the square to be carved as representations of the Badlands. The 10 stones on the west side are the Black Hills. The spires sitting between them would then represent Rapid City.

For this project, 81 artists from around the world responded to the call for qualifications. In the course of a year, the field was eventually reduced to five finalists. The chosen artist will add to the growing list of rock carvings in the Black Hills, one sculpture at a time. It's a great opportunity to witness artistic creation in progress.

has it all. The beautiful displays are a pleasure to view, and if you fall in love with a piece, you can take it home with you.

◖ Journey Museum

The Journey Museum (222 New York St., 605/394-6923, www.journeymuseum.org, Memorial Day–Labor Day daily 9 A.M.–6 P.M., winter Mon.–Sat. 10 A.M.–5 P.M., Sun. 1–5 P.M., admission fees adult $8, senior $4.60, student 11–17 $5.75, child 10 and under free, *Into the Cosmos* tickets adult $5.75, senior $4.60, student $3.45, child 10 and under $2) is a great resource for visitors interested in the cultural, historical, and environmental aspects of the Black Hills. Collections include archaeology, geology, paleontology, Lakota history, and pioneer history. Museums can sometimes feel stagnant and dusty, but not the Journey. It's a dynamic space with many interactive exhibits that visitors can touch, as well as view. *Into the Cosmos,* held in the on-site theater, offers a digital trip from the Black Hills to the edge of the universe and back in a near three-dimensional environment. With lots of science and spectacular imagery, it's a reminder that Earth is one small planet in a very large and beautiful galaxy. The Journey can be overwhelming, so it might be best to pick a couple of collections, give them the full attention they deserve, and call it a day. The gift shop is marvelous, with a tasteful collection that includes jewelry, books, science toys, T-shirts, and other items.

City of Presidents

The City of Presidents sculpture exhibit is impossible to miss in downtown Rapid City. Life-sized bronze sculptures of U.S. presidents adorn many of the street corners. The project began in 2000, with the goal of adding four presidents to the exhibit each year. In 2013, President Barack Obama will be added to the collection, and the project will be finished—until the next election! The **City of Presidents Information Center** (631 Main St., June–early Oct. Mon.–Sat. noon–9 P.M., closed in winter) provides maps, and staff can answer questions about the sculptors, the presidents, and the project. Statues in public places are usually larger than life-size, which seems to have an impact on our perception and makes the presidential statues look small. Watch as people walk by, or stand or sit next to one and you'll see that they are, indeed, about the size of a normal person.

in a circular space, cycloramas were usually designed to provide a panoramic view of a historic scene, battle, or site. The form eventually fell out of favor and only a few of the original cycloramas remain. The Dahl cyclorama is an unusual and interesting return to an art form from an earlier time. Today, the Dahl has been expanded to encompass three separate galleries, a children's interactive gallery, a 250-seat event center, and art classrooms, in addition to the Thomas mural. Exhibitions at the galleries are rotated on a regular basis and are eclectic in nature. The event center hosts literary events and music and theater presentations.

Museum of Geology

One of the best collections of South Dakota's ancient resources resides at the Museum of Geology at the **South Dakota School of Mines and Technology** (501 E. Joseph St., 605/394-2467 or 800/544-8162, ext. 2467, http://museum.sdsmt.edu, open year-round, May–Aug. Mon.–Fri. 9 A.M.–5 P.M., Sat. 9 A.M.–6 P.M., Sun. noon–5 P.M., winter Mon.–Fri. 9 A.M.–4 P.M., Sat. 10 A.M.–4 P.M., closed Sun., free). The museum opened in 1885 and today, the collection includes over 350,000 specimens of fossils, rocks, and minerals from the Black Hills' ancient past. Displays also include minerals from around the world, fluorescent minerals, and local agates, meteorites, and native gold. There are also several life-sized models of dinosaurs on display. Many of the museum's extensive collections are on loan to the Journey Museum.

Dinosaur Park

There are several sites in the Rapid City area that are fun for both kids and adults. Dinosaur Park (940 Skyline Dr., 605/343-8687, open year-round, daily dawn–dusk, free) is likely one of the odder projects funded by the WPA in the 1930s. Built in 1936, the park is on the National Register of Historic Places. For decades, these

© LAURAL BIDWELL

Meet Andrew Jackson at the City of Presidents. The sculpture was created by South Dakota native James Michael Maher.

The Dahl Arts Center

Also downtown is the Dahl Arts Center (713 7th St., 605/394-4101, www.thedahl.org, open year-round, summer Tues.–Fri. 10 A.M.–6 P.M., Sat. 10 A.M.–5 P.M., closed Sun. and Mon., winter Mon.–Wed. and Fri. 9 A.M.–5 P.M., Thurs. 9 A.M.–8 P.M., Sat. and Sun. 1–5 P.M., suggested donation $5). In the mid-1970s, Arthur E. Dahl commissioned artist Bernard Thomas to paint a 180-foot-long, 360-degree cyclorama depicting 200 years of American history. Dahl was a prominent banker in Rapid City and his intention was to gift the cyclorama and the building it was housed in to Rapid City. Bernard Thomas was a Western artist born near Sheridan, Wyoming, in 1918. He was very active in mural painting and painted several in the Wyoming region, though the Dahl building is the only art-in-the-round that he created. The cyclorama was an extremely popular art form in the late 19th century. Painted

© LAURAL BIDWELL

Dinosaur Park

concrete sculptures—including a T. rex, bronto-saurus, stegosaurus, and triceratops—have been watching the prairie horizon and welcoming visitors every day, year-round. The dinosaurs were originally gray, but now are painted green and white. They aren't biologically accurate, but they are designed for good climbing. Have a seat on a dinosaur tail and enjoy the view.

The park's visitors center (970 Skyline Dr., 605/343-8687, June–Aug. daily 8:30 A.M.–8 P.M., May and Sept.–Oct. daily 9 A.M.–5 P.M., closed in winter) carries a nice collection of dinosaur books and gifts, rocks, and fossils, and also has a snack bar with sand-wiches and ice cream.

◖ Storybook Island

Another great place to bring the kids is Storybook Island (1301 Sheridan Lake Rd., 605/342-6357, www.storybookisland.org, Memorial Day–Labor Day daily 9 A.M.–7 P.M., closed in winter, free). Established in 1959 by

the Rapid City Rotary Club, Storybook Island is populated by life-sized characters from fairy tales and other children's books. Meet the Cat in the Hat, Humpty Dumpty, the Three Little Pigs, Winnie the Pooh, Huck Finn, and more than 100 other stars of children's fiction. The Children's Theater at the park presents four dif-ferent plays five days a week throughout the summer; tickets are $1. The park is in a lovely setting next to Rapid Creek and the city-wide bike path. There is a snack bar on the grounds and a small gift shop, as well.

South Dakota Air and Space Museum

Seven miles east of Rapid City, off I-90, exit 67, the South Dakota Air and Space Museum (235 Main Gate Rd., 605/385-5189, www.sdairandspacemu-seum.com, summer daily 8:30 A.M.–6 P.M., winter daily 8 A.M.–4:30 P.M., free) is located just out-side the main gate to **Ellsworth Air Force Base.** This is a site for fans of military aviation. There are over 25 aircraft displays ranging from WWII bombers to the contemporary B-1B Lancer. Some of the planes are displayed inside the hangar, but most are outside on the grounds. (In January and February, only the outside grounds are open and the museum's indoor hangars and gift shop are closed.) Since the museum is located outside of Ellsworth Air Force Base, a military or other ID is not required for entry. However, a bus tour (mid-May–mid-Sept., adult $8, child $5) enters the grounds of the base, so all visitors over the age of 18 must bring valid identification in order to clear a security checkpoint. The bus tour takes about 50 minutes and includes a tour of the base and a visit to a Minuteman II training launch facility.

◖ Reptile Gardens

Reptile Gardens (8955 S. Hwy. 16, 605/342-5873 or 800/335-0275, www.reptilegar-dens.com, Memorial Day–Labor Day daily 8 A.M.–6 P.M., Apr. 1–Memorial Day and Labor Day–mid-Oct. daily 9 A.M.–4 P.M., Nov.–Dec. hours vary, closed Jan.–Mar., admission prices

a giant tortoise at Reptile Gardens

vary seasonally, adult $12–16, child $8–11) is a great family attraction in the hills. This assessment is seconded by both the Midwest Travel Writers Association and *USA Today*, which called it one of the top 10 roadside attractions in the United States. The grounds of Reptile Gardens include a large gift shop, the Sky Dome, an outdoor stage, and several outdoor exhibit areas, including an area for raptors and another for crocodiles. From Labor Day–Memorial Day, three rotating presentations are given throughout the day at the exhibit areas. Wild Wings is a presentation on raptors and other birds. The Crocodilian Show is an exciting look at the differences between alligators, crocodiles, and caimans, presented by the keeper as he's wading among them, demonstrating their strength—and their teeth—when they are fed. The third show is all about snakes. You can see a mangrove, Burmese python, cottonmouth, cobra, and prairie rattlesnake up close as the handler talks about their unique

characteristics. All of the shows are highly interactive, humorous, and filled with facts. The presentations rotate so that you can wander from one to another while you are there. Also roaming the grounds during the summer are the giant tortoises, a personal favorite.

The Sky Dome is landscaped and temperature controlled to create two separate environments: a desert and a tropical jungle. Lizards and frogs hop freely about the lush tropical plants and finches fly throughout the dome. In the desert zone, cactus and other succulents are planted, and the Safari room of the dome is filled with orchids and other colorful flowers. Large parrots, macaws, and pythons complete the display. The Sky Dome also houses some of the rarest snakes in the world, and there are more species of reptiles at Reptile Gardens than at any other place in the world.

Reptile Gardens opened its doors in 1937, the brainchild of the somewhat nutty Earl Brocklesby (who would surprise visitors by removing his hat to display a coiled up rattlesnake on his head!). Earl passed away in 1993, but the gardens remain family-owned and -operated to this day.

◖ Bear Country U.S.A.

More than 20 species of animals roam the grounds of Bear Country U.S.A. (13820 S. U.S. 16, 605/343-2290, www.bearcountryusa. com, May–late Nov. daily 8 A.M.–6 P.M., May and Sept.–Oct. daily 9 A.M.–4 P.M., closed in winter, adult $16, child $10, maximum charge $60 per vehicle), located about eight miles south of Rapid City off of U.S. 16. The first part of the park is a drive-through wildlife-viewing area. Expect to get an intimate view of the over 200 bears on-site, as well as elk, reindeer, cougars, deer, bighorn sheep, and other North American mammals on this three-mile drive-through adventure. The animal habitat is carefully designed to give the animals an environment much like the one they would experience in the wild. It takes about two hours, with many stops, to travel the loop. At the end of the drive, stop at the Wildlife Center and at Babyland, which houses baby animals and smaller animals that would not be visible otherwise. A very large gift shop features souvenirs, art prints, mugs, and other items, most of which follow a wildlife theme.

Cosmos Mystery Area

Everyone over the age of seven approaches the Cosmos Mystery Area (24040 Cosmos Rd., 605/343-9802, www.cosmosmysteryarea.com, open seasonally, June–Aug. daily 8 A.M.–dusk, Apr.–May and Sept.–Oct. daily 9 A.M.–5 P.M., closed in off-season, child aged 12 and older $9.50, child under 11 free when accompanied by a parent) with a healthy dose of skepticism. After all, visitors are told that they will change heights, water will run uphill, and a mysterious force will create all sorts of mind-boggling experiences. It's a fun tour (about 30 minutes) where skepticism turns to confusion. Children

are confounded and hooked after the first narrated demonstration. Adults take a little longer, but by the time the tour is over, everyone is scratching their heads wondering "How did they do that?"

RECREATION
Golf

There are several nice public golf courses in the Rapid City area. The **Golf Club at Red Rock** (6520 Birkdale Dr., 605/718-4710, www.golfclubatredrock.com, 18 holes $51, 9 holes $29) was ranked as the number one public course in South Dakota in 2009 by *Golf Week* magazine. It is ranked as the most difficult course in the area by local golfers. The 7,000-yard, par-72 course is marked by rolling fairways with dramatic elevation changes and surrounded by prairie grasses and ponderosa pines. **Hart Ranch Golf Club** (23645 Club House Dr., 605/341-5703, www.hartranch.com, summer 18 holes $48, cart $34, 9 holes $27, cart $19, spring and fall 18 holes $42, 9 holes $25) is another fine choice. The 6,841-yard, par-72 course has been listed as one of the "Places to Play" by *Golf Digest* magazine. Both courses are located about nine miles southwest of town off of Mount Rushmore Road (U.S. 16).

Closer to town is **Meadowbrook Golf Course** (3625 Jackson Blvd., 605/394-4191, www.golfatmeadowbrook.com, 18 holes $38, 9 holes $24), which was chosen to host the 2009–2010 Women's National Championships. The 7,100-yard, par-72 course is located in western Rapid City near Canyon Lake Park off of Jackson Boulevard (Hwy. 44). It is a very pretty course. Nestled into the foothills of the Black Hills, Rapid Creek runs through the property, coming into play on five holes.

Biking and Hiking

Rapid City has over 13 miles of municipal biking and walking trails that wind through the city following Rapid Creek. Contact the

City Parks and Recreation Department (Recreation Dept., 125 Waterloo St., 605/394-4168, www.rcgov.org/parks-and-recreation) for information and maps, or check with local bike shops. For the most part, you need to bring your own bike to Rapid City; however, on the west side of town, **Acme Bicycles** (1727 W. Main St., 605/343-9534, www.acmebicycles. com) rents bicycles from whatever used bicycle stock the shop has available. The charge for a rental is $20 per day, but since Acme Bicycles is not really in the business of rentals, it charges the full sale price of the bike and then credits back all but $20 when the bike is returned.

Other Recreation

Canyon Lake Park (4181 Jackson Blvd., 605/394-4175) is a municipal park in western Rapid City. Activities at the park include fishing, paddle boating, and biking. Paddle boats can be rented from **Canyon Lake Resort** (2720 Chapel Ln., 605/343-0234 or 800/646-5603, www.canyonlakeresorts.com, 2-seat $8 per half hour, $12 per hour, 4-seat $10 per half hour, $15 per hour).

Clustered around the hotels located off of I-90 on the northern side of town are two fun family recreation sites. The best mini golf can be found at **Pirate's Cove Adventure Golf** (1500 La Crosse St., 605/343-8540, www.piratescove.net/rapid-city, May–mid-Oct. daily 9 A.M.–10 P.M., closed in winter, adult $8.50, child $7.50), located in the northeast corner of the city off of exit 67B from I-90. The course is like a small theme park and players will find themselves putting into caves, from behind waterfalls, and around other pirate-themed obstacles. It's a charming setting and elevates mini golf to a new level of aesthetics.

The largest water park in a four-state region, the **Watiki Indoor Waterpark Resort** (1314 N. Elk Vale Rd., 877/545-2897, www.watikiwaterpark.com, open year-round, summer Sun.–Thurs. 8 A.M.–9 P.M., Fri.–Sat. 8 A.M. to 10 P.M., off season Mon.–Thurs. 4–9 P.M.,

Fri. 4–10 P.M., Sat. 8 A.M.–10 P.M., Sun. 8 A.M.–8 P.M., $19.95) is located off of I-90, exit 61, on the north side of Rapid City. At 30,000 square feet, the park includes an arcade and concession stand. The park adjoins La Quinta Inn & Suites and Fairfield Inn & Suites.

ENTERTAINMENT
Chuck Wagon Dinners

A decidedly Western phenomenon, the chuck wagon dinner and show generally features music, corny jokes, and food served as diners walk through a line, plates in hand. There are two chuck wagon dinner venues in the Rapid City area. The format is similar, but the two places are quite different.

The **Flying T Wranglers** (8971 S. U.S. 16, 605/342-1905 or 888/256-1905, www.flyingt. com, Memorial Day–mid-Sept., ticket office opens at 3 P.M., dinner at 6:30 P.M., adult $24, child aged 7–11 $12, child aged 3–6 $6, show without dinner adult $12, child $6) is located just south of Reptile Gardens. While most chuck wagon establishments serve steak or chicken with a potato, the Flying T has branched out into more creative cuisine. The menu includes your choice of buffalo stew (from a fabulous source, **Wild Idea Buffalo Company**), chicken and dumplings, or vegetable stew with a dessert offering of blackberry pudding. It stays classic with corn bread and coleslaw side dishes. The show is also classic. Close to the original chuck wagon format, the music is old style country with a few contemporary country songs in the mix. The show is just about an hour long and starts right after dinner.

The **Fort Hayes Chuck Wagon & Show** (2255 Fort Hayes Dr., 888/394-9653, www. mountrushmoretours.com, mid-May–Oct., daily dinner 6:30 P.M., show at 7:15 P.M., adult $21, child aged 5–12 $10.50, child 4 and under $5) provides more traditional chuck wagon food, including sliced barbecue beef or baked chicken with potatoes, beans, and biscuits and

Fort Hayes Chuckwagon & Show

© LAURAL BIDWELL

honey. The show features a more contemporary country music selection. The grounds of the Fort Hayes chuck wagon dinner include some of the sets from the movie *Dances with Wolves*. There is also a rope making shop, a tin plate making shop, a brick maker and a Christmas/Western-themed gift shop.

Rushmore Plaza Civic Center

The Rushmore Plaza Civic Center (444 N. Mt. Rushmore Rd., 605/394-4115, www.gotmine.com) plays host to rodeos and music, sports, dance, and theater productions. It has an ice arena and the Don Barnet arena, which seats 10,000 and is a flexible space that can transform itself from a circus tent to a rodeo to a concert venue. The **Black Hills Symphony Orchestra** (1202 E. St. Francis St., 605/348-4676, www.bhsymphony.org, adult $12–25, student $5–15), established in the early 1930s, plays a concert series that runs October–April at the Civic Center. Be sure to check with the center when you are

traveling to the Hills to see if there are any special shows you wouldn't want to miss.

EVENTS
Summer Nights

Every Thursday night, June–September, several blocks in downtown Rapid City are closed off to traffic and are opened up to pedestrians. Music, local artisans, gallery walks, and activities for children and adults are organized from 5:30–8:30 P.M. Activities and music for this extremely popular event change every week. More information is available at www.rapidcitysummernights.com.

Central States Fair

The Central States Fair (800 San Francisco St., 605/355-3861, www.centralstatesfair.com, last week in Aug.) is a week-long celebration that features lots of free entertainment and livestock shows, plus concerts, rodeos, and other events, like a demolition derby and supercross dirt bike races. There are also carnival rides, pig races, food, and hobby and craft competitions. The cost to get into the grounds is just $3. All concerts are $28–34, and other events (such as the demolition derby, and supercross races, and the PRCA Range Days Rodeo) are $15 for adults and $5 for children. Carnival ride passes cost $27 per day. Alternatively, tickets can be purchased for individual rides. It's all delightful noise and lights, cheap rides, and junk food—a great way to end the summer.

Black Hills Stock Show Rodeo

The Black Hills Stock Show Rodeo, which shares a website with the Central States Fair (www.centralstatesfair.com, click on the stock show option), is a one-week rodeo and stock show that occurs the last few days of January and the first week of February. It is held at the Rushmore Plaza Civic Center (444 N. Mt. Rushmore Rd., 605/394-4115, www.gotmine. com). Ticket prices range $10–40. The stock

show events include a banquet and ball, livestock shows, horse events, a Western art show, sheepdog trials, and nightly concerts and rodeo performances. Vendors sell everything from horse trailers to handcrafted jewelry.

SHOPPING
Downtown Boutiques

The best way to discover unique shops in the downtown area is to put on some walking shoes and roam around. Most of the cute boutiques are in the six-block area bordered by 5th Street, Main Street, Kansas City Road, and Mount Rushmore Road. Many of the shops are run by owners who are more than happy to talk about their products, about their businesses, and about the best of Rapid City. As in many cities nationwide, there has been an increased focus on energizing the downtown district and new boutiques are popping up on a regular basis.

A recent addition to downtown is a complete city block called **Main Street Square**

Main Street in Rapid City offers shopping and dining.

© LAURAL BIDWELL

(512 Main St., Ste. 100, 605/716-7979, www. mainstreetsquarerc.com). Outdoors, the square sports a dancing water fountain and other water features, along with several rock formations waiting for the selection of a winning design and a sculptor to convert the rocks into representations of the Black Hills and the Badlands. There are tables, umbrellas, and chairs available to the public for picnics or for a place to sit for a spell. In the summer time, people are welcome to step into the fountain and enjoy the cool spray. Also in the summer, the square organizers sponsor events almost every weekend. Events include wine and beer tastings, concerts, free movies under the stars, theatrical performances, and a farmers market. In the winter, the water feature turns into a small ice rink. It's a festive and fun corner downtown.

In addition to the events and the open space, Main Street Square is also home to several small shops. **Mitzi's Main Street Books** (510 Main St., 605/721-2665, www.mitzisbooks.com, Mon.–Sat. 9 A.M.–8 P.M., Sun. 11 A.M.–5 P.M.) is a great location for folks who support independent bookstores and love paper over plastic when it comes to the reading experience. This is a great place to pick up a book, grab some coffee, and take advantage of the square's outdoor tables. Right next door is **Roam'n Around** (512 Main St., 605/716-1660, www. roamnaround.com, Mon.–Sat. 10 A.M.–9 P.M., Sun. 11 A.M.–4 P.M., winter hours Mon.–Sat. 10 A.M.–6 P.M., Sun. 11 A.M.–4 P.M.), a great little travel store that carries travel gear, like backpacks, and some adventure gear, like rock climbing equipment. The shop also carries *Moon Handbooks* travel guides.

In addition to Prairie Edge, one of the must-see locations in town, there are several other art galleries in the downtown area, including the **James Van Nuys Gallery** (516 6th St., 605/343-2449, www.jamesvannuys.com, Mon.–Sat. 10 A.M.–6 P.M.). Van Nuys is a multitalented musician, writer, and artist of many mediums, including oil, acrylic, and watercolor. Of particular note is his mastery of the beauty of prairie skies. Van Nuys also works with bronze, and he crafted two of the presidents in the City of Presidents display: Millard Fillmore (the 13th president of the United States, who served 1850–1853) and Franklin Pierce (the 14th president, who served 1853–1857). Van Nuys' gallery is also his studio, and stopping by will likely result in an opportunity to watch the artist at work.

Reflections of South Dakota Art Gallery

WHAT IS BLACK HILLS GOLD?

Just about every community in the Black Hills has a shop that sells "Black Hills Gold." Exactly what is that? Legally, all products sold with that label must be manufactured in South Dakota. However, it does not mean that the gold used to create the piece was *mined* in South Dakota. In addition to the legal definition, the Black Hills Gold designation has a traditional meaning. Simply put, traditional Black Hills Gold combines pink, green, and yellow gold in a design that incorporates grapes, grapevines, and grape leaves. The design originated in the gold mining towns of California (hence the grapes), migrated with the jewelers to the gold camps of Montana, and finally, followed the last gold rush in the United States to the Black Hills of South Dakota. The signature colors of traditional Black Hills Gold are created using alloys. To obtain pink gold, 24-karat yellow gold is alloyed with copper. To obtain green gold, 24-karat yellow gold is alloyed with silver.

To see Black Hills Gold jewelry crafted by hand, visit **Landstrom's** (405 Canal St., Rapid City, 605/343-0157 or 800/343-0157, www.landstroms.com, Mon.-Fri., free tours twice daily at 10 A.M. and 1 P.M.) and go on the factory tour, which takes 30-45 minutes.

(605 Main St., 605/341-3234, www.reflectionsofsouthdakota.com, Memorial Day–Sept. Mon.–Sat. 9 A.M.–9 P.M., Sun. noon–5 P.M., Oct.–Memorial Day Mon.–Sat. 10 A.M.–6 P.M., Sun. 10 A.M.–5 P.M.) features over 30 local and national artists who work in a wide variety of mediums, including painting, sculpture, photography, jewelry, pottery, leather, and woodwork. The gallery is owned by photographer Joe Lowe, who served as the state of South Dakota's wildland fire coordinator for many years (and still gets called out of retirement to help when the fire danger rises), and Wendy Lowe, who is a painter in her own right.

The **Alex Johnson Mercantile** (608 St. Joseph St., 605/343-2383, www.shopalexjohnson.com, May–Sept. daily 8 A.M.–9 P.M., Oct.–Apr. daily 9 A.M.–5 P.M.) features an eclectic mix of arts and crafts, jewelry, and gift items. Several Lakota artists are represented here, and the shop prides itself on carrying products made in the United States. It offers lobby access to Hotel Alex Johnson, so it also carries items of interest to the traveler, including stamps, newspapers, and souvenirs.

Landstrom Jewelers (620 St. Joseph St., 605/342-6663, Mon.–Fri. 9 A.M.–5:15 P.M., Sat. 9 A.M.–5 P.M.) is the oldest full-service jewelry store in Rapid City and carries a significant collection of Black Hills Gold. The owner knows his business and is more than happy to chat about what the "Black Hills Gold" designation means. I asked why the shop was open until 5:15 P.M., since it's the first I've heard of such an interesting closing time. The owner said, "Well, we have a lot of people who need to pick things up or drop things off after work, but we noticed that we didn't really do any business between 5:15 and 5:30, so this works." That's efficient management!

Outdoors Specialty Shops

Two sports superstores in Rapid City grapple for your shopping dollars by making a visit to their establishment more of an adventure than a shopping excursion.

Scheel's Sports (1225 Eglin St., 605/342-9033, Mon.–Sat. 9 A.M.–9 P.M., Sun. 11 A.M.–6 P.M.) in Rapid City is part of an eight-state chain that opened in 1902. The store has over 100,000 square feet of merchandise in its location off of Highway 79, north and east of town. It's made shopping for equipment a bit of an expedition, with sports simulators, an archery range, and on-site specialists available to answer questions. Somewhat incongruously, a fudge shop called Gramma Ginna's has been added to the offerings of the store, so if the thought of hiking leaves you hungry, you can fill up on the likes of amaretto, praline, almond, maple walnut, or any of several other flavors of fudge.

Cabela's (3231 E. Mall Dr., 605/388-5600, summer Mon.–Sat. 8 A.M.–9 P.M., Sun. 9 A.M.–6 P.M., shorter hours in off-season) is most famous for the museum-quality animal displays in its retail outlets. The store had humble beginnings as a kitchen table mail-order enterprise in Chappell, Nebraska, back in 1951. Today, the flagship store is located in Sidney, Nebraska, and occupies more than 250,000 square feet. Cabela's, also famous for its catalog sales, now has retail outlets in more than 30 locations throughout the United States. The Rapid City store has more than 80,000 square feet of sports shopping entertainment. In addition to sales, the store is full of events for outdoor people. Want to know what your gun is worth, buy live bait for fishing, learn how to prepare for a disaster, or try your hand at archery? All of these various learning experiences are available at the store. It is located off of I-90, exit 61; from there, head north on Elk Vale Road and take a left on Mall Drive.

ACCOMMODATIONS

Hotels in the Rapid City area are clustered around exits off of I-90 on the north side of town, and along Mount Rushmore Road near downtown. In both locations, chain hotels dominate. The western edge of the city, off of Highway 44, is closest to the wooded Black Hills, and cabins and campgrounds are available here. For access to the best attractions in the Central and Southern Hills, the best places to stay are near the downtown area or just south of downtown off of U.S. 16. Downtown locations provide easy access to boutique shopping, galleries, restaurants, and pubs. Hotels located near the I-90 corridor provide easy access to the Northern Hills and the Badlands.

$50-100

The **◖ Big Sky Lodge** (4080 Tower Rd., 800/318-3208 or 605/348-3200, www.bigskylodge.com, open year-round, summer rates $79–99, shoulder and winter rates $39–69) is one of the few small family-owned and -operated motels off of U.S. 16A. A one-story, well-maintained building located close to Sky Ridge Drive (and Dinosaur Park), the 31-room motel rests on the edge of a ridge overlooking the city. There is parking in front of each of the rooms for easy access and unloading. In the evening, you can sit in the hot tub and watch the city lights and the stars. It's an absolutely beautiful view. There are also plenty of benches arranged on the outdoor deck for taking in the views. The rooms are simple but attractive, with nice quilts. Amenities include free wireless Internet access, a playground, and a picnic area. The owners, Jay and Alicia Culbertson, love the hospitality business, their lodge, and meeting people from around the country.

On the western side of town, **Canyon Lake Resort** (2720 Chapel Ln., 605/343-0234 or 800/646-5603, www.canyonlakeresorts.com, open year-round, motel rooms and small cabins summer $99, Sept.–Memorial Day $54–64) is located next to one of Rapid City's prettiest parks. The location is very nice, and while the rooms are nothing fancy, they are a good

deal. Each motel room has two queen-sized beds and a kitchenette. The single cabins have one queen bed. There is a fire pit located outside the rooms, and guests can paddleboat on the lake for free. Located on two acres, this is a quiet spot, close to the Meadowbrook Golf Course and Canyon Lake City Park. There is cable and free wireless Internet, and a special bonus is that the Rapid City Trolley stops here at 30-minute intervals. It's a great way to spend a day downtown without having to drive.

$100-150

Most of the hotels in this price range are chains, but the **Grand Gateway Hotel** (1721 N. LaCrosse St., 605/342-8853 or 866/742-1300, www.grandgatewayhotel.com, summer rates $129–149, winter rates $59–79) is a family-owned and -operated property right off of I-90 on the north end of town. It is an older hotel, built in the early 1980s, but the rooms are clean and elegant and the staff is comprised of five of the founder's grandsons and one granddaughter. The property features an indoor pool and water slide, and 24-hour access to an attached Perkins Restaurant. It makes a good base camp for day trips to the Badlands or to the Northern Hills.

In the downtown area, the 99-room **Howard Johnsons** (950 North St., 605/737-4656, www.hojorapidcity.com, summer $129–149) is a modern facility with a nice marble and wood lobby. Built in 2002, the hotel features an indoor pool and hot tubs, free Wi-Fi, and a fitness center. Complimentary continental breakfast is included. The standard rooms are spacious and nicely decorated with plenty of lighting. A small desk and work area is incorporated into each room. The hotel is just on the other side of Rapid Creek near Mount Rushmore Road and is within walking distance to downtown and the Rapid Creek walking/biking path and parks.

The **◖ Hisega Lodge B & B** (23101 Triangle Trail, 605/342-8444, www.hisegalodge.net, open year-round, $109–149, weekend rates $199–209) is located just seven miles west of Rapid City on Highway 44. A historic property that has served tourists since 1908, the lodge has a gorgeous wraparound deck and a fireplace in the common area. There are nine rooms, all with private baths. The rooms are meant to be soothing and are light and airy in style. There are wood floors and warm quilts on the beds. Some of the rooms have light wood paneling, some are painted; each is rustic and different from its neighbors. Every room opens directly onto the wraparound porch or to Rapid Creek, which runs through the property. Amenities include free Wi-Fi and, of course, a fabulous breakfast. Plan a Monday–Thursday stay for a great deal.

Another great choice in terms of location and value is the **Sweetgrass Inn Bed & Breakfast** (9356 Neck Yoke Rd., 605/343-5351, www. sweetgrassinn.com, $125–135). It's located about six miles south of central Rapid City off of Mount Rushmore Road (U.S. 16), the main route to the best Black Hills attractions and Mount Rushmore—and is almost directly across the street from Reptile Gardens. The eight rooms feature private entrances and private baths. The rooms are romantic, with light, floral décor. The Prairie Star Room is a pleasant place of rest for just about any taste.

Construction of the 143-room **Hotel Alex Johnson** (523 6th St., 605/342-1210 or or 888/729-0708, www.alexjohnson.com, summer $129–159, shoulder season $89–129, winter $49–89) began one day before work began on Mount Rushmore. One year later, in 1928, the hotel opened. Over the course of its history, the hotel has hosted six United States presidents. The building exterior is primarily brick, but the upper floors and roof are in Tudor style, painted white and crossed with dark wood framing. The lobby of the hotel is truly striking, with an interesting mix of Native American decor and German Tudor architecture. Now on the National Register of Historic Places, the

Alex Johnson recently underwent a major restoration. Based on old photographs and hotel plans, the hotel has returned to its 1920s-era decor. All of the furnishings were replaced, and fixtures include marble countertops and foyers, luxury bedding, in-room espresso makers, and large flat-screen televisions (a modern addition to the 1920s theme). Open to the hotel, **Seattle's Finest** is available for coffee and pastries. There is lobby access to the Mercantile Gift Shop and to **Paddy O'Neill's Pub,** considered one of the best nightspots in town.

The 177-room **Adoba Eco** (445 Mt. Rushmore Rd., 605/348-8300, www.adobarapidcity.com, summer $139–159) is another hotel within walking distance of downtown Rapid City. Previously a Raddison Hotel, the Adoba Eco is in the process of renovating the entire hotel to create as small a carbon imprint as possible. First to go was the swimming pool. The only floor that has been completely converted to recycled materials is the 8th floor. These are not your ordinary chain hotel rooms. The design work is a cross between metal pop and log cabin. Amenities include free Wi-Fi, new flat-screen TVs, a full breakfast buffet, airport shuttle, car rental service, and restaurant. The walls are covered with recycled Wyoming snow fences. Trays are made of traffic signs. And the windows open for fresh air. The hotel restaurant **Enigma** serves organic and locally grown foods for breakfast, lunch, and dinner daily. Breakfast is served beginning at 6 A.M.

$150 and up

On the northern side of town, the 93-room **Fairfield Inn & Suites by Marriott** (1314 N. Elk Vale Rd., 605/718-9600 or 888/236-2427, www.marriott.com, $150–209) is located off of I-90 at exit 61. Amenities include in-room coffee, microwave, wireless Internet, free continental breakfast, a fitness center, and direct access to the Watiki Indoor Water Park, making this a good choice for families. The rooms are modern and the beds are luxurious with firm mattresses and very soft pillows.

Also located on the northern end of town is the **Best Western Ramkota Hotel** (2111 N. LaCrosse St., 605/343-8550, www.rapidcity. ramkota.com, 267 rooms $160–170), at exit 59 off of I-90. The rooms are decorated with a Western theme and amenities include an indoor heated pool and whirlpool, a fitness room, free high-speed and wireless Internet access, and complimentary airport shuttle. The hotel also has an award-winning restaurant, Minerva's, and a cocktail lounge. This hotel is close to the Rushmore Mall for easy shopping access.

Cabins and Campgrounds

The Happy Holiday Resort (8990 S. U.S. 16, RV park reservations 605/342-7365 or 888/342-7365, motel and cabins 605/342-8101 or 888/674-2779, www.happyholidayrvresort. com, mid-May.–mid-Sept. tent sites $24, RV sites $27–37, motel rooms $70–99, sleeping cabins $55) is conveniently located about eight miles south of Rapid City near Reptile Gardens. There's a large pool and spa, lots of trees, an arcade, laundry, free wireless Internet, a convenience store, and car rentals; rates are reasonable and the property is close to all of the Central Hills attractions.

Mystery Mountain Resort (13752 S. U.S. 16, 605/342-5368 or 800/658-2267, www.mysterymountain.us, tent sites $19–28, RV sites $32–38, cabins $69–89) is nestled in the pines about nine miles south of Rapid City, just past Bear Country U.S.A. The facility is located on 38 acres and has free Wi-Fi, a playground, a 50-foot swimming pool, a hot tub, and mini golf. There is also a small convenience store and laundry services.

The **Lake Park Campground & Cottages** (2850 Chapel Ln., 605/341-5320 or 800/644-2267, www.lakeparkcampground.com, tent sites $28.50, RV sites $35–42, cabins $79–99, rates are $35 more per night if staying less than three nights) comprise a well-maintained property close to Canyon Lake on the west side of Rapid City. The tent sites feature 12-by-14-foot elevated tent pads on sandy soil and are fully shaded. The RV sites are forested sites, as well. The cabins are fully furnished, and simply decorated in lodge style with rustic pine furniture. There are no phones in the cottages, but wireless Internet and cable television are available. All RV sites have full hookups. There is paddle boating and trout fishing available on the lake, and the Rapid Creek bike path runs right past the facility for hiking and biking.

FOOD
Family Fare

The **Colonial House** (2501 Mt. Rushmore Rd., 605/342-4640, summer Mon.–Sat. 7 A.M.–9:30 P.M., Sun. 7 A.M.–9 P.M., winter Mon.–Sat. 7 A.M.–9 P.M., Sun. 7 A.M.–2 P.M., breakfast $9, lunch $9, dinner $15–20) is a local favorite for dining out in Rapid City. Located near many of the motels along Mount Rushmore Road, the very bright canary-yellow exterior is deceiving. Inside, you'll find a large, spacious restaurant, with a lot of wood paneling, dark green carpet, wood booths and tables, and brass trim in the small bar. It's casual and comfortable. The house specialties include chicken noodle soup and delicious hot caramel rolls. The menu includes a full range of sandwiches, burgers, and salads. Dinner specialties include buffalo rib eye and various cuts of steak.

Dakota Thyme (502 Main St., Ste. 200, 605/716-3354, www.dakotathyme. com, summer Mon.–Sat. 7 A.M.–8 P.M., Sun. 9 A.M.–4 P.M., $10) on Main Street Square is a deli-style restaurant serving a wide variety of soups, sandwiches, fresh pastries, and breakfast items. The food is great, the interior is painted in warm colors, the light is by Tiffany, and there are two outdoor decks. The restaurant has a beer and wine license and carries the widest variety of bottled beers I've seen anywhere.

The wine collection is equally impressive. This is a fabulous addition to downtown.

Tally's Silver Spoon (530 6th Street, 605/342-7621, www.tallyssilverspoon.com, daily 7 A.M.–9 P.M., kitchen closed 2–5 P.M. with a limited selection of items available, breakfast $9–13, lunch $9, dinner $13–30) is a great selection for breakfast downtown. Located across the street from the Hotel Alex Johnson, it is one of the few sit-down restaurants open for breakfast in the downtown area. Menu options range from traditional comfort foods to more creative foods, like the "Fish Monger's breakfast," which is a combination of mussels, shrimp, salmon, potatoes, avocado, lemon, poached eggs, and toast. It's an unusual but delicious breakfast. Standard breakfast fare is available, as well. The chef calls it "fine diner" cooking. The restaurant is black and stainless steel, a completely modern look.

For those staying on the north end of town, **Dakota Steak House** (1325 N. Elk Vale Rd., 605/791-1800, www.dakotahsteakhouse.com, daily 11 A.M.–10 P.M., lunch $10–14, dinner $16–35) is located off of exit 61 of I-90, just south of the highway. The restaurant is new, like most of the neighborhood here, and is near several new large chain hotels. Inside, the restaurant is a combination of casual and elegant, with wood floors, olive walls, and cherry accents. In the winter, there's a roaring fire. The signature dishes here are the steaks, of course. There are several cuts and serving sizes available. The menu includes wine suggestions for each entrée suggestion.

Also on the north end of town is the award-winning **Minerva's Restaurant & Bar** (2111 N. LaCrosse St., 605/394-9505, Mon.–Sat. 6:30 A.M.–10 P.M., Sun. 6:30 A.M.–9 P.M., breakfast $8, lunch $10, dinner $16–30, Sun. brunch $13). Minerva's is a large facility that manages to maintain an intimate feel with the well-planned use of room dividers and lighting. Rich greens and burgundy colors, and hardwood tables, chairs, and booths give the restaurant an intimate feel. The bar area, which is also used for dining, is warmed by a stone fireplace. The Sunday brunch is a local favorite. A full range of hot breakfast dishes, including omelets made to order, complimented by lunch selections—such as ham, roast beef, hot potato dishes, and pasta—make for a nice Sunday morning out on the town. During the week, there are plenty of choices on both the breakfast and lunch menus. Lunch offerings include a wide array of soups, salads, and sandwiches. Dinner selections are standard American fare, including chicken, pasta, and steak.

Ethnic Fare

The **Hunan Chinese Restaurant** (1720 Mt. Rushmore Rd., 605/341-3888, summer daily 11 A.M.–10 P.M., winter daily 11 A.M.–9:30 P.M., lunch $7, dinner $10) offers a huge selection of Chinese food. In addition to the extensive menu, there is also a buffet that is carefully maintained to ensure that the food is hot and fresh. The walls are decorated with the photography of owner Robert Wong, an international award-winning photographer. Make sure to take a spin around the restaurant to view his work.

The **Golden Phoenix** (2421 W. Main St., 605/348-4195, daily 11 A.M.–9 P.M., lunch $7, dinner $9–12) is another local favorite for Chinese food. Located west of downtown, the restaurant specializes in Mandarin-style Chinese cuisine. Diners can choose to eat in at the restaurant or carry out their meals. The family-owned restaurant features large tables and booths with lazy Susans provided for easy sharing of meals. Service is fast and friendly. There is a full range of menu items featuring beef, pork, chicken, and seafood entrées; from pot stickers and pan fried dumplings to cashew chicken or beef and broccoli, all of it is good. The restaurant has a beer and wine license and serves a Sunday brunch. Vegetarian options are available.

If you crave Italian food, try **Botticelli Ristorante Italiano** (523 Main St., 605/348-0089, Mon.–Fri. 11 A.M.–2:30 P.M. and 5–9 P.M., Sat. 11:30 A.M.–9 P.M., Sun. 5–9 P.M., lunch $10, dinner $14–25). Located right in the center of downtown, this small, intimate restaurant offers over 18 different pasta selections in addition to salads, pizza, veal, chicken, salmon, and steaks.

The best sushi in town can be found at **Hana Restaurant** (3550 Sturgis Rd., 605/348-0299, www.hanarestaurantrc.com, Mon.–Sat. 11 A.M.–9 P.M., lunch $10, dinner $15–20), just minutes from downtown. The owner is from Korea, where she was a sushi chef. The restaurant features meats grilled Korean-style, plus a full sushi bar. Seating is Japanese style: pillows, low tables, and no shoes.

Curry Masala (605/716-7788, www.currymasalainc.com) offers fine, fresh Indian food at two locations: 2050 West Main Street, Suite 7 (mid-May–Sept. Mon.–Sat. 11 A.M.–2 P.M. and 5–9 P.M., Sun. 11 A.M.–2 P.M., Oct.–mid-May Mon.–Sat. 11 A.M.–2 P.M. and 5–8 P.M., Sun. 11 A.M.–2 P.M.) and 510 St. Joseph Street (Mon.–Thurs. 11 A.M.–2 P.M., Fri.–Sat. 11 A.M.–2 P.M. and 5–8 P.M.). The décor is plain, but the food is fabulous. Old family recipes are the secret to the menu's success. While curry is a major component, many other dishes are available as well. Specify the level of spice you would prefer, from mild to super-hot. The owners believe that rice and fresh bread are at the center of a great meal. They also offer cooking lessons to interested parties.

Fine Dining

The 🅒 **Corn Exchange Restaurant & Bistro** (727 Main St., 605/343-5070, www.cornexchange.com, Tue.–Sat. from 5 P.M., last dinner reservation at 9 P.M., $25–35) is one of the finest restaurants in Rapid City. It's also one of the smallest, with just 12 tables (seating for 32) and five bar seats; reservations are highly recommended. Inside the historic 1886 building, walls of exposed brick, tin/copper ceilings, white tablecloths, and carefully designed lighting create a warm and cozy dining environment. Using organic and local ingredients, this is one location where the menu is not limited to beef and walleye. Dishes here include the likes of buttermilk, white corn, and scallion pancake topped with house-smoked South Dakota trout from Clarke Trout Farm, a cucumber crème fraiche, and horseradish compote. After receiving French Culinary Institute training, Chef M. J. Adams learned her trade in several New York City eateries before packing up and moving back to the Midwest.

Look for the **Potted Rabbit** (725 Main St., 605/343-5050, Tues.–Friday 9 A.M.–5 P.M. Sat. 9 A.M.–3 P.M., $10), also owned by Chef M. J. Adams, next door to the Corn Exchange. This gourmet shop stocks fine foods, including cheeses and breads, as well pastries baked daily. Linger at the espresso bar where you can also enjoy a meal of the daily homemade soup. New menu items are expected to be added in the future.

At the **Wine Cellar** (513 6th St., 605/718-2675, www.winecellarrestaurant.com, Tues.–Wed. 3:30–10 P.M., Thurs.–Fri. 3:30–11 P.M., Sat. 5–11 P.M., closed Sun.–Mon., wine service continues one hour after dinner service ends, $25), dinner is complete only if served with the perfect wine. Located in a historic building near Hotel Alex Johnson, right in the center of downtown Rapid City, the Wine Cellar sports white tablecloths, hardwood floors, and tin ceilings. In the summer, wire tables are set outside for sidewalk café dining. Owner and executive chef Pamela Light features seasonal menu offerings every week, in addition to a creative menu of California and European choices (such as gourmet pizza, calzones, pasta, and traditional pork, chicken, and salmon dishes). There are over 50 wines available by the glass and 70 wines available by the bottle. This delightful restaurant is cozy and elegant.

Pubs and Nightlife

The **Firehouse Brewing Company** (610 Main St., 605/348-1915, www.firehousebrewing. com, Mon.–Thurs. 11 A.M.–11 P.M., Fri.–Sat. 11 A.M.–midnight, Sun. 11 A.M.–10 P.M., lunch $9–11, dinner $15–25) has been brewing its own ales since 1991. It is a large venue, with two floors and an outdoor patio dedicated to the lounge and restaurant. The third floor hosts a small theater. There is live music all summer. The cheesy artichoke dip is delicious, as are most of the items on the menu. This is a hot social spot in town and tends to the noisy side, which is not surprising when you mix ales, music, and food.

The **Independent Ale House** (625 St. Joseph St., 605/718-9492, www.independentalehouse. com, Mon.–Sat. 3 P.M.–close, closed Sun.) is a new addition to downtown. For beer tasting at its finest, the ale house has 28 rotating beers on tap, and over 100 different bottle selections. In case you get hungry while here, there is hand-crafted pizza available ($9 personal size). Brick and wood paneled walls, a very *very* long bar, and lots of booths are the interior features. Happy hour is 3–6 P.M.

Another downtown favorite is the **Dublin Square Irish Pub and Grill** (504 Mt. Rushmore Rd., 605/791-1600, www.mydublinpub.com, Tues.–Thurs. 3–11 P.M., Fri.–Sat. 3 P.M.–2 A.M., closed Sun. and Mon.), which specializes in Guinness, Irish whiskey, and scotch. With live music and dancing on weekends and a variety of menu items priced $9–12, this is a popular nightspot.

Paddy O'Neill's Pub and Casino (523 6th St., 605/342-1210, ext. 1232, summer daily 2 P.M.–2 A.M., winter Mon.–Sat. 2 P.M.–2 A.M., Sun. 6 P.M.–2 A.M.) is one of the best-loved pubs in Rapid City. Part of Hotel Alex Johnson, Paddy O'Neill's has a cozy ambience, with a lot of brass and wood, and outside tables in the summer. Live folk-style music is frequently offered late in the week and on weekends.

INFORMATION AND SERVICES

Information

The **Rapid City Chamber of Commerce** (605/343-1744, www.rapidcitychamber.com) and the **Rapid City Convention & Visitors Bureau** (605/718-8484 or 800/487-3223, www.visitrapidcity.com) are both located at 444 North Mount Rushmore Road, inside the Civic Center Complex.

Tour Companies

From half-day tours to weeks-long adventures, there are several tour companies in the area that can provide guided tours to the local attractions and activities. Each company has a slightly different offering. Some tour in small groups in vans, and others utilize full buses. Large bus tours are less expensive, while the smaller tours are easily customizable and flexible.

ABS Travel Group (945 Enchantment Rd., 605/791-2520 or 888/788-6777, www.abstravelgroup.com, $70–125) specializes in half-day, small-group tours. All tours are available in the morning or the afternoon. Generally, each tour includes two sites. For example, Rapid City and Mount Rushmore or Mount Rushmore and Crazy Horse, Wall Drug and the Badlands or Custer State Park and the Wildlife loop. Evening tours include the Crazy Horse laser show, the town of Keystone, the Mount Rushmore lighting ceremony, and Fort Hayes dinner and show.

Affordable Adventures (5542 Meteor St., 605/342-7691 or 888/888-8249, www.affordableadventuresbh.com, $45–125), another small-group tour company, offers guided tours to as few as two people at a time. The tours range from introductions to Rapid City to a wide selection of tours in the hills. This is one of the few tour companies that provides tours of the **Pine Ridge Reservation** ($240) and to **Devils Tower** ($125) in Wyoming.

Mount Rushmore Tours (605/343-3113 or 888/343-3113, www.rushmoretours.com)

utilizes full bus tours. The company's primary offering is nine hours long, with two options. Option one begins with a cowboy breakfast in the morning, makes stops at Mount Rushmore, Custer State Park (including Needles Highway and Sylvan Lake), and Crazy Horse Mountain, and finishes with a chuck wagon dinner and show at Fort Hayes in the evening. The cost is $40 for children and $81 for adults. Option two is the same tour without meals and is $30 for children and $59 for adults.

Gray Line of the Black Hills (1600 E. St. Patrick St., 605/342-4461 or 800/456-4461, www.blackhillsgrayline.com, adult $73, child $47–30) offers classic motorcoach tours in vehicles that seat close to 60 people. All admissions are included in the tour price and breakfast is also included. The basic nine-hour tour includes a ride on the 1880 Train between Hill City and Keystone, Mount Rushmore, Crazy Horse, and Iron Mountain Road in Custer State Park.

Three "non-standard" tour companies in Rapid City offer completely different experiences. **Black Hills Adventure Tours** (201 N. 44th St., 605/209-7817, www.blackhillsadventuretours.com, $110–175) offers traditional sightseeing tours, as well as tours geared toward the active visitor. Guided tour selections include Mickelson Trail bike rides, Badlands hikes, Spearfish Canyon hikes, Pactola Lake kayaking, and other action-oriented tours.

Go Native Tours (406/850-3747, www.gonativeamerica.com, average $185 per day, $3,500 per week) offers small-group tours throughout the Native American West. Tours focus on history and cultural education, and range 1–14 days. You can see Paha Sapa (the Black Hills) from the perspective of a Native American guide, or visit the reservation lands and people, including Cheyenne Country in Wyoming, Navaho and Hopi lands in New Mexico, Apache land in Arizona, the Pine Ridge Reservation (including Wounded Knee), and Maco Sica (the Badlands).

Emergency Services

For quick access to emergency services, including police or ambulance, call 911. For nonemergency situations, the **police station** is located downtown (300 Kansas City St., 605/394-4131). **Rapid City Regional Hospital** (353 Fairmont Blvd., 605/719-1000) is located south of downtown. To find the hospital, drive south on Mount Rushmore Road to Cathedral Drive and turn left. Cathedral Drive will turn into Fairmont Boulevard. The hospital is on the right just past 5th Street.

Other Services

The most convenient **post office** location for visitors is located at 909 St. Joseph Street, one block south of Main Street and one and a half blocks west of Mount Rushmore Road downtown.

Small grocery stores are scattered throughout the city. For visitors staying near I-90 on the north end of Rapid City, the most convenient place to stock up on groceries is the **Walmart Superstore** (1200 N. LaCrosse St., 605/342-9444), which is a few blocks south of I-90, exit 59. **Safeway** (2120 U.S. 16, 605/348-5125) can be found on the way to Mount Rushmore from the downtown area.

Many campgrounds and hotels provide laundry services for guests, but some do not. For visitors staying on the west side of town near Canyon Lake, the most convenient laundry is the **Dew Drop Laundromat** (3618 Canyon Lake Dr., 605/343-0900). For visitors staying on the north side of town, and for folks staying downtown, the closest Laundromat is **Laundry World** (1315 Haines Ave., 605/348-5121), which is south of I-90, exit 58. From downtown, head north on 5th Street, which turns into Haines Avenue.

GETTING THERE AND AROUND
Rapid City Regional Airport

The Rapid City Regional Airport (4550

Terminal Rd., www.rcgov.org/airport) is located about 11 miles from downtown, off of Highway 44 headed east. Call 605/393-9924 for airport information, and 605/393-2850 for flight information. Shuttle service between the airport and downtown is provided by **Airport Express Shuttle** (605/399-9999 or 800/357-9998, within city limits rates are $20 for one person, $30 for two, and $13 each for three or more).

Car Rental

The Black Hills are a driving destination. Car rental companies at the airport include **Alamo/ National** (605/393-2664), **Hertz** (605/393-0160), **Avis** (605/393-0740), **Budget** (605/393-0488), and **Enterprise** (605/393-4311).

Public Transportation

The **Rapid City Transit System** (300 6th St., 605/394-6631, www.rapidride.org, information available Mon.–Fri. 7 A.M.–6 P.M., adult and student $1.50, senior $0.75, child under 4 free) has five major routes that carry passengers within the city limits. It's a great transportation deal if you want to spend a morning downtown or near the I-90 shopping district. Buses run Monday–Friday 6:30 A.M.–6:30 P.M. and Saturday 9:30 A.M.–4:30 P.M.

Taxi Service

There is only one cab company in Rapid City, **Rapid City Taxi** (605/348-8080). The cost of a cab ride from the airport to the downtown district of Rapid City averages $26.

THE SOUTHERN HILLS

The landscape of the Southern Hills is easy on the eyes. Soft hills fade into the surrounding plains. The sky is a dominant feature of the landscape. There is a sense of great distance here and the presence of humans is small. Approaching storms are visible for miles as lightning and rainbows color the vast plains.

For scenic beauty, wildlife-viewing, and outdoor activity, there is no place better in the region than 71,000-acre Custer State Park. Hiking trails to lakes and peaks crisscross the park, and bison ramble unfettered throughout. Reminiscent of the great architecture of our national parks, four beautiful lodges provide international dining and accommodations that range from simple cabins to luxury rooms.

The Southern Hills are also home to the monumental work-in-progress mountain carving honoring Lakota warrior and leader Crazy Horse. Two of the world's longest caves, the calcite crystal–encrusted Jewel Cave National Monument and Wind Cave (in Wind Cave National Park) offer exciting looks at the world below the surface. The historic town of Hot Springs looks and feels much as it did 100 years ago, with beautiful sandstone buildings, a river walk, and warm, spring-fed "healing waters" that inspired early-20th-century train travelers to come and "take the cure."

HIGHLIGHTS

◖ **Crazy Horse Memorial:** The most ambitious mountain carving project in the world demonstrates what a dream and a jackhammer can accomplish (page 87).

◖ **Jewel Cave National Monument:** There are many caves in the Black Hills, but Jewel Cave, named after the sparkling calcite crystals of its interior, is one of the prettiest – and it's estimated to be the second-longest cave in the world (page 90).

◖ **Needles Highway:** Scenic byways abound in the Black Hills, but the Needles Highway section of the Peter Norbeck Scenic Byway ranks as number one in my book. It winds and climbs the hills past Cathedral Spires, squeezes through the Needles formation, and ends at peaceful Sylvan Lake (page 104).

◖ **Wildlife Loop:** Along this 18-mile loop in Custer State Park, bison, pronghorns, prairie dogs, mule deer, whitetail deer, and wild turkeys graze placidly, undisturbed by their many admirers (page 106).

◖ **Harney Peak Trail:** Harney Peak is the highest point in the Black Hills and the trail there provides the best hike in the hills. It's just the right length and difficulty level to make you feel like you've earned the vast and inspiring views at the top (page 108).

◖ **Black Hills Playhouse:** Located deep within Custer State Park, the Black Hills Playhouse features wonderful performances in a charming and historic venue, surrounded by scenic beauty (page 114).

◖ **Mammoth Site:** It started with one tusk overturned by a bulldozer. Today, the skeletal remains of 58 mammoths, a short-faced bear, and other Pleistocene-era animals are displayed (page 121).

◖ **Cave Tours at Wind Cave National Park:** Beneath the surface of Wind Cave National Park is the fifth-longest cave in the world. There are five tours on offer, including a candlelight tour (page 134).

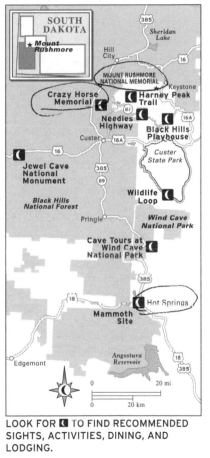

LOOK FOR ◖ TO FIND RECOMMENDED SIGHTS, ACTIVITIES, DINING, AND LODGING.

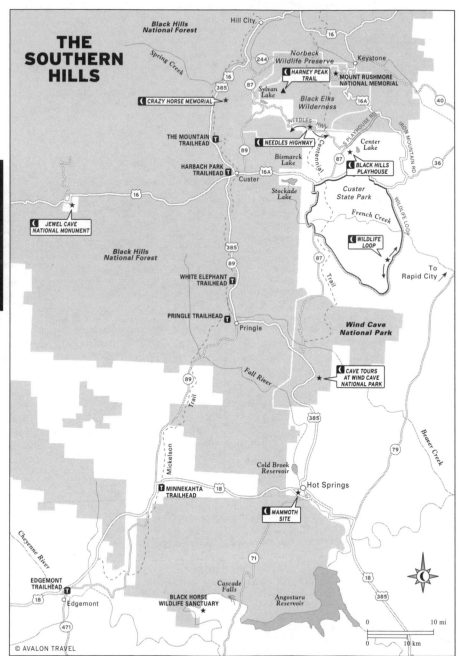

THE SOUTHERN HILLS

PLANNING YOUR TIME

Planning to tour anywhere in the Black Hills involves thinking in circles. And, for the most part, touring involves driving. In order to minimize driving time and maximize fun, plan on at least three days in the Southern Hills. No matter which tour strategy is selected—a base camp with day trips into different regions or a slow meander through the hills—it's good to mix in sights and activities with the scenic.

Close to both the Southern Hills and Central Hills sights and attractions, the town of Custer and Custer State Park are both great base camp options. Plan on a minimum of two hours for each sight, three hours for each scenic route, a good five hours to hike Harney Peak, two hours for cave tours, and an evening for the Playhouse. Throw in time for picnics, hiking, biking, golfing, horseback riding, or swimming, and it's easy to see that 3–5 days can easily and happily be spent in this region.

Custer

For a long time, the northern great plains were highlighted on maps as the "Great American Desert." It took the discovery of gold and the subsequent railroad lines to bring people to the region. The gold rush began when the ore was discovered east of Custer in French Creek. At the time, and by treaty, the land belonged to the Lakota.

The Fort Laramie Treaty of 1868 had delineated a district to be "set apart for the absolute and undisturbed use and occupation" of the Great Sioux Nation, and the land described included the entire Black Hills region. In 1874, Lieutenant Colonel George Armstrong Custer, in the company of over 1,000 troops, was charged with the mission of exploring the Black Hills of South Dakota, officially to scout out a potential location for a military outpost to control "unsigned" Native Americans. In addition to the troops, the expedition included a scientific corps comprised of a geologist, a botanist, a zoologist, and two miners. A photographer and several news correspondents were also expedition participants.

In July 1874, Horatio Ross, one of the expedition's miners, made the gold discovery near French Creek. In just four days, the news was broadcast to newspapers all over the country. The gold rush was on, and, unable to stop the onslaught of miners to the area, the military was eventually charged with protecting them. The Fort Laramie Treaty was broken. By January 1875, just six months after the discovery of gold, an estimated 10,000–15,000 miners had invaded the Black Hills. The U.S. government tried to buy the land but its offers were rebuffed. The miners couldn't be stopped and the Indian Wars began again in earnest.

The population of the town of Custer peaked in 1875 and then, when richer discoveries of gold occurred in the Northern Hills, it rapidly crashed, as miners rushed north to seek their fortunes elsewhere. Today, Custer's population hovers around 1,900 and a good part of the community's income is generated by tourism. Custer sits on the edge of the Central and Southern Hills and is well situated to serve as a home base for day trips into every region of the hills. Custer provides easy access to Mount Rushmore, Custer State Park, Jewel Cave National Monument, and is 30 minutes from Wind Cave and 45 minutes to the city of Hot Springs at the southernmost edge of the Black Hills—and it offers a wider variety of shopping, dining, and lodging than nearby Custer State Park.

SIGHTS
◖ Crazy Horse Memorial

For 14 years, Native Americans watched the

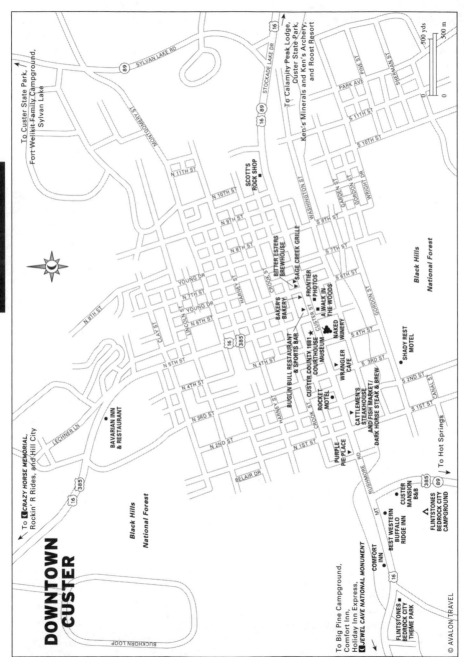

THE SOUTHERN HILLS

DOWNTOWN CUSTER

To CRAZY HORSE MEMORIAL,
Rockin' R Rides, and Hill City

To Custer State Park,
Fort Welikit Family Campground,
Sylvan Lake

SYLVAN LAKE RD

MONTGOMERY ST

STOCKADE LAKE DR

To Calamity Peak Lodge,
Custer State Park,
Ken's Minerals and Ken's Archery,
and Roost Resort

SCOTT'S
ROCK SHOP

N 11TH ST
N 10TH ST
N 9TH ST
N 8TH ST
N 7TH ST
N 6TH ST
N 5TH ST
N 4TH ST
N 3RD ST
N 2ND ST
N 1ST ST

YOUNG DR
N 7TH ST
YOUNG DR
N 6TH ST

N 8TH ST
CLAY ST
LINCOLN ST
HARNEY ST
CROOK ST

BITTER ESTERS
BREWHOUSE
SAGE CREEK GRILLE

BAKER'S
BAKERY

FRONTIER
PHOTOS

A WALK IN
THE WOODS

NAKED
WINERY

CUSTER COUNTY 1881
COURTHOUSE
MUSEUM

BUGLIN BULL RESTAURANT
& SPORTS BAR

WRANGLER
CAFE

ROCKET
MOTEL

CATTLEMEN'S
STEAKHOUSE
AND FISH MARKET/
DARK HORSE STEAK & BREW

SHADY REST
MOTEL

BAVARIAN INN
& RESTAURANT

LECHNER LN

Black Hills
National Forest

PURPLE
PIE PLACE

BELAIR DR

RUSHMORE RD

To Hot Springs

WASHINGTON ST
S 8TH ST
S 7TH ST
S 6TH ST
S 5TH ST
S 4TH ST
S 3RD ST
S 2ND ST
S 1ST ST

GORDON ST

CANAL ST

PARK AVE
PINE ST
SHERMAN ST
S 11TH ST
S 10TH ST
GARDEN ST
GORDON ST
WRIGHT DR

Black Hills
National Forest

500 yds
500 m

CUSTER
MANSION
B&B

FLINTSTONES
BEDROCK CITY
CAMPGROUND

BEST WESTERN
BUFFALO
RIDGE INN

COMFORT
INN

To Big Pine Campground,
Comfort Inn,
Holiday Inn Express,
JEWEL CAVE NATIONAL MONUMENT

FLINTSTONES
BEDROCK CITY
THEME PARK

BUCKHORN LOOP

MT

© AVALON TRAVEL

carving of Mount Rushmore, a tribute to white American leaders, in the sacred Black Hills. In 1948, seven years after Mount Rushmore was completed, Chief Henry Standing Bear approached sculptor Korczak Ziolkowski about creating a mountain carving to show the world that Native Americans had great leaders, too. Ziolkowski, who had worked on Mount Rushmore with Gutzon Borglum, agreed, and the plans to build the Crazy Horse Memorial (12151 Avenue of the Chiefs, Crazy Horse, 605/673-4681, www.crazyhorsememorial.org, summer daily from 7 A.M. until after the laser light show, winter daily 8 A.M.–5 P.M., $10 per person or $27 per car; $5 bicycles, motorcycles, and walk-ins) were born.

Inspired by the stories of Chief Henry Standing Bear, Ziolkowski imagined a memorial that would include the largest mountain carving in the world, a museum, a university, and a medical center. The carving was to be of Crazy Horse on horseback, pointing to the Black Hills, his homeland. Ziolkowski, working alone, started carving in 1948. The carving is still underway today, with the third generation of Ziolkowskis working on the mountain. When completed, the carving will be 641 feet long by 563 feet high. No federal funds have been used to finance the work. Today, the carving remains far from complete and there is no estimated finish date on the memorial. However, the carving has seen a great deal of progress in the past decade. The face, 87 feet high, is virtually complete and much work has been accomplished on the horse's head. The carving is a fascinating project and it provides visitors with a one-of-a-kind opportunity to view an extraordinary piece of artwork in progress. This is the only ongoing mountain carving in the world. It captures the imagination.

In addition to the mountain carving, the grounds of the Crazy Horse Memorial include

© CRAZY HORSE MEMORIAL

Crazy Horse Memorial

many of the attractions that Ziolkowski originally envisioned. The **Welcome Center** has an
information desk, conference facilities, and
a small theater. Be sure to see the 20-min-
ute orientation video. The historic film footage follows Ziolkowski as he climbs hundreds
of stairs to start carving a granite mountain
with a jackhammer. It adds a human perspective to the project. Connected to the Welcome
Center, the wood-paneled **Native American
Museum** is filled with Native American artwork and artifacts, most of which were donated to the facility. There is also the **Native
American Educational and Cultural Center,**
where visitors are encouraged to participate in
Lakota games, and listen to staff and Native
American vendors discuss Lakota history and
culture. Native American artists are provided
free booth space within the center to display
and sell their artistic creations.

Other facilities on-site include a gift shop, a
restaurant, and Ziolkowski's original home and
studio on the mountain. The studio displays
some of his other artistic works, and the lobby
of the original welcome center has been preserved, as well. One of the favorite souvenirs of
the memorial is available here: Inside the lobby
fireplace, there is a pile of rocks blasted off the
mountain, and visitors are encouraged to take a
stone home with them when they leave.

A bus ($4) brings visitors close to the base of
the sculpture to get a different perspective of
the carving. The bus leaves every 15 minutes
or so, depending on weather and the mountain
blasting schedule, and includes a narrative of
the history of the carving. It's a short ride, no
longer than three-quarters of a mile, and the
bus stops at a parking lot right at the base of
the carving where the presentation continues.

In early June, hikers are allowed to climb Crazy
Horse Mountain during the annual **Volksmarch.**
For an entry fee of $3 per person, around 10,000
hikers are allowed to climb the mountain and
stand on Crazy Horse's outstretched arm.

During the summer months, a laser light
show is presented nightly. The show begins as
soon as it's dark, so the start time varies with
the time of sunset.

Crazy Horse Memorial is located about five
miles north of Custer off of U.S. 16/385.

◖ Jewel Cave
National Monument

Named for the glittering calcite crystals that
line the walls, Jewel Cave National Monument
was discovered by miners Frank and Albert
Michaud in 1900. The brothers filed a mining
claim, but it seems clear that their intention
was always to create a tourist attraction. Over
the next few years, the brothers, with family
friend Charles Bush, widened the entrance to
the cave with dynamite and constructed a ru-
dimentary trail. They built a lodge on the rim
of the nearby Hell Canyon, and established the
Jewel Cave Dancing Club in 1902. At the time,
however, travel was difficult and the local population was not large enough to provide enough
financial support for the cave. Bush was bought
out for $300, and after the brothers died, the
claim was sold to the government for a nominal
amount. While the cave was small, with just a
half-mile mapped, and the attempt at tourism
wasn't a success, the beauty of the cave was well
known and in 1908, Theodore Roosevelt declared the cave a national monument.

The cave remained virtually unexplored
through 1959, when the cave had only been increased in size to two miles in length. A local
geologist decided to take exploration of the cave
more seriously and convinced two avid rock
climbers, Herb and Jan Conn, to join him in
mapping out the cave. In less than two years,
the length of the cave expanded to 15 miles.
This sparked the interest of the National Park
Service and mapping of the cave continued in
earnest. Today, the cave is the second-longest
cave in the world and growing, currently mea-
suring 161.07 miles in length, honeycombed

THE LEGACY OF CRAZY HORSE

Sitting Bull, Red Cloud, Spotted Tail, and Crazy Horse were all Native American leaders deserving of recognition, but the choice of Crazy Horse was an easy one for those planning to honor a Lakota leader with a mountain carving.

Crazy Horse was born in the early 1840s near Bear Butte, South Dakota. The Lakota kept no written records, so much of what is known of his youth was carved out of the memories of elders many years after his death.

Crazy Horse lived his entire life under the shadow of encroachment on the lands of his people: the central plains of Nebraska, South Dakota, and Wyoming, and the northern plains of eastern Montana, all of which surround the Black Hills. What began as a trickle of white men with Lewis and Clark in 1804 turned into a flood. Between 1843-1869, it is estimated that somewhere between 300,000-500,000 white travelers passed though the plains on their way west. With these travelers came the military, the forts, the settlements, and the inevitable skirmishes with Native American tribes trying to preserve their hunting grounds and way of life. Treaties were signed and broken; the most significant of those was the Fort Laramie Treaty signed in 1868. All white people were banned from the Powder River area of Montana, and the Lakota, Dakota, and Arapahoe tribes were to maintain ownership and hunting rights of the Black Hills and other lands in South Dakota, Wyoming, and Montana. This treaty lasted only until the 1874 discovery of gold.

Crazy Horse, by that time in his thirties, had already distinguished himself as a warrior and as a great hunter. Involved in the victory against the soldiers near Fort Phil Kearney in Nebraska (the "Fetterman Massacre"), Crazy Horse would also be identified as one of the strategic leaders of the 1876 Battle of the Little Big Horn, also known as "Custer's Last Stand," where George Armstrong Custer was killed with all of his troops. From this battle began the relentless military attacks on the Native American tribes in the area.

Constant battle, a harsh winter, and the scarcity of bison drove the tribes to despair. Crazy Horse could have escaped into Canada alone, but he chose not to abandon his people. In May of 1877, Crazy Horse and 900 followers rode into Camp Robinson in northwestern Nebraska and turned over their weapons and horses. Four months later, Crazy Horse was dead, killed by the bayonet of a soldier when he struggled against being locked up in the guard house. It was a devastating loss to his community.

A hunter, a warrior, a leader, and a protector, Crazy Horse lived his life in the Lakota way. He was not interested in renown. He did not allow others to photograph him. He did not go to Washington to negotiate. He did not give speeches, and he never signed a treaty. He died trying to maintain his freedom, shortly before all of his people were forced to abandon their way of life and move onto reservation lands. Crazy Horse became a symbol of all that they had lost.

---

under just three square miles of land. The largest room in the cave is over 570 feet long, 180 feet at its widest and 30 feet tall. In addition to the sparkling calcite crystals that gave the cave its name, the cave also features popcorn (small round clusters of calcium carbonate that looks like...popcorn), stalactites, and stalagmites.

VISITORS CENTER

The first place to stop when visiting Jewel Cave is the visitors center (13 miles west of Custer, 605/673-8300, www.nps.gov/jeca, May daily 8:30 A.M.–4:30 P.M., June–mid-Aug. daily 8 A.M.–7 P.M., mid-Aug.–mid-Sept. daily 8:30 A.M.–5:30 P.M.) mid-Sept.–Apr. daily 8:30 A.M.–4:30 P.M.). Information about the available cave tours and ranger-led educational programs can be obtained at the visitors center. Park rangers offer educational programs during the high summer months (early June–mid-Aug.). These programs include a variety of guided walks on the surface of the Jewel Cave property, and a series of talks about cave exploration, wildlife, fire ecology, and the wildflowers, plants, and animals of the area. All cave tours originate in the visitors center.

A small bookstore, operated by the Black Hills Parks and Forests Association, offers books and maps specific to Jewel Cave, as well as books on local and regional flora, fauna, and history.

CAVE TOURS

More than 80,000 people per year take the cave tours here. If you plan on taking a tour, remember to bring a sweater. Jewel Cave is one of the colder caves in the hills, reaching only 49°F, even during the hottest days of summer. There are four tours available.

The **Discovery Tour** (adults 16 and over $4, children and seniors free) is offered year-round and is wheelchair accessible. One room of the cave is visited, with elevator access, and a park ranger provides a 20-minute introduction to the cave's history and formation.

The **Scenic Tour** (adult $8, child 6–16 $4, child under 5 free), also offered year-round, takes about 1.3 hours and is moderately strenuous. There are 723 stairs to climb in a half-mile loop. The trail is paved and there is electric lighting along the path. This is one of the most popular tours. The glittering calcite crystals that gave the cave its name can be viewed in several rooms. Other cave formations (speleothems) on this tour include knobby calcite formations called popcorn, boxwork, flowstone, stalactites, and stalagmites, and cave bacon. (Many formations are named for what they look like.) Most of the formations in Jewel Cave are calcite or gypsum related.

The **Lantern Tour** (mid-June–Labor Day, adult $8, child $4, minimum age 6) is designed to replicate the experience of the early cave explorers. Park employees wear historic uniforms and lighting for the tour is provided only by lanterns carried in by the participants. The tour lasts 1.75 hours and is considered strenuous. It begins at the cave's natural entrance and includes walking up wooden staircases, bending,

stooping, duckwalking, and climbing steep ladders. The trail is unpaved, and sturdy shoes with rubber soles and long pants are recommended. Reservations are highly recommended.

The **Wild Caving (Spelunking) Tour** (mid-June–early Oct., adult $27, minimum age 16) is an extremely strenuous, 3–4-hour tour. Participants must be in good health and physical condition. Tour participants are also required to wear sturdy, leather over ankle boots, elbow and knee pads, gloves, long pants, and a long-sleeved shirt. (Bring extra clothes, as you will get very dirty.) The tour provides a hard hat and head lamp. This tour is designed for thrill seekers. It will give participants a real feel for what it is like to explore and map a cave in its natural state. Participants will scramble over rough rock, belly crawl through tight passages, rope climb semi-vertical rocks, and chimney between cave walls. Do not even think about this tour if you are even mildly claustrophobic. Before taking the tour, participants must demonstrate that they can fit through a passage 8.5 inches high by 24 inches wide. During the course of the tour, participants will learn about safe caving, caving equipment, and techniques. Advance reservations are required.

1881 Custer County Courthouse Museum

The 1881 Custer County Courthouse Museum (411 Mt. Rushmore Rd., 605/673-2443, www.1881courthousemuseum.com, Jun.–Aug. Mon.–Sat. 10 A.M.–7 P.M., Sun. 1–7 P.M., early May and Sept. Mon.–Sat. 10 A.M.–4 P.M., Sun. 1–4 P.M., closed in winter, adult $5, senior $4, child 12 and over $1, child under 12 free), an original 1881 courthouse and jail, explores the history of the city and county of Custer and of the Black Hills. Museum artifacts include photos of the 1874 Custer expedition, a hunting gun used by George Armstrong Custer, and some items found at the expedition campsite. Other displays include a Native American room,

Custer reenactors in front of the 1881 Custer County Courthouse Museum

a mining industry room, weapons of the West, and the original courthouse and judge's quarters.

Flintstones Bedrock City Theme Park

In 1960, the cartoon series *The Flintstones* hit prime-time television as the first animated television series aimed specifically at adults. Mixing blue-collar humor with Stone Age imagery and sight gags, the show ran for six years. In spite of adult themes, the series was a hit with kids, as well. When the television series disappeared, the Flintstones Bedrock City Theme Park (422 W. Mt. Rushmore Rd., 605/673-4079, www.flintstonesbedrockcity. com, mid-May–mid-June and mid-July–Labor Day daily 9 A.M.–5 P.M., mid-June–mid-July daily 9 A.M.–6 P.M., $11, child under 5 free) appeared, making its debut in South Dakota in 1966. Over a period of a few years, there were four theme parks built, two in the United States and two in Canada. Today there are only two parks remaining, one in Arizona and this one. Of interest, however, is the announcement by Fox Television of the debut of a new 21st-century version of *The Flintstones*. A whole new generation of children may once again know Fred, Wilma, Barney, Betty, and Dino.

The Flintstones Bedrock City Theme Park features a small train that travels the perimeter of the property, a playground, and statues of all of the characters from the TV show. Visit Fred, Wilma, Barney, and Betty at their homes and then take a peek at some of Bedrock's businesses. Children under six especially seem to appreciate the talking parrot statue that greets visitors at the entrance. In keeping with the theme park's location, there is a Mount Rockmore, with four carved faces, one of which is a dinosaur. There is also a small theater where you can see old *Flintstones* reruns and eat popcorn. At the entrance to the park is a *Flintstones*-themed gift shop and a restaurant where you can dine on brontoburgers, dino dogs, and chickasaurus sandwiches.

The property also includes a campground. Campground guests who wish to visit the theme park pay admission fees once, after which access to the theme park is free for the length of their stay.

RECREATION
Tours

Golden Circle Tours (12021 U.S. 16, 605/673-4349, www.goldencircletours.com), based in Custer, offers several different tours throughout the Black Hills and the Badlands. The company uses either a 7- or 14-passenger van to transport visitors to many of the major sights in the hills. The basic tour lasts a full day and visits Sylvan Lake, the Needles Eye and Needles Highway, Cathedral Spires, part of the Wildlife Loop, and then heads north on Iron Mountain Road up to Mount Rushmore. The final stop is Crazy Horse. Adult tickets are $96 and include all entry fees. Passengers are on their own for lunch. The tour is flexible, stopping whenever the group decides it's time for another photo. Passengers are picked up and dropped off at their Custer area locations. This is a great way to get a peek at the hills without having to do the driving. Tours are also offered to the Northern Hills and to the Badlands. The company is happy to custom-design tours for visitors who are interested in specific sites. They also offer shuttle service to the Mickelson Trail bike path and to the Rapid City Regional Airport.

Ballooning

Custer is the home base for **Black Hills Balloons** (605/673-2520, P.O. Box 210, blackhillsballoons@gmail.com, www.blackhillsballoons.com, scheduled flights May–Sept., other months by arrangement, adult $295, child 12 and under $245), the longest-running, single-owner balloon company in the United States. The owner, Steve Bauer, an experienced balloonist, incorporated his company Black Hills Balloons in 1987 and safety is his first priority. Potential riders meet at a designated parking lot in Custer at sunrise, where a helium balloon is released to test wind speed and direction. There are no steering wheels on hot air balloons, so the results of the test determine the best launch site for the day. The most common route includes drifting over the Wildlife Loop in Custer State Park, but the whimsy of the wind currents rule and each flight is unique. Plan to take three hours for a balloon experience from launch to an end-of-ride champagne celebration. In-air time is usually about an hour. Balloon capacity ranges 2–12 passengers. Specialty flights are available and can be arranged by quote only. Reservations are required for the flights.

Horseback Riding

Rockin' R Rides (605/673-2999, www.rockingrtrailrides.com, Memorial Day–Sept., adult $28–65, child $25–60) is located at Heritage Village, three miles north of Custer and just one mile south of Crazy Horse on U.S. 385/16. It operates under permit from the U.S. Forest Service. Owners Peggy and Randy have been outfitting riders in the Black Hills since 1998 and their staff is experienced and knowledgeable. It is recommended that reservations be made one or two days in advance, but Rockin' R Rides will accommodate walk-ins if possible. Rides, lasting from one hour to half a day, will bring riders through all kinds of terrain, from open fields to forested hillsides. Views of the Crazy Horse Memorial, just a mile away, are visible intermittently along the ride.

Biking

The closest bike trails include the Mickelson Trail, the Centennial Trail, and trails in Custer State Park. Bike rentals are available at **Frontier Photos & Bike Rentals** (512 Mt. Rushmore Rd., 605/673-2269, www.frontierphotos.com, Memorial Day–Labor day daily 8 A.M.–8 P.M.). Rates are $18 for 2–3 hours, $27 for half a day, and $32 for a full day.

If you need bike shuttle service to any Mickelson trailhead (or any other trailhead) or need to arrange a pick-up after a day of riding, **Golden Circle Tours** (605/673-4349, www.goldencircletours.com) offers this service. Fees depend on distance to the trail, number of riders, and type of service desired.

SHOPPING

Custer is a small town and most of the shopping is located in the downtown area along U.S. 16/385 (Mt. Rushmore Rd.). Many of the shops are open year-round, but know in advance that if you are visiting in winter, it is best to call before stopping in as shopkeepers will vary their hours based on weather and foot traffic.

One of the finest gift shops in Custer, **A Walk in the Woods** (506 Mt. Rushmore Rd., 605/673-6400, summer daily 9:30 A.M.–9 P.M., winter daily 10 A.M.–5 P.M.) features country-style home decor, gifts, clothing, and the work of local and regional artists. Right next door and part of the same complex, you'll find **Custer County Candy Company** (506 Mt. Rushmore Rd., 605/673-3911, daily 9:00 A.M.–8 P.M.), filled with hand-dipped chocolates, fudge, candies, ice cream, and specialty coffees. If you prefer a little salt with your sweet, check out **Kernel Custer's Popcorn** (440 Mt. Rushmore Rd., 605/673-3636, Mon.–Sat. 9 A.M. 7 P.M., Sun. 1–5 P.M.), serving over 40 varieties of gourmet popcorn, as well as espresso coffee drinks and light snacks.

For a taste of something completely different, stop in at the **Naked Winery** (430 Mt. Rushmore Rd., 605/673-2733, open year-round, summer daily 11 A.M.–8 P.M., off season Sun.–Thurs. 11 A.M.–7 P.M., Fri.–Sat. 11 A.M.–9 P.M.), a somewhat controversial newcomer to Custer. With a black and red exterior framed by cowgirl silhouettes reminiscent of Playboy mud flaps and very suggestive wine labels, the shop raised some eyebrows when it first opened outlets in both Custer and Hill City. The interior of the Custer shop is quite nice, however, and the wines are from Oregon and Washington. Wine tastings are $5 for six different wine samples. With wine purchase, the tasting is free. Microbrew beers are available for those who prefer handcrafted beers.

Don't forget to stop by **Frontier Photos & Bike Rentals** (512 Mt. Rushmore Rd., 605/673-2269, www.frontierphotos.com, Memorial Day–Labor Day daily 8 A.M.–8 P.M.) for souvenirs or to create your own memory with an old-time photo shoot. The shop has a wide variety of costumes and props on hand and since it is a full-service photography studio, it can handle large groups. Deb Waite, the owner of the establishment, is also a wildlife photographer and her work is available framed or highlighted on souvenir mugs. You will find a wide variety of T-shirts here, as well.

© LAURAL BIDWELL

THE SOUTHERN HILLS

a beautiful display of glass and stone at Ken's Minerals

There are two rock shops in Custer. **Scott's Rock Shop** (1020 Mt. Rushmore Rd., 605/673-4859, summer daily 9 A.M.–6 P.M., winter Tues.–Sat. 10 A.M.–5 P.M., closed Sun.–Mon.) has a small museum featuring rocks and minerals in addition to agates, jewelry, and jewelry-making supplies. **Ken's Minerals and Ken's Archery** (12372 U.S. 16A, 605/673-4935, Apr.–Sept. daily 9 A.M.–6 P.M., closed Oct.–Mar.) features Diamond bows and other archery equipment in addition to rocks, minerals, and fossils.

ACCOMMODATIONS

Custer is full of hotels, motels, cabins, and campgrounds. Many of the chains are present, and there are several nice family-run hotels, as well. Prices are generally less than $150 per night, except during Sturgis Motorcycle Rally week, when a room with a standard summer rate of $99.99 can cost as much as $220.

Most of the lodging is located along Mount Rushmore Road, the main street through town. There is also some lodging along U.S. 385 headed north out of town. And, as in many regions of the Black Hills, most of the lodging establishments are closed in winter or keep a limited number of rooms available; if you are traveling anytime between October and May, make sure to call first.

$50-100

The 1950s and the automobile road trip go together like peanut butter and marshmallow fluff. That is why it's fun to spend some time in a 1950s' historic motel or cabin. The **⟨ Rocket Motel** (211 Mt. Rushmore Rd., 605/673-4401, www.rocketmotel.com, open year-round, summer rates $76–89, limited rooms available in winter with rates starting at $50) fits the bill. Family owned since 1950, it is a AAA-rated hotel with 27 rooms, free wireless Internet, refrigerators, microwaves, clean rooms, and really friendly service. The owners have gone out of their way to keep the rooms authentic to the era with furniture and lamp fixtures from the 1950s and black, grey, and white checked 1950s-style carpet. Several of the rooms are designed especially for families, with a queen bed in one room, one bath, and a second bedroom with either two double beds or a double and a twin. It's a great way to enjoy a family vacation that leaves mom and dad with a little privacy. If you are passing through the area off season, call and check to see if they have a room available. They do allow dogs; however, there are only three pet rooms available.

The **⟨ Shady Rest Motel** (238 Gordon St., 605/673-4478, www.shady-rest-motel.com, mid-June–Sept., $75–140 with a 10 percent discount for stays longer than three days, pets add $10 per night) is actually a collection of charming cabins that date back to the 1930s. The original owners believed that since the establishment was nestled up against the hill

and away from the main street of Custer, they needed to be brightly colored to be seen. To this day, the cabins remain the same historic colors of bright yellow with red trim that they were painted when they were first opened. Inside, the cabins are all pine and very cozy. There are 10 cabins available, Wi-Fi is free, and each has a full or partial kitchen. Views from the cabins extend to the Cathedral Spires of Custer State Park and the backyard is national forest. There is a hot tub, a city park across the street, and access to the Custer City Pool is prepaid for all guests. Restaurants and downtown activities are just blocks away. Outgoing and friendly owners complete the experience.

The **Chief Motel** (120 Mt. Rushmore Rd., 605/673-2318, www.chiefmotel.com, May–Sept., $75–100) has been operated by the same family since 1995. The rooms are clean and comfortable and there are several configurations available for families. Amenities include Wi-Fi, a microwave and refrigerator in every room, a very large swimming pool, a breakfast arrangement with a local restaurant for just $1.99, and coupons for half off of pie at the Purple Pie Place just down the street.

The **Bavarian Inn** (U.S. 16/385 N., 605/673-2802 or 800/657-4312, www.bavarianinnsd.com, Apr. 15–Nov. 15, $89–109, pets add $10 per night) is a chalet-style property located one mile north of Custer on U.S. 385/16. The rooms are fairly standard hotel issue, but come with many amenities. Every room has a microwave and refrigerator. There is free wireless Internet, a guest laundry, and free continental breakfast. The grounds include a heated pool inside and a heated pool outside. A hot tub is located next to the indoor pool. The property also sports a tennis court. The Bavarian Inn Restaurant is on-site. (A word of warning from the owners: While the physical address for the Bavarian Inn is 907 N. 5th Street, many guests have gotten lost when using it in their GPS devices, which for some reason completely misidentify their location.)

The **Calamity Peak Lodge** (12557 U.S. 16A, 605/673-2357, www.blackhills.com/calamitypeak, June–Aug. $55–110, May and Sept.–Oct. $40–70) is an older but well-kept property located two miles east of downtown Custer on U.S. 16A. Located just minutes from the west entrance to Custer State Park, the views are great, the rooms are clean, and the price is right. The rooms are pine-paneled and cozy and evoke feelings of summer camp. Most of the rooms have kitchenettes. Free wireless Internet is included. For a historical touch, French Creek, where gold was first discovered in the Black Hills, winds through the property.

$100-150

Mid-range hotel rooms are primarily chains. The 88-room **Best Western Buffalo Ridge Inn** (310 W. Mt. Rushmore Rd., 605/673-2275, May–Sept., $109–139) provides spacious and clean rooms. Amenities include a free continental breakfast, indoor heated pool and hot tub, and free high-speed Internet access, with a microwave and refrigerator available. Many of the rooms have drive up access, which is a nice feature when you have a lot of luggage and equipment to unload.

The **Comfort Inn** (339 W. Mt. Rushmore Rd., 605/673-3221 or 800/424-6423, $115–149) has 83 very spacious rooms with light wood furnishings. Overall, the feel is somewhat spare and elegant. Hotel amenities include an indoor pool and hot tub, free high-speed Internet, free local calls, free local newspaper, guest laundry, a small exercise room, and a free hot or continental breakfast. Hair dryers and coffee makers can be found in all of the rooms; suites provide microwaves and refrigerators.

The **Custer Mansion Bed & Breakfast** (35 Centennial Dr., 605/673-3333 or 877/519-4948, www.custermansionbb.com, open year-round, $90–140) is a great choice in this price category. Built in 1891, the Victorian-style house has been beautifully restored and is listed on the National Register of Historic Places. There are five rooms, each named and decorated based on a different theme song, and each has a private bath. During the busy summer months, guests are required to stay for a minimum of two nights. Breakfast specialties include a variety of cooked fruit (grilled grapefruit, cooked oranges, or maple bananas), breakfast casseroles, or homemade waffles. The property is located on the west side of town, at the traffic light at the corner of Mount Rushmore Road and U.S. 385 south (where U.S. 385 heads south to Hot Springs and Mt. Rushmore Rd. continues west to Jewel Cave). Note that while the Custer Mansion is open year-round, the owners vacation now and again during the winter months. When they are gone, the inn is closed. Be sure to call first.

$150 and up

The **Holiday Inn Express** (433 W. Mt. Rushmore Rd., 605/673-2500 or 800/315-2621, May–Oct., $150–180) is one of the newest properties in Custer. Built in 2008, it is equipped with a fitness center, pool, and hot tub and is completely nonsmoking. A hot breakfast is included in the room rate, as is high-speed Internet access. An interesting feature of the hotel is a nightly bonfire on the outdoor patio where guests roast marshmallows and enjoy the landscaping.

Cabins and Campgrounds

The **⚅ Roost Resort** (12462 U.S. 16A, 605/673-2326 or 800/294-4603, www.blackhills.com/roost, May 15–Oct. 1, RV sites $30–33, cabins $69–89, $5–10 charge for pets in cabins) is a pretty property. Located just off of Mount Rushmore Road close to the entrance to Custer State Park, the site has a very secluded feel. The back of the property is all meadow views and ponderosa pine. There are 10 cabins and 12 RV spaces with hookups. The cabins have kitchenettes, a grill, cable TV, and Internet access.

The **Flintstones Theme Park & Campground** (U.S. 16/385, 605/673-4664, www.flintstonesbedrockcity.com, mid-May–early Sept., tent sites $23, RV sites $29 with full hookups, sleeping cabins $45) is a favorite of children, even though Fred, Barney, Wilma, and Betty are not as famous as they used to be. The campground is located on a hilltop meadow with good views, but not much shade. The facility includes showers, a laundry room, a game room, and an outdoor swimming pool. The campground is affiliated with the adjacent theme park; campers who wish to visit the theme park pay the full admission once, after which admission to the park is free for the duration of their stay. To find the campground from Mt. Rushmore Road in Custer, head south toward Hot Springs on U.S. 16/385 for a quarter-mile. You'll see the campground on the hilltop on your right.

Close to Custer State Park, the **Fort Welikit Family Campground** (24992 Sylvan Lake Rd./Hwy. 89, 605/673-3600 or 888/946-2267, www.fortwelikit.com, open year-round, rates shown are based on two-person occupancy: tent sites $25, RV sites $32–40, tipis and covered wagons $32, fully equipped cabins $125–135, small pets allowed in cabins, $5 per pet per night) has location, location, location going for it. Nestled in ponderosa pines, the campground is just minutes from Sylvan Lake in Custer State Park. Showers, horseshoes, badminton, and basketball are available. Tents, tipis, and all kinds of RV sites are offered. There is also a covered wagon available, but it is very narrow and is best for children. This might well be a good way for parents to carve out a little privacy and provide fun for the kids, as well. This property also has horse stalls available for $3 per head and there is direct access from the property to the Black Hills National Forest. An RV repairman is on-site and the campground also has propane for sale on-site.

The **Big Pine Campground** (12084 Big Pine Rd., 605/673-4054 or 800/235-3981, www.bigpinecampground.com, open year-round, tent sites $24, RV sites $33–35, based on 2 adults, 2 children) is a large campground with 90 wooded sites nestled into the hillside. The sites are well spaced and large enough for any size RV, with plenty of roof clearance. Two large, well-maintained restroom facilities are available. Amenities include DSL cable Internet service, a playground, volleyball court, shower house, horseshoe pits, a recreation room with video games, and a grocery and gift shop, which also provides RV supplies and firewood. The campground is located two miles west of the downtown area of Custer.

FOOD
Family Fare

The ◖ **Baker's Bakery** (541 Mt. Rushmore Rd., 605/673-2253, www.bakersbakery.biz, summer daily 6:30 A.M.–4 P.M., off-season Tues.–Sun. 6:30 A.M.–2 P.M., closed mid-Dec.–Mar. 1, breakfast $8, lunch $10) in downtown Custer is a favorite for breakfast and lunch. The small but choice breakfast menu includes omelets, pancakes, biscuits and gravy, and egg dishes; the specialties of the house include homemade bread, great coffee, pastries, and caramel rolls. The restaurant is a cozy, friendly place to start the day. Breakfast is served until 11 A.M. Sandwiches and burgers, wraps, and salads comprise the lunch menu. Vegetarians will be able to find choices on both the breakfast and lunch menus, including omelets, veggie burgers, or a portobello mushroom sandwich.

Another great place to eat breakfast is the **Cattlemen's Steakhouse and Fish Market** (140 Mt. Rushmore Rd., 605/673-4402, May–Oct. daily 7 A.M.–10 P.M., closed Nov.–Apr., breakfast $6–10, lunch $9–10, dinner $13–23). Even though it's a very large restaurant, the wood-paneled walls and booth arrangements make for cozy dining. The restaurant has an extensive menu with flavorful entrées that go beyond the standard bacon and egg dishes; the sausage, cheese, and portobello mushroom omelet is a personal favorite. Lunch entrées include salads, burgers, and barbeque sandwiches. Dinner entrées include buffalo, elk, and beef steaks, as well as salmon, trout, and barbecue.

Behind the Cattlemen's and up the stairs, look for the **Dark Horse Steak & Brew** (140 Mt. Rushmore Rd., 605/673-3833, only open in summer daily 11 A.M.–10 P.M. lunch $10, dinner $12–20). Locally known for its great prime rib, steaks, and burgers, the Dark Horse has dark wood furnishings and a great pub-like atmosphere. There are over 100 beer selections available and for entertainment, there is a pool table, dart boards, and several televisions tuned to sports events.

The **Buglin' Bull Restaurant and Sports Bar** (511 Mt. Rushmore Rd., 605/673-4477, www.buglinbull.com, winter Mon.–Thur. and Sun. 11 A.M.–8 P.M., Fri.–Sat. 11 A.M.–9 P.M., lunch $9–15, dinner $13–20) is situated in a beautifully remodeled historic building. The restaurant and bar are cozy, sporting old brick walls, wood tables, and tin ceilings. A sweet bonus is the rooftop deck that overlooks the main business district. Look for a wide variety of lunch items, including sandwiches, wraps, and south-of-the-border selections. Dinner offerings include steaks, fish, pasta, and pizza.

The **Wrangler Cafe** (302 Mt. Rushmore Rd., 605/673-4271, summer Mon.–Sat. 5 A.M.–9 P.M., Sun. 6 A.M.–9 P.M., winter Mon.–Thurs. 5 A.M.–8 P.M., Fri.–Sat. 5 A.M.–8:30 P.M., Sun. 6 A.M.–2 P.M., breakfast $7, lunch $8, dinner $9) is a local favorite. Clean and spacious, this homey, family-oriented restaurant offers great service, generous portions, and an extensive menu of good, solid American fare (breakfast items, sandwiches, soups, burgers, and steaks). The house specialty is buffalo burgers and rib eye.

Bobkat's Purple Pie Place (19 Mt. Rushmore Rd., 605/673-4070, www.purplepieplace.com,

May 1–Oct. 15 daily 11 A.M.–10 P.M., closed in winter, lunch and dinner $8, pie slice $4.25, whole pie $14.95) serves standard American fare, including burgers and sandwiches, but as the name implies, it is a great place to get dessert. A wide variety of homemade pies are served with or without ice cream. A local favorite is the bumbleberry pie, which is made from rhubarb, apples, strawberries, blueberries, and raspberries. The exterior is painted with bright purple and white stripes, which gives the restaurant its name. Inside, the small dining area is more subtly colored, with wood paneling and Western-themed art on the walls.

Fine Dining

The **⊂ Bavarian Inn Restaurant** (U.S. 16/385, 605/673-2802 or 800/657-4312, www. bavarianinnsd.com, May–Oct. daily 4:30–10 P.M., Nov.–Apr. Sat.–Sun. 4:30–9 P.M., $11–18) is a great dinner location for German food, featuring schnitzel, sauerbraten, and brats. There are two separate dining rooms at the facility. The main dining room was renovated in 2008 and the bar and entry areas were renovated in 2009. Think fireplaces and wood furnishings accented with large outdoor scenic paintings. The German food is based on family recipes, but American options (including steaks, chicken, and seafood dishes—try the walleye) are also available. Make sure to save room for dessert. Rose Marie, the owner, makes homemade apple strudel daily. The restaurant is located just north of Custer on U.S. 16/385.

The **⊂ Sage Creek Grille** (611 Mt. Rushmore Rd., 605/673-2424, summer Mon.–Sat. 11 A.M.–2 P.M. and 4:30–9 P.M., winter Tues.–Sat. 11 A.M.–2 P.M. and 4:30–9 P.M., lunch $8, dinner $19–25) is a very attractive restaurant with a light and airy feel to it. With hardwood floors, light oak tables and chairs, and walls painted in warm shades of rose accented with slate blue, the restaurant is a contemporary and casual place to dine. The high ceilings can sometimes make the room a bit noisy. There is a great wine list, and there is a small bar area where a glass of wine complemented by a cheese plate is a nice option. The restaurant features a variety of salads, soups, and sandwiches for lunch. The soup, dressings, and desserts are all homemade. The menu changes weekly and the dishes are not the standard South Dakota steak and potatoes, but instead feature selections like an open-faced grilled wild salmon melt sandwich. Dinner entrées include creative chicken, fish, and steak selections.

The first brew pub in Custer is located right next door to Sage Creek. **Bitter Esters Brewhouse** (607 Mt. Rushmore Rd., 605/673-3433, Mon.–Sat. 3–11 P.M., Sun. 4–10 P.M., $10) handcrafts beer on-site from South Dakota hops. The beer is excellent, modeled after British and Belgian beers. The space features a long, wide wooden bar, as well as some tables along the walls. The food features designer pizza, salads, burgers, and other sandwiches.

INFORMATION AND SERVICES

Many of the campgrounds and bed-and-breakfasts in the Custer area provide accommodations for travelers bringing horses to the region. For information about what information to carry with you regarding your horse, be sure to contact your local veterinarian before you leave town. Your vet will know what certificates and tests will be required for livestock being transported across state lines.

Summer temperatures can soar to the 80s and 90s, an unsafe temperature for your pets. If you are considering boarding your animal companions in the Custer area on a daily or weekly basis, try **Lynn's Pet Motel** (12227 Lynn Dr., 605/673-3347), two miles south of Custer on U.S. 385.

Custer comes complete with basic services. Picnic supplies and groceries can be found at the independently owned and operated **Custer County Market** (444 Mt. Rushmore Rd.) which features South Dakota buffalo products and a good selection of organic foods along with the basics. There is also **Lynn's Dakota Mart** (800 Mt. Rushmore Rd.), a regional grocery chain. The **post office** is located at 634 Mount Rushmore Road, and **The Lost Sock** laundry can be found at 242 Mount Rushmore Road.

For more information about the city of Custer, including vacation guides to Custer and to the Southern Hills, the **Custer Area Chamber of Commerce** (P.O. Box 5018, Custer, SD 57730, 605/673-2244 or 800/992-9818, www.custersd.com) is open Labor Day–Memorial Day Monday–Friday 9 A.M.–5 P.M. The chamber is also open Memorial Day–Labor Day Saturday 9 A.M.–4 P.M. and Sunday 10 A.M.–4 P.M. The **Visitor Center** is located at 615 Washington Street.

GETTING THERE AND AROUND

Golden Circle Tours (12021 U.S. 16, 605/673-4349, www.goldencircletours.com) provides shuttle service from Rapid City Regional Airport. **Fort Welikit Car and Camper Rentals** (675 W. Mt. Rushmore Rd., 605/673-6600 or 888/978-2267) rents automobiles and campers.

Custer State Park

Some of the most beautiful locations in all of the Black Hills can be found in Custer State Park (13329 U.S. 16A, headquarters 605/255-4515, resort reservations 888/875-0001, campground reservations 800/710-2267, www.custerstatepark.info). Encompassing 71,000 acres, Custer State Park is one of the largest state parks in the United States and offers much in the way of scenic diversity and outdoor activities. In the southernmost areas of the park, the landscape is all soft rolling hills, with fields of prairie grasses and small stands of ponderosa pine scattered throughout. Vast views and big skies dominate. It is here that grassland wildlife abounds. Bison, pronghorn, deer, and prairie dog populations are common sights. Traveling north, the elevation rises and the scattered stands of ponderosa pine turn into dense forest. The rolling low hills turn into craggy peaks with steep canyon walls and sheer granite outcroppings. The deer remain, but the bison are scarce in the northern sections of the park. Instead, look for Rocky Mountain sheep and mountain goats.

The park is accessible year-round although most of the park facilities are closed mid-October–May. During the winter months, fees are collected on the honor system, with envelopes and deposit boxes located at several park entrances. One time admission fees (good for seven days in any South Dakota state park) are $15 per vehicle or $10 per motorcycle. An annual pass is $28. There are access roads to the park from every direction. Highway 87 runs north–south through the park from Wind Cave just north of Hot Springs to just south of Hill City. Scenic U.S. 16A circles through the park and has exit/entry points near the city of Custer and in the most northeastern corner of the park. Highway 36 enters the park from the east, as well. Highway 79 runs north–south along the front range of the Black Hills, and

many of the gravel county roads and Forest Service roads, including Forest Service Road 16 and County Roads 14 and 12 headed west, will bring you into the park.

Custer State Park provides some of the best lodging, dining, and outdoor recreation opportunities (including hiking, biking, horseback riding, rock climbing, fishing, and boating) in the Black Hills. Add exceptional wildlife-viewing opportunities, a summer playhouse, a chuck wagon dinner, and many scenic drives and it is understandable why Custer State Park is a must-see for any visitor to the Black Hills.

There are four major lodging and campground areas within the confines of the park boundaries, each with a distinctly different feel. If you are planning to stay at the park, one of the four regions is likely to suit your personal preferences: the Western feel of the Blue Bell Resort with its hayrides, horseback riding, and chuck wagon dinners; the elegant State Game Lodge, the center of many of the park's activities; the casual fishing-, boating-, and swimming-centered Legion Lake area; or the majestic beauty and high peaks near Sylvan Lake Lodge. There is a perfect spot for everyone. Whether staying in the park or in the nearby communities of Hot Springs or Custer, plan to spend a minimum of two days in the park.

VISITORS CENTERS
Peter Norbeck Visitor Center

The main location for information about the park's educational programs and activities is the Peter Norbeck Visitor Center (U.S. 16A just past the State Game Lodge at the east entrance to the park, 605/255-4464, Apr.–Memorial Day daily 9 A.M.–5 P.M., Memorial Day–Labor Day daily 8 A.M.–8 P.M., Labor Day–Sept. 30 daily 8 A.M.–6 P.M., Oct. daily 9 A.M.–5 P.M., closed Nov.–Mar.). The visitors

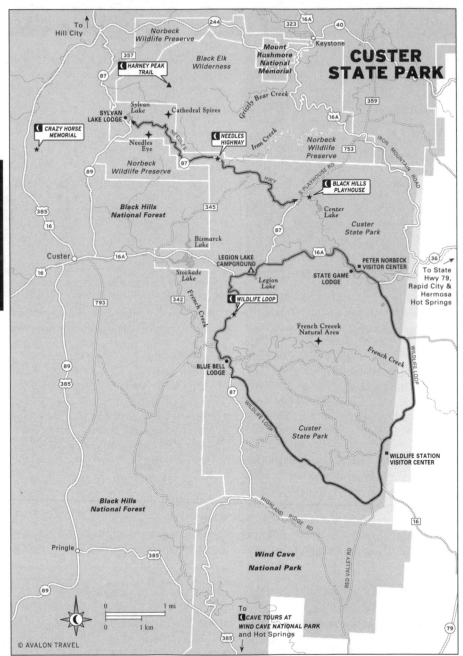

© AVALON TRAVEL

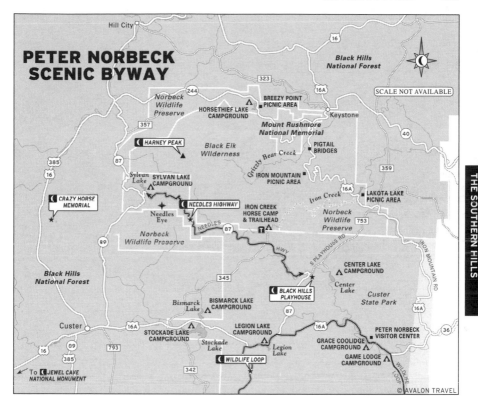

PETER NORBECK
SCENIC BYWAY

center was built by the Civilian Conservation Corps in 1934–1935. Inside are interpretive exhibits and displays about the history, geology, and ecology of the park, in addition to park maps and information about ranger-led programs and activities.

Wildlife Station Visitor Center

The Wildlife Station Visitor Center (Memorial Day–Labor Day daily 8 A.M.–8 P.M., Labor Day–Sept. 30 daily 10 A.M.–4 P.M., closed in winter and spring) is located about midway through the Wildlife Loop on the southeastern corner of the park. Park rangers located at the Wildlife Station have information about the current location of the park's buffalo herd and can answer any questions visitors might have about the flora

and fauna they view along the loop. There are restrooms available at the station, as well.

SIGHTS

Peter Norbeck was the governor of South Dakota in the early 1900s and was enamored with western South Dakota. It was his conservationist vision that created Custer State Forest, which was converted to Custer State Park in 1919. The **Peter Norbeck Scenic Byway,** named in his honor, winds 68 miles through the Black Hills. Segments of that byway, including the Needles Highway and Iron Mountain Road, traverse sections of Custer State Park. The byway is not long in terms of mileage and the entire scenic route can be driven in about four hours—but the road is

© WWW.TRAVELSD.COM

You may see buffalo in their natural state – in this case, in the middle of a massive back scratch.

narrow and winding, and it is more comfortable and relaxing to drive the route in short stretches, taking time to stop and enjoy the wildlife and other scenic attributes of the drive.

◖ Needles Highway

Peter Norbeck wanted to simultaneously preserve and provide access to some of the most beautiful regions of the Black Hills. In 1919, he designed the route for the Needles Highway, a road that many engineers deemed impossible to build. Two years and 150,000 pounds of dynamite later, the road was opened to automobiles. The most dramatic way to travel the Needles Highway is from south to north. Begin in Custer State Park at the junction of U.S. 16A and Highway 87. Highway 87 north turns into the scenic highway. The 14-mile highway slowly climbs in elevation as it winds through narrow tunnels and weaves its way through towering granite spires and ponderosa

pine forests. The road is named for the many towering, pointed rock columns that look like needles of rock piercing the sky.

Several turnouts along the way allow viewing some spectacular formations. **Cathedral Spires** is a massive collection of rock towers pointed to the heavens. The **Eye of the Needle** is a narrow spire over 30 feet tall; time, wind, and water have eroded it to create a three-foot-wide slit in the top of the formation that looks like the eye in a sewing needle. There is parking at the base of the eye. There is also a tunnel leading to the formation that is so narrow that busses driving the route look to have less than two inches of clearance on each side.

Initially, it was this region that was suggested as a location for massive stone carvings in South Dakota. Doane Robinson, considered to be the father of Mount Rushmore, visualized a series of heroic characters carved into the spires. His vision included both Native

© LAURAL BIDWELL

THE SOUTHERN HILLS

Sylvan Lake is a jewel in the hills.

American and white leaders. When sculptor Gutzon Borglum came to investigate the area, he rejected the Needles due to the fragility of the towering spires. Borglum selected nearby Mount Rushmore instead.

The Needles Highway ends at **Sylvan Lake,** the most northern and western spur of the park. Sylvan Lake is not a natural lake. It was created in the 1930s when a dam was constructed by the Civilian Conservation Corps. This high-elevation lake is surrounded by towering granite peaks and ponderosa pine. It is one of the jewels of the park.

The Needles Highway is the only road in the park that is closed with a locked gate in the winter time. Officially, the road is closed November–April, but the actual closing time depends on the weather. Once the gate is closed, the road remains closed until spring.

Iron Mountain Road

Peter Norbeck worked closely with Gutzon Borglum, the man who carved Mount Rushmore, to design Iron Mountain Road. The result of their combined efforts resulted in a road with several pigtail bridges and three tunnels, each of which frame the Mount Rushmore sculpture as you drive through them. At 17 miles in length, Iron Mountain Road connects the northeastern corner of Custer State Park to Mount Rushmore. It's not the fastest route, but it is certainly the most scenic and dramatic approach to the memorial. There are two picnic areas and many scenic overlooks along the way.

Bring some carrots or apples with you on this journey, as one of the park's two herds of feral burros frequently blocks traffic along this route. The burros are not native to the region and therefore aren't considered wildlife, so feeding them is not against park rules. Keep in mind, though, that burro stomachs are not really designed to digest potato chips and marshmallows, as much as they enjoy them. The burros were introduced to the region when they were used to provide rides to the top of Harney Peak. When the rides were stopped, the burros were set free. While the burros aren't wild, they aren't exactly domestic either, so keep a close eye on them and on your children. If they display any aggressive behavior, including ears flattened against their heads, or if there are too many of them crowding close, just toss them apple slices from the car.

◖ Wildlife Loop

The Wildlife Loop, at 18 miles long, is the longest of the three byways in the park. On the north side of the park, the Wildlife Loop begins just east of the State Game Lodge off of U.S. 16A. The southwestern entrance to the Loop is located off of Highway 87, just about one mile south of the Blue Bell Lodge area. It doesn't matter which end of the loop you start from—what matters is the time of day. Wildlife is most active and visible early in the morning or near dusk. Pronghorn, bison, whitetail deer, mule deer, and prairie dogs are common along the route. On lucky occasions, the elusive elk herd will make an appearance, or a coyote will slink into the underbrush. The Wildlife Loop runs through the rolling prairie regions of the park, so visibility is exceptionally good.

Bring carrots on this drive. One of the park's two herds of burros is usually found somewhere along this route. While the burros are not wild animals, these burros have lived in the wild for decades. They are used to visitors and are generally friendly, but keep an eye out for overly aggressive behavior and watch your children. In their enthusiasm to grab carrots, especially early in the spring and summer when visitors come by less frequently, burros could knock over a child.

There are several turnouts along the route to allow for photographs and wildlife-viewing. Expect "traffic jams" when bison herds decide to cross the road. Keep in mind that bison are wild, dangerous animals that are quite capable of turning on a dime and of reaching speeds

of up to 45 miles per hour in a matter of seconds. You cannot outrun them if they choose to charge, so keep your distance.

OUTDOOR RECREATION
Ranger-Led Programs

There's nothing like an expert to make any experience more rewarding. The park offers several ranger programs for visitors May–September. Programs include a **guided tour through the Wildlife Loop** (Memorial Day–mid-Aug. daily 9 A.M. and 6 P.M.). On this tour, visitors will create a car caravan, led by one of the park naturalists, who will speak at various locations along the route. The **gold panning demonstrations** (Peter Norbeck Visitor Center, Memorial Day–Labor Day, 9 A.M. and 1 P.M.) include a talk about the gold rush of the 1870s and provide participants with the opportunity to try panning for gold in one of the park's creeks. **Guided nature walks** (June–mid-Aug. daily) are held throughout the day and provide visitors with information about the park's geology, history, birds, and wildflowers. Park naturalists also provide hands-on tips for trout fishing in the Black Hills through the **Hook 'Em & Cook 'Em fishing program** (June–Labor Day, times and locations vary). The number of participants in the fishing program is limited, and space and equipment are provided on a first-come, first-served basis. A South Dakota fishing license is required for the program and costs $9 for state residents and $16for non-residents. They are available at each of the four resort areas.

Evening programs are presented by naturalists at each of the four campgrounds in the park. Topics vary but generally include information about the wildlife, plants, geology, astronomy, park history, or outdoor recreation activities in the park. Schedules are available at the two visitors centers in the park.

Artists in Residence

During the summer, the park hosts several artists at Sylvan Lake Lodge, the State Game

THE PRONGHORN

A pronghorn buck surveys his territory.

Antilocapra americana means American goat-antelope, but the pronghorn is unrelated to New World goats or to Old World antelopes. Native only to North America, this beautiful animal has been roaming the plains since the days of saber-toothed tigers. If our enemies make us what we are, the predatory cat may well have made the pronghorn what it is today.

A skittish animal, the pronghorn can detect motion up to four miles away. If startled, it can attain speeds of 55 miles per hour in a quick sprint, with a stride that can exceed 20 feet. It is the second-fastest land mammal in the world, second only to the cheetah. While a cheetah could outrun a pronghorn, it could not outlast it. At half its top speed, the pronghorn can run for hours and travel vast distances. As nimble as this beautiful animal is, the pronghorn will generally not leap over fences, preferring instead to crawl under them.

Pronghorn stand about three feet tall at the shoulder. The males are distinguished by black patches on the lower jaw below the eye and by a black mask from the nose back. Both the male and female of the species have horns, though only the male horns grow large enough to split. They are the only animals that shed their horns, which they do annually. They will live 9-10 years in the wild.

THE SOUTHERN HILLS

Lodge, and the Coolidge Store in the Game Lodge area. The artists work on-site and answer questions from visitors. Recently featured artists have included photographers, painters, water colorists, potters, and sculptors.

Hiking

There are over 63 miles of marked trails in the park ranging in difficulty from wheelchair accessible to strenuous. Hiking off of designated trails is allowed and, as a matter of fact, hiking is allowed anywhere in the park. Trail maps are available at both of the visitors centers.

Bring water with you as there is no water available along the trails. Do not drink from any of the streams. Remember to keep your distance from buffalo and other wildlife, and be careful of poison ivy along the trail. Camping is allowed only in the campgrounds, and open fires are not allowed along the trails, except in designated picnic areas. (Check at one of the visitors centers or look for signs that broadcast the fire danger level. In case of high danger, fires are not allowed anywhere.) Remember that afternoon thundershowers are not uncommon in the summer, so bring light rain gear. Watch where you step, as prairie rattlesnakes live in the Black Hills. They are not aggressive snakes, but will strike if threatened. Finally, the only predator in the Black Hills is the mountain lion. They are shy of people and have never attacked anyone, but if you do see a lion, do not run. Maintain eye contact, make yourself as large as possible, and throw rocks and sticks. Keep children close. Do not allow them to run too far ahead or lag too far behind the group. Hiking and biking are both allowed just about everywhere in the park.

⟨ HARNEY PEAK TRAIL

- **Distance:** 6.6 miles round-trip
- **Duration:** 4–5 hours
- **Elevation Gain:** 1,100 feet
- **Effort:** Moderate to strenuous
- **Trailhead:** Sylvan Lake, north of Highway 87 (Needles Hwy.)
- **Directions:** To find the trailhead from the entrance gate, drive past the park store located at Sylvan Lake off of Highway 87 and take your first left. (This would be a right onto the road if you are traveling Needles Highway and are entering the lake area from the south.) There is a parking lot at the end of this short road. Park there and cross the footbridge leading to the swimming area. To your right is a trail information board and the start of the trail.

The hike to Harney Peak from the Sylvan Lake trailhead (Trail #9) is one of the best in the park. Moderate in difficulty, it is a six-mile round-trip hike that provides spectacular views of both the plains and the hills. The peak elevation is 7,242 feet, the highest point in South Dakota and, for that matter, the highest point between the Rocky Mountains and the Eastern Seaboard.

Trail #9 is marked by blue diamonds. The trail is well traveled and is wide enough at the start for two to hike side by side. The trail was closed late in 2009 for a short time to allow removal of a large number of trees with pine beetle infestation. The tree removal is noticeable, but doesn't affect the overall scenic impact of the hike. The trail begins in Custer State Park and crosses into the Black Elk Wilderness area.

The elevation climb is constant but not steep in the earlier sections of the trail, and small forest meadows and marshes glitter in the sunlight that filters through the pine and spruce trees in the area. Small streams of water cross the path and, as the trail progresses, large rock formations loom to the left and right. As the elevation increases along the way, more and more granite outcroppings become evident and the sky opens up. By the time you reach the Black Elk Wilderness area, the trees are thinner and the views encompass great distances.

When you reach the peak, what you see is a 360-degree panorama. The views extend past the Black Hills into Wyoming to the west, and as far as the eye can see over the plains to the east. Harney Peak is crowned with a fire tower that was built entirely of stone by the Civilian Conservation Corps in the 1930s. The tower is open for exploration, though it is no longer manned.

SYLVAN LAKE SHORE TRAIL

- **Distance:** 1-mile loop
- **Duration:** 30 minutes
- **Effort:** Easy
- **Trailhead:** Pick up the trail at any point near the shore of Sylvan Lake. The trail is a loop around the lake.
- **Directions:** Sylvan Lake is located north of Highway 87 (Needles Hwy.) in the park, near the intersection of Highways 87 and 89.

If there isn't enough time to hike to Harney Peak, the Sylvan Lake Shore Trail is a relaxing alternative. This is an easy but very scenic one-mile loop trail around the lake. A level path for the most part, there is a moderately strenuous section behind the dam with a short but steep climb on a stone staircase. Views from the trail are primarily of the granite-circled lake, though on the top of the rocks near the dam side of the trail, some of the spires of the Needles formation can be seen, as well.

SUNDAY GULCH TRAIL

- **Distance:** 2.8-mile loop
- **Elevation Gain:** 500 feet
- **Duration:** 2 hours
- **Effort:** Strenuous
- **Trailhead:** Between the swimming area and the dam at Sylvan Lake
- **Directions:** The trail begins and ends at Sylvan Lake, though there are two trailheads to choose from. One is just behind the dam to the left (with the lake behind you). The other is between the dam and the swimming area of the lake. The left-side trailhead starts easier and ends strenuous, and the right-side trailhead starts with a steep descent into the gulch.

The Sunday Gulch Trail passes through some of the greatest diversity of plants, trees, and scenery in the park, and was designated a National Recreation Trail in 1971. National Recreation Trails are designated by the Secretary of the Interior or the Secretary of Agriculture to recognize trails of local and regional significance. For dramatic impact, begin the trail at the northwest trailhead and hike counterclockwise. The first part of the trail descends steeply and requires some scrambling over huge granite boulders. It's just 0.25 mile to the bottom of the gulch, but take the trail with caution. It can be slippery here as overflow from Sylvan Lake cascades down the rocks. The Park Service has carved stone steps into the boulders and has provided hand rails. This trail is closed in winter due to the likelihood of extremely icy conditions. Once the bottom of Sunday Gulch is reached, the trail meanders through the valley surrounded by towering granite cliffs and crosses the streambed many times. In addition to the ponderosa pines that dominate the hills, you will find birch, aspen, and spruce in this region. The last half-mile or so of the loop is a little too close to roads and power lines, but overall, it's a spectacular hike.

LOVER'S LEAP TRAIL

- **Distance:** 3-mile loop
- **Duration:** 3–3.5 hours
- **Elevation Gain:** 500 feet
- **Effort:** Moderate to strenuous
- **Trailhead:** South side of U.S. 16A, across the street from the Peter Norbeck Visitor Center
- **Directions:** In the State Game Lodge area in the northeastern quadrant of the park, the Lover's Leap Trail begins behind the schoolhouse, across the street from the Peter Norbeck Visitor Center.

The Lover's Leap Trail starts with a very steep climb to the top of a ridge. Hiking along the ridge provides beautiful views of the Cathedral Spires rock formation and of Harney Peak in the distance. The hardest part of the hike comes early, so don't be discouraged. At the top of the first ridge, about 45 minutes into the hike, there is a sign marking the spot where legend has it that two lovers leapt to their deaths. The summit of this hike is near 4,800 feet and the views are spectacular. The trail descends to Galena Creek. There are several creek crossings here and no bridges, so be prepared to get wet. The trail ends back at the road, a short walk from the schoolhouse where the hike begins.

CREEKSIDE TRAIL

- **Distance:** 4 miles round-trip
- **Duration:** 1.5 hours
- **Elevation Gain:** None
- **Effort:** Easy (wheelchair accessible)
- **Trailhead:** The trail runs from the State Game Lodge to Grace Coolidge Campground and can be accessed at many points along U.S. 16A.

The wheelchair-accessible Creekside Trail runs parallel to U.S. 16A near the Game Lodge Campground. The hard-surfaced trail follows the Grace Coolidge Creek and connects the Game Lodge Campground and the Grace

THE SOUTHERN HILLS

Coolidge Campground. The trail covers about two miles and passes by the State Game Lodge, the Peter Norbeck Visitor Center, the Coolidge General Store, and the park office. It is not uncommon to see buffalo along this trail.

Mountain Biking

Mountain biking is allowed on all of the trails in the park unless closed for maintenance or restoration. Check at the visitors center for any closures. Mountain bike rentals ($10 per hour, $30 per half-day, $50 per day) are available in the park at both Legion Lake Lodge and at the State Game Lodge. Bikers must yield to both horseback riders and hikers. These trails are multipurpose trails but due to their length or location, they are great for biking.

The **Centennial Trail,** Trail #89, is a 111-mile trail that runs from just south of Bear Butte in the Northern Hills to Wind Cave National Park in the south. Almost 22 miles of the trail runs through Custer State Park. Three trailheads in the park (Iron Creek, Badger Hole, and French Creek) provide access to the Centennial Trail. The trail is marked by brown fiberglass posts and gray diamonds. The trail enters the park in the northwest corner of the main section of the park off of Highway 87 and ends near the spot where Highway 87 enters Wind Cave National Park.

IRON CREEK TRAILHEAD

- **Distance:** 7.3 miles to Badger Hole Trailhead
- **Duration:** 5 hours
- **Elevation Gain:** 600 feet
- **Effort:** Strenuous
- **Directions:** North of Highway 87 (Needles Hwy.) on Camp Remington Road

This segment of the Centennial Trail begins at the northern end of Custer State Park and ends near a historic cabin (once lived in by Badger Clark, South Dakota's first poet laureate) just south of Legion Lake. The trail rises and falls

with the gently rolling hills of the area. There are several small stream crossings. About six miles in, the trail climbs steeply and enters an area that was burned in the 1988 Galena fire, a lightning strike fire that burned over 17,000 acres of park land. The trail continues on to the Badger Hole, the nickname for the cabin once occupied by Badger Clark.

BADGER HOLE TRAILHEAD

- **Distance:** 4.2 miles to French Creek Trailhead
- **Duration:** 3 hours
- **Elevation Gain:** 700 feet
- **Effort:** Strenuous
- **Directions:** This trailhead is located one mile off of U.S. 16A on CSP Road 9, near Legion Lake.

The distance between the Badger Hole Trailhead and the final trailhead at French Creek is only 4.2 miles, but it is the most difficult segment of the Centennial Trail in the park. The trail winds near CSP Road 9 for about a mile and then heads south and begins to climb up a steep rocky hill. The entire park can be seen from the summit. The trail descends into the French Creek Natural Area. The trail is very steep and rocky as it descends and can be very muddy at the bottom. The trail follows French Creek, crossing the creek several times.

FRENCH CREEK TRAILHEAD

- **Distance:** 10.3 miles to the border of Wind Cave National Park Highland Creek Trailhead
- **Duration:** 3.5 hours
- **Elevation Gain:** 750 feet
- **Effort:** Moderate
- **Directions:** This trailhead is located three miles from the Bluebell Stables on CSP Road 4. Follow the signs to the horse camp/Centennial Trail. You will pass through the camp to reach the trailhead.

This section of the trail crosses the Wildlife Loop and enters the open grasslands of the park. Pronghorn and prairie dogs will be frequent companions. There are large herds of bison in this region, so be sure to keep a good distance. Bison are especially protective in the spring, when the calves are born, and aggressive in late August, when the rut season begins. You cannot outrun or outride them, so keep at least 100 yards between you and them. The trail passes through a gate and then ends at the border of Wind Cave National Park. Wind Cave does not allow mountain biking; only hikers are allowed south of this point.

GRACE COOLIDGE WALK-IN FISHING AREA TRAIL

- **Distance:** 6 miles round-trip
- **Effort:** Moderate
- **Trailheads:** Center Lake or Grace Coolidge Campground
- **Directions:** The trail can be accessed from the north near the Center Lake swimming beach shower house, or from the south from the parking lot located across U.S. 16A from the Grace Coolidge Campground.

Bring a bathing suit or a fishing pole and ride the Grace Coolidge Walk-In Fishing Area Trail. The trail runs between the Grace Coolidge Campground and the Center Lake Campground, a distance of 2.8 miles, and follows Grace Coolidge Creek the entire distance. From the south, the trail parallels the creek, with several crossings along the way. Be careful as the crossings can be challenging, especially in the spring when stream flow is high. This is also a popular creek for trout fishing, so try not to create too much mud when splashing through the water. As you near Center Lake, the trail begins to climb sharply. From the top of the hill, you can see the lake nestled in the pines. The descent is steep and will bring you to the swimming beach near the shower house at the lake.

This is a nice ride for those who need to rent bikes. Pick up a bike at the State Game Lodge, follow the Creekside Trail to the Grace Coolidge Campground, and then head up this trail to Center Lake. Remember there are several stream crossings that require hopping on and off the bike, but it's a great way to ride, go for a refreshing swim, and return the bike to the lodge.

BIG TREE ROBBERS ROOST DRAW

- **Distance:** 15.5 miles
- **Elevation Gain:** 500 feet
- **Effort:** Moderate
- **Directions:** Turn into the Blue Bell stables and immediately turn right onto CSP Road 4. Follow the signs to the horse camp and to the French Creek Trailhead. Drive through the horse camp and park at the French Creek Trailhead.

The trail is 15.5 miles long and is a nice loop. You'll be traveling over all kinds of terrain on this loop, including the western areas of the rolling grass prairie near the Wildlife Loop and up and down dry streambeds. You'll have an opportunity to see and photograph the second-largest ponderosa pine in the United States on this route. The trail starts out on the Centennial Trail through Horse Camp, crossing French Creek once. Just before the second crossing of the creek, the trail turns left and heads up and over a steep hill. Descend the hill and the trail will parallel the Wildlife Loop for about two miles. The trail will take a fairly sharp left and head up a dry streambed. About a quarter-mile up the streambed, you'll find the large ponderosa pine. Stop long enough to take a photo and have some water, then continue up to the top of the ridge. This section of the trail is pretty steep and rocky. Follow the ridge until the trail takes a left, and then follow the trail down into the Robbers Roost Draw. From here, the trail will meet up with CSP Road 3 until that meets up with CSP Road 4, which will return you to the French Creek Trailhead where you started.

Horseback Riding

Horseback riding is allowed in most areas of the park, with the exception of the Sylvan Lake watershed and the Grace Coolidge Walk-In Fishing Area. Guided trail rides are available at **Blue Bell Stables** (605/255-4700, one-hour ride adult $33, child $28, two-hour ride adult $45, child $38, half-day $120 per person, full-day $190 per person, half-day and full-day rides include lunch, reservations required). The Blue Bell area is nicely forested. There is a pretty stream (French Creek) that meanders through the trees, and all rides provide a little of every kind of terrain. Children must be at least 5 years old for the one-hour ride, 7 for the two-hour ride, and at least 10 to participate in the half-day and full-day rides.

Rock Climbing

Rock climbing is not a park-sponsored activity but climbing is allowed. Most climbing takes place in the northern spur of the park and includes routes near Sylvan Lake, the Needles rock formations, and Cathedral Spires. The **Sylvan Rocks Climbing School & Guide Service** (605/484-7585, www.sylvanrocks.com) has permits with Custer State Park to teach and guide climbers in the park. The school offers classes for every level of climber, including beginners, and provides all equipment for the climb. Cost for beginners is $78 per person with a minimum of two persons per class, or $110 for a single-person class. Expect the class to last 3–4 hours.

Water Sports

With the exception of the area around Blue Bell Resort in the southwestern corner of the park, there is a lake or pond located near each of the major lodging areas in the park. **Swimming** is allowed at all locations, but be aware that there are no lifeguards on hand. The park admission fee includes use of all of the beaches. **Fishing** is permitted in all of the park waters with a valid

climbing off of Needles Highway with the Sylvan Rocks Climbing School

South Dakota fishing license, which can be obtained at any of the resort areas in the park. Non-resident licenses are $16 per day, $34 for three days. (Residents pay a $9 per day fee or a $27 annual license fee.) **Fly-fishing guided trips** can be arranged in the park with **Dakota Angler & Outfitter** (605/341-1457, www.flyfishsd.com, half-day $250 for two people, $125 for each additional person, full-day $425 for up to two people, $125 for each additional person.) **Boat rentals** are provided at some of the lakes and may include paddleboats, kayaks, rowboats, canoes, or hydro-bikes. Hourly rates for rentals are per person and are $9 for a half-hour, $14 for an hour. Half-day boat rentals are $40, and full-day boat rentals are $80. Fees are the same for all locations in the park. Life jackets are included with the rental fees.

Sylvan Lake is located in the high-elevation area near Harney Peak in the most northwestern spur of the park. From the town of Custer, head east on Mount Rushmore Road and then turn left (north) onto Highway 89 and follow the signs. From Hill City, head south about three miles on U.S. 385 and turn left on Highway 87. From within the park, the lake is the end point of the Needles Highway, Highway 87 headed north. It is a small lake but is the prettiest lake in the park, with wonderful views of the surrounding granite formations. Large boulders line the lake. An easy, one-mile walking trail meanders around the lake and trailheads for hikes to Harney Peak, the Little Devils Tower Trail, and the Sunday Gulch Trail are found here. There is a small beach area for swimming. There are ducks to watch and mountain goats are frequently visible on the high granite outcroppings nearby. Paddleboats, canoes, kayaks, and rowboats are available for rental here. The **Sylvan Lake general store** (605/574-2561, May–Oct. daily 7 A.M.–9 P.M.) sells bait and fishing licenses, in addition to souvenirs, gifts, and fast food. Brook and rainbow trout are the most likely

catches here. Boats with small electric motors are allowed on the lake, but as small as the lake is, it seems more suited to rowboats.

Stockade Lake is the biggest lake in the park and is located on the far west boundary of the park. The town of Custer is just down the road (Mt. Rushmore Rd./U.S. 16A). Stockade Lake offers the best fishing in the park. In addition to the rainbow, brown, and brook trout found everywhere in the park, it is not uncommon for anglers to catch northern pike, bass, perch, crappie, and bullhead here. This is the only lake in the park that allows gas-powered engines on boats, and there is a boat ramp available. This is still a very small lake, however, so don't expect to go waterskiing. There are camping facilities near the lake, and there is a small sandy beach for swimming.

Legion Lake is located along U.S. 16A in the northern third of the park. There is a restaurant and gift shop on-site that sells bait and other fishing supplies during the summer months, and cabins are available for rent. Paddleboats, kayaks, and hydro-bikes are available right next to the lodge. There is a swimming beach here that is tucked back from the lodge and away from view of the road, which makes it feel nice and secluded. Look to catch rainbow and brook trout. Boats with electric motors are allowed.

Center Lake is the most remote of the lakes in the park. A three-mile hike from the Grace Coolidge Campground parking lot, just past the park office on U.S. 16A, will bring you to the lake. Drive-in access to the lake is available, as well. From U.S. 16A in the park, take Highway 87 north to the intersection with County Road 753 and follow signs for the Black Hills Playhouse. Go past the turnoff to the Playhouse and take your next right on Center Lake Road. This will bring you straight to the lake. There is a picnic area and swimming beach located on the north end of the lake. This is one of the quietest areas in the park. Rainbow, brown, and brook trout are the most common catches.

ENTERTAINMENT AND EVENTS

◖ Black Hills Playhouse

Since 1946, the Black Hills Playhouse (605/255-4141 or 855/584-4141, www.blackhillsplayhouse.com, evening performances Tues.–Sat. 7:30 P.M., matinees Sat. and Sun 2 P.M., adults $28–35, child aged 4–12 $10–15) has been entertaining visitors to Custer State Park. Located off the beaten track in the north end of the park, the theater can be reached from the State Game Lodge by taking U.S. 16A west to the junction of Highway 87. Take Highway 87 north to County Road 753 and follow the signs to the Playhouse.

The theater originated in 1946, when Dr. Warren Lee, director of the University of South Dakota theater program, brought a traveling troupe of actors to the Black Hills. The troupe lodged at the old Civilian Conservation Corps (CCC) facility, built in the park in 1933, while it presented plays in other theaters in the hills. In 1947, the University of South Dakota became actively involved in the theater and performances began to be held in the park. The first venue was a 50-seat theater that served as the dining hall when the CCC camp was active. By 1955, the current facility was built and in recent years, air conditioning and heating capabilities were added. Now with seating for over 300 patrons, the theater remains an intimate, warm performance venue with low balconies and beautiful wood beams throughout. There isn't a bad seat in the house. Tickets can be purchased at any of the resort lodges in the park, online, or at the ticket booth located next to the theater.

There is something very special about the Black Hills Playhouse. Set at a dead-end road in the middle of the forest, the remote location adds to the mystique of the experience. While theater is high culture, there's nothing formal about an evening here. The air smells like pine instead of perfume. The snack bar serves brats and hot dogs before the performance. Shorts and jeans are as comfortable as dresses and diamonds. The quality of the performances is generally high and set design is consistently delightful. The theater has tackled many a Broadway play, and musical productions have included *Fiddler on the Roof, A Chorus Line,* and Neil Simon's *Brighton Beach Memoirs.* After the performance, drive slowly and carefully through the park. Be alert for shining eyes in the dark; bison and elk will be wandering the roads.

Annual Buffalo Roundup

Custer State Park winds down the summer season with a task that started as buffalo herd management and is now an event that attracts thousands of people. At the end of September, the buffalo are herded into corrals for vaccinations, tests, branding, and sorting. Most bison are returned to the park, but many will be auctioned off. Park management noticed early on that the sight of 1,500 bison being rounded up was fairly impressive and elected to open the process to the public.

Roundup weekend begins with the **Buffalo Roundup Arts Festival.** On Saturday and Sunday, hundreds of artists and craftspeople set up booths near the State Game Lodge. There's a pancake breakfast, and the **Chili Cookoff** (in which buffalo meat must be included in the recipe) is a festival highlight. Entertainment is scheduled throughout the day. Dancing, music, and a buffalo chip toss are other festival favorites.

Monday morning brings the roundup itself. The Wildlife Loop provides access to the viewing areas from either end of the loop, though the south viewing area provides more extended bison views. Park employees direct visitors to parking areas. Go early as the crowds start to arrive at 6:30 A.M. Bring coffee and snacks since bison aren't always amenable to being herded and the wait can be unpredictable. The bison are guided to the corrals by men and women on horseback, a dangerous task for both horse and rider. Behind the horses are the pickup trucks

© WWW.TRAVELSD.COM

The annual Buffalo Roundup occurs each September.

and ATVs, which take away from the ambience of the event but add to its expediency.

ACCOMMODATIONS

Accommodations in the park are centered around four lodge and campground communities in different regions of the park. Each area has a different feel and each location is somewhat self-contained with dining, convenience stores, and other amenities provided close by. Pick a place that suits your personal style. They are all beautiful and while the prices vary, they are comparable. Each area has a variety of cabins. Sleeping cabins do not have a kitchen, while housekeeping cabins do, though they are not equipped with pots, pans, or utensils. There are many different cabin configurations that can sleep 8–16 people. Rates provided here are for lodging that can sleep 1–4 people per cabin, or a double for lodge and motel rooms.

It is possible to enjoy Custer State Park year-round at Creekside Lodge near the State Game Lodge. Camping cabins are available at the Game Lodge Campground, and limited campground facilities (including drinking water, vault toilets, tables, and fire grates) are available at both the State Game Lodge campground and the French Creek Horse Camp.

State Game Lodge

The State Game Lodge (13389 U.S. 16A, 605/255-4541 or 888/875-0001, www.custer-resorts.com, May 1–Oct. 31, $115–315) is a beautiful granite and frame structure reminiscent of the style of early National Parks. Built in 1922, the lodge is now on the National Register of Historic Places. Nicknamed the "Summer White House" after President Coolidge spent the summer season at the lodge in 1927, the lodge is set next to Grace Coolidge Creek and is surrounded by ponderosa pine forest. The property features seven historic lodge rooms, motel rooms, sleeping cabins, and housekeeping cabins. There is a gorgeous dark wood and stone porch that runs along the front of the lodge and inside, the lobby has hardwood floors, wood-beamed ceilings, a stone fireplace, leather furnishings, and fine art prints on the walls. The rooms are painted in soft colors and decorated with wildlife prints and scenic prints of the Black Hills. All the rooms have television and air-conditioning, and free wireless Internet is available on request. (It is possible to reserve President Coolidge's room.)

In 2008, the **Creekside Lodge** ($200) was added to the accommodations provided at the State Game Lodge and features large rooms with either two queens or one king bed. This property is open year-round.

The State Game Lodge features its own elegant restaurant. The Peter Norbeck Visitor Center is located across the street from the lodge, and bicycle rentals and gold-panning demonstrations are held at this site. The Coolidge General Store and Gift Shop is located here and offers groceries, deli items, fishing licenses, gasoline, camping supplies, and souvenirs. Nondenominational services are held at the State Game Lodge Chapel every Sunday June–August.

Legion Lake Lodge

Legion Lake Lodge (12967 U.S. 16A, 605/255-4521 or 888/875-0001, www.custerresorts. com, sleeping cabins $140, housekeeping cabins $175–204) is the most casual of the park's lodges. The lodge is situated next to Legion Lake, which got its name from the American Legion, which leased the land for years. Built in 1913, the lodge pre-dates the region's status as a state park. At the time it was built, the area around the lodge was a game preserve situated within what was then Custer State Forest. Custer State Forest became Custer State Park in 1919. Close to Needles Highway and to the park exit to the town of Custer, Legion Lake Lodge is a quiet area where family picnics, swimming, and fishing are the activities of choice. Sleeping and housekeeping cabins are nestled into the side of the hill behind the lodge, tucked away from sight

of the road. Sleeping cabins do not have kitchens. The housekeeping cabins have kitchens, but neither cooking nor dining supplies are provided. It's very secluded and feels like a summer camp. All of the rooms have air-conditioning. Bicycles can be rented from the lodge, and a casual café and small gift shop are on-site.

Blue Bell Lodge

Blue Bell Lodge (25453 Hwy. 87, 605/255-4531 or 888/875-0001, www.custerresorts. com, sleeping cabins $210, housekeeping cabins $150–175, $10 per pet per night) is the southernmost lodge in the park; its theme is decidedly Western. The main lodge holds the dining room and lounge. Sleeping and housekeeping cabins are located along French Creek, nestled in the ponderosa pine forest. The cabins have two-burner hot plates and a small refrigerator but no pots, pans, dishes, glassware, or flatware are provided for the bulk of the cabins. The lodge was built in the early 1920s by an executive of Bell telephone. The logo for the phone company, a blue bell, inspired the resort's name. The only horseback riding stable in the park is located here. Chuck wagon dinners and hay rides are offered nightly. There is a dining room and lounge, general store, and gift shop located near the cabins. There are fire grates at every cabin, and free wireless Internet is available. The Blue Bell Lodge is close to the southern entrance of the Wildlife Loop and is not far from Wind Cave National Park.

Sylvan Lake Lodge

Perched on the top of a hill with a fabulous view of Harney Peak, Sylvan Lake Lodge (24572 Hwy. 87, 605/574-2561 or 888/875-0001, www.custerresorts.com, $140–220) is within reach of some of the best hiking, rock climbing, and mountain scenery in the hills. The lodge interior has the feel of a woodland hunting lodge, with high cross-beamed ceilings and hunting trophies displayed on the walls. There are 35 rooms in the lodge, as well as sleeping cabins and housekeeping cabins on the property. Sylvan Lake Lodge is also the closest location for easy access to Hill City, Keystone, and Mount Rushmore. Today's lodge was not the original lodge in this area. The first Sylvan Lake Lodge was built in 1895 right on the shoreline. Unfortunately, the original lodge burned down in 1935. The current lodge opened in 1937. It is about a quarter-mile walk to the shores of Sylvan Lake and that short distance ensures an air of peaceful relaxation on the lodge grounds. There is a beautiful, outdoor stone patio behind the lodge, and a dining room and lounge are on-site, as well. At the lake, a general store and gift shop provide casual dining, groceries, fishing licenses, and souvenirs. Paddle boats and kayaks are available for rental.

Campgrounds

There are nine campgrounds in the park (800/710-2267 or www.campsd.com for reservations) located near the four major lodge areas or near the lakes in the park. The campgrounds are run by the South Dakota Department of Game, Fish and Parks. Most of the campsites are gravel or paved, and have electricity, a fire grate, and a picnic table. Prices are $18–20 without electricity and $24–27 with electricity for each "camping unit" at the site. Two tents equal two units, as in one camper trailer and one tent. In other words, two tents on one site results in being charged for two units, unless the second tent is for family members. Every site has warm showers and toilets. Electric hookups are available at all campgrounds with the exception of the Center Lake. One-room camping cabins are also available at some of the locations. These run $47 per night and do not have bathrooms or kitchens. They are, in the words of a reservation agent, "hardsided tents."

Tent campers who are looking for a deal and don't mind primitive camping with no facilities should head for the **French Creek Natural Area,** located just east of the Blue Bell horse camp off of CSP Road 4. Camping is allowed anywhere in this area for just $6 per person per night. Evening campfire programs occur at all of the campgrounds.

Activities and amenities vary near the campgrounds, depending on which lodge the grounds are affiliated with. The **Blue Bell Resort Campground** has 30 tent or RV sites and 23 camping cabins. Within a mile of the campground are laundry facilities and a park store, which provides fuel, basic supplies, and gifts. Nearby activities include fishing, horseback riding, chuck wagon dinners, and hay rides. There is a dining room/restaurant and lounge at the resort. The southwestern entrance to the Wildlife Loop is within one mile of the Blue Bell Resort area.

At the **Legion Lake Campground,** there are 21 sites and no camping cabins. There is a casual dining facility at the lodge, and a park store nearby. This store does not have a fuel pump. There is a swimming beach and paddleboats, kayaks, and hydro-bikes are available for rental. Bike rentals are provided here, as well. Activities include biking, hiking, swimming, and fishing.

The **Game Lodge Campground** has 55 sites and 11 camping cabins. It is the only campground on park grounds with an RV dump station. This campground is close to everything. There is a small pond nearby for swimming and fishing. The lodge has a restaurant and lounge. The park store and gift shop, with fuel, is within a mile, as are laundry facilities. Activities near the State Game Lodge include bike rentals, guided wildlife caravans through the Wildlife Loop, and gold-panning demonstrations. The Peter Norbeck Visitor Center is located across the street from the State Game Lodge.

The **Sylvan Lake Campground** has 38 sites and no camping cabins. There are several hiking trailheads near Sylvan Lake. Fishing and swimming and boat rentals are available here. There is a restaurant and a lounge at the Sylvan

Lake Lodge near the campground, and a general store and gift shop at the water's edge.

Campers with horses are allowed at **French Creek Horse Campground,** which is located close to the Blue Bell Resort. This campground has 28 sites and three camping cabins.

Center Lake Campground, located in the northern section of the park near the Black Hills Playhouse, has 71 sites and no camping cabins. The sites are all available on a same-day reservation basis or first-come, first-served. There are no sites with electricity, but, according to park employees, camping here is almost always available with the exception of Sturgis Motorcycle Rally week and the July 4 weekend. It is also a great site for fishing and swimming, and it is close to both the Needles Highway and Iron Mountain Road.

FOOD

The **State Game Lodge Dining Room** (13389 U.S. 16A, 605/255-4541, www.custerresorts. com, May–Oct. daily 7 A.M.–9 P.M., breakfast $12, lunch $13–16, dinner $19–32) is a casual place for breakfast and for lunch. Dinner has a more elegant and formal atmosphere. Breakfast offers all of the standard items, but there are a few interesting specialty items here, as well, including banana-stuffed French toast and a buffalo Benedict. Lunch features an array of soups, stew, sandwiches, and pasta. House specialties include buffalo stew, buffalo burgers, and a salmon BLT. At night, the lodge seems to gleam. The lobby's hardwood floors shine with rich polish, the dining room tables are covered with white tablecloths, and tables are spaced well, giving each party a sense of privacy and intimacy. The dinner menu is extensive. Highlights include local game, such as bison, pheasant, and trout, as well as a wide variety of salads and pasta. The restaurant has an extensive wine list, and wine recommendations are included with every entrée listing. There is also a full bar for cocktails.

The **Legion Lake Lodge Dining Room** (12967 U.S. 16A, 605/255-4521, www.custer-resorts.com, May–Oct. daily 7 A.M.–9 P.M., closed in winter, breakfast $9, lunch and dinner $9–15) is the most casual dining facility in the park. Red checkered table cloths, tile floors, and light wood tables and chairs are homey and inviting. Dine inside or out on the deck overlooking the lake. Free wireless Internet is available.

Breakfast includes the basics, such as buffalo sausage and eggs, omelets, French toast, and pancakes. Lunch and dinner share the same menu, with a selection of burgers, sandwiches, salads, and pizza. One of the specialty choices is trout grilled in pecan butter.

The **Blue Bell Lodge Dining Room** (25453 Hwy. 87, 605/255-4531, www.custerresorts. com, early May–mid-Oct. daily 7 A.M.–9 P.M., closed in winter, breakfast $9, lunch and dinner $10–18) is casual and keeps with the very Western theme of the Blue Bell Resort. The lodge, a dark brown and cream log cabin structure, is set back from the road, surrounded by tall pines. The inside is all Western, with chinked log walls, wooden tables, and trophy animals displayed on the walls. The menu looks like a newspaper tabloid and food selections have Western-style titles. Appetizers become "Bits & Spurs" and you are invited to "Saddle Up" for salads. Any of the sandwiches can be requested to go for a box lunch in the park. Supper features a large number of steak dishes, pasta, and a variety of buffalo and fish entrées. There is a bar on-site where you can "Wet Your Whistle" with wine, beer, or cocktails. The **Chuck Wagon Dinner** (adult $45, child under 12 $35, child under 3 free) includes a hay ride out to a nearby meadow. Long lines of picnic tables await patrons, who can choose to dine on either an eight-ounce sirloin steak or a half-pound hamburger with cowboy beans, cornbread and honey, potato salad, coleslaw, watermelon, cookies, coffee, and lemonade. After dinner, a sing-along country/folk band entertains throughout the evening. Participants meet at the lodge to load the wagons. Check departure time with the lodge. Generally the ride, dinner, and show run 5–8 P.M. All participants receive a souvenir cowboy hat and bandana.

The **Sylvan Lake Lodge Dining Room** (24572 Hwy. 87, 605/574-2561, www.custerresorts.com, May–mid-Oct. daily 7 A.M.–9 P.M., closed in winter, breakfast $9, lunch $10–15, dinner $18–38) is lined with windows, and the furnishings are light wood. The best feature, though, is right outside. Perched high above the lake, views of Harney Peak are clear from every spot. Dine outside on the veranda and you are in paradise. The breakfast menu is fairly limited, with just a few standard egg and pancake dishes. Lunch includes a variety of soups, salads, and sandwiches; the staff can pack you a lunch to go, so that you can enjoy an outdoor picnic in the park. Dinner specialties include elk medallions and buffalo rib eye, as well as trout, walleye, and salmon.

INFORMATION AND SERVICES
Information
Park Headquarters are located at 13329 U.S. 16A, one mile west of the State Game Lodge, and can be reached at 605/255-4515. The park website is www.custerstatepark.info, which redirects to the South Dakota Department of Game, Fish and Parks website. Campground reservations can be made by calling 800/710-2267 or accessing www.campsd.com. Lodge reservations, managed by a private company, can be made at 888/875-0001 or online at www.custerresorts.com.

Services
There are a variety of general services available within the park boundaries. **Laundry facilities** are located at the State Game Lodge Campground. **Fuel** is available at the Coolidge General Store and Gift Shop, one mile west of the State Game Lodge, and at the park store across from the Blue Bell Lodge. There are three **nondenominational chapels** that provide Sunday services. These are located near the State Game Lodge and the Sylvan Lake Lodge, and there is an outdoor chapel next to the Blue Bell Restaurant. There are three **convenience stores** that carry limited grocery, deli, and snack items, as well as gifts, souvenirs, and camping supplies. These are located at the State Game Lodge, at Sylvan Lake, and across the street from the Blue Bell Restaurant. **Restrooms** are located at the visitors centers, the park headquarters, the lodges, and campgrounds.

Hot Springs

While many Black Hills communities were founded as a result of the 1874 gold rush, the founding of Hot Springs was different. No gold was ever discovered there. By 1875, when a second geologic expedition was exploring the region, reports of warm springs in the Fall River Valley began to surface. The healing powers of warm mineral springs had long been in the prescription bags of medical doctors at the time, but the area where the springs were discovered was virtually uninhabited and unreachable.

The rush of miners to the Black Hills brought the railroads, the ranchers, and other support industries. Transportation and population created an environment in which development of a spa resort became possible.

In 1879, one of the members of the expedition that found the warm waters of Hot Springs decided to return, and this time he brought a young reporter from Deadwood with him. The reporter wrote an article about the warm springs and published it in the Deadwood

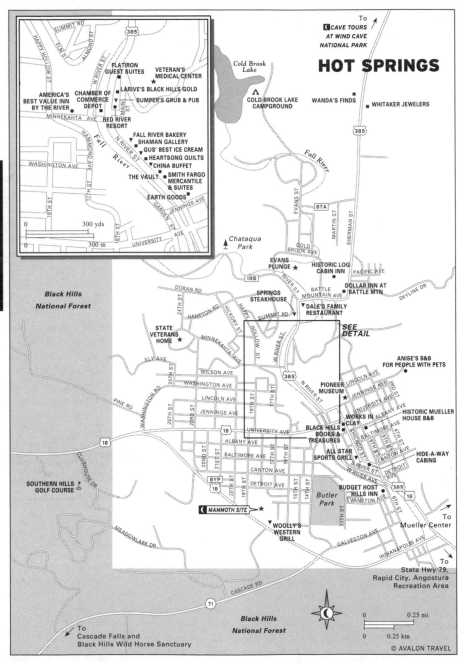

HOT SPRINGS

To
☕ CAVE TOURS
AT WIND CAVE
NATIONAL PARK

THE SOUTHERN HILLS

Cold Brook
Lake

FLATIRON
GUEST SUITES
VETERAN'S
MEDICAL CENTER
LARIVE'S BLACK HILLS GOLD
CHAMBER OF
COMMERCE
DEPOT
BUMPER'S GRUB & PUB
AMERICA'S
BEST VALUE INN
BY THE RIVER
RED RIVER
RESORT

COLD BROOK LAKE
CAMPGROUND

WANDA'S FINDS

WHITAKER JEWELERS

MINNEKAHTA AVE

FALL RIVER BAKERY
SHAMAN GALLERY
GUS' BEST ICE CREAM
HEARTSONG QUILTS
CHINA BUFFET
SMITH FARGO
MERCANTILE
& SUITES
THE VAULT
WASHINGTON AVE

EARTH GOODS

Fall River

JENNINGS AVE

UNIVERSITY AVE

0   300 yds
0   300 m

Fall River

385

87A

EVANS ST

MARTIN ST

SHERMAN ST

Chataqua
Park

COLD
BROOK AVE

EVANS
PLUNGE

HISTORIC LOG
CABIN INN

PACIFIC AVE

18B

RIVER ST

BATTLE
MOUNTAIN AVE

DOLLAR INN AT
BATTLE MTN

SKYLINE DR

DORAN RD

SPRINGS
STEAKHOUSE

DALE'S FAMILY
RESTAURANT

Black Hills
National Forest

HAMPTON RD

HICKORY ST

SUMMIT RD

SEE
DETAIL

STATE
VETERANS
HOME

MINNEKAHTA AVE

HAPPY HOLLOW

W RIVER ST

385

ANISE'S B&B
FOR PEOPLE WITH PETS

ELY AVE

WILSON AVE

LINCOLN AVE

PIONEER
MUSEUM

PINE RD

WASHINGTON BLVD

WASHINGTON AVE

LINCOLN AVE

N RIVER ST

JENNINGS AVE

3RD ST

UNIVERSITY AVE

ALBANY AVE

HISTORIC MUELLER
HOUSE B&B

JENNINGS AVE

WORKS IN
CLAY

BALTIMORE AVE

CHICAGO ST

6TH ST

5TH ST

4TH ST

18

UNIVERSITY AVE

BLACK HILLS
BOOKS &
TREASURES

ALBANY AVE

18

22ND ST

21ST ST

20TH ST

19TH ST

17TH ST

16TH ST

BALTIMORE AVE

CANTON AVE

ALL STAR
SPORTS GRILL

CANTON AVE

DETROIT ST

HIDE-A-WAY
CABINS

BYP

18

DETROIT AVE

Butler
Park

W RIVER AVE

BUDGET HOST
HILLS INN

385

18

MAMMOTH SITE

15TH ST

14TH ST

11TH ST

EVANSTON AVE

6TH ST

To
Mueller Center

WOOLLY'S
WESTERN
GRILL

MEADOWLARK DR

GALVESTON AVE

INDIANAPOLIS AVE

To
State Hwy 79,
Rapid City, Angostura
Recreation Area

SOUTHERN HILLS
GOLF COURSE

CLUBHOUSE DR

CASCADE RD

71

Black Hills
National Forest

0   0.25 mi
0   0.25 km

To
Cascade Falls and
Black Hills Wild Horse Sanctuary

© AVALON TRAVEL

newspaper. The article attracted the notice of a local physician named Jennings, but it would be another year before Jennings would venture south to investigate.

The springs were discovered, claimed, and sold for nominal sums two or three times before Dr. Jennings finally revisited the area in 1881. He formed a stock company with Fred Evans, E. Dudley, and L. Graves, then bought the springs and set out to make improvements. During the next few years, word got out about the warm waters of the region and a slow but steady stream of visitors began to visit the area with the goal of improving their health. By this time, those who were going to be lucky enough to strike it rich in the Northern Hills had already done so, and many of those individuals were looking for new opportunities. The idea of a pleasure resort resonated with many of them, and a lot of the historical founders of Hot Springs arrived here after spending some years in Deadwood first.

Most of the buildings that exist in the Historic District today were built in a period of rapid growth between 1890 and 1910. Many of the first buildings were hotels, built to house those seeking the cure from the warm mineral waters of the community. The elegant Evans Hotel was completed by 1886. All of the sandstone used in construction was quarried locally. In 1888, Hot Springs became the county seat of Fall River (and remains so to this day). Hot Springs was selected as the site for the Soldiers' Home and the Battle Mountain Sanitarium due to the common belief in the healthy environment of the community's air and water. By 1890, the railroad came to town, a defining moment and a requirement for growth for any prairie town. By 1891, the Evans Plunge was built. It remains a cornerstone of Hot Springs tourism.

Today, Hot Springs, perched on the southern edge of the Black Hills, is one of the prettiest towns in the region. With steep red canyon walls, a warm water river meandering through

town, pine-covered hills, and an aura of history wrapped around its sandstone buildings, it will never be one of those prairie towns that flourish for a bit and then fade away, abandoned by its residents for greener pastures. The history of the town community lives on in the beautiful architecture. In 2009, Hot Springs was named by the National Trust for Historic Preservation as a Distinctive Destination.

Hot Springs is a bit dusty and its edges are still a little rough, but there is something special here. For those seeking a sense of another era and a quiet respite from the hectic pace and crowds of the communities geographically closer to Mount Rushmore, Hot Springs is a great place to visit.

SIGHTS
◖ Mammoth Site

The fascinating Mammoth Site (1800 Hwy. 18, 605/745-6017, www.mammothsite. com, open year-round mid-May–mid-Aug. daily 8 A.M.–8 P.M., mid-Aug.–Labor Day daily 8 A.M.–6 P.M., Labor Day–Oct. daily 9 A.M.–5 P.M., Nov.–Feb. Mon.–Sat. 9 A.M.–3:30 P.M., Sun. 11 A.M.–3:30 P.M., Mar.–mid-May daily 9 A.M.–5 P.M., adult $9, senior $8.00, child aged 4–12 $6.50, child under 4 free) is a must on any vacation to the Black Hills. The first mammoth tusk discovered at the site was overturned by accident. Early in 1974, a bulldozer, working to level out the hill for a planned real estate development, uncovered the tusk. Thankfully, the owner of the property was willing to halt development until the site could be evaluated. Since then, the skeletal remains of 60 mammoths have been found and are displayed where they were uncovered. In addition to the mammoths, 85 other species of animals, plants, and several unidentified insects dating back 26,000 years to the Pleistocene Age have been archived. The latest exhibit features Lyuba, a baby mammoth found in Siberia by a reindeer herder. The frozen little mammoth's skin, internal organs, and stomach were intact.

A guided tour of the **Sink Hole and Dig Site** takes about 30 minutes, after which visitors are free to wander the site as long as they please. The **Self-Guided Tour** pamphlet is available in Dutch, English, French, German, French, Russian, and Italian for those who elect not to participate in a group tour. During the month of July, the site is alive with activity as members of Earthwatch come to continue the dig. It's fascinating to watch the dedicated volunteers at work with tiny tools that look much like dental equipment.

The Mueller Exhibit Hall, adjacent to the dig site, features replicas of many of the animals found at the dig, a mammoth bone hut, and a collection of some of the oldest North American arrowheads. There are also skeletons of now-extinct carnivores on display, including the short-faced bear and the American lion.

The Mammoth Site offers a **Junior** **Paleontologist Excavation Program** for children aged 4–12 (June–July 4 daily at 10 A.M., 11 A.M., 2 P.M., and 3 P.M., Aug. daily at 2 P.M., $10 in addition to site admission fee). This program allows children to dig at a simulated excavation site with the same tools that are used at the real dig. The program takes about 1.5 hours and includes lessons on Ice Age animals and specimen identification. Children will get dirty during the dig, so spare clothing is recommended. Advance reservations are required for this program. Reservations can be made as early as January in the year plans are made to visit the site.

Older children (aged 13 and up) might enjoy the **Advanced Paleontology Program** (June and July daily at 4 P.M., $20 in addition to site admission fee), which teaches participants bone identification and excavation techniques, including how to map and jacket a bone.

Evans Plunge

One of the favorite family spots in town is the **Evans Plunge Indoor Pool and Mineral Spa** (1145 N. River St., 605/745-5165, www.evansplunge.com; Apr. 2–Memorial Day: Mon.–Fri. 8 A.M.–7 P.M., Sat. 10 A.M.–7 P.M., Sun. 1–7 P.M.; Memorial Day–mid-Aug.: Mon.–Fri. 8 A.M.–9 P.M., Sat.–Sun. 10 A.M.–9 P.M.; mid-Aug.–Labor Day: Mon.–Fri. 8 A.M.–8 P.M., Sat.–Sun. 10 A.M.–8 P.M.; Labor Day–Oct. 1: 8 A.M.–7 P.M., Sat.–Sun. 10 A.M.–7 P.M., closed Oct. 2–Apr. 1; adult $12, child $10, child under 2 free, health club access add $3.50). The Evans Plunge, a 50-by-150-foot gravel-bottomed mineral pool, came into being at a time when mineral springs were believed to have great medicinal value. Doctors recommended that patients drink mineral water to cure all kinds of internal ailments and prescribed soaking in it to cure joint problems. The warm mineral springs cure has been with us almost as long as recorded history. That all changed with the creation of synthetic drugs in the 1930s. Why

© LAURAL BIDWELL

60 mammoths have been discovered at this dig site…so far.

travel uncomfortably for hundreds of miles when a cure is waiting in your bathroom medicine cabinet? And so began the slow decline in medical tourism.

There are whispers that old-fashioned pools like the Evans Plunge have no future in the highly competitive water-park market of the 21st century. But that would be unfortunate. The inside of the Evans Plunge today looks much as it did 100 years ago. The water is crystal clear since the spring-fed pool has a complete change of water 16 times a day. Very little chlorine is needed in the pool because of the constant water change, so there is no chlorine smell, and no burning red eyes. The Evans Plunge has two water slides, a set of rings to swing out over the pool, basketball hoops, inflatable alligators and rafts to float on, a children's shallow pool, a small outdoor pool, and a great mural of the Mammoth Site painted on the wall. The gravel bottom is a refreshing change from the bright aqua color of most standard swimming facilities. There are lifeguards on duty at all times. The pool is big enough for the kids to have a great time and small enough to keep an eye on them. In the summertime, there is also an outdoor pool available.

The first amenity at the site where the Evans Plunge now stands was a bathtub-like structure picked out of the rock about three feet wide by three feet deep and eight feet long. Guests generally brought their own towels and accommodations included a tent by the side of the spring. The original soaking site was outdoors. In 1891, Fred T. Evans, one of the original founders of Hot Springs, opened the luxurious Evans Plunge complex. Unlike most of the bathhouses of the time, which were somewhat serious institutions of healing, Evans built the plunge with slides and rafts for guests to enjoy. Over time, the original wood frame building had to be replaced as the damp and warped rafters surrendered to the wet environment; today,

the exterior of the plunge is a rather uninteresting concrete block. But inside, the slides, the rafts, and the fun remain.

Pioneer Museum

In 2011, the Library of Congress accepted a copy of the "Square Earth Map" created by Professor Orlando Ferguson of Hot Springs, South Dakota, thinking it was the only copy of this map in the world. They were wrong. You can view the map and all kinds of items of historical interest at the Pioneer Museum (300 N. River St./U.S. 385, 605/745-5147, www.pioneer-museum.com, mid-May–mid-Oct. Mon.–Sat. 9 A.M.–5 P.M., closed in winter, adult $5, senior $4, child under 12 free if accompanied by an adult, family pass $15). The museum is housed in a beautiful historic building that was built in 1893 of pink sandstone from the local Burke Quarry. The building was active as a school until 1961. There are three floors of exhibits. The museum collections include artifacts from pioneer and town life from the 1880s through the 1970s; it's an eclectic collection of items that represent life in everyday Fall River County. The museum has an extensive collection of turn-of-the 20th century artifacts, including furniture, glassware, farm implements, photographs, and clothing from that era. Three rooms of the museum include re-creations of everyday life in a schoolroom, kitchen, and parlor. There is also a fully stocked general store and post office. Not surprisingly, the museum has a collection of medical equipment, too, including an iron lung and an early 1900s dentist's office. The Pioneer Museum also owns one of the early sculptures created by Gutzon Borglum, the artist behind the carving of Mount Rushmore. The museum is very family friendly, with special activities just for children. Kids especially enjoy participating in the museum's scavenger hunt and ringing the schoolroom bell.

one of many fascinating artifacts at the Pioneer Museum

Black Hills Wild Horse Sanctuary

Wild horses are icons of the American West. In 1971, as a result of public outcry at their shrinking populations, Congress enacted a law to protect wild horses (and burros) and to charge the Bureau of Land Management with their protection. Populations began to recover as a result of the law and, in order to manage herd size, animals were removed from the range and sold at auction. For horses that were "unadoptable," generally meaning over 10 years old or offered for auction three times without success, slaughter was allowed.

In 1988, Dayton Hyde, an author and conservationist, established a sanctuary for unadoptable horses. The Black Hills Wild Horse Sanctuary (Hwy. 71 S., 605/745-5955 or 800/252-6652, www.wildmustangs.com) is situated on 11,000 scenic acres bordering the Cheyenne River and is located about 12 miles south of Hot Springs off of Highway 71.

Historically the sanctuary has offered guided bus tours to the general public. In recent years, the Black Hills region has not been getting enough rainfall or snow to replenish the prairie grasses. In order to preserve whatever grasses may grow for use by the horses, the larger bus tours have been temporarily suspended while a new range management plan is put into place. Several plans are being considered for the future of the sanctuary. Visitors are encouraged to call ahead to see what programs are available at the time of their visit. Private tours are still available.

The **3-Hour Cross Country Tour** ($150 per person) is a private guided tour for one to seven people. More time is spent with the horses and more stops for photographs are made at scenic locations on the wild horse sanctuary property. It is a very beautiful piece of land. The Cheyenne River runs through the property and the views of the Black Hills just to the north are lovely.

The **Adventure Tour** ($750 for up to three people) is a six-hour guided tour that explores some of the more remote areas of the sanctuary by four-wheel-drive. This tour is limited to three people, lasts around six hours and includes a picnic lunch.

The **Photographer's Tour** ($300) is a four-hour guided tour by four-wheel drive specially designed for photographers. There are many stops and photographers are allowed to exit at several locations to take close-up photos of the herd.

Visitors are allowed to visit the property without taking a tour. The on-site visitors center and gift shop are open year round. The beautiful gift shop offers Wild Horse Sanctuary t-shirts, caps, and other unique horse-related gifts, as well as books written by Dayton Hyde, the founder of the sanctuary. All proceeds from tours and gift shop sales benefit the horses. In the near future, the Wild Horse Sanctuary plans to add a small café and picnic area to the grounds. Expect a lovely outdoor deck and picnic table seating.

RECREATION
The Springs

One of the most frequently asked questions in Hot Springs is, "Is there somewhere outdoors that I can go and sit in the hot springs?" For the most part, the answer is no. Most of the springs here are warm, not hot, and aren't concentrated in one place. However, there are places where you can enjoy the springs at no charge. Take a walk along the **Freedom Trail,** a paved pathway about a mile long that follows **Fall River** from the corner of North River Street and Minnekahta Road down to the Mueller Civic Center. Fall River is fed by over 100 warm springs and maintains an average temperature of 87°F year-round. Wading is allowed anywhere along the river, although the best spot is behind the Brookside Apartments (201 S. River St.). There are picnic tables there and it is a safe, fun spot to let the kids get wet.

Another favorite spot is **Cascade Falls,** located about 12 miles south of town off of

Highway 71. From the road, it looks like an ordinary roadside rest stop. Walk to the western edge of the area, though, and look down to see a good sized pond and a fast-flowing shallow stream cascading over the rocks. The falls aren't big, but there is something appealing about this hidden stream. There are no lifeguards or services other than picnic tables and restrooms, and there is no fee.

Angostura Recreation Area

For those who love serious boating, fishing, and swimming, there is the Angostura Recreation Area (13157 N. Angostura Rd., 605/745-6996, www.gfp.sd.gov/state-parks, for camping reservations 800/710-2267 or www.campsd.com, open year-round, day fee $4 per person or $6 per vehicle, annual pass $28, camping $14–18). Located 10 miles southeast of Hot Springs off of U.S. 385/18, Angostura is part of the South Dakota State Park system and requires a park pass for entrance. With 36 miles of shoreline, Angostura is the largest reservoir in western South Dakota. Single and double kayaks are available for rental at the northern entrance to the area. There are four campgrounds at the lake (with a total of 169 sites), showers, water, and dump stations.

Golf

If swinging a club sounds more satisfying than swimming, try golf at the **Southern Hills Municipal Golf Course** (W. U.S. 18, 605/745-6400, www.hotspringssdgolf.com). This beautiful par-70 course was cited by *Golf Week* as one of the "2009 Best You Can Play" golf courses, and given 4.5 stars by *Golf Digest.* The Seven Sisters range of hills are just east of the course, prairie views are to the south, and ponderosa pines and scenic hills are to the north. Green fees are $20 for 9 holes on weekdays, $23 on weekends; $33 for 18 holes on weekdays, $37 on weekends. Cart rentals range from $13.50 for 9 holes to $27 for 18 holes.

Spa

The **Red Rock River Resort** (603 N. River St./ U.S. 385, 605/745-4400 or 888/306-8921, www. redrockriverresort.com, open year-round, day spa guests daily 10 A.M.–6 P.M., overnight guests 24 hours) is housed in one of the many restored historic sandstone buildings in town. The facility has some interesting offerings, including a granite heat room, sand heat room, dry sauna, whirlpool/hot tub, and tranquility tea room (a place to sip tea, read, and relax), and has several well-appointed treatment rooms. Massage services include Swedish style, deep tissue, hot stone, craniosacral, gemstone, reflexology, Reiki, and others. A day pass for use of the facility is $25. Spa treatments range in price based on the time and treatment selected, but generally run $35–45 per half-hour and $65–120 for 60- and 90-minute sessions. Package deals are available and change regularly.

Other Activities

The sandstone architecture in Hot Springs is truly stunning and both the Pioneer Museum and the Chamber of Commerce have a booklet that will direct you through town on a **self-guided walking tour.** The booklet, called *Step Back in Time,* describes many of the historic buildings along River Street and other areas in town.

The **Freedom Trail** parallels Fall River through town. The path is lit after dark so it's great for a nice after-dinner walk of about a mile in length. On hot days, if you start at the northern end and head south, you can reward yourself with a Dairy Queen ice-cream cone. If you start at the south end of the trail and head north, you can treat yourself to an ice cream at Gus' Best Ice Cream.

The **Hot Springs Theater** (241 N. River St./U.S. 385, 605/745-4169), built in 1910, offers movies year-round Friday–Sunday at 7 P.M. The fabulous feature of this theater is that the seats are spaced so far apart, it is possible to stretch your legs straight out and still not come close to the row in front of you.

EVENTS

Lean Horse Marathon

For die-hard physical fitness fans, join the fun in late August, when the annual Lean Horse Marathon (www.leanhorsehundred.com, registration 100-mile $199, 50-mile $99, 50K $99) takes place. The course is changed slightly every year but always finishes near the Hot Springs Chamber of Commerce office at the **Mueller Center** (801 S. Sixth St., 605/745-4140 or 800/325-6991, www.hotsprings-sd.com). There are three separate races—a 100-mile race, a 50-mile race, and a 50K race.

All three races are run primarily along the Mickelson Trail, though the starting point changes from year to year. In most cases, the 100-miler runners travel from the Southern Hills all the way to Hill City and back. This is not a race for the weak at heart—literally.

SHOPPING

It is along U.S. 385, which cuts through the middle of Hot Springs, that most retail venues will be found. All stores with addresses on River Street, Jennings Avenue, and Chicago Street are on U.S. 385.

Hot Springs is small and a little farther from the heart of tourism, but its special kind of beauty appeals to artists. There are many local jewelers, potters, and painters who live in the community, but it isn't always easy to find them. Galleries tend to have unpredictable hours, so keep an eye out for their open signs. The **Shaman Gallery** (405 N. River St./U.S. 385, 605/745-6602, www.shamangallery.com) specializes in native works from both Alaska and the plains and has over 4,000 square feet of display space. The building that houses the gallery was originally the Morris Grand Theater. **Works in Clay** (108 N. Chicago St./U.S. 385, 605/745-7338) is owned by potter Tom Eastburn. Historically, the hours of the gallery space have fluctuated with the workload of its owner. Beautiful

EDGEMONT: RODEOS, RAILROADS, AND REDNECKS

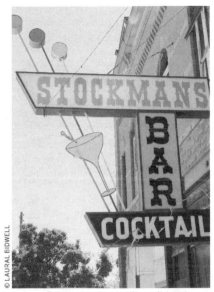

© LAURAL BIDWELL

a sign of Edgemont's earlier, wilder days

Situated on the southwest corner of the Black Hills, Edgemont, South Dakota, is a small community of less than 1,000 people. Like many plains communities, the town has seen more than its share of boom and bust. Currently in a quiet phase of the cycle, Edgemont is determined to inspire another economic recovery. As a result of much brainstorming, energy, and enthusiasm, the community has managed to come up with some very creative and sometimes crazy ideas. If you are in the southern hills and like to enjoy small towns at their best, head to Edgemont for some old-fashioned fun. (Check your calendar first, as the dates of these events vary.)

The **Edgemont Theatre Company** (809 2nd Ave., 605/662-6275, www.edgemont-sd. com/edgemont-theatre.html, $25 per ticket includes dinner, general admission $4-6, dinner at 7 P.M., performances at 8 P.M.) presents melodrama to full houses for two weekends (Thurs.-Sat.) in both June and July. It's an audience participation event: You are required to sigh when the beautiful heroine appears, boo at the villain, cheer the handsome hero, and, in an activity that may well be unique to this theater, throw peanuts (gently!) at the actors whenever they utter a really corny line. Given that melodrama is, by nature, corny, ducking flying peanuts is one of the prime activities of the evening. Dinner consists of steak, baked potato, a lettuce wedge, and angel food cake, served by the cast. Reservations are required for dinner. General admission tickets can be bought at the theater on the night of the performance.

The **Edgemont Redneck Rally** is held in July. The event features a golf tournament, poker run, an ATV obstacle course, an art show, a Redneck Parade (with cash prizes and interesting trophies for the best in redneck design), lawn mower races, a garden tractor pull, sanctioned Mud Bogging (driving though a pit of mud for a set distance), and poker tournaments. The day ends with a redneck appreciation dance. This event will frequently dovetail with a melodrama weekend so you could spend the entire day in town!

Seeing a rodeo is a must for many visitors to the west, and Edgemont plays host to several different rodeos throughout the summer and fall. The **Cheyenne River Run Series** features local rodeo riders one evening a week in June. There is no fee to attend. August brings both the **Fall River County Fair and Rodeo** and the **Little Britches Rodeo,** a nationally sanctioned rodeo for youngsters in three divisions: Little Wranglers aged 5-7, Juniors aged 8-13, and Seniors aged 14-18.

Railroad fans and train photographers will delight in the high activity levels of the BNSF line that rumbles through town. While most of the trains are hauling coal, sometimes the freight can be pretty interesting. Over 100 tons of it come through town on an annual basis.

pottery, local jewelry, and other works are featured here.

Every community in the Black Hills has a shop that specializes in Black Hills Gold. In Hot Springs, seek out **Larive's Black Hills Gold** (713 N. River St./U.S. 385, 605/745-7936, May–Labor Day Mon.–Sat. 9 A.M.–6 P.M., closed Sun., winter Mon.–Fri. 9 A.M.–4 P.M., closed Sat.–Sun.). In addition to Black Hills Gold jewelry, Larive's offers souvenirs and T-shirts.

Quilters and quilt lovers will enjoy **Heartsong Quilts** (345 N. River St./U.S. 385, 605/745-5330, www.heartsongquilts.com, open year-round daily Mon.–Sat. 10 A.M.–6 P.M.).

Another fun place to poke around is the **Smith Fargo Mercantile** (321 N. River St./U.S. 385, 605/745-4233 or 605/890-0585, Apr.–Nov. Wed.–Mon. 10 A.M.–5 P.M., closed Tues., closed in winter). It's set up flea market–style, divided into dozens of individually operated booths selling everything from used LPs, furniture, antiques, candles, and other treasures.

Around the corner, you'll find **Earth Goods** (738 Jennings Ave./U.S. 385, 605/745-7715, www.earthgoodsnaturalfoods.com, Mon.–Fri. 10 A.M.–6 P.M.), which specializes in organic foods and quality supplements. The store hosts herb walks from time to time, and Jackie, who has studied herbal medicine for over 20 years, is happy to discuss traditional and contemporary uses of the herbs and supplements found on the shelves.

Located in "lower" downtown, **Black Hills Books and Treasures** (112 S. Chicago St./U.S. 385, 605/745-5545, www.blackhills-books.com, May–Sept. Mon.–Fri. 10 A.M.–6 P.M., Sat. 10 A.M.–3 P.M., Oct.–Dec. Mon.–Fri. 11 A.M.–5 P.M., Sat. 10 A.M.–3 P.M., Jan.–Mar. Tues.–Fri. 11 A.M.–5 P.M., Sat. 10 A.M.–3 P.M., closed in Apr.) specializes in antique, out-of-print, and used books. In addition, the store carries an interesting gift selection including CDs by local musicians and craft items created by local artisans.

Just north of town is **Wanda's Finds &**

Morgan Saddlery (27237 Wind Cave Rd./U.S. 385 N., about a mile north of town, 605/745-4040, www.wandasfinds.com, open year-round Mon.–Sat. 9 A.M.–4 P.M., Sun. 11 A.M.–4 P.M.). This is one of the larger stores in the area, with both new and used merchandise including jewelry, clothing, antiques and collectibles, and furniture. Wanda runs the store and her husband runs the saddlery shop. Across the street from Wanda's is **Whitaker Jewelers** (27162 Wind Cave Rd., 605/440-0078, daily 10 A.M. to 5 P.M.), owned by Eugenia Whitaker. Look for handcrafted wire wrapped jewelry and pieces made of mammoth ivory and gemstones.

ACCOMMODATIONS

There's something about Hot Springs that attracts the creative and independent entrepreneur. This is evident in the interesting assortment of lodging options available here. While chain hotels and motels are amply represented, the most interesting places are the bed-and-breakfasts and independently run establishments tucked here and there about town. All rates are for summer season, double occupancy, or by the room, as appropriate.

$50-100

If you are looking for an authentic log cabin experience, check out the **Historic Log Cabin Inn** (1246 Sherman St., 605/745-5166, www.historiclogcabins.com, open year-round, $69–99). Located on the northern edge of town just off of U.S. 385, the cabins were built in the late 1920s. To this day, they retain a rustic charm with nice decks overlooking the VA hospital campus and the community. Amenities include free wireless Internet access, continental breakfast, an outdoor hot tub, picnic tables, and gas grills. Decorated for Christmas year-round, this is a pet-friendly property.

Hide-A-Way Cabins (442 S. Chicago St./U.S. 385, 605/745-5683, open year-round, summer season kitchenettes $75, house $115, winter season kitchenettes $65, house $95) located in "Lower Hot Springs" has three units with full kitchenettes, one unit with a microwave and refrigerator, and a small two-bedroom house available for travelers. The property backs up to the Freedom Trail and Fall River, close to a very nice picnic area.

Clean and economical hotel rooms can be found at **Dollar Inn at Battle Mountain** (402 Battle Mountain Ave./U.S. 385, 605/745-3182 or 888/745-4149, www.dollarinnhotsprings.com, May–Oct., closed in winter, $69–79). Continental breakfast is included, and rooms come with a microwave and fridge. The rooms are fairly standard, but they are spacious and clean. Free wireless Internet is available. The hotel is within walking distance of Evans Plunge.

America's Best Value Inn by the River (602 W. River St./U.S. 385, 605/745-4292, open year-round, $90, hefty discounts for booking in advance or with AARP membership) is a pretty property with a great central location near the Historic District of town. The hotel is also located at the northern end of the Freedom Trail. At one time, the property was a Best Western hotel, so the rooms are standard-issue chain-style. Amenities include free continental breakfast, cable TV, and a nice outdoor pool. Three log cabins with kitchenettes ($135) are also available on the property.

The **Budget Host Hills Inn** (640 S. 6th St., 605/745-3130 or 800/283-4678, www.budgethosthillsinn.com, Mar.–Oct., closed in winter, $89), located on the south end of Hot Springs, is another reasonable option. The 35-room facility has a small pool, free Internet, microwaves and refrigerators, free continental breakfast, and is located close to Fall River and the Freedom Trail. **Putt-for-Fun,** a nice, little, mini golf course is run by the hotel and is right next door.

The **Historic Mueller House Bed and Breakfast** (201 S. 6th St., 605/745-5272, www.muellerhousebedandbreakfast.com, open year-round, $99–129), built in 1888, is a Victorian-style building with a homey feel. It is located just a few blocks from the main street in town, close to shopping and dining. There are three rooms available, one with a Native American theme, one in country style, and one in Western style. A hearty home-cooked breakfast is prepared by the owners every morning. Upon request, they are happy to serve a gluten-free breakfast. There is a resident dog there and friendly guest dogs are welcome. (Please bring proof of vaccinations!) Free wireless Internet is provided.

$100-150

The **Red Rock River Resort** (603 N. River St./U.S. 385, 605/745-4400 or 888/306-8921, www.redrockriverresort.com, open year-round, $95–125) is located in the historic Minnekahta Block, another project of early Hot Springs pioneer Fred Evans. Built in 1891, this beautiful historic sandstone building now houses a spa facility and several renovated rooms, each with a private bath. With high ceilings and deep windows, the rooms feature luxurious bedding and feather-down pillows. Amenities include air-conditioning and cable television. The spa has hot tubs, a warm sand room, a dry sauna, and a granite heat room.

Opened in 2009, the **Smith Fargo Suites** (321 N. River St./U.S. 385, 605/890-0585, www.smithfargosuites.com, May–Oct., closed in winter, $99–135), located in the historic Fargo Mercantile Building (which was built in 1910), are the newest additions to the Hot Springs collection of esoteric lodging. There are five beautiful and elegant suites positioned on the second floor above the retail-level flea market shops. The common areas and the suites are all quite beautiful, featuring hand-painted murals, stained glass, lots of tile, and theme-appropriate furnishings in each room (Oriental, Miner, Victorian, Cowboy, and Mission). The fully appointed kitchen is shared by all, and room rates include a free continental breakfast. All rooms

THE SOUTHERN HILLS

have 42-inch flat-screen televisions, high-speed wireless Internet, microwaves, and refrigerators.

The **FlatIron Guest Suites** (745 N. River St./U.S. 385, 605/745-5301, www.flatiron.bz, open year-round, suites $115–160, guest rooms $39–74) are beautifully decorated by the owner, Kara Hagen. The rooms all have a contemporary feel and the fabrics used for the curtains, bedspreads, and linens are all plush. Fine-quality wood furnishings, light fixtures, ceiling fans, beautiful kitchen tiles, countertops, and tile and hardwood flooring throughout create a luxurious feel to all of the suites. There are a total of three guest rooms (which share a bathroom) and five suites in the historic sandstone Gibson Building, a hotel originally built in 1911. Although the three guest rooms share a bathroom, they're luxurious for the price.

Campgrounds

The Army Corps of Engineers is responsible for the tucked-away, lovely, primitive **Cold Brook Lake Campground** (27279 Larive Lake Rd., 605/745-5476, $7), just one mile north of Hot Springs. There are 13 sites and a beach area, and the lake is stocked with trout. While the feeling is remote, the grounds are only 10 minutes from town. There are no showers or electricity; however, there are vault toilets and drinking water is available at the site. To find the campground, follow North River Street past Evans Plunge. Take your first right after Evans Plunge on Cold Brook Road. Then take the second left on Evans Road and follow the signs to the lake.

Keep an eye on **Larive Lake Resort** (27291 Larive Lake Rd., 605/745-3993, tents $14, RV sites $25–35). It's quiet, scenic, and very rustic. The resort has a private lake with a dock, swimming, and small boat rentals ($10 per hour). Campers have access to showers and flush toilets, as well as picnic tables and outdoor grills. RV sites come with electric or full hookups. There are also a few small cabins available for

rental (starting at $59). To get to the resort, follow the directions to Cold Brook Lake, but after the second left on Evans Road, keep an eye out for a gated gravel road that heads up a hill on the left side. On the gate, you'll see the sign for the resort.

The **Hot Springs KOA** (27585 Hwy. 79, 605/745-6449 or 800/562-0803, www.koa.com/where/sd, RV sites $34–39, cabins $64, deluxe cabin with full bath $84) is the best place for RVs in the area. In a wooded location, the campground facility includes showers, restrooms, a snack bar, mini golf, laundry, a game room, free wireless Internet, and a heated outdoor pool. There are camping cabins on-site, as well.

In the mood to spend a night in a tipi? **Allen Ranch** (27531 Hidden Nook Trail, 605/745-1890, www.gwtc.net/~allenranch/, tents $25, tipi $35, RV sites $35) is located right on Fall River. Full RV hookups and showers are available. Tent sites are nestled into the cottonwoods that line the river banks. It is a working ranch and the sounds of bleating sheep may well be your morning wake-up call. Nonguests are welcome to shower at the campground for $10.

FOOD

South Dakota is not famous for creative dining. It's a land of comfort food where beef, chicken, meatloaf, pork chops, and the occasional salmon are the main fare in many of the restaurants. Portions are more than generous, prices are low, and salad bars frequently feature Jell-O, pastas, and beans over greens. However, most every restaurant in town has something special to offer.

Family Fare

Dale's Family Restaurant (745 Battle Mountain Ave., 605/745-3028, summer Mon.–Fri. 5:30 a.m.–8 p.m., Sat.–Sun. 5:30 a.m.–2 p.m., winter Tues.–Fri. 5:30 a.m.–7 p.m., Sat.–Sun. 5:30 a.m.–2 p.m., breakfast $6, lunch $7–9, dinner $8–12) is the kind of place that still offers a breakfast special for as little as $3.99. There's nothing fancy about Dale's. The booths and tables are Formica, and on the walls hang chimes and souvenir items available for purchase. Every holiday, the decorations come out: Spiders and singing ghouls materialize at Halloween, dancing Santa Clauses and Christmas villages show up in December, and bunnies make their appearance in the spring. Every year, Cindi, the owner, finds some new singing or dancing figure to add to the scene. You'll likely get caught up in local chatter at the restaurant because the regular crowd meets there every morning. Breakfast items are available all day and it's the only place in town that can poach an egg. Lunch includes hot and cold sandwiches and soup. Dinner choices include steaks, meatloaf, chicken, and hot turkey and roast beef sandwiches with mashed potatoes. The best deal is the senior menu, which is available to anyone who wants it and includes an entrée and a trip through the soup and salad bar. This is a place that serves good basic American comfort food and you can't beat the prices.

The **All Star Sports Grill** (310 S. Chicago St./U.S. 385, 605/745-7827, open year-round, summer daily 7 A.M.–9 P.M., breakfast $8, lunch $9, dinner $12) is a mid-priced family restaurant that serves a variety of sandwiches, salads, chicken, pasta, and beef dishes. There are two outside dining areas at the All Star, one small deck on the side and a nice sized covered patio in the front. Inside, there are televisions all around the dining room for tracking sports events, but the volume is set very low and the sets are placed fairly high on the walls, so they are fairly unobtrusive. The bar area is segregated from the dining room and has a few slot machines. The restaurant has a beer and wine license and serves several good beers on tap.

There is nothing fancy about the **Fall River Bakery** (407 N. River St./U.S. 385, 605/745-6190, open year-round, summer daily 6 A.M.–3 P.M., reduced hours in winter, breakfast $7, lunch $9), but it is the best place in town to get a morning breakfast burrito, pastry, or homemade toast. In addition to breakfast, the bakery serves a variety of soups and sandwiches into the afternoon, all of which are homemade by Diane, the proprietor of the place. There are a few tables (again, nothing fancy) outside on the sidewalk and it is a great place to watch the waterfall, slow down, and participate in small town life. It is a local favorite morning hot spot.

China Buffet (333 N. River St./U.S. 385, 605/745-4126, open year-round, summer daily 10:30 A.M.–9 P.M., winter daily 10:30 A.M.–8 P.M., lunch $7, dinner $9) has both a lunch buffet and an evening buffet (although in the winter, the evening buffet is only served on Friday and Saturday nights). The buffet is good, but food is best when ordered off the menu. The facility isn't fancy and the booths are a little beat up, but the food is authentic and tasty and portions are generous. (Entrées ordered off the menu easily serve two.) The buffet usually includes two different soups (wonton and egg drop), a choice of fried or steamed rice, egg rolls, and six or seven main courses, including sweet and sour pork, sweet and sour chicken, Happy Family (a mix of shrimp, chicken, and beef), almond chicken, and beef with broccoli, among other dishes. A fortune cookie is served with every meal.

◖ **Woolly's Western Grill** (1648 U.S. 18 truck bypass near the Mammoth Site, 605/745-6414, Tue.–Sat. 11 A.M.–9 P.M., lunch $9, dinner $12) has something for every traveler with very reasonable prices and a very comfortable atmosphere. The restaurant specializes in steaks, burgers, and other grilled entrées, but also has a nice selection of Italian and Mexican items, sandwiches, and salads. A trip to the soup and salad bar is included with most entrées. One of the prettiest restaurants in town, it has a small deck for those who love outdoor dining, along with lovely views of the Seven Sisters range of hills located on the south side of Hot Springs.

The ⚫Springs Steakhouse (902 N. River St./U.S. 385, 605/745-3187, May–Oct. Tue.–Sat. 4:30–9 P.M., closed in winter, $10–22) is located in the historic sandstone Braun Hotel. When the hotel was being built in 1910, builders encountered a large granite boulder that could not be removed, so the hotel was built around it and the boulder protrudes today, taking up residence in the dining area of the hotel. There is an outside patio that looks out over Fall River. The soups are homemade and are quite good. In addition to steak, the restaurant serves a variety of game dishes, including elk, bison, and venison. Fine German beers are also available. One of the specials of the house is a delicious small filet mignon, wrapped in bacon.

At one time, "the bar" was a place where motorcyclists held races indoors, the music was loud, and the smoke was thick—for many, it was just not a place to hang out. But all of that has changed. The Vault (329 N. River St./U.S. 385, 605/745-3342, www.thehotspringsvault. com, Sun.–Thurs. 11 A.M.–9 P.M., Fri.–Sat. 11 A.M.–10 P.M., lunch and dinner $9–16) is a delightful addition to the night life of Hot Springs. With a 60-foot bar, rustic pine walls, heavy wooden tables, and wildlife trophies hanging on the walls, this is the place to go for a beer in the afternoon, an early dinner, and late-night music. The Vault offers open mics, live music, and karaoke on the musical side, pool and darts for the sports minded, and a fairly extensive and creative menu.

For dessert, there is Gus' Best Ice Cream (345 N. River St./U.S. 385, 605/745-6506, www.gusbesticecream.com, Mon.–Sat. noon–8 P.M., $3–5), which features hard-packed ice cream served in waffle cones or bowls, fruit smoothies, milk shakes, and shave ices. Ice cream flavors vary from time to time, but Rocky Road, Cookies & Cream, Butter Pecan, Mint Chocolate Chip, Vanilla, Chocolate, and Strawberry are always on hand. The interior of Gus' is small, but there are some nice wrought iron tables outside. On a warm summer day, there is nothing better.

INFORMATION AND SERVICES

The Hot Springs Chamber of Commerce (801 S. 6th St., 605/745-4140 or 800/325-6991, www.hotsprings-sd.com) is located inside the Mueller Civic Center. In the summer (Memorial Day–Labor Day), the Chamber also operates a visitors center on North River Street at the old train depot.

Campers can find laundry facilities at Quality Cleaners Laundromat (1605 University Ave., 605/745-6201), or next door at Mike's Place (1645 University Ave., 605/745-6228), and groceries at Sonny's Superfoods (801 Jensen Hwy., 605/745-5979) or Lynn's Dakota Mart (505 S. 6th, 605/745-3203). The post office is located at the corner of Chicago Street and Jennings Avenue (146 N. Chicago St./U.S. 385, 800/275-8777).

There are two hospitals in the community. The Hot Springs VA Medical Center (500 N. 5th St., 605/745-2000) is available for veterans. The other is Fall River Health Services (1201 Hwy. 71, 605/745-3159).

For folks traveling with pets, Anise's B & B for People with Pets (1 Canyon View Cir., 605/745-7455 or 800/794-4142, www.bnb-4pets.com, open year-round) has to be the finest location in the hills for boarding services or even day care services for dogs. Located on 15 acres, much of it fenced, it is a safe and beautiful place to leave your animals during the day while you're out wandering the hills. There is someone on hand at all times. Doggie day care is available for just $2 per hour, and overnight stays are $20 for the first pup and $10 for each additional pup. Just a few blocks from town, the property is nestled up against Battle Mountain and is surrounded by ponderosa pine, giving the whole place a sense of seclusion. The dogs will feel pampered. Just be sure to bring proof of current vaccinations!

Wind Cave National Park

Wind Cave has been considered sacred by Native Americans for centuries. It wasn't until 1881, however, that the cave was discovered by Europeans. Two brothers, Jesse and Tom Bingham, heard a loud whistling noise while passing through the region. Upon investigation, they discovered a small hole in the ground, from which a strong gust of wind was emanating. This small hole is the only natural entrance to the cave that has ever been found.

After the cave's discovery, several mining claims were established in the area. J. D. McDonald managed one of those claims for the South Dakota Mining Company. Mining operations at Wind Cave turned out to be an unsuccessful venture, but McDonald and his family discovered that they could make money by giving cave tours and selling cave formations. In 1891, the McDonalds teamed up with John Stabler and formed the Wonderful Wind Cave Improvement Company. The company widened the entrance to the cave, built a wooden staircase, erected a hotel near the cave entrance, and started offering stage coach rides to the cave from Hot Springs.

In 1893, there were stirrings of trouble between the Stabler and McDonald families. J. D. and Alvin McDonald headed off to an exposition in Chicago to promote the cave. Alvin got typhoid fever on the trip and died shortly thereafter. After his death, arguments broke out between the families about how profits were being split and the fight ended up in court. After years of courtroom battles, the Department of the Interior decided that since there was no mining and no homestead activity involved, neither party held any ownership in the cave; in 1901, it withdrew the property from availability as a homestead. In 1903, Theodore Roosevelt, a frequent visitor and supporter of conservation, signed a bill creating Wind Cave National Park.

Wind Cave became the eighth National Park in the federal park system and was the first to be set aside to preserve a cave. In 2011, the National Park Service increased the size of the park with the purchase of an additional 5,555 acres adjacent to the original park boundaries. The acquisition includes a thousand-year-old buffalo jump and a historic homestead. Limited access to the new areas is available while the park develops a land management plan for the acquisition. Check at the information desk when you arrive to see if new hiking or interpretive activities have been developed for the area. The park is located just 11 miles north of Hot Springs on U.S. 385, and today presents two faces to the visitor.

On the surface, Wind Cave National Park, at more than 33,000 acres, boasts over 30 miles of hiking trails. The mixed grass prairie ecosystem supports abundant wildlife, including bison, mule deer, whitetail deer, prairie dogs, pronghorn, wild turkeys, and elk. The topography of the park is vastly different from that of the Northern Hills. Lower elevation and eroded round hills provide scenic viewing as far as the human eye can see. It is a place where east meets west, the Great Plains prairie meets the ponderosa pine forest. It's a wonderful place to watch the not infrequent summer thunderstorms cross the plains.

Below the surface, under just one square mile of the park, lies over 136 miles of explored cave passages. Wind Cave is the third-longest cave in the United States and the fifth-longest cave in the world. It may move up in the standings, however, as it is estimated that only 10 percent of the cave has been explored and mapped.

Wind Cave is famous for its boxwork, an unusual type of speleothem (cave formation). Most cave formations are created when dripping or seeping water deposits calcium on the cave walls and ceilings, forming the stalactites (which hang from the ceiling like icicles) and stalagmites (built up from the floor) that most visitors expect to see in a cave. Since Wind Cave is relatively dry, the formations in the cave are more subtle. Boxwork is made of thin slices of calcite that project from the cave walls and intersect with each other in a honeycomb-like fashion. The pattern looks like a collection of diamond and rectangular boxes protruding from the walls and ceilings. It is suspected that boxwork formation results from the uniform seepage of water, literally through the pores of the rock, instead of from larger cracks and crevices. Other common formations found in the cave include popcorn (knobby deposits of calcite) and frostwork (thin needles of calcite crystals in patterns that resemble a three-dimensional version of frost on a window).

VISITORS CENTER

The first place to stop is the **Wind Cave Visitor Center** (26611 U.S. 385, 605/745-4600, www.nps.gov/wica, May.–mid-June daily 8 A.M.–6 P.M., mid-June–mid-Aug. daily 8 A.M.–7 P.M., mid-Aug.–Sept. daily 8 A.M.–6 P.M., Oct.–Apr. daily 8 A.M.–4:30 P.M.). From the north, the visitors center is on the right just past the junction of U.S. 385 and Highway 87. From the south, the road to the visitors center is a left off of U.S. 385 and is clearly marked with park signage. It is here that you can find maps, arrange your cave tour, obtain free backcountry camping permits, or purchase National Parks and Federal Recreation Lands Passes. An annual National Parks and Federal Recreation Lands Pass costs $80 and is valid for one year from the date of purchase. The pass allows the holder entry into parks and federal lands that charge an entry or standard amenity fee.

Rangers at the visitors center can provide you with information about activities going on at the time of your visit and answer any questions you may have about the park and its environment. They are usually aware of where the bison herd has roamed and will provide updates if seeing the herd is on your agenda. A nice bookstore is on-site and carries a wide selection of local interest books and field guides.

◖ CAVE TOURS

There are five different cave tours to choose from at Wind Cave. Cave tours are available year-round, though in the summer, there is a wider variety of tours offered. The tours vary in difficulty and in price. The temperature in the cave hovers around 53°F, so bring a sweatshirt or sweater. It is possible to arrange tours for mobility-impaired visitors, as there are limited areas of the cave that are wheelchair accessible. Be sure to call the park in advance to make arrangements. Tours for visitors with special needs are just $5 for adults over 17, $2.50 for children 6–16. Sign language tours are also available at the park.

The **Natural Entrance Tour** (Memorial Day–Labor Day daily every hour, adult $9, child aged 6–16 $4.50, child under 6 free) is a 1.25-hour tour that is moderately strenuous, requiring about a half-mile of hiking. There are 300 stairs along the route, most of which are downward climbs. (Exit from the cave is via elevator.) This tour brings visitors to the only natural entrance to the cave to discover why the cave got its name. Entry is via an artificially constructed entrance, and the tour takes visitors to the middle level of the cave where the boxwork formation, for which the cave is famous, is abundant.

The **Garden of Eden Tour** (year-round, 3–4 tours daily, adult $7, child aged 6–16 $3.50, child under 6 free) is the shortest and least strenuous of all the cave tours, with just 150 stairs to navigate. The tour takes about one hour and requires about a quarter-mile of walking. Entry and exit to the cave is by elevator. Small amounts of popcorn, boxwork, and flowstone (a calcite formation that looks as if it is flowing over the rocks) are seen along the trail.

A tourguide points out some unusual boxwork at Wind Cave.

The **Fairgrounds Tour** (Memorial Day–Labor Day, 3–8 tours daily, adult $9, child aged 6–16 $4.50, child under 6 free) takes about 1.5 hours to complete and requires about a half-mile of hiking. This tour is the most strenuous of the walking tours, as there are over 450 stairs to climb, including a single staircase of more than 90 stairs. The tour visits the upper and middle levels of the cave. Boxwork is abundant in the middle section, and the upper level of the cave features large rooms in which popcorn and frostwork are common.

The **Candlelight Tour** (Memorial Day–Labor Day, 1–2 tours daily, adult $9, child aged 8–16 $4.50) is a two-hour tour that requires about one mile of hiking. This is a strenuous tour that takes place in a less-developed area of the cave along a fairly rugged trail. Participation is limited to 10 people per tour. Participants are required to wear shoes with non-slip soles, so no sandals are permitted. During this tour, visitors explore Wind Cave the way that early cavers did, without benefit of electricity. Each participant carries a candle bucket, which is the only lighting for the tour. Cave walls loom into the light and shadows dance along the walls, heightening the sensation of visiting another world below the surface of our day-to-day lives. Advance reservations are recommended for this tour.

For the adventurous soul, the **Wild Cave Tour** (Memorial Day–Labor Day, one tour daily, $23) is the tour of choice. Be prepared to get dirty, as this tour requires crawling through some very narrow spaces while learning the basics of safe caving. Wear old clothes. Long pants, long sleeves, and sturdy, lace-up boots or shoes with non-slip soles are required. The park will provide kneepads, hard hats, and lights. Note that participants must be at least 16 years old, and that young adults aged 16 and 17 must have a signed parental consent form to participate. This tour takes about four hours and covers about a half-mile, much of it spent crawling.

This is not a tour for people with claustrophobia! Advance reservations are required.

RANGER-LED PROGRAMS

There are several ranger-led programs available at the park during the summer months. Times and hours vary, so be sure to check with the visitors center to determine the what, where, and when of activities occurring during your visit. The **Prairie Hike** is a two-mile hike that begins at the visitors center. Bring water and wear hiking boots or sturdy shoes. During the course of the hike, you'll learn about the varied habitats of the park and about the plants and animals that inhabit them.

Evening **Campfire Programs** take place most every evening at the Elk Mountain Campground amphitheater. Rangers and interpreters present 45-minute programs that range in topic from wildlife to plants, cave exploration, history, geology, or astronomy. In July, the **Evening Hike** is added to the campfire program schedule. It is an interesting night-time visit to a prairie dog town. The hope is that participants will get to see the endangered black-footed ferret. Hikers meet at the amphitheater, located at the Elk Mountain Campground, and then drive to a nearby site. Be sure to bring a flashlight and wear hiking boots.

The newest addition to the park is a ranger-guided tour of the **Sanson Buffalo Jump** location at the park. Currently, the tour is offered only on weekends during the summer. Participants meet at the visitors center at 9 A.M. on Saturday or Sunday morning and car caravan out to the jump site for a three-hour tour. There is a moderate hike involved, so wear good hiking shoes and bring water and sunscreen.

Children up to age 12 may enjoy participating in the **Junior Ranger Program.** Junior Ranger booklets are available at the park bookstore and contain activities designed to help kids understand the park's ecosystem, the cave, and local animals. On Wednesdays and

Saturdays during the summer, Junior Ranger hikes leave at 9 A.M. from the visitors center. Participants who complete the activities receive a Junior Ranger badge.

Throughout the day, rangers present **Discovery Activity Programs.** These programs are given at the visitors center. Topics vary and demonstrations and presentations may include discussions of local wildlife, plants, geology, area history, and cave surveying.

HIKING

There are over 30 miles of marked hiking trails in the park that range from easy to strenuous in effort. Visitors are also welcome to leave the trails and wander the park at whim. Topographic maps can be purchased at the visitors center, but visibility at the park is good and it is not a difficult place to navigate.

Remember that buffalo can be found in most areas of the park. Do not approach them. They are wild animals, and though their size may give the impression that they are slow reactors, they aren't. Weighing in at around a ton, buffalo can reach speeds of up to 35 miles per hour in just a few strides. Keep 100 yards between you and a buffalo!

For a short hiking excursion, try one of the three **Nature Trails** in the park. The trails are marked with interpretive signage and displays and each is about one mile long. The Elk Mountain Trail begins at the end of the Elk Mountain Campground road and circles up through the forest near the park's boundary. This trail highlights the intertwined ecologies of the meeting of prairie grasslands with the forest habitat. The Prairie Vista Trail begins at the visitors center and the interpretive signage focuses on information about the prairie grasses. The Rankin Ridge Trail is located off of Highway 87 in the northwestern corner of the park. The hike begins and ends at the parking lot of the Rankin Ridge Lookout Tower. The ridge provides beautiful views in all directions—open prairie to the east and the Black Hills to the west.

Lookout Point-Centennial Trail Loop

- **Distance:** 4.5 miles round-trip
- **Duration:** 3 hours
- **Elevation Gain:** Minimal
- **Effort:** Moderately strenuous
- **Trailhead:** Southern trailhead of the Centennial Trail
- **Directions:** From the visitors center, head north on U.S. 385 and take an almost immediate right on Highway 87. The trailhead is 0.7 mile down on the east (right) side of road.

This nice loop trail exposes the hiker to all of the diversity of the park. From the trailhead, the hike begins in a stand of ridge top pines and then descends rapidly to the valley floor. From there, it meanders along Beaver Creek winding between the low hills of the park. About two miles in, the Centennial Trail takes a fairly sharp left. Continue straight on at this point and you will be on a short stretch of the Highland Creek Trail. This trail will loop around to join up with the Lookout Point Trail. Where the Highland Creek Trail veers south, continue heading west along the Lookout Point Trail and it will return you to the Centennial Trail trailhead. Throughout the hike, you will traverse a streambed, pass through prairie grasslands and rolling hills, and climb into some of the pine forests of Wind Cave National Park.

Wind Cave Canyon

- **Distance:** 3.6 miles round-trip
- **Duration:** 1.5 hours
- **Elevation Gain:** None
- **Effort:** Easy

- **Trailhead:** The trailhead is on the east side of the road one mile north of the junction of the southern entrance to the Wind Cave Visitor Center and U.S. 385.

This easy hike follows what used to be a service road in the park and trails Wind Cave Canyon to the park's boundary fence. It is one of the best places in the park for bird-watching as it winds along limestone cliffs filled with cliff swallows and great horned owls. Dead stands of trees make great nesting places for several varieties of woodpeckers.

ACCOMMODATIONS

The only accommodation available in Wind Cave National Park is the **Elk Mountain Campground.** Located one mile north of the visitors center, the campground has 75 sites available on a first-come, first-served basis. Each site can accommodate two vehicles and up to eight people. There are two wheelchair-accessible sites. Facilities include restrooms with flush toilets and cold running water. There are no showers and there are no hookups for RVs, although there are some pull-through sites available for RV use. In the summer, fees are $12 per site per night. In the winter, once the water is turned off, fees drop to $6 per night. Pets must be kept on a leash but are allowed in the campground.

Backcountry camping is allowed in the northwestern part of the park. Campers must have a permit, which is free, and which can be obtained at the visitors center. Pets are not permitted in the backcountry. If you elect to go hiking or camp in the backcountry section of the park, bring water with you or carry equipment to boil and purify and water found in local streams.

Located 11 miles south of the park, the city of Hot Springs has many hotels and other accommodations for park visitors.

THE SOUTHERN HILLS

THE NORTHERN HILLS

Life seems more adventurous, wilder, and flashier in the Northern Hills. From the tattoos, leather, and roaring bikes of the Sturgis Motorcycle Rally in August, to the year-round ringing bells and flashing casino lights in Deadwood, the high-energy, late-night crowd has a home here.

Gambling keeps the energy level high and the hours long; its legalization in 1989 breathed new life into an area that was starting to fall into disrepair. The funds generated from the gambling industry allowed the area to revitalize its historic buildings. The entire town of Deadwood is now a registered National Historic Landmark and it embraces its Wild West past with daily gunfights and historic reenactments.

Check out the local museums (and cemetery!) for information about some of South Dakota's most famous and infamous characters who at one time called Deadwood home.

Sister mining community, Lead (pronounced Leed), just three miles down the road from Deadwood, was once home to the largest and deepest gold mine in North America. Closed in 2002, the mine is being reborn as the Deep Underground Science and Engineering Laboratory. A mining museum and guided tour of the grounds reminds visitors of what inspired people to trespass on Native American land, break the law, and risk their lives in the hope of finding great wealth.

Diversity is the watchword of the Northern

HIGHLIGHTS

◖ D. C. Booth Fish Hatchery: A surprisingly delightful site in Spearfish, the hatchery features a museum, a fish railcar, an underground viewing window, a park-like setting, and thousands of trout waiting to be fed. There is even a fish rescue boat (page 143).

◖ Termesphere Gallery: Dick Termes is an internationally acclaimed artist who has chosen an unusual canvas. His paintings are done in the round, on spheres of all sizes. Hanging from the ceiling and spinning, these tiny painted worlds are captivating. A visit here is a one-of-a-kind gallery experience (page 144).

◖ Spearfish Canyon Scenic Byway: Waterfalls, wildlife, and recreational opportunities abound on this beautiful drive connecting the communities of Spearfish and Lead (page 152).

◖ Homestake Visitor Center: The center provides a surface tour of the Homestake Mine, the richest mine in the region in terms of production and longevity (page 160).

◖ Adams Museum: The oldest museum in the Black Hills features a great collection of early mining artifacts, including the first steam locomotive in the hills and memorabilia from some of the town's most infamous characters, including Wild Bill Hickok and Calamity Jane (page 168).

◖ Historic Adams House: The Adams House was built in 1892, and was closed – with all contents stored inside – for over 50 years after Adams's death. It offers a fascinating peek into a more elegant side of Victorian-era Deadwood (page 170).

◖ Saloon No. 10: Billed as the only museum with a bar, Saloon No. 10 reenacts the killing of Wild Bill Hickok every day during the summer and is chock-full of Old West artifacts. Downstairs, it's bars, beers, and rock and roll,

while upstairs, it's all fine dining and martinis in the **Deadwood Social Club** (page 174).

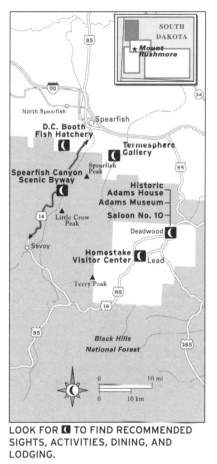

LOOK FOR **◖** TO FIND RECOMMENDED SIGHTS, ACTIVITIES, DINING, AND LODGING.

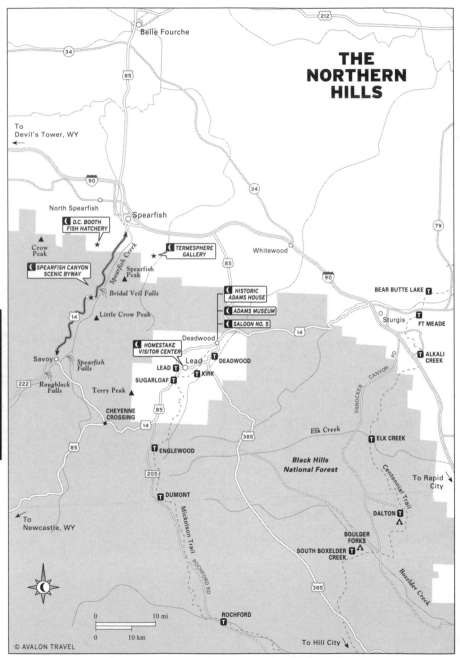

THE NORTHERN HILLS

212

34

85

To Devil's Tower, WY

90

34

North Spearfish   Spearfish

D.C. BOOTH FISH HATCHERY

79

Crow Peak

Spearfish Creek

TERMESPHERE GALLERY

Whitewood

SPEARFISH CANYON SCENIC BYWAY

Spearfish Peak

85

90

Bridal Veil Falls

BEAR BUTTE LAKE

HISTORIC ADAMS HOUSE

14   Little Crow Peak

ADAMS MUSEUM

SALOON NO. 5

Sturgis

FT MEADE

Deadwood

HOMESTAKE VISITOR CENTER

14

Savoy

Spearfish Falls

Lead   DEADWOOD

ALKALI CREEK

222   Roughlock Falls

LEAD   KIRK

SUGARLOAF

VANOCKER   RD

Terry Peak

CANYON

CHEYENNE CROSSING

85

Elk Creek

14

385

ELK CREEK

Black Hills National Forest

ENGLEWOOD

Centennial Trail

To Rapid City

205

To Newcastle, WY

DUMONT

DALTON

Mickelson Trail

BOULDER FORKS

ROCHFORD RD

SOUTH BOXELDER CREEK

Boxelder Creek

385

0   10 mi

ROCHFORD

0   10 km

© AVALON TRAVEL

To Hill City

Hills, as adventure extends itself to the great outdoors. Harney Peak, the highest peak in the hills, is located in the Central Hills region, but there are several peaks in the Northern Hills that reach heights of 6,900 feet and above. Here you can explore some of the best rock climbing, hiking, and biking trails in the state. Tired of trying your luck at the blackjack table? Head to Spearfish Canyon and try your hand at fly-fishing in Spearfish Creek instead. The Spearfish Canyon Scenic Byway is a dramatic 22-mile route that cuts though steep canyon walls, drops more than 2,000 feet in elevation, and winds along Spearfish Creek to connect the historic mining community of Lead to the educational, arts, and historic ranch community of Spearfish.

PLANNING YOUR TIME

Offering history, gaming, and scenic byways, the Northern Hills attracts a diverse audience. For those seeking the excitement of the casinos and Wild West shows, Deadwood is just 45 minutes from Rapid City and makes for an easy day trip if time is limited. But to enjoy the historic and scenic beauty of the region, you'll want to spend at least one night and two days. Start in Spearfish, drive the scenic byway, spend a night in Lead, visit the mining museums, and then spend the rest of the day in Deadwood.

Spearfish

Spearfish, staked out and founded in 1876, sprang into existence because of the 1874 gold rush. Thousands of people streamed east from California and west across the plains in search of that precious metal. The founders of this community, however, saw their gold in the form of timber, crops, cattle, horses, and other livestock. Gold camps need food and supplies, after all, and life above ground is more enticing to many than digging below the surface. Unlike many of the gold rush towns, growth for this community was comparatively slow.

Calling itself the Queen City (a popular choice out west) due to the crown of mountains to the south and west of the town proper, Spearfish was one of the first Black Hills communities to host a post high school educational institution. In 1883, this small community was funded by the state legislature to start the Spearfish Normal School, which would eventually become Black Hills State University. Later, the railroad brought a new kind of commerce. When the Grand Island and Wyoming Central Railroad completed a spur between Spearfish and Deadwood through Spearfish Canyon in 1893, the transport of timber and tourists flourished. (A note for train aficionados: Shortly after completing this amazing railroad highway, the spur was sold to the Chicago, Burlington, and Quincy Line.)

Only one train per day traveled through the canyon between the gold camp of Deadwood and the city of Spearfish. It was a spectacular ride filled with tight turns, steep elevation gains and descents, and a number of breathtaking creek crossings. The train conductor was more than happy to stop and let people on and off the train at various points throughout the canyon. Passengers would disembark for a day of creek-side picnicking and fishing. One of the favorite stops was atop a trestle that crossed over Spearfish Falls. Passengers would step off the train to feel the shaking of the tracks as the waterfall thundered below them.

By 1899, a national fish hatchery was opened in Spearfish. The creek and other Black Hills lakes were stocked with trout, and fish were shipped all over the country. Frank Lloyd Wright visited the area and declared Spearfish Canyon to be as majestic as the Grand Canyon.

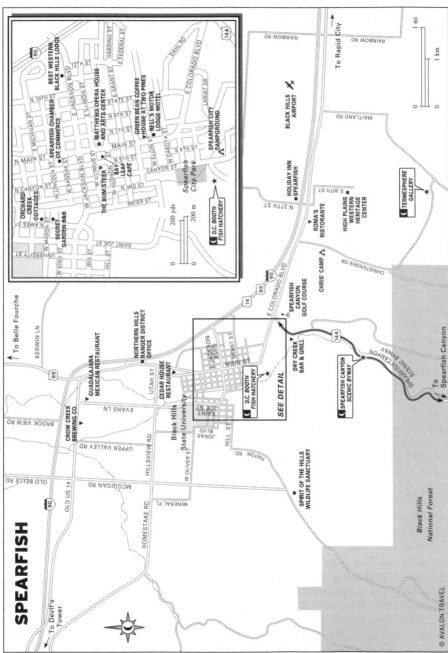

SPEARFISH

To Devil's Tower

To Belle Fourche

KERWIN LN

NORTHERN HILLS
RANGER DISTRICT
OFFICE

GUADALAJARA
MEXICAN RESTAURANT

CEDAR HOUSE
RESTAURANT

UTAH ST

EVANS LN

CROW CREEK
BREWING CO.

BROOK VIEW RD

UPPER VALLEY RD

HILLSVIEW RD

Black Hills
State University

W OLIVER ST

JONAS
BLVD

SAINT
JOE ST

HILL ST

MCGUIGAN RD

OLD BELLE RD

OLD US 14

HOMESTAKE RD

MINERAL PL

SPIRIT OF THE HILLS
WILDLIFE SANCTUARY

TINTON RD

Black Hills
National Forest

JACKSON
BLVD

MAIN ST

GRANT ST

D.C. BOOTH
FISH HATCHERY

SEE DETAIL

DRY CREEK
BAR & GRILL

SPEARFISH
CANYON
GOLF COURSE

E COLORADO BLVD

CHRIS' CAMP

CHRISTENSEN DR

SPEARFISH CANYON
SCENIC BYWAY

SPEARFISH CANYON
SCENIC BYWAY

To
Spearfish Canyon

Spearfish Canyon

14A

HOLIDAY INN
SPEARFISH

N 27TH ST

S 27TH ST

ROMA'S
RISTORANTE

HIGH PLAINS
WESTERN
HERITAGE
CENTER

S 30TH ST

TERMESPHERE
GALLERY

MAITLAND RD

BLACK HILLS
AIRPORT

To Rapid City

RAINBOW RD

RAINBOW RD

1 mi

1 km

BEST WESTERN
BLACK HILLS LODGE

SPEARFISH CHAMBER
OF COMMERCE

MATTHEWS OPERA HOUSE
AND ARTS CENTER

GREEN BEAN COFFEE
HOUSE AT TWO PINES

BELL'S MOTOR
LODGE MOTEL

SPEARFISH CITY
CAMPGROUND

N 10TH ST

N MICHIGAN ST

N MAIN ST

N CANYON ST

ORCHARD
CREEK
COTTAGES

SECRET
GARDEN B&B

W AMES ST

N MASON ST

W MASON ST

W KING ST

UNIVERSITY ST

IRIS ST

HILL ST

SAINT JOE ST

MEIER ST

W JACKSON BLVD

W LINCOLN ST

W KANSAS ST

W ILLINOIS ST

N HUDSON ST

W ELGIN ST

THE BUM STEER

BAY
LEAF
CAFE

N 3RD ST

W 5TH ST

N DAKOTA ST

CANYON ST

Spearfish
City Park

S 5TH ST

MAIN ST

N 7TH ST

N 8TH ST

STATE ST

N GRANT ST

E GRANT ST

N 9TH ST

12TH ST

HARDING ST

E FEDERAL ST

DAHL RD

LARIAT DR

E COLORADO BLVD

14A

D.C. BOOTH
FISH HATCHERY

200 yds

200 m

© AVALON TRAVEL

© LAURAL BIDWELL

D.C. Booth Fish Hatchery

Unfortunately, in 1933, two miles of track washed out. By then, the expense of rebuilding far outweighed the need for train transportation for supplies. Outdoor lovers continued to visit the canyon, however, and eventually, the canyon would be paved. The road, Spearfish Canyon U.S. 14A, was declared a National Forest Scenic Byway and a South Dakota Scenic Byway in 1989.

Today, Spearfish is one of the fastest-growing communities in the hills. Located at the mouth of Spearfish Canyon, it is surrounded on three sides by Black Hills National Forest. Spearfish Creek winds through the heart of the city. With easy access off of I-90, art galleries, coffee shops, great dining, lots of students and their energy, and easy access to the canyon, it's the recreational and cultural heart of the Northern Hills.

SIGHTS
◖ D. C. Booth Fish Hatchery

The D. C. Booth Historic National Fish Hatchery (423 Hatchery Cir., 605/642-7730, www.fws.gov/dcbooth, grounds open year-round daily dawn–dusk; museum, visitors center, and gift shop May 15–mid-Sept. daily 10 A.M.–4 P.M., free) is a surprisingly delightful experience. Opened in 1899, and functioning as a hatchery until 1989, the hatchery was originally called the Spearfish National Fish Hatchery. Its mission was to propagate, stock, and establish trout populations in the Black Hills of South Dakota and Wyoming. While trout are not native to the region, the fast-flowing, cold spring water of the region is a perfect environment for them.

The hatchery is situated on 10 acres of land a few blocks from downtown Spearfish and adjacent to Spearfish City Park. Beautiful landscaping—including ponds, wooden bridges, rock walls, and flower gardens—complement the attractive **Von Bayer Museum of Fish Culture** and historic superintendent's residence, the 1905 **Booth House**. All of the ponds are stocked with trout; food is available from dispensers located near the ponds for $0.25, and small bags of food can be purchased from the gift shop for $1–3. Near the entryway to the park, a below-surface walkway allows visitors to watch some very large trout swimming about in the stock pond. Feeding the trout is a fun and inexpensive source of entertainment for both kids and adults.

Thoughtfully designed displays and interpretive signs are scattered throughout the grounds, including a **Yellowstone Boat** and a replica of a **Fish Car.** The Yellowstone Boat on display is a Great Lakes–style cabin cruiser. It was used at Yellowstone Lake to collect fish eggs. The boat was originally designed to rescue fish stranded by receding floodwaters when the Mississippi River flooded. These boats were selected for the Yellowstone project because they were sturdy enough to withstand the heavy waves on Lake Yellowstone. The Fish Car is a replica of the rail cars that were used to transport fish ready for stocking in the days before refrigeration. Volunteers walk visitors through the replica, explaining how fish were kept alive and how the cars evolved at a time when the only way to keep the fish cool was ice and the only way to keep the water aerated was with hand pumps. Today, fish are transported from hatcheries in specially designed tanker trucks that are filled with refrigerated, aerated, and constantly circulated water. In the 1880s, that was not yet an option. Over 72 billion fish were transported from the fisheries to destination streams by fish rail cars in 1873–1947.

The Von Bayer Museum of Fish Culture houses a collection of more than 175,000 artifacts related to the fisheries industry. Guided tours of the museum and the 1905 Booth House, which served as the superintendent's residence, are available daily. The tours are not scheduled and the guides are volunteers. The tour starts whenever visitors are interested in taking one and lasts as long as the visitors like. And even

after the tour begins, anyone can tag along. Guides provide information about the history of fisheries in the United States, as well as the D. C. Booth Historic Site, and explain what many of the artifacts in the museum were used for.

◖ Termesphere Gallery

Dick Termes is an internationally acclaimed and award-winning artist whose three-dimensional paintings on spheres make for a stunning artistic display. Lauded for his work from San Francisco to Paris, Termes acknowledges M. C. Escher and Buckminster Fuller as early influences. His work is on display at the Termesphere Gallery (1920 Christensen Dr., 605/642-4805 or 888/642-4805, www.termespheres.com, Mon.–Sat. 9 A.M. to 5 P.M., Sun. noon–5 P.M.) and is a delight for the eyes. Colorful spheres, ranging in size from a small Christmas ornament to 24 inches in diameter, hang from the ceiling of the gallery and quietly spin, the result of a small electric motor, giving the viewer a 360-degree view of a hand painted scene created by Termes. His work has included depictions of the Globe Theater in London, the Pantheon, and St. Marks Square in Venice. Termes continues to experiment, using mirrors and painting scenes from the inside of the sphere out. Some are brightly colored scenes and some are intricate graphical designs. It's hard to begin to explain the six-point perspective approach that Termes uses to create his spherical masterpieces, but the results are absorbing. Housed in a geodesic dome built by the Termes family, the hanging and spinning paintings are available for sale. When he isn't on the road doing shows or giving lectures, Termes can be found on-site, happy to chat about his work. The gallery space is located in his home, as is his studio.

The Matthews Opera House and Arts Center

The Matthews Opera House and Arts Center

(612 N. Main St., 605/642-7973, www. spearfishartscenter.org, Arts Center Mon.–Sat. 10 A.M.–5 P.M., Opera House self-guided tours during gallery hours, events $15–25 per ticket) share a building in downtown Spearfish. The gallery features paintings and photographs by local Spearfish and regional Black Hills artists, and hosts artists receptions on a regular basis.

The Matthews Opera House hosts concerts and community theater events. Opened in 1906, the Opera House was built on the second floor of a sandstone building owned by Wyoming rancher Thomas Matthews. The theater featured colorful prefab murals, tin columns painted a rich cream color and accented in gold, incandescent lighting, hardwood floors, box seats, a balcony, and paintings of several playwrights, including Shakespeare. The Opera House was used for stage productions and traveling shows through the 1920s. The next decade saw rapid declines in live performances as the general public became enamored with "moving pictures." For about a decade, the Opera House was used as a movie house, but it was abandoned when the owner moved the movie house into a new and larger facility down the street. Hard times continued to plague the small Opera House after the theater department of Black Hills State University built a theater that could seat twice as many patrons. Many small arts groups made efforts to revive the Opera House over the years, but it required more work than small arts groups could afford. The community came together in 1985 to start restoring the Opera House and completed the historic restoration of the little jewel of a theater in time for its centennial in 2006. The restoration added air-conditioning, dressing rooms, and gallery space on the first floor, which now houses the Spearfish Art Center. Concerts at the Opera House have included everything from "Guys with Guitars" to tango, zydeco, and folk music events.

Tours of the Opera House (free, donations accepted) are by appointment only and can be arranged through the Arts Center. The tours take about half an hour and include information about the history and design of the theater.

Spirit of the Hills Wildlife Sanctuary

At the Spirit of the Hills Wildlife Sanctuary (500 N. Tinton Rd., 605/642-2907 or 877/761-7754, www.spiritofthehillssanctuary.org, tours May–Labor Day, Tues.–Sat. 8:30 and 10 A.M., adult $15, senior, military, and student $10, youth 4–18 $7), unwanted, abused, abandoned, and unadoptable animals are given lifetime sanctuary. The refuge specializes in wild animal care but also assists local shelters with ranch and domestic animals. As long as there is room and resources, any animal in need is provided shelter. Located on 200 acres of rocky hillside terrain, the grounds are a mix of open meadow and forest. In the cleared areas, there are wonderful views of the Spearfish river valley to the north and the high plains to the west.

The sanctuary is a labor of love for founder Michael Welchnyski, who opened the facility in 1999. The first impression of the sanctuary is a little unsettling. There are all kinds of birds, cats, and dogs freely roaming the grounds in apparent peaceful coexistence. The corrals and fenced areas seem cobbled together with whatever sturdy materials are at hand. It has a homemade feel that makes the place seem a little impoverished. But a second look takes in the important elements of the facility. This is not a sanctuary designed for visitors. It is designed for the animals. With glossy coats, clear eyes, and relaxed demeanors, the animals look extraordinarily healthy. Their cages are spacious and clean. The animals have far more room to roam here than those in the average zoo.

Every animal at the sanctuary has a story and the volunteers know them all. On the tour, the stories are revealed. There are many tigers, leopards, and lions here. Most were originally purchased to serve as exotic pets and then surrendered when their owners couldn't control them. There are colorful, noisy parrots. There is a camel at the sanctuary, one of the retired cast members of the *Passion Play,* a long-running theatrical performance in Spearfish that closed in August 2008. The animals at the sanctuary were all born in captivity and abandoned, or rescued by state agencies and transferred here. Any young at the facility are the result of pregnant animals transferred in, as the sanctuary neuters most all of the animals onsite. It is not a place to breed animals; it is a place created to allow unadoptable animals the opportunity to live out the remainder of their lives in relative peace.

The sanctuary is a clear demonstration of why it is not right to try and raise wild animals as pets. It doesn't work. The sanctuary survives on volunteer labor, tour fees, and donations, and the voluntary veterinarian care of Dr. David Elsom. While public tours are offered only in the summertime, people interested in contributing to the organization are invited to call and make an appointment to visit at any time.

To get to the sanctuary from I-90, take Spearfish exit 8 and head south to Tinton Road. Bear right on Tinton Road. The entrance to the sanctuary is on the left.

High Plains Western Heritage Center

The High Plains Western Heritage Center (825 Heritage Dr., 605/642-9378, www.westernheritagecenter.com, Nov.–Mar. daily 9 A.M.–4 P.M., Apr.–Oct. daily 9 A.M.–5 P.M., adult $7, child aged 6–16 $3, family $15) opened in 1989. The mission of the museum is to preserve the history of the early pioneers in the five states of South Dakota, North Dakota, Wyoming, Montana, and Nebraska. Displays in the museum include a fully stocked blacksmith shop and saddlery.

Western artifacts include one of the original Cheyenne–Deadwood stagecoaches, photographs from early rodeos in the region, and artifacts from the agricultural and timber industries. A small bookstore and gift shop are on-site. Outside displays include live longhorn cattle and buffalo, a fully furnished log cabin, a rural schoolhouse, and antique farm equipment. When the facility was built, a 200-seat theater complex was included. Several times a year, concerts and other special programs are presented at the center. In addition, the local historical society or traveling shows give lectures and workshops at the facilities. (Ticket prices vary from free admission to $40 per ticket, depending on the program.) Call for information about lectures, workshops, and concert performances occurring during the time of your visit.

RECREATION

Some of the best recreation in the Black Hills is concentrated along the Spearfish Canyon Scenic Byway, which runs south from Spearfish to Lead. Hiking trails, rock climbing routes, and fly-fishing are all activities enjoyed within the bounds of the canyon walls. The canyon road was designed to allow safe biking. The shoulders on both sides are about four feet wide. It's a wonderful 20-mile trek. The fastest access to the byway is to take exit 14 off of I-90, and then stay on U.S. 14, which parallels I-90 headed west. Just past the Spearfish Country Club, take a left (heading south) on U.S. 14A—this highway is the **Spearfish Canyon Scenic Byway.**

Hiking

There are several scenic hiking and biking trails southwest of Spearfish in the Black Hills National Forest. And there are several peaks that afford spectacular views. The Crow Peak Trail is one of the best and, not surprisingly, one of the most popular hikes in the region.

© WWW.TRAVELSD.COM

hiking near Spearfish, overlooking Spearfish Canyon

CROW PEAK TRAIL

- **Distance:** 7 miles round-trip
- **Elevation Gain:** 1,600 feet
- **Duration:** 6 hours
- **Effort:** Strenuous
- **Trailhead:** Crow Peak Trailhead
- **Directions:** From Spearfish, take Forest Service Road 214 (Higgins Gulch Rd.) about seven miles south of town. The trailhead is located at a good sized parking lot on the right.

The trail starts off winding west though ponderosa pine, aspen, and birch trees. The path quickly turns steep, ascending the mountain through a series of tight switchbacks. At higher elevations, the trees thin and the trail becomes rocky. At the summit, the views encompass several peaks including Terry Peak (second only in elevation to Harney Peak in the central hills), Cement Ridge, Spearfish Peak, and Bear Butte in the distance to the east. The name Crow Peak comes from the Lakota name Paha Karitukateyapi, which means "the hills where the Crow were killed," a reference to a battle between Crow and Lakota warriors.

OLD BALDY TRAIL

- **Distance:** 5.7 miles round trip
- **Elevation Gain:** 300 feet
- **Duration:** 4 hours
- **Effort:** Moderately strenuous
- **Trailhead:** Old Baldy Trailhead
- **Directions:** The trailhead is located 13 miles south of Spearfish off of Forest Service Road 134.

Do not let the modest elevation gain fool you. While the gain is only about 300 feet, the entire hike takes place above 5,800 feet. High-elevation hiking can be wearing. Add 0.7 mile for the spur to the summit of Old Baldy Mountain. The trail loop winds through quaking aspen, ponderosa pine, and paper birch. From the top, there is a stunning panoramic view of Crow Peak to the north, Terry Peak to the east, and the stone tower of the Cement Ridge fire lookout tower in Wyoming to the west.

Biking and Cross-Country Skiing

The Big Hill Trails present a great selection of trails for bike riders of all skill levels and for cross-country skiers. Five interconnected loops allow for an easy family ski trip in the winter or an all-day difficult bike ride covering more than 13 miles for mountain bikers in the summer season.

BIG HILL TRAILS

- **Distance:** A loop plus A1 loop 3.3 miles round-trip; A-C-D outer loop 10.9 miles; B loop 3.6 miles; Loop C 6.9 miles; Loop D 4.5 miles; 7.1 miles total from trailhead
- **Elevation Gain:** 400 feet
- **Duration:** Varies from 2 hours to a full day of combining interconnecting loops
- **Effort:** Easy to moderately strenuous
- **Trailhead:** Big Hill Trailhead
- **Distance:** From Spearfish, exit 10 off of I-90 and head toward town on North Main Street. Just past the forest service office (2014 N. Main), take a right on Utah Street. Continue to a four-way stop. Drive south 0.5 mile on the gravel road until the intersection with Forest Service Road 134. Drive south on Forest Service Road 134 for 7.8 miles until you reach the trailhead.

These trails range in difficulty from easy to strenuous. During the winter, some portions of the trails are groomed for cross-country skiing and cross-country ski racing. Loops A (2.8 miles, easy to moderate) and A-1 (0.5 mile, easy) are fairly level, are groomed in the winter, and meander through stands of quaking aspen and birch trees. Loop B (3.5 miles, difficult) starts out on Loop A (head right on Loop A) and then veers off about 0.5 mile into the trail. At that point, the trail earns its difficult rating as it gets fairly steep in spots. Loop B is not groomed in winter, is a more challenging trail, and is popular with mountain bikers. Loop C (6.9 miles, difficult) also starts out on Loop A (head left on Loop A from the trailhead), and is another groomed trail that

extends past the aspens into the ponderosa pines. The longest trail here is Loop D, which is 7.5 miles of groomed trail with a 0.2-mile un-groomed spur that offers a scenic overlook of Spearfish Canyon and Spearfish Mountain. This trail is rated as moderately strenuous and winds through extensive ponderosa pine forests. Hikers will enjoy Loop D best for its views. Novice mountain bikers will enjoy Loops A and A1. All of the other loops are fine for intermediate riders.

Fly-Fishing

Spearfish Creek is a fast-moving creek with fly-fishing access year-round. The river is stocked with rainbow, brown, and brook trout. A fishing license is required and can be obtained from Queen City Liquors, Wal-Mart, Iron Lake General Store, and the K-Mart in Spearfish, or at the Spearfish Canyon Lodge in Savoy. A one-day license is $9 for state residents and $16 for nonresidents. Perfectly good fish can be caught right in the heart of Spearfish.

Golf

Spearfish Canyon Country Club (120 Spearfish Canyon Dr., 605/717-4653, www.spearfishcanyoncountryclub.com, 9 holes $27–30, 18 holes $48–53) is the only 18-hole golf course (6,667 yards, par 71) in the Northern Hills. The semi-private club is open to the public six days a week and is for members only on Wednesdays. Amenities include a heated swimming pool and a full-service bar and grill.

ACCOMMODATIONS
$50-100

Bell's Motor Lodge Motel (230 N. Main St., 605/642-3812 or 800/880-2095, www.bellsmotorlodgemotel.com, $60–78) harkens back to another era and provides basic accommodations in a family-run motel. There are 30 rooms available, and in some of the rooms, microwaves and small refrigerators are available.

© WWW.TRAVEL.SD.COM

fly-fishing at Spearfish Creek

There are two kitchenettes. Coffeemakers, hair dryers, and irons can be checked out at the office if desired. Small pets are allowed. The outdoor pool is very small, but the property is close to town, safe, offers free high-speed Internet access, and features a friendly, helpful staff.

Orchard Creek Cottages (514 W. Mason St., 605/642-4234 or 877/642-2400, www.orchardcreekcottages.com, $94–105) are located right on Spearfish Creek. Cabins are available at nightly or weekly rates mid-May–mid-August only. Once Black Hills State College semesters start up in the fall, the cabins are rented on a monthly basis to students. All of the cabins are kitchenettes and all have free wireless. The cabins are close together, but the communal grounds are very attractive. The cabins are clean and the environment is smoke free. There are 12 cabins available. Pets are not allowed.

For a rustic setting just inside Spearfish Canyon, **Rimrock Lodge Cabins** (U.S. 14A, Spearfish Canyon, 605/642-3192, www.rimrocklodge.com, $72–96) offers six cabins tucked into the canyon with gorgeous views. The cabins range from one full-sized bed to two queen-sized beds, and all include microwaves, mini-refrigerators, and coffeemakers. There are no televisions, Internet, or telephones. The property is just five miles from downtown Spearfish shops and restaurants, but feels worlds away. All of the cabins are smoke free. Pets are allowed with a cleaning deposit.

Days Inn of Spearfish (240 Ryan Rd., 605/642-7101 or 800/225-3297, www.daysinn.com, $80–100) is easy access from the interstate and is located within walking distance of several Spearfish restaurants and bars. The property allows pets for a small fee. There are hair dryers, coffeemakers, and free wireless Internet in all the rooms; a continental breakfast is included with the room charge. The rooms are pretty standard mid-level hotel fair, but are spacious and clean.

$100-150

Holiday Inn Spearfish (305 N. 27th St., 605/642-4683 or 800/465-4329, $129–166) offers a large heated pool, whirlpool, and fitness center. There is a small video game room to entertain the kids and a restaurant and pub are on-site. Pets are allowed with a one time $25 cleaning fee. The clean and comfortable rooms are nice, fairly standard hotel rooms with free wireless Internet.

The 50-room **Best Western Black Hills Lodge** (540 E. Jackson Blvd., 605/642-7795, www.bestwestern.com/blackhillslodge, $139) is an outdoors-themed hotel located off of I-90 at exit 12. Amenities include an outdoor heated pool, indoor hot tub and dry sauna, free continental breakfast, microwave and refrigerator in every room, coffeemakers, and hair dryers. The rooms are extra large and have either a small dining table or desk. There is free Wi-Fi in every room, and there are laundry facilities on-site. Dogs are allowed for a one-time cleaning fee of $15. (Other animals are allowed at the hotel's discretion.) The entire property is smoke free.

The **Secret Garden Bed & Breakfast** (938 N. Ames St., 605/642-4859 or 800/321-1466, www.bbonline.com/sd/secret, $95–150), open year-round, is a large historic Victorian-style home built in 1892 that has four rooms available. All of the rooms have a private bath and all are smoke free. There is a hot tub available in the garden area. A gourmet breakfast is served in the dining room, or outside in the garden, or in your own room upon request.

Campgrounds

C Spearfish City Campground (404 S. Canyon St., 605/642-1340, www.spearfishparksandrec.com/campground, RV hookups $32–37, tent sites $21) is a beautiful site not far from the town center and across the street from a city park. Spearfish Creek runs through the grounds and since the campground is located at the end of a dead end street, there is no traffic in the area except for fellow campers. Amenities include Wi-Fi, picnic tables, restrooms, showers, fire grills, and lots of trees.

Another nice spot is **Chris' Camp** (701 Christensen Dr., 605/642-2239 or 800/350-2239, www.blackhills.com/chriscampground, open May 1–Oct. 15, tent sites $19, water and electric hookups $30, full hookups $33, camping cabins $50), which has been family owned and operated here for 48 years. Amenities include a pool, recreation room, playground, convenience store, free wireless, and a petting zoo. Pets are welcome at the campground.

FOOD
Family Fare

Healthy eaters may want to fire up their energy at **C Green Bean Coffee House** (304 Main St., 605/717-3636, Mon.–Thu. 6 A.M.–8 P.M., Fri.–Sat. 6 A.M.–6 P.M., Sun. 8 A.M.–6 P.M., $7), where a full array of great coffee and espresso drinks are served with an assortment of wraps, sandwiches, and soups. The specialty of the house is homemade focaccia bread for the panini sandwiches. It's a comfortable place within walking distance of downtown, with a nice front porch and interesting decor.

The **Cedar House Restaurant** (130 E. Ryan Rd., 605/642-2104, www.cedarhousespearfish.com, Mon.–Sat. 6:30 A.M.–9 P.M., Sun. 6:30 A.M.–3 P.M., $7–10), a family-run restaurant since 1988, specializes in homemade soups and reasonably priced family dining.

The **Dry Creek Bar and Grill** (523 Spearfish Canyon Rd., 605/642-1134, Mon.–Sun. 11 A.M.–10 P.M., lunch $9–15, dinner $16–26) is the local steakhouse and bar but there are also pasta dishes, salads, walleye, and salmon, with a few vegetarian options, as well. Willing to alter a dish without much fuss, it is a very casual establishment (leaning toward funky!) with great food.

Fine Dining

The **Bay Leaf Café** (126 W. Hudson St., 605/642-5462, www.bayleafcafe.net, Mon.–Thurs. 11 A.M.–8 P.M., Fri.–Sat. 11 A.M.–9 P.M., Sun. 4–8 P.M., lunch $9–11, dinner $11–25) has been serving Spearfish diners since 1993 in a lovely historic building built in 1892 as the Queen City Hotel. The menu is decidedly continental, including several Mediterranean selections (humus, falafels, tabbouleh), as well as more traditional fare (sandwiches). Dinner features native game and fish specialties, steaks, Alaskan seafood, and creative pasta selections. The restaurant is happy to vary menus to suit customer preferences, including vegetarian, gluten-free, and/or allergy-specific needs.

The ❰ **Bum Steer** (701 N. 5th St., 605/717-8337, daily 11 A.M.–9 P.M., $16–30) is located in a historic sandstone building built in 1893. The interior features gorgeous hardwood floors, lots of contemporary art, and a salad bar that is over 15 feet in length. The restaurant's signature dish is steak, but seafood, pork, and chicken have found a place on the menu, as well. On Sunday, the restaurant serves brunch. It's a beautiful restaurant that has developed a reputation for great service and fabulous food.

Ethnic Fare

Roma's Ristorante (2281 E. Colorado Blvd., 605/722-0715, www.romasristorante.net, Mon.–Sat. 11 A.M.–2 P.M. and 4–9 P.M., Sun. 4–8 P.M., lunch $9, dinner $18–25) is in a brand new building in a brand new location. The interior is warm with golden-hued walls, white tablecloths, tall windows, and lots of wood. Lunch includes a normal array of sandwiches, plus calzones and pasta offerings including ziti, lasagna, primavera, alfredo, and meatballs with linguini. Dinner broadens the offerings and includes steaks, fish, and chicken. Not too surprisingly, however, the chef specials features pasta, including Cajun shrimp and sausage with linguini, buffalo ravioli, seafood lasagna, and many other Italian dishes.

Guadalajara Mexican Restaurant (83 Old U.S. 14, 605/642-4765, daily 11 A.M.–9:30 P.M., $10–13) has to be one of the most colorful restaurants in town. The high wooden booths are carved with brightly colored suns and sunflower motifs, and flags hang from the ceiling; it's just plain festive. It is also a family-run restaurant where all of the food is made from scratch and the atmosphere is casual. All of the Mexican food favorites can be found here, including tostadas, fajitas, burritos, enchiladas, and many combinations featuring chicken, pork, seafood, and beef.

Pubs

The **Crow Peak Brewing Company** (125 W. Old U.S. 14, 605/717-0006, www.crowpeakbrewing.com, Mon.–Thurs. 2–10 P.M., Fri. 2 P.M.–midnight, Sat. noon–midnight, Sun. noon–8 P.M.) brews beverages that range from pale ales to pitch black porters for pleasing the palate of any beer drinker. Located in a beautiful building with large second-story decks and outdoor tables, Crow Peak, which started as a small five-barrel operation in 2007, has built a successful fan base and is now distributed throughout South Dakota. The barroom itself is large with wood tables, stone decor, and a very long bar.

INFORMATION AND SERVICES

The **Spearfish Visitor Information Center** (603 N. Main St., 605/717-9294, www.visitspearfish.com, Memorial Day–Labor Day Mon.–Fri. 8 A.M.–5 P.M., Sat.–Sun. 10 A.M.–3 P.M., off-season closed Sat.–Sun.) has information available on Spearfish and the Black Hills for visitors to the region. The **Spearfish Chamber of Commerce** (106 W. Kansas St., 605/642-2626 or 800/626-8013, www.spearfishchamber.org) is located downtown and is open Monday–Friday. For maps and information on hiking, biking, and camping in the Black Hills National Forest, contact the **Northern Hills Ranger District Headquarters** (2014 N. Main St., 605/642-4622).

Groceries can be found at **Leuders Food Centers** (620 7th St.) or at **Safeway Stores** (1606 N. Ave.). There are also two **post office** locations in Spearfish—one at 120 Yankee Street, and one at 810 North Main Street.

Transportation services are provided by **Canyon Cab** (605/717-9997).

◖ SPEARFISH CANYON SCENIC BYWAY

Spearfish Canyon is a State and National Forest Scenic Byway that winds for 20 miles along Spearfish Creek between the communities of Spearfish and Lead. The byway is U.S. 14A, which is also a commercial highway, so be sure to pull well off the road when stopping to view the scenery. All of the views are straight up the canyon walls to heights of over 1,000 feet, but don't forget to keep an eye on the road as many bicyclists and hikers may be riding or walking along the highway shoulders.

Over two billion years ago, the area that is now the Black Hills was covered by an inland sea. Over time, as the sea receded and returned and receded again, layers of sediment were deposited on the ocean floor. As these layers hardened, different sedimentary layers were created. Around 65 million years ago, a dome-shaped uplift in the earth's crust formed the Black Hills. In the Northern Hills, crevasses within the limestone layer, created by the uplift, filled with magma. These magma flows, called intrusions, cooled forming igneous rocks. Limestone and other sedimentary layers erode faster than the harder igneous rock, so while the sea receded, the overlying sedimentary layers were eroded, exposing the igneous intrusions. Crow Peak, Spearfish Mountain, and Terry Peak in the Spearfish area are all igneous intrusions, as is Bear Butte, the easternmost igneous peak in the region.

About five million years ago, the erosion of the

limestone layer near Spearfish was accelerated by the power of water. Many of the streams that flow out of the hills begin as springs within the limestone plateau on the western side of the hills. Spearfish Creek is one of those streams. Today, the streambed of Spearfish Canyon is more than 1,000 feet below the highest canyon walls.

The river runs south–north and passes through four different plant communities on its way. The Northern Coniferous Forest, featuring white spruce trees, merges into the dominant biome of the region, the Rocky Mountain Pine Forest, which includes the ponderosa pine and which covers 85 percent of the Black Hills region. Next, the Eastern Deciduous Forest makes inroads into the hills with stands of quaking aspen and birch. As the creek spills into the Spearfish river valley, the northern plains habitat of oak and cottonwood trees and prairie grasses appears. Of the 1,585 plant species found in the state of South Dakota, 1,260 are found in the Black Hills, and most of these can be found in Spearfish Canyon.

When the communities of Spearfish and Lead were founded in 1876, the canyon between the two communities was impassable, even on horseback. It wasn't until 1893 that the Grand Island and Wyoming Line Railroad built a direct rail line through the canyon which made the area accessible for day trips. Visitors to the canyon could ride the train to any point they wished and the train would stop and pick them up on the return trip.

Driving from Spearfish: Take exit 10 or exit 14 off of I-90 and follow the signs to the Spearfish Canyon Highway. At the intersection of U.S. 14 and U.S. 14A (the scenic byway), head south. The National Forest Service has created a self-guided tour brochure that is available at the Spearfish Ranger District office (2014 N. Main St., Spearfish, 605/642-4622).

Natural Features

Spearfish Canyon is beautiful from start to

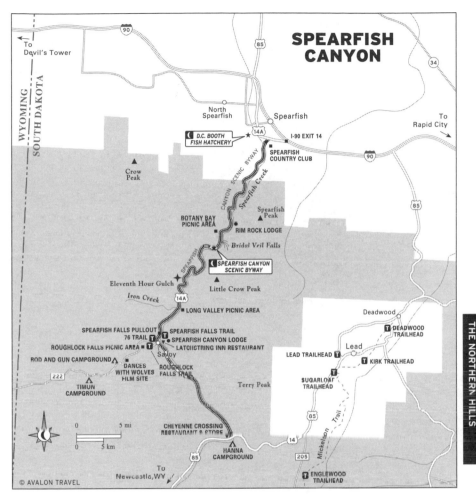

SPEARFISH CANYON

THE NORTHERN HILLS

finish, but you'll want to keep an eye out for some of these special features. **Bridal Veil Falls** is located about six miles into the canyon, just south of the **Botany Bay picnic area.** The falls are on the left side of the canyon. There is a pullout on the right-hand side, across from the falls, for safe parking. In the spring, water cascades over the canyon wall (look up!), but by late summer, the stream of water slows to a trickle. The rock over which Bridal Veil Falls cascades is part of the igneous intrusions that occurred during the uplift. At one time, Spearfish Creek ran level with the falls, but as erosion ate away at the softer limestone formations, the streambed burrowed deeper and deeper, creating the canyon. Continue south along the byway and at about 3.3 miles past Bridal Veil Falls, **Eleventh Hour Gulch** meets Spearfish Canyon. The canyon rims of Eleventh Hour Gulch are so close together that it is said that the canyon floor only receives one hour of daylight per day and that the sun

© WWW.TRAVELSD.COM

Bridal Veil Falls one of three waterfalls in Spearfish Canyon.

THE NORTHERN HILLS

doesn't enter the canyon until at least 11 A.M. The narrow canyon and high rim walls of the gulch present a striking formation.

In addition to Bridal Veil Falls, there are two other easily accessed waterfalls in the canyon. Both are located near the small community of Savoy. The trail to **Spearfish Falls** is located at the north corner of the Latchstring Inn Restaurant. **Roughlock Falls** are located on the other side of the byway. There is a gravel road just before the Spearfish Canyon Lodge. Take a right onto the road and drive until you reach a picnic area. Just a few short feet away are the cascading falls of Little Spearfish Creek.

Hiking

There are several beautiful hiking, biking, and horseback riding trails along U.S. 14A (the Spearfish Canyon Scenic Byway). Remember to carry water and wear sunscreen and a hat. Keep an eye on the sky for thundershower activity as lightning storms are not uncommon in

the summer season. If a storm does arise, head down the trail as fast as you can.

DEVIL'S BATHTUB TRAIL

- **Distance:** 0.75 mile
- **Elevation Gain:** None
- **Duration:** 1–1.5 hours
- **Effort:** Easy
- **Trailhead:** From Spearfish, take U.S. 14A south about eight miles to Cleopatra Place. Take a left on Cleopatra Place and look to your left for the small parking area that marks the trailhead.

This is a great hike for interesting geology and water features. The hike follows Cleopatra Creek, and there are several stream crossings. Be prepared to get wet. It is an easy, relatively flat hike that ends at two pools of blue-green water carved into the rock. The trail is hard-packed dirt, well worn, and easy to follow. At one time, it was possible to slide down the stream right into the pool, but a large boulder fell into the chute, blocking the slide. The pool is still a nice place to dangle your feet for a bit—but just a short bit, because the stream water is very cold.

Near Savoy, about 13 miles south of Spearfish on the scenic byway, there are three great trails to choose from. There are two different waterfalls to visit in this area, and since both are short and easy hikes, it's worthwhile to do them both. There is also a hike to the canyon rim that provides the best views to be found within the canyon proper.

SPEARFISH CANYON FALLS

- **Distance:** 1.5 miles round-trip
- **Elevation Gain:** 400 feet
- **Duration:** 1 hour
- **Effort:** Easy to moderate
- **Trailhead:** The trailhead is located on the north side off of the Latchstring Inn Restaurant parking lot.

The hike to Spearfish Canyon Falls is a backwards one. You will travel down first, and then climb back up the slope when you return. As you travel down the gently sloping trail, keep a watchful eye out for *Oreo helix*, a miniature snail. There are thousands of these located here near Spearfish Canyon Falls. As the trail descends, the vegetation changes first to the ponderosa pine forest that blankets most of the hills, then to the aspen and birch of the Eastern Deciduous Forest. Since birds are very particular about the environmental niches that they occupy, a wide variety of birds make their home in the multifaceted habitat here, including mountain bluebirds, grosbeaks, warblers, goldfinches, and even golden eagles.

At the bottom of the trail, continue over the bridge that crosses Spearfish Creek to the point where Little Spearfish Creek cascades into Spearfish Creek. From a nearby clearing, you'll see the falls from the bottom. The trail begins to climb here, 400 feet up to a beautiful bridge that crosses a 120-foot gorge over Spearfish Creek. On the other side of the gorge, the trail winds another 400 feet to an arched bridge crossing Little Spearfish Creek. You have arrived at the top of Spearfish Canyon Falls. At this point, you can continue along the trail to finish a strenuous loop that winds back to the Latchstring Inn Restaurant via a steep incline, or return the way you came. Just about all of the plant communities in the hills meet here. At the rim, 80 feet above the creekbed, see the towering spruce trees of the Northern Coniferous Forest, some over 120 feet tall.

ROUGHLOCK FALLS TRAIL

- **Distance:** 2 miles round-trip
- **Elevation Gain:** None
- **Duration:** 1.5 hours
- **Effort:** Easy
- **Trailhead:** Located behind the Spearfish Canyon Lodge at the far end of the parking lot.

This is a wheelchair-accessible trail that follows Little Spearfish Creek. The packed-dirt trail starts off in a forested area paralleling the creek. In this region, ponderosa pine, spruce, aspen, and oak trees line the trail. There are several wooden benches tucked along the trail for rest stops. The path opens onto a marshy area with willow and high grasses. Look for blue heron in this area. At the end of the trail, wooden bridges allow close access to the falls. Little Spearfish Creek cascades over large boulders on its way to join Spearfish Creek a couple of miles down the canyon. At the end of the trail, a wooden bridge crosses over the stream and inclines slowly to a parking lot and picnic area. Walk down the road back to the lodge or turn around and return along the trail.

76 TRAIL

- **Distance:** 1.5 miles round-trip
- **Elevation Gain:** 1,000 feet

THE NORTHERN HILLS

- **Duration:** 1.5–2 hours
- **Effort:** Strenuous
- **Trailhead:** Across the gravel road from Spearfish Canyon Lodge at Savoy

The 76 Trail is the only formal hiking trail to climb to the top of the rim of Spearfish Canyon. The trail is short, but it climbs more than 1,000 feet from start to finish. There are benches tucked into the side of the trail for catching your wind. The panoramic view from ridge at the top of the canyon makes the effort well worthwhile.

Biking

The Spearfish Canyon Scenic Byway sports four-foot-wide shoulders specifically to allow bikers safe use of the highway. From Spearfish to Lead, the byway is about 19 miles and is a beautiful bicycle ride road-trip. Bridal Veil Falls is visible from the road and near Savoy (about 13 miles into the canyon), and at the Spearfish Canyon Lodge, there is a mile-long road to Roughlock Falls that is passable by both road and mountain bikes which makes a nice side trip.

Rock Climbing

Spearfish Canyon has started to develop a reputation for climbing and has been featured in many rock climbing magazines. With more than 300 routes up the limestone walls, there is suitable climbing for all skill levels. Climbing in the canyon is accessible year-round. There are no rock climbing tour companies allowed in the canyon, but there are climbing guidebooks available. Look for *Rock Climbing Guide, Spearfish Canyon Limestone* by Bruce Junek.

Fly-Fishing

Spearfish Creek provides some of the best trout fishing in the Black Hills. A fast-moving creek with fly-fishing access year-round, the river is stocked with rainbow, brown, and brook trout. A fishing license is required and can be obtained from Queen City Liquors, Wal-Mart, Iron Lake General Store, and the K-Mart in Spearfish, or at the Spearfish Canyon Lodge in Savoy. A one-day license is $9 for state residents and $16 for nonresidents. Visitors wishing to try their luck for more than one day can get a three-day fishing license for $34.

Snowmobiling

There are 350 miles of groomed snowmobile trails in the Northern Hills. Within Spearfish Canyon, the most accessible trail is Trail #4, located just west of the Spearfish Canyon Lodge (877/975-6343 or 605/584-3435). Snowmobile rentals are available at the lodge for guests and nonguests alike. Renters must be at least 18 years of age, however, and have a valid driver's license. Snowmobile rentals can be for a half- or a full-day (full-day: $140 single seat, $160 double seat; half-day: $80 single seat, $100 double seat). For those who have their own machines, a registration fee must be paid if the owner is not licensed in another state. The fee is $40 for a five-day permit. These can also be purchased at the lodge. Snowmobiles that are licensed in another state can be operated in South Dakota without the permit.

Weather in the Black Hills can be very unpredictable, especially in the Northern Hills, where the wind comes whipping across Wyoming! Be sure to wear plenty of layers, and keep a minimal amount of food and water on hand. For trail conditions, call 800/445-3474. Information about the trails can be obtained from the South Dakota Department of Game, Fish and Parks (605/773-3391) and printable trail maps can be obtained at www.gfp.sd.gov.

Picnic Areas

There are three picnic areas along the scenic byway. Traveling from Spearfish to Lead, the first, **Botany Bay Picnic Area,** is located 5–6 miles from the intersection of U.S. 14A and U.S. 14, inside the mouth of the canyon. This picnic area is named for the wide variety of unusual and rare plant species (including ancient ferns) that can be found there. The **Long Valley Picnic Area** is another 5.2 miles past Botany Bay and has tables right next to the creek. **Roughlock Falls Picnic Area** is located near the Spearfish Canyon Lodge in Savoy. Take a right just to the north of the lodge and follow the road one mile back. From the parking lot there, a short walk will take you to picnic tables and to the cascading Roughlock Falls.

Accommodations and Food

There isn't much food available along the byway. Look for the town of Savoy. It isn't big, but you'll find food and lodging there, about 13 miles into the canyon, measured from the intersection of U.S. 14 and U.S. 14A in Spearfish, or about 5.5 miles into the canyon from Cheyenne Crossing in the south.

◖ Spearfish Canyon Lodge (10619 Roughlock Falls Rd., Lead, 605/584-3435 or 877/975-6343, www.spfcanyon.com, open year-round, standard double queen rooms summer rates $152–172, winter rates begin Oct. 15 $89–109) has it all in terms of beauty and location for those seeking a quiet place near the best scenery, hiking, and biking in the region. The facility features large log construction and a light and airy lobby with a huge stone fireplace. The large log motif is carried into the full-service lounge. Several trailheads are located within walking distance of this site, including the Roughlock Falls Trail, Spearfish Falls Trail, and 76 Trail. Guests can take advantage of bike rentals, arrange for fly-fishing packages, obtain fishing equipment and licenses, and rent snowmobiling equipment. The lodge also has conference facilities.

The **Latchstring Inn Restaurant** (10619 Roughlock Rd. and U.S. 14A, 605/584-3333, www.spfcanyon.com/dining.html, open year-round, daily 7 A.M.–9 P.M., breakfast $8, lunch $10, dinner entrées $20–26) is a beautiful log cabin with high ceilings, a fireplace, large windows, and simple wood tables. The restaurant is run by the same folks who run the Spearfish Canyon Lodge across the street. In the summer, dining is available on the wood deck on the back of the restaurant overlooking the canyon, as well as the inside dining room. The breakfast menu is limited, but includes a little bit of everything. Lunch features a variety of sandwiches, buffalo stew, and a daily soup offering. The Inn enjoys offering a variety of breads, including flatbread, ciabatta buns, and whole-grain bread. The chips are homemade and soups are served with corn cakes. Dinner entrées range from walleye, trout, salmon, and scallops to buffalo rib eye, beef rib eye, and chicken and pasta dishes. For dessert, think chocolate decadence. The establishment has a beer and wine license.

Just barely on the edge of the scenic byway at the intersection of U.S. 14A and Highway 85, look for **◖ Cheyenne Crossing** (21415 U.S. 14A, 605/584-3510, www.cheyennecrossing. org, summer Mon.–Wed. 7:30 A.M.–4 P.M., Thurs.–Sun. 7:30 A.M.–8 P.M., winter Thurs.–Sun. 7:30 A.M.–8 P.M., breakfast $7, lunch $9, dinner $9–13), which has the best breakfast around. Choose from sourdough pancakes, buttermilk biscuits, buffalo sausage, and homemade cinnamon rolls, among other items. Lunch and dinner are great, as well. The house specialty is Indian Tacos, which start with a homemade base of WoodenKnife Indian Fry Bread—a family recipe from Interior, South Dakota—topped with a wide variety of options including pulled pork, veggies, shredded roast beef, or traditional taco toppings (ground beef, lettuce, red onions, tomato, olives, cheese, picante sauce, and sour cream). The dinner menu includes salmon, cod, top sirloin and rib eye steaks, and shrimp. On the lighter side, choose from chicken dishes, fish, and beef sandwiches. The restaurant also has a very nice wine selection. It's a real country-style kind of restaurant—cozy and warm with delicious food.

Campgrounds

There are three National Forest Service campgrounds near the southern end of the canyon. None of them require reservations. Contact the Black Hills National Forest office at 605/642-4622 for more information. Reservations can be made at 877/444-6777 or online at www.recreation.gov. All are primitive sites with no electricity. There are restrooms and running water. The maximum length of stay at any of the campgrounds is 14 nights. Two of the campgrounds are located south of Savoy, off of Forest Service Road 222. The **Rod and Gun Campground** (Apr.–Dec.,

$15) offers seven sites just three miles down Forest Service Road 222 on the left. Located beside Little Spearfish Creek, this is a high-elevation campground sitting at about 5,500 feet above sea level. It is very close to where the winter scenes in *Dances with Wolves* were filmed. The **Timon Campground** (Apr.–Dec., $15) is another 1.5 miles past the Rod and Gun Campground. It also has seven sites right beside Little Spearfish Creek and is at an elevation of more than 5,600 feet.

The **Hanna Campground** (closed in winter, $15) is located off of U.S. 14A about 3.5 miles south of Savoy (about 0.5 mile north of Cheyenne Crossing). The campground has 13 sites and is located next to Spearfish Creek. In the summer, there's an on-site host.

Lead

The city of Lead (pronounced Leed), like many Black Hills communities, traces its founding back to the discovery of gold. In February 1876, Thomas Carey discovered placer gold in Gold Run Gulch. As was always the case with the discovery of gold, as soon as the word got out, other prospectors rushed to the gulch. By July 1876, the residents laid out the town between the north and south forks of Gold Run Creek. The town was named after the large number of ore outcroppings (called "leads") in the area. The gold rush lasted about two years in the Deadwood/Lead area. However, the discovery of gold at the Homestake Mine would have an impact on the community for several decades.

The Homestake Mine was originally claimed by brothers Moses and Fred Manuel and a partner, Hank Harney, in April 1876. In June 1877, George Hearst purchased the claim from the brothers for $70,000. The mine went on to produce approximately 40 million ounces of gold; before it closed, it was the oldest, largest, and deepest mine in the Western Hemisphere,

reaching more than 8,000 feet below the town of Lead.

By the time Hearst invested in Homestake, mining was second nature to him. A graduate of the Franklin County School of Mining in Missouri, he already had interests in mines in Missouri, California, Montana, Nevada, and Utah. Hearst headed the company Hearst, Haggin, Tevis and Co., which became the largest private mining company in the United States. Hearst and his wife Phoebe were the parents of William Randolph Hearst, who elected not to operate his father's mining interests and instead took over the *San Francisco Examiner,* which was to become the foundation of the Hearst publishing empire.

George Hearst died in 1891 and left Phoebe Hearst as his sole heir. Phoebe took over his business investments, including the controlling interest in the Homestake Mine. Though she didn't spend all that much time in Lead after George's death, she became one of its biggest benefactors. In 1894, Phoebe Hearst gave the

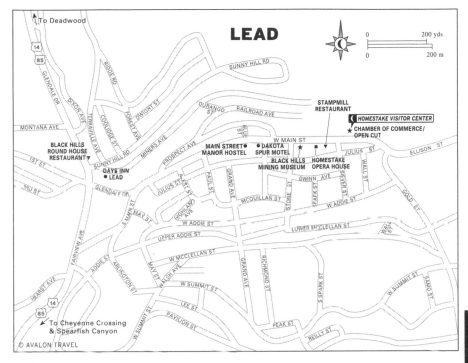

city a library, with over 8,000 books and public documents, which she maintained at her personal expense until she died (and which she endowed through 1925 in her will). In 1900, she endowed and then continued to support the Hearst Kindergarten. In 1914, the Homestake Opera House and Recreation Building were gifts to the town from the Homestake Mine. It housed an opera house, bowling alley, swimming pool, library, social rooms, billiards and pool tables; with the exception of the opera house, all were free to the public. The Homestake Mine also provided free medical care to employees and their families at the Homestake Hospital. Phoebe Hearst died in 1919.

By 1910, Lead had become one of the largest cities in South Dakota, weighing in with a population of over 8,000 people, most of whom were affiliated with the Homestake Mine. Even through the Great Depression of the 1930s,

miners did well at Homestake. Eventually, however, the rich deposits of ore were mined out and what was left was not economical to extract; and so, in 2002, the mine closed.

Today, the Homestake Mine, the deepest, oldest mine in the West, is in the process of being transformed into the Deep Underground Science and Engineering Laboratory (DUSEL). The same year that the mine officially closed, Dr. Ray Davis was awarded the Nobel Prize for a neutrino detector that he had installed 4,850 feet below the surface at Homestake Mine. An experiment that spanned decades of collaboration between the mine and Davis made the mine famous in the world of science. When the mine was closed, a proposal to convert the mine into an underground laboratory spread quickly. By July 2007, Homestake Mine was chosen for the new location of the underground laboratory, at which experiments will take place deep below the earth's surface—where cosmic rays can't affect their outcome. The laboratory plans to conduct experiments in the areas of particle physics, astrophysics, biology, geosciences, and engineering.

The town of Lead has an alpine feel to it, with houses carved into the hills and the streets built on precariously steep inclines. It's hard to imagine driving these streets in winter without visualizing cars sliding out of control down perilous slopes and through intersections. There is little room for expansion here, but lots of room for improvement—and the town may develop into a quaint and historic host for visitors, though it will be years before the Deep Underground Science and Engineering Laboratory will contribute to the economic recovery of Lead. The population of the community is around 3,000 people. It is an optimistic population. Residents are hoping that the science lab and the tourism generated by its sister city, the gambling community of Deadwood, and by the great outdoor recreation in the region will restore the community to financial health.

SIGHTS
◖ Homestake Visitor Center

The Homestake Visitor Center (160 W. Main St., 605/584-3110, www.homestakevisitorcenter. com, Sept.–mid-May daily 8 A.M.–5 P.M., mid-May–Aug. daily 8 A.M.–6 P.M., free) sits on the edge of a huge gouge in the surface of the hillside; known as the "Open Cut," the gouge was created by miners hauling out tons of rock from the Homestake Mine to process into gold. The Homestake Visitor Center features mining artifacts, including cyanide pellets(!), carbide hats, old helmets, and air packs. A free informational video on mining plays on demand and there is a nice display of the rocks and minerals of the region. Gold panning is offered on the observation deck and a small gift shop is on-site.

The most popular offering of the center is the one-hour guided tour (May–Sept., adult

hoist for the mine shaft elevator at Homestake Visitor Center

LOOKING FOR GOLD

The Homestake Mine, the biggest and longest-lasting gold mine in the United States, closed in 2002 after pulling and processing over 39.8 million ounces of gold from the ground. It's not likely that a mine of that sort will ever be found again, but there is gold in the hills, and considering current prices, it might be fun to go looking for it. At the very least, it would certainly be a different way to approach a weekend creek-side picnic in the hills.

The Black Hills National Forests are open to prospecting for gold. Begin your initial foray by spending a day panning or sluicing (using specially designed boxes that channel water over gravel to separate out the lighter materials from the denser gold). No permit is required for this as long as only hand tools and no motorized equipment is used. Remember to check in with the local forest service office for maps to avoid trespassing on private property, claim jumping, or panning in wilderness areas where it may not be allowed. They might even volunteer some hot location tips!

There are several places to learn how to pan for gold in the hills. In the Northern Hills, be sure to look to the Black Hills Mining Museum for instruction. You can buy a starter kit there, or check with local rock shops. Another local source of information is the **Black Hills Prospector's Club** (www.blackhillsprospectors.com). Check some of the South Dakota forums on www.treasurenet.com, too. Even if you never go searching for gold, they are fun to read. On a national level, the Gold Prospectors Association of America (www.goldprospectors.org) sells starter kits, as well.

On July 6, 2010, a nugget was found "within 20 miles of Rapid City." It weighed 5.27 ounces. It was named the "Icebox Nugget." It was the first time a nugget that size had been found in over 120 years. But it was found – and you might be the next lucky gold prospector. Grab a pan, find a mule, and head for the hills!

$7.50, student $6.50) of Lead and of the surface operations of the Homestake Mine. The tour starts at the Open Cut behind the center, where a presentation about the open mine is given. After the presentation, the group boards a trolley. As the trolley travels through town, the guide provides information about the historic buildings, the history of the town, and the geology of the region. A stop at the Yates Hoisting Room and at the surface area of the mine inspires a discussion of mining processes, including the hoisting, crushing, and milling of the ore. There is always something to be learned from a tour of this sort. Two items of note struck me: When looking at the Open Cut, there are several small round holes in the side of the cut, visible from the visitor center deck. We discovered that those tiny round holes were actually exposed mine shafts, eight feet high by eight feet wide. This adds a great deal of perspective to the actual size of this gouge in the side of the mountain. Another interesting fact is that Mary Baker Eddy, one of the founders of Christian Science, lived in Lead.

It's a fascinating history as the scope of the Homestake Mine is revealed. During 1875–2001, the mine reached depths of more than 8,000 feet below the town and pulled 39.65 million ounces of gold out of the hills. By comparison, the entire Black Hills region in that period produced a total of 46.5 million ounces of gold.

The tour also covers the problem of subsidence in Lead. At one time, there was so much excavation under the town that parts of the community began to sink into the earth as old mine shafts collapsed. The entire eastern portion of the town moved west as parts of the community started to sink as much as 35 feet.

Black Hills Mining Museum
The Black Hills Mining Museum (323 W.

Main St., 605/584-1605, www.mining-museum.blackhills.com, May–Sept. daily 9 A.M.–4 P.M., winter hours vary, adult $6.50, student and senior $5.50, child under 5 free) was established to preserve the mining heritage of the Black Hills. The upstairs area of the museum contains a collection of old photographs, maps, displays of equipment, and informational exhibits of mining techniques. The museum also has a mining document archive of mining records from 1876–1940. Gold panning instruction ($8 per gold pan) is also provided upstairs. Elect to try your hand at gold panning here and the discovery of some placer gold is guaranteed. A small theater presents a 20-minute mining video on request.

Tours (included with museum admission fee) run every hour beginning at 9 A.M.; the last tour starts at 3 P.M. The tour begins as visitors take 17 steps down into the lower levels of the building. The building disappears into a simulated underground mine, where the equipment used to dynamite and mine the rock is explained. Participants wear mining lights and hard hats as they descend into the mining environment. The 45-minute guided tour is an education in the evolution of mining technology, from the earliest days of mining in the 1870s to the present. The underground mine was created by 140 miners working together to provide an accurate rendition of the environment of a mining operation. The information is fascinating. Did you know that the temperature of a mine goes up about 15 degrees every 150 feet down and that the temperature at the lowest levels of the Homestake Mine was 138°F? The very knowledgeable guides here add to the experience.

Homestake Opera House

The Homestake Opera House (313 W. Main St., 605/584-2067, www.leadoperahouse.org, guided tours by reservation only $5 per person) is a work in progress. The opera house's construction was orchestrated by Phoebe Hearst, the widow of mining magnate George Hearst. Built in 1914 as a gift to the city, the complex included the opera house and an attached recreation center. The opera house was called the "Jewel of the Black Hills" and no expense was spared in building the beautiful hall. The 1,016-seat opera house had eight private boxes and a balcony in addition to the floor seating. The box seats were high-backed chairs upholstered in black leather. The floor seating featured mahogany wood upholstered in dark green velvet. Hand stenciling and hand-painted murals decorated the ceilings, ornate plaster columns adorned the walls, and glass chandeliers hung from the ceilings. The recreation facility included a bowling alley, swimming pool, library, and billiards room.

For 70 years, the opera house served as the community center. Everything from vaudeville shows and silent movies to musical concerts and boxing competitions was presented. In 1984, fire struck and severely damaged the building, caving in the roof. The town voted to save the structure, but it sat empty for 20 years until serious restoration began in 2004. Today, visitors are free to visit the building and see the restoration in process. In the summertime, the Homestake Opera House sponsors a series of "Concerts in the Courtyard." In addition, the opera house hosts several community theater productions by the Gold Camp Players, which are held in-house. In 2012, productions ran from March–November and included *Five Women Wearing the Same Dress, Some Enchanted Evening: The Songs of Rogers & Hammerstein,* and *Steel Magnolias,* among others.

RECREATION
Horseback Riding

One of the best horseback riding locations in the hills is **Andy's Trail Rides** (11186 Deer Mountain Rd., 605/645-2211, www.andys-trailrides.com, custom trail rides $20 per person per hour for four or more riders, $30 per

There are hundreds of miles of snowmobile trails in the Northern Hills.

© WWW.TRAVELSD.COM

Mountain Biking

The **George S. Mickelson Trail** is a 109-mile biking, hiking, and horseback riding trail that was once a "Rails to Trails" project. The trail travels between Deadwood in the north and Edgemont in the south. There is a daily usage fee of $3, or an annual fee of $15 to use the trail, payable by drop-off envelope at any trailhead. There are three trailheads near Lead. The **Kirk Trailhead** is located a half-mile south of Lead on Highway 85; the **Lead Trailhead** is a 0.8-mile spur that starts in town off of Hearst Avenue (across from the high school); and the **Sugarloaf Trailhead** is one mile southwest of Lead on Highway 85. All of the trailheads are well marked and the paths are packed gravel, great for mountain bikes.

There are no bike rental locations in the Northern Hills, so bring bikes with you or plan on renting bikes in Hill City (Mickelson Trail Adventures, 605/574-4094, or Rabbit Bike, 605/574-4302).

hour per person for fewer than four riders, call for reservations), where Andy and his staff go out of their way to make your ride a personal experience and a memory to savor. Generally speaking, the rides are arranged for just your family and friends. This is not a nose-to-tail kind of outfit. Rides may take in the vistas of Terry Peak, or follow the historic railroad beds. Arrange for a breakfast ride to the Cheyenne Crossing Restaurant or a sunset honeymoon ride by the creek. If you're comfortable on the horse, feel free to trot or gallop. The pace is not fixed. In one case, a couple of families traveling together designed their own trip. They all rode to Spearfish Creek carrying fishing poles. The men were dropped off and the women continued to ride. On the way back, they stopped to gather up the men and everyone had a great day. That is what a custom ride is all about. Weather permitting, rides are available year-round, including sleigh rides in the winter time.

Snowmobiling

There are more than 350 miles of groomed trails dedicated to snowmobiles in the Northern Hills. Snow season generally runs mid-December–March. Three trails (Trail #7, Trail #5, and Trail #4) are easily accessible from Lead. From Lead, drive four miles southwest on U.S. 85 to Rochford Road. Take a left onto Rochford Road and continue on for half a mile. The parking lot for Trail #5 will be on your right. Continue south on Rochford Road for another five and a half miles and you'll be at the Dumont Parking lot at the trailhead for Trail #7. The parking lot for Trail #4 is in Spearfish Canyon, just west of the Spearfish Canyon Lodge at Savoy.

Snowmobiles can be rented at **Mad Mountain Adventures** (five miles south of Lead on Hwy. 385, 605/578-1878, www.madmountainadventures.com, $100–160) or in Spearfish Canyon at the Spearfish Canyon Lodge.

THE NORTHERN HILLS

Snow Skiing

TERRY PEAK

South Dakota is not the first place you'd think of when you think snow skiing, but there can be some fine skiing in the Northern Hills. **Terry Peak Ski Area** (21120 Stewart Slope Rd., Lead, 605/584-2165 or 605/342-7609, snowline 800/456-0524, www.terrypeak.com, lift tickets adult $47 full-day, $40 half-day, child aged 6–12 $35 full-day, $30 half-day) has five lifts and over 30 trails for skiers and snowboarders that range in difficulty from green-marked beginner trails to black diamond expert trails. Elevations around the ski area range 5,900–7,000 feet, and this region gets more snow than any other in the Black Hills. In addition, 60 percent of the mountain is maintained with snowmaking equipment when Mother Nature disappoints.

All equipment needed to ski or snowboard is available at the rental shop, including helmets, boots, poles, snowboards, and skis. Lessons are also available for every level of experience on either the snowboard or on skis. Opening day is tentatively scheduled every year for the day after Thanksgiving.

The ski area also sports two day lodges where tired and hungry skiers can come inside for food and drink.

SKI MYSTIC

Located between Lead and the Spearfish Canyon Scenic Byway, the **Ski Mystic Resort** off of U.S. 14 (11187 Deer Mountain Rd., 605/580-1169, www.skimystic.com, lift tickets adult $38 full-day, $25 half-day, child $30 full-day, $20 half-day, Zero Gravity Tubing $41 all day) is located on the 6,850-foot Deer Mountain. Founded in 1968, the resort offers a triple chairlift and a tow rope to skiing and snowboarding enthusiasts. The mountain has over 40 trails available. In addition to the standard ski trails, the resort offers "Zero Gravity Tubing," an area set aside specifically for sliding down a hill especially landscaped for riding in a tube. (The price of the tubing ticket includes the tube.) Andy's Trail Rides, which provides superb horseback riding in the summer, is available in the winter for sleigh rides.

Ski lessons and equipment rentals are offered at the resort. The facility also provides a lodge complete with a fireplace, café, and pub, and free wireless.

ACCOMMODATIONS
$50-100

There are 13 attractive rooms to choose from at the ◖ **Dakota Spur Hotel** (509 W. Main St., 605/571-1011, www.dakotaspurhotel.com, $50 weeknights, $75 weekends). The rooms are light and most offer full or queen size beds with attractive, light pine bedsteads. The feel is a combination of contemporary and country style. There is an outdoor patio and a downstairs lounge area which includes a pool table, a foosball game, a video game, a long bar and counter for sitting or eating at, and a small stage. Guests are welcome to use the microwave, coffeemakers, refrigerator, and toaster located there, as well. There is free Wi-Fi in all of the rooms. Pets are not allowed, and the rooms are smoke free. There is off street parking and a couple of the rooms have Jacuzzis!

The **Main Street Manor Hostel** (515 W. Main St., 605/717-2044, www.mainstreet-manorhostel.com, Memorial Day–Labor Day $25 per person, Labor Day–Memorial Day $15–20 per person, closed in Dec.–Jan.) has to be one of the best deals in the hills, and one of the more attractive properties, although the rooms are not particularly suited to couples. There are four rooms with twin beds and one room with bunk beds, and there is Wi-Fi access, a shared bath, and a common room with cable television access. Family-owned and -operated, the hostel is decorated in "French chateau" style. It is in walking distance to local attractions and dining in downtown Lead.

The **White Tail Court Motel** (11295 U.S. 14A, 605/584-9085, www.blackhills.com/ whitetailcourt, summer $65–99, winter $45–99) is located two miles west of Lead on U.S. 14A/Highway 85. There are seven cabins, some with kitchen units. The rooms aren't fancy, but they are clean and spacious, and free wireless Internet is available. There are a couple of hot tubs available to guests, as well as picnic tables and grills. The property is really pretty, with lots of trees and a babbling brook, and has a great location for outdoor recreation enthusiasts. A shower house is provided for tenting/RV guests (sites are $15–29) and picnic tables are located throughout the property. The motel is located on White Tail Creek and at the base of Trail #5W, a snowmobile-only trail. In the wintertime, the motel provides fuel and oil for snowmobilers, as well as a heated garage for repairs.

A more traditional style of lodging can be found at the **Days Inn Lead** (900 Miners Ave., 605/584-1800, www. daysinn.com, summer $89–99, winter $49–59). The Days Inn sports fairly standard chain hotel–style rooms, but the service here seems a cut above. The hotel has 100 rooms available and has a bar and restaurant, the **Copper Mountain Grill** (dinner 4–9 P.M. weeknights, open until 11 P.M. on weekends, $9–12, bar 4–11 P.M. weeknights, open until 2 A.M. on weekends), on-site. There is free wireless in the rooms, a continental breakfast, and pets are allowed for an additional nonrefundable $10 per night per pet. The hotel offers a shuttle service to Deadwood for $6 per person on weekends. During the week, it has arrangements with Dakota Taxi for $4 per person. There is also direct access to the Mickelson Trail from the hotel grounds.

$100-150

Cheyenne Crossing (21415 U.S. 14A, 605/584-3510, www.cheyennecrossing.org, $95–135) is located at the southern edge of the Spearfish Canyon Scenic Byway. A three-bedroom, one-bath, pine-paneled apartment is located over the restaurant and is available for nightly rental. Guests can elect to use one, two, or three bedrooms; the rate varies based on the number of rooms used. This is not set up like a bed-and-breakfast, as the apartment is available for just one guest/family at a time. It's a nice alternative for large parties traveling together. It's a great location for sports enthusiasts wanting close access to Spearfish Canyon and those seeking great dining. (The downstairs restaurant serves one of the best breakfasts in the region, and great lunches and dinners, too.)

FOOD

For the best burgers in town, go to **Lewie's Saloon & Eatery** (711 S. Main St., 605/584-1324, daily 11 A.M.–11 P.M., $7), located just south of Lead on Highway 85. A rustic bar, Lewie's is decorated with antiques, old motorcycles, old signs, and all kinds of interesting artifacts hanging from the walls and rafters, and sitting on shelves. The place is famous for the burgers and beer, and also for having (at last count) 38 televisions for all of the sports enthusiasts in the neighborhood. Lewie's is also popular locally as the host site of a trivia competition held on Friday nights during the winter months (Oct.–early spring). The long-running competition has been held at various venues in Lead over the years; Lewie's has been hosting the games since 2005. Watch the local teams (Uncivil Servants, Bumper Car Cowboys, and Alcohol Was Involved, among others) compete or chime in! Finally, wireless Internet service is also provided to customers.

Food and theater go together at the **Black Hills Round House Restaurant** (106 Glendale Dr., 605/722-1901, www.blackhillsroundhouse.com, summer Sun.–Thur. 11 A.M.–8 P.M., Fri.–Sat. 11 A.M.–9 P.M., winter Tues.–Sat. 11 A.M.–8 P.M., lunch $10–15, five course fixed menu dinner $35, a la carte $25). Meals are served in a train environment, where you may be waited on by a conductor, a wandering hobo, or waiters dressed in Victorian attire. If you sit in the right train seat, you may see scenery passing by your window as you dine. Lunch includes a wide variety of salad, sandwich, and pasta selections. Dinner guests have the option of selecting a fixed price, five course gourmet meal, or ordering a la carte. Menu items include swordfish, buffalo dishes, walleye, and seafood. One of the more unusual items is a rattlesnake and rabbit sausage, which can be served with pasta or with potatoes.

Pizza lovers will be happy to find **Pizza Lab** (124 U.S. 14A, 605/578-9933, www.thepizza-lab.com, Sun.–Thur. 11 A.M.–9 P.M. Fri.–Sat. 11 A.M.–10 P.M., $8–18 depending on pizza size and toppings, lunch buffet daily 11 A.M.–2 P.M., $8), which not only has all of the standard pizzas available but also offers some interesting specialty combinations. There are vegetarian pizzas, a thai chicken pizza with peanut sauce, clam and tomato pizzas, and a barbeque chicken club pizza. The restaurant has a full bar and seating is available for up to 150 people. Pizza Lab will deliver, or you can call ahead and carry out. Dessert comes in the form of 17 different flavors of hand-scooped hard ice cream. If that isn't enough, there are a couple of pool tables on hand ($0.75 per game) and a wall full of arcade games.

The **Stampmill Restaurant & Saloon** (305 W. Main St., 605/584-1984, www.thestamp-mill.com, Mon.–Sat. 11 A.M.–9 P.M., Sun. 11 A.M.–3 P.M., lunch $8, dinner $13–15) is located near downtown and is housed in an 1897 historic sandstone building that was originally a boardinghouse. The inside is brick and light wood, and in the winter, there's a roaring fire. Everything served is made from scratch, and the beef is from nearby Harding County. Dine inside or outside on the patio in the summertime. The owners are originally from Louisiana, though they've been out West for more than 20 years. The menu features sandwiches, soups, and salads for lunch. Dinner entrées include steaks, fish and chips, several pasta dishes, and the specialty of the house, jambalaya.

INFORMATION AND SERVICES

The **Lead Chamber of Commerce** (605/584-1100 or 877/428-5590, www.leadmethere.org) is located at 160 West Main Street and is open Monday–Friday 9 A.M.–5 P.M. The main **post office** is located at 329 West Main Street. Groceries can be found at **Lynn's Dakota Mart** (145 Glendale Dr., 605/584-2905). The taxi service in town is **Dakota Taxi** (605/920-2020); for about $7 one-way, you can be dropped off in Deadwood. The taxi service also serves Spearfish and most other locations in the hills, and includes shuttle service to the Rapid City airport.

Deadwood

Gold was first discovered in the Black Hills in the city of Custer in 1874 by two members of the Custer expedition. As prospectors flocked to the region, gold was discovered all over the hills, but the richest claims and longest-running mines resided in Deadwood and its sister city of Lead, just three miles away. Life was wild in all of the gold camps, but Deadwood managed to attract the most colorful characters, including James Butler "Wild Bill" Hickok and Calamity Jane.

It's hard to tell how much of Wild Bill Hickok's past was hype and how much true, but by the time he reached Deadwood in 1876, his reputation as a gambler, womanizer, and gunfighter preceded him. Just 39 years old at the time, he was already suffering from too much time spent in saloons. He continued that pattern in Deadwood. Most of his time there was spent drinking and gambling. The story is told that one day a man named Jack

McCall, playing poker at Wild Bill Hickok's table, lost a lot of money. It is said that Hickok gave him back enough to get something to eat and warned him against gambling if he didn't have enough to cover his losses. The next day, Wild Bill Hickok was playing poker at the same table, with his back to the door, a seat he would rarely agree to accept. Jack McCall, drinking heavily at the bar, came up behind him and shot Hickok in the back of the head. As he died, Wild Bill Hickok spilled his poker hand on the table—a pair of aces and a pair of eights—a hand that has since that day been called the "dead man's hand."

Calamity Jane, born Martha Canary in Missouri in 1862, was another famous character that made her way to Deadwood. After both her parents died within a year of each other, Calamity Jane found herself, at the age of 15, the head of a household that included five younger siblings. To support the family, Calamity Jane took whatever work

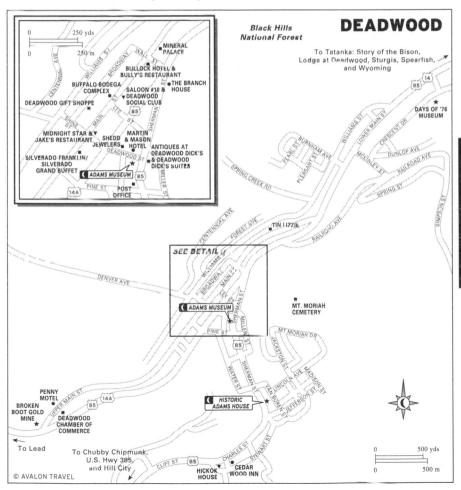

© WWW.TRAVELSD.COM

Days of '76 Rodeo

she could find, including cook, nurse, dance hall girl, waitress, ox-team driver, and prostitute. In 1870, she joined Lieutenant George Armstrong Custer as a scout; this is when she first began dressing as a man, a habit she maintained throughout her life. By the time she joined Custer, she was known as a fearless rider and formidable markswoman. Calamity Jane stayed with the western cavalry, fighting Native Americans for several years.

In 1876, Calamity Jane was ordered to the Black Hills with General Crook. Once there, she became severely ill and spent two weeks in the hospital at Fort Fetterman. After her recovery, she headed to Laramie, Wyoming, and met up with Charles Utter's wagon train headed to Deadwood. With Utter was Wild Bill Hickok. Both heavy drinkers and both prone to great exaggeration, it seems Calamity Jane and Hickok hit it off. While there are stories that they were romantically linked, there are also stories that this was just wishful

thinking on the part of Calamity Jane. At any rate, she joined the wagon train on its trip to Deadwood. Calamity Jane took a job with the Pony Express when she arrived, delivering mail between Custer and Deadwood.

At the age of 52, Calamity Jane died a natural death—at least as "natural" as a death that is caused by the ravages of alcohol can be. This fearless rider, champion cusser, deadly shot of a woman was another character of the West loved by dime store novelists. As she died, she had one last request—to be buried next to Wild Bill Hickok. And so she was. She got her wish. Both Wild Bill Hickok and Calamity Jane are buried in Mount Moriah Cemetery in Deadwood.

To this day, Deadwood remains one of the edgiest and dynamic towns in the hills. The entire town was designated a National Historic Landmark in 1976, yet it wasn't until 1980 that the last four brothels in town were closed. Refusing to be tamed, small stakes gambling was legalized in 1989 and the stakes were upped in 2000.

Deadwood Gulch is a fairly narrow canyon and most of the town is squeezed in along just a few main streets. In 1879, fire (the plague of many a rickety wooden mining community) roared through the narrow gorge and destroyed 300 buildings in an area just 0.5 mile by 0.25 mile. Over 2,000 people were left homeless. The town was quickly rebuilt upon the ashes, but this time, most of the buildings were of solid brick and sandstone construction. The historic district of the town looks much as it did after the fire, as most of the existing buildings trace their construction to post-fire rebuilding. Today, Deadwood is a center for historic reenactments (including the daily shooting of Wild Bill Hickok), fine dining, rodeos, special events, and gambling.

SIGHTS
◖ Adams Museum
William Emery Adams was born in 1854 and moved to Deadwood at the age of 23 with his

the Historic Adams House

brother. Like most, Adams went looking for gold, but eventually teamed up with his brother to run the Banner grocery store. The store was destroyed, along with 299 other buildings in a fire in 1879. Undaunted, Adams and his brother rebuilt, and Adams remained a successful businessman, serving as mayor for several terms over the course of his residency in Deadwood. Convinced that a museum was necessary to preserve Deadwood's past, Adams donated over $75,000 to construct the Adams Museum (54 Sherman St., 605/578-1714, www.adamsmuseumandhouse.org, May–Sept. daily 9 A.M.–5 P.M., Apr. and Oct. Mon.–Sat. 9 A.M.–5 P.M., closed Sun., Nov.–Mar. Tues.–Sat. 10 A.M.–4 P.M., closed Sun.–Mon., suggested donation: adult $5, child $2) in honor of his first wife and two daughters.

W. E. Adams married Alice Burnham, from the nearby community of Fountain City, in 1880. Their daughter Lucile was born in 1884, and daughter Helen followed in 1892. Lucile died of typhoid in 1912. In 1925, Alice went to Pasadena, California, to assist Helen, who was about to give birth to their first grandchild. Alice, who had recently been diagnosed with cancer, died unexpectedly while she was there. Distraught, Helen went into early labor and died the next day. The baby lived only a few hours. In the course of just 48 hours, W. E. Adams lost his entire family. He was grief-stricken.

Adams was to find happiness again, however. In 1927, he married his second wife, Mary Mastrovich Vicich. He was 73, and she was just 29. It was also in 1927 that a group of businesspeople decided that a museum was needed to preserve the history of Deadwood. It was Mary who encouraged Adams to contribute to the project in honor of his first wife and his daughters. The Adams Museum was completed in 1930, and is considered to be the oldest museum in the Black Hills.

The museum has three floors of pioneer, mining, and Lakota artifacts; artwork; old

THE THOEN STONE

In 1887, brothers Louis and Ivan Thoen were hauling building stone from the base of a mountain near Spearfish when they found a sandstone slab inscribed with a message. On one side of the stone was carved:

Came to these hills in 1833
seven of us
DeLacompt
Ezra Kind
G. W. Wood
T. Brown
R. Kent
Wm. King
Indian Crow
all dead but me Ezra Kind
killed by Ind beyond the high hill got our gold June 1834

On the reverse:

Got all the gold we could carry

our ponies all got by Indians
I have lost my gun and nothing to eat
and Indians hunting me.

There is no controversy surrounding the idea that gold might have been found by someone before Custer announced its discovery in 1874. But the stone's authenticity is questionable. After all, if you were weaponless, hungry, and being hunted, would you stop and carve a relatively long message into stone? And the men who found the carved message were, coincidentally, stone workers, who very well might think about inscribing a message in stone.

Researchers have been trying to determine if the Thoen Stone is a hoax or if it is real ever since its discovery. To date, research has determined that many of the men named on the stone did, in fact, head West in the 1830s and were never heard from again. And, apparently, it is possible to carve wet sandstone fairly easily with just a knife. So, perhaps this was the equivalent of a desperate miner's last words. Or...perhaps not. See the stone at the Adams Museum in Deadwood and decide for yourself.

photos; maps; and cultural items outlining Deadwood's wild and diverse history. There are also artifacts left by some of the local town characters. Look for Wild Bill Hickok's gun collection, and N. C. Wyeth pencil sketches of Hickok. A highlight on the main floor of the museum is the first steam train ever used in the Black Hills. Weighing in at about five tons, it makes for an impressive display. The controversial Thoen Stone (is it real or a hoax?) is also on display at the museum.

◀ Historic Adams House

Sister site to the Adams Museum, the Historic Adams House (22 Van Buren Ave., 605/578-3724, www.adamsmuseumandhouse.org, May–Sept. daily 9 A.M.–5 P.M., Apr. and Oct. Mon.–Sat. 9 A.M.–5 P.M., closed Nov.–Mar.,

adult $7, child $2) is shown by guided tour only. The house was built in 1892 and is one of the finest examples of a Queen Anne–style Victorian home in Deadwood. W. E. Adams bought the house in 1920 with his first wife, Alice. It was closed in 1936 by his second wife, Mary Mastrovich Vicich, after W. E. Adams died in 1934 at the age of 80. Mary closed up the house, contents intact, and never lived in the house again. She moved to California, but returned frequently to supervise the activities of the Homestake Mining Company, a company in which she now held controlling interest. When she returned to town, she stayed in local hotels. For 50 years, the house remained empty and fully stocked. For a brief period, 1987–1992, the house was opened and used as a bed-and-breakfast. The proprietors,

gravestone of "Wild Bill" Hickok in Mount Moriah Cemetery

© WWW.TRAVELSD.COM

understanding the historical importance of the contents of the house, carefully stored everything in the attic. In 1992, the house was sold to the city for preservation.

The house was opened to the public in 2000 after careful restoration. Today, guided tours (every half-hour June–Aug., hourly May and Sept.) give visitors a peek into the wealthier side of Deadwood's early days. Imagine entering a home where virtually nothing has changed since the late 1920s, the style in which the home was decorated. The original silverware, found in a safe, is on display, as are all of the furnishings, knick-knacks, artwork, and other personal possessions of Mary and W. E. Adams, all relatively undisturbed to this day. It's a fully authentic walk through another era.

Mount Moriah Cemetery

While W. E. Adams represented the more refined side of Deadwood, a large part of the town's historic appeal can be attributed to the shady characters that were drawn there. The Mount Moriah Cemetery (10 Mount Moriah Dr., 605/722-0837, daily, requested donation: adult $1, child $0.50) on the hillside above Sherman Street in the southeast corner of town is the resting site of many of Deadwood's famous and infamous characters. During the summer, admission is collected at a ticket booth on-site. A brochure of the layout of the cemetery is provided to visitors. It is possible to access the cemetery after hours. A donation box is set up near the entry gate for contributions to be made on the honor system.

James Butler "Wild Bill" Hickok and Calamity Jane are two of the famous residents of the cemetery. Mount Moriah is actually the second resting spot for Wild Bill Hickok. Originally interred in the Whitewood Gulch Cemetery, he was moved to Mount Moriah, with the rest of the Whitewood Gulch inhabitants, when the town fathers decided that the relatively flat land of Whitewood was better suited for building than for graves.

It is actually quite pretty in the cemetery. A short walk to the top of the hill provides nice views of Deadwood and is a great spot for photographs.

Days of '76 Museum

The Days of '76 Museum (18 76 Dr., 605/578-1657, www.daysof76museum.com, May–Sept. daily 9 A.M.–5 P.M., Apr. and Oct. Mon.–Sat. 9 A.M.–5 P.M., Nov.–Mar. Tues.–Sat. 9 A.M.–5 P.M., adult $7, child $4) is an offshoot of the Days of '76 Rodeo and Parade that started in 1923 to honor the memory of the wild days of the gold rush, and the founding of Deadwood in 1876. The museum started out housing many of the horseless vehicles that were in the original rodeo parade, including one of the original Deadwood Stages, and has continued to add to that collection. Photographs and artifacts from more than 80 years of the Days of '76 Rodeo comprise another of the museum's major collections. The crown jewel of the museum's displays, however, is the Clowser collection. Don Clowser first came to Deadwood in 1926 when he was just 12 years old. Clowser became an avid collector of historic artifacts and Native American art, and eventually ran the Deadwood Trading Post. His personal collection included thousands of pioneer, mining, and Native American artifacts. A member of the Days of '76 committee for 35 years, Clowser asked if the organization would be interested in housing his collection. The response was an enthusiastic yes. Some of the artifacts are priceless and some are just interesting, but all of them contribute to the preservation of the history and culture of the region.

Tatanka: Story of the Bison

Tatanka: Story of the Bison (Hwy. 85, one mile north of Deadwood, 605/584-5678, www.storyofthebison.com, open seasonally, May 15–Sept. 30 daily 9 A.M.–5 P.M., adult $7.50, child $5.50) is a facility dedicated to the history of the bison and the native culture built around it. The facility includes a dramatic sculpture by local artist Peggy Detmers of 14 life-sized bison pursued by three Native Americans on horseback, an interactive interpretive center, a gift shop featuring the arts and crafts of Native American and regional artists, and a snack bar. Start a visit at the center by viewing the 20-minute DVD that runs throughout the day in a small theater; it covers the creation of the sculpture and the mission of the center. Created by actor Kevin Costner to serve as an education center, the Tatanka story is an interesting approach to learning about the culture and social history of a people. On the simplest level, just about everything you'd ever want to know about the bison is explained. Beyond that, interpreters and displays demonstrate how native culture depended on the bison for food, clothing, and housing, and how the near extinction of the bison affected the Native American

people. Artifacts including tipis, sinew, and clothing are displayed to support the discussion, and Native American interpreters are on hand to answer any questions.

Broken Boot Gold Mine

It wouldn't be right to visit a famous gold mining town without visiting an old gold mine. The Broken Boot Gold Mine (Upper Main St., U.S. 14A, 605/578-1876, www.brokenbootgoldmine.com, open seasonally, mid-May–mid-Sept. daily 8 A.M.–6 P.M., adult $5, senior $4.50, child $3), established in 1878, was a mine that made its owners more money selling fools gold than the real thing, but about 15,000 ounces of gold were extracted from what was originally known as Seim's Mine. Tours leave every 30 minutes and take about 30 minutes. The guides are knowledgeable and demonstrate how some of the mining equipment, including dynamite, is used in the mine. The history of the Broken Boot Gold Mine is presented, as is a general history of mining in the Deadwood area. At the end of the tour, participants can pan for gold ($7 per person). Every visitor receives a replica of a stock certificate in the mine at the completion of the tour as a souvenir.

TOURS

To get an overview of the sites in Deadwood, hop the **Deadwood Trolley** (102 Sherman St., 605/578-2622, Sun.–Thurs. 7 A.M.–1:30 A.M., Fri.–Sat. 7 A.M.–3 A.M., winter Sun.–Thurs. 8 A.M.–midnight, Fri.–Sat. 7 A.M.–3 A.M.). It's just $1 per ride and stops by most of the main attractions in the community. See what looks interesting to you and then plan your own walking tour. The trolley stops at most every street corner and can be boarded or left at any location. The trolley runs 365 days per year. during the week, only two trolleys run, while Friday–Saturday, three trolleys circle the town, and run late into the night (until midnight Friday, and until 3 A.M. Saturday!).

There are several in-town tour companies that provide narrated tours through town. **Boot Hill Tours** (662 Main St., 605/578-3758, www.boothilltours.com, June–Oct., adult $8, child $4) offers one-hour tours. It's owned by two local historians and is endorsed by the Lawrence County Historical Society. Five tours are scheduled daily (9:30 and 11 A.M.; 1, 3, and 5 P.M.) as long weather permits.

Kevin Costner's **Original Deadwood Tour** (677 Main St., 605/578-2091, www.originaldeadwoodtour.com, daily May–mid-Oct., adult $9, child $5) provides a one-hour guided tour of the history of the town and its major characters. There are four tours daily (10:30 and 11:30 A.M., 1:30 and 3:30 P.M.). Obtain tickets and board in front of the Midnight Star casino. Admission to Mount Moriah Cemetery is included in the tour fee.

GAMING

In 1989, small stakes gambling was legalized in Deadwood and revitalized the entire region. With over 80 gaming establishments in town, most of which are side by side on the two central streets of town, there are plenty of casinos to choose from. Gambling was initially limited to very small stakes with a $5 bet limit in 1989. That was increased to $100 in 2000, and in 2012, the bet limit was increased to $1,000. Games offered include slot machines, blackjack, and poker. Many of the casinos are also hotel and dining establishments with very reasonable prices. Smoking was recently banned in Deadwood, though smoking right outside the buildings is still allowed. It does clean up the air inside, though. The entire town is on the National Register of Historic Places, and feels much as it did in the late 1800s with, of course, the addition of a lot of flashing lights.

The **Midnight Star** (677 Main St., 605/578-1555 or 800/999-6482, www.themidnightstar.com, Sun.–Thurs. 8 A.M.–1 A.M., Fri.–Sat. 8 A.M.–2 A.M.) is a casino with strong Hollywood ties. Actor Kevin Costner has a stake in the establishment. Costner filmed *Dances with Wolves* in the Northern Hills and enjoyed the experience enough to invest in several businesses here. At the Midnight Star, the decor is elegant, with plenty of etched glass and polished brass, and the walls are lined with memorabilia from several of Costner's movies. Look for the 10-foot-tall "Pharaoh's Gold" machine. The payout on one pull of the handle could be $50,000.

Voted the best casino in Deadwood by local area residents, **The Lodge at Deadwood** (100 Pine Crest Rd., 605/584-4800 or 877/393-5634, www.deadwoodlodge.com, 24 hours daily) is an elegant facility located about three-quarters of a mile from the downtown district. Nestled into the side of Mount Roosevelt, the lodge is best described as classy. Lots of natural stone, tile, and wood highlight all areas of the facility. The casino floor is spacious, with plenty of elbow room for gamblers. Over 300 games are available, including blackjack and poker.

The **Mineral Palace** (601 Main St., 605/578-2036 or 800/847-2522, www.mineralpalace.com, 24 hours daily), with over 350 slot machines, blackjack, three card poker, and double-deck blackjack are the featured table games. The property also has a restaurant and a 75-room hotel.

With less glitz but plenty of games, the **Tin Lizzie** (555 Main St., 605/578-1715 or 800/643-4490, www.tinlizzie.com, 24 hours daily) is a favorite of locals. When asked what makes it a local hangout, the most common response is "great people." There are plenty of state-of-the-art slot machines and live blackjack games. The owners are well-known, active community members.

A favorite of gamblers is the **Silverado-Franklin** (709 Main St., 605/578-3670 or 800/584-7005, www.silveradofranklin.com, 24 hours daily), the largest casino on Main Street. The building doesn't have the historic background of some of its neighbors, but it was built in 1933 by businessman W. E. Adams to house Hills Chevrolet. It was purchased and renovated by Silverado after the legalization of gambling. It's almost as famous for its crab and prime rib buffet as for its large table gaming and poker rooms.

The **Buffalo Bodega Complex** (658 Main St., 605/578-1162, www.buffalobodega.com, daily 9 A.M.–2 A.M., steakhouse daily 11 A.M.–10 P.M.) has three casinos. The complex was completely remodeled in 2007. In addition to the casinos, there is a nice lounge, saloon, and restaurant on-site.

ENTERTAINMENT AND EVENTS
◖ Saloon No. 10

Saloon No. 10 (657 Main St., 605/578-3346, www.saloon10.com, daily 8 A.M.–2 A.M.) is an Old West saloon with a great bar and restaurant in addition to its gaming rooms. Billed as the only museum with a bar, the saloon is filled with historic artifacts and bears the name of the place where Wild Bill Hickok was killed while playing poker in 1875. The original Saloon No. 10 burned down in the fire of 1879, and was across the street from the current location—but that doesn't seem to bother anyone, as the new Saloon No. 10 reenacts Wild Bill Hickok's death several times a day during the summer months (Tues.–Sun. 1, 3, 5, and 7 P.M., free).

The downstairs bar is a favorite of the younger crowd, featuring rock and roll most nights of the week. Upstairs, you'll find fine dining at the **Deadwood Social Club** (daily 11 A.M.–10 P.M., $15–25) and cocktails at the quieter **Martini Bar** (summer daily 11 A.M.–midnight, winter Sun.–Thurs. 11 A.M.–9 P.M., Fri.–Sat. 11 A.M.–10 P.M.).

Nightlife

The **Deadwood Mountain Grand** (1906 Deadwood Mountain Dr., 605/559-0386 or 877/907-4726, www.deadwoodmountaingrand.com) sports a hotel, casino, restaurant, and a bar and lounge, but the best aspect of this addition to Deadwood nightlife is the event center that the Grand brings to town. With 2,500 seats, the event center is capable of bringing a wide variety of well-known acts to town, including the likes of Willie Nelson, George Jones, and Roy Clark. Something is going on most every night at the Grand.

If you're up for dancing, check out the **Buffalo Steakhouse & Saloon** (658 Main St., 605/578-1162, www.buffalobodega.com, summer Sun.–Thur. 9 A.M.–12:30 A.M. Fri.–Sat. 9 A.M.–1:30 A.M., winter Sun.–Thur. 9 A.M.–11 P.M. Fri.–Sat. 9 A.M.–1:30 A.M.). On Friday and Saturday nights (10 P.M.–1:30 A.M.), you'll find a DJ and a dance floor. It's all about buffalo in this saloon. There are portraits on the wall made out of buffalo nickels and there are some buffalos hanging from the ceiling—rope buffalos, that is, made from over three miles of rope.

Looking for a comfortable, cozy, small bar tucked away from all the casino noise? **Bully's** (Bullock Hotel, 633 Main St., 605/578-1745, www.historicbullock.com, daily 6 A.M.–1:30 A.M./last call) serves a limited breakfast and brunch during the daylight hours, but at night, it turns into a wonderful little bar for having a drink and sharing stories with friends.

Events

Casinos and flashing lights are definitely the draw, but in the summer, the Old West environment keeps both adults and children entertained. There are gunfights in the streets Memorial Day–Labor Day; Wild Bill Hickok is killed several times a day; and Jack McCall, his killer, is tried for his murder almost as often. It's all fun and the historic reenactments add to the Wild West atmosphere of the community.

Everyone loves a good **Gunslinger Shootout** (2 P.M. in front of Four Aces Casino, 531 Main St.; 4 P.M. in front of the Celebrity Hotel, 629 Main St.; 6 P.M. in front of the Franklin Hotel, 709 Main St.; free), especially the kids.

The **Trial of Jack McCall** (Masonic Temple, 715 Main St., Memorial Day–Labor Day 8 P.M., adult $5, child $3) mixes a lot of historical facts with a lot of fun and audience-participation-oriented fiction.

For additional information on the reenactments and the trial, call the Chamber of Commerce (605/578-1876 or 800/999-1876). Something is always going on in Deadwood. One of the best local events is the **Days of '76 Rodeo** that takes place in late July and which was selected by the Professional Rodeo Cowboys Association as the Midsize Rodeo of the year 2004–2008. **Kool Deadwood Nites** is a late-August event that brings classic cars to town. With live concerts of 1950s- and 1960s-era music, street dances, and a classic car parade, it's a popular family-oriented weekend.

SHOPPING

While there are souvenir shops galore in Deadwood (since every casino sells *something*, particularly branded items), there are a few great specialty shops in town that are not casinos. The place to buy Black Hills Gold in Deadwood is at **Shedd Jewelers** (21 Deadwood St., 605/578-2494 or 800/578-2494, www.sheddjewelers.com, daily 8 A.M.–5 P.M.), a family-owned and -operated business since 1950. For South Dakota–made gifts, books, pottery, jewelry, foods, and other prairie-oriented products, stop by the **Deadwood Gift Shoppe** (666 Main St., 605/722-4975, www.deadwoodgiftshoppe.com, summer daily 9 A.M.–9 P.M., winter daily 10 A.M.–6 P.M.). The published mission statement of **Chubby Chipmunk** (420 Cliff St., 605/722-2447, www.chubbychipmunk.net, summer Mon.–Sat. 10 A.M.–6 P.M., Sun. 11 A.M.–5 P.M., winter Mon.–Sat. 10 A.M.–5 P.M., Sun. noon–4 P.M.) is "to provide the most decadent truffles you will ever experience." This is an honorable goal and one worth supporting. All the chocolates are homemade and hand-dipped

in Deadwood by owner and chocolatier Mary "Chip" Tautkus.

The largest shopping venue in Deadwood is **Antiques at Deadwood Dick's** (51–55 Sherman St., 605/578-3224 or 877/882-4990, www.deadwooddicks.com, Memorial Day–Labor Day daily 10 A.M.–9 P.M., winter Mon.–Thur. 10 A.M.–6 P.M., Fri.–Sat. 10 A.M.–10 P.M., Sun. noon–6 P.M.). In addition to 12,000 square feet of antique booths, the facility also houses a bar, restaurant, and lodging. According to the manager, this is one of the few places you can browse and carry a cocktail while you shop.

ACCOMMODATIONS
$50-100

The **Penny Motel** (818 Upper Main St., 605/578-1842 or 877/565-8140, www.pennymotel.com, summer $70–105, winter weekends only $40–76), a family-owned motel with 15 rooms, offers one of the better bargains in Deadwood. Just a couple of blocks away from the busiest sections of Main Street, the rooms are clean and the owners are friendly. Penny, by the way, was the name of the daughter of the original owner of the hotel and was never a reference to the motel's bargain prices. The current owners purchased the motel in early 2008. No pets are allowed. There are some smoking rooms. Some of the rooms have microwaves, coffeemakers, and small refrigerators. Free Wi-Fi is available.

Deadwood Dick's (51 Sherman St., 605/578-3224, www.deadwooddicks.com, summer $80–90, winter $40–60) is just two blocks off of Main Street. Check out the queen rooms and the king room for a great place to stay at a reasonable price in town. The decor leans toward Victorian. The third floor location of the rooms provides great views of either downtown Deadwood or the mountains and forests out back. All of the 10 rooms are spacious and clean, and the owners Mary and Dave are frequently on-site to make sure all is going well for their guests. In addition to lodging, the building, built in the late 1800s by W. E. Adams to serve as his grocery warehouse, has a small saloon and dining room; it advertises itself as the smallest casino in town, with just three slot machines in the bar.

$100-150

Just a few blocks from downtown, the **Cedar Wood Inn** (103 Charles St., 605/578-2725 or 800/841-0127, www.cedarwoodinn.com, summer $99–109, winter $39–69) is a well-maintained property that has been family owned for over 17 years. It is beautifully landscaped, the rooms are large, and each is uniquely decorated. There is no smoking in any of the rooms. Free Wi-Fi is available in all the rooms and a continental breakfast is served in the morning.

The 28-room **(C Bullock Hotel** (633 Main St., 605/578-1745 or 800/336-1876, www.historicbullock.com, summer $120–140), winter $75) was built by the man credited with bringing law and order to Deadwood. Seth Bullock moved to Deadwood one day before Wild Bill Hickok was shot to death. A former lawman, Bullock was appointed sheriff seven months after his arrival. But commerce is what brought him to town and his first endeavor, with his business partner Sol Star, was a hardware store. The building survived the fire of 1879, but wasn't so lucky in 1894, when fire razed the building. Bullock decided to replace the store and aimed to build the finest hotel in Deadwood. In 1895, the Bullock Hotel was built. Today, beautifully restored, it is one of the most photographed locations in town. It is also on the itinerary for folks who like to stay in haunted hotels. Reputedly, Seth Bullock, who died in 1919, still visits the hotel. According to most guests, his ghost is mischievous but friendly. The rooms at the hotel are Victorian in style. Colors are emerald green, red, and gold. All of the furnishings are Victorian replicas. Amenities include free wireless Internet and coffeemakers.

The **(C Branch House** (633 Main St., 605/578-1745 or 800/336-1876, summer $140, winter $75) is another Bullock property; check-in is at the Bullock Hotel. The rooms are very different from the main hotel, however. Decorated with Mission-style furniture and with a brick wall interior, the eight deluxe rooms are cozy, warm, and very comfortable. Downstairs in the basement is a full fitness center. There is parking right next to the hotel and, even though it's only one block off of the main street of town, it's very quiet.

$150 and up

When the **Martin & Mason Hotel** (33 Deadwood St., 605/722-3456, www.martin-masonhotel.com, $180 king) was renovated in 2007, the owners went beyond the ordinary in restoring it to its Victorian splendor. There are eight rooms available for guests. Most of the rooms have king beds, but other configurations are available, as well. All of the rooms have authentic furnishings and decor from the 1890s. It's elegant and all of the rooms' accoutrements are first class, including 100 percent Egyptian cotton sheets, cable TV and wireless internet, and fresh scones and coffee in the morning.

The **(C Lodge at Deadwood** (100 Pine Crest Ln., 605/584-4800 or 877/393-5634, www.deadwoodlodge.com, summer $160–180, winter $99–104) opened in December 2009. The 140-room facility includes the hotel, a sports bar, a restaurant, an indoor water park, and a casino. The hotel has a natural feel, with lots of wood and stone incorporated into the decor. The artwork displayed includes wildlife paintings and scenic photographs of the Black Hills. The rooms are luxurious and spacious, with pillow-top beds, LCD televisions, refrigerators, coffeemakers, and free wireless Internet. Many of the rooms have patios or balconies. There is an outside seating patio for guests, a fitness

STURGIS MOTORCYCLE RALLY

© LAURAL BIDWELL

Some of the biggest bars in the world are set up in Sturgis.

In 1938, nine Sturgis motorcyclists and their families got together for the first Black Hills Motor Classic and camped on a lawn belonging to one of the participants. Today, approximately 400,000-500,000 bikers converge annually on the Black Hills the first full week of August (the first Saturday of the month and the subsequent week), filling every campground, hotel, and motel in the Northern and Central Hills.

Thousands of bikes line the streets of Sturgis. Bikers and nonbikers alike shuffle along the sidewalks admiring paint jobs, leather work, gleaming chrome, and each other. Wild hats, bikinis, leather, and not much else adorn more than a few of the celebrants. Beautiful young women, hired by the large motorcycle companies, stroll by in branded leathers and little else. Tattoos and piercings, food on a stick, rally T-shirts, and beer are the purchases of choice. It's crowded. It's noisy. It's a party. And for the most part, it's a jovial, fun-loving, and friendly crowd.

There are races and poker runs, and daily rides into the hills. Every motorcycle manufacturer in the world is there, from the smallest custom bike creator to Harley-Davidson. At night, there are world-class concerts, and the parties lean toward the raucous. It's the biggest event in South Dakota, doubling the population of the state for about 10 days. Some of the

venues that are synonymous with or unique to Sturgis include the following:

- The **Sturgis Motorcycle Museum** (999 Main St., 605/347-2001, www.sturgismuseum.com, Mon.-Fri. 9 A.M.-5 P.M., Sat. 9 A.M.-4 P.M., Sun. 10 A.M.-4 P.M., $5) has a great collection of vintage motorcycles dating back to the early 1900s and a hall of fame to honor those who have contributed to the sport of motorcycling.

- The **Buffalo Chip Campground** (20622 131st Ave., 605/347-9000, www.buffalochip.com) is a small city unto itself about five miles east of Sturgis. Famous for both its campground and concerts, the Buffalo Chip provides several different on-site dining options, tent camping, RV camping, cabin camping, four shower houses, and plenty of restrooms. Concerts in the past have included acts like Toby Keith, ZZ Top, and George Thorogood and the Destroyers. Weekly passes or daily admissions are available; both include camping and concerts.

- The **Full Throttle Saloon** (12997 Hwy. 34, 605/423-4584, www.fullthrottlesaloon.com) bills itself as the world's largest biker bar. With 100 beautiful and scantily clad female bartenders and 200 other employees on hand for the rally, it may well be true. This huge venue hosts concerts and contests and provides rental cabins on its grounds. It also leans toward an R rating. Where else can you get "hot" models painted to look like your bike?

- **The Knuckle Saloon** (931 1st St., 605/347-0106, www.theknuckle.com) is filled with Sturgis memorabilia and antiques from the town's early days. With the longest bar in town, live music, and poker and pool tournaments, it's the hottest spot downtown.

The best information about the rally, including lodging and schedules of events, can be found at www.sturgismotorcyclerally.com, a website created by the **Sturgis Chamber of Commerce** (2040 Junction Ave., 605/347-2556, www.sturgis-sd.org).

center, and a large pool and whirlpool. Pets are allowed at no additional charge. The lodge can be found just off of Mt. Roosevelt Road, before you reach the city center. From exit 17 off of I-90, take Highway 85 south.

FOOD

Truth be told, it is almost impossible to separate food from lodging and casinos in Deadwood. After all, almost all establishments offer all three. In any case, most of the food is reasonably priced. No one wants you to leave!

Family Fare

Bully's Restaurant (633 Main St., 605/578-1745, daily 6 A.M.–1 P.M., $7–10) is located in the historic Bullock Hotel and is one of the nicest spots in town for an early and tasty breakfast. The menu is limited, but the restaurant, tucked away in the small bar at the Bullock Hotel, is away from the hustle and noise of the casino. Breakfast offerings include a six-ounce sirloin; bacon or sausage with two eggs, hash browns, and toast; and the daily special. Lunch is a steak sandwich, cheeseburger, or grilled cheese. Don't look for a meal after lunch, however, as Bully's turns into a bar in the evening.

Family dining away from a bar atmosphere can be found at the **Hickok House** (137 Charles St., 605/578-1611, daily 6:30 A.M.–9 P.M., $9–15), located at the Best Western Hotel. Away from the hustle and bustle of downtown Deadwood, the Hickok House features large windows on three sides of the restaurant. It's an all-American restaurant, and an especially great choice for breakfast. Omelets, ham steak, chicken-fried steak, corned beef hash, pancakes, and breakfast burritos are served all day. Lunch features salads, sandwiches, and wraps. Dinner offerings include fried chicken, liver and onions, fried fish, and marinated steak tips. It's a casual and comfortable environment, perfect for families.

Miss Kitty's Cantina (649 Main St.,

605/578-2828, daily 8 A.M.–10 P.M., later on weekend nights, breakfast $7, Mexican specialties $7–9) is located inside Miss Kitty's Casino. The room itself is surprisingly quiet, given all the activity just outside the door. It's not fancy, but the prices are reasonable and the quantities are huge. Kids will be happy with the corn dogs, hot dogs, chicken strips, grilled cheese, and burger offerings.

For the best buffet in Deadwood, check out the **Silverado Grand Vegas-Style Buffet** (709 Main St., 605/578-3670 or 800/584-7005, www.silveradofranklin.com, Mon.–Sat. 7–10:30 A.M., breakfast buffet $11, 11 A.M.–2:30 P.M., lunch buffet $13, Sun. brunch 8 A.M.–2:30 P.M., $16, Sun.–Thurs. 4:30–9 P.M., dinner buffet $18, Fri.–Sat. 4:30–10 P.M., crab buffet $22, buffet is half-price for child under 12). The restaurant is located inside the Silverado-Franklin Hotel and Gaming Complex. The buffet includes over 80 feet of buffet items to choose from. Look for made-to-order items, wood fired pizzas, and soup, salad, and dessert selections. The highlight of the week is the all-you-can-eat crab buffet on Friday and Saturday nights.

Fine Dining

The **Deadwood Social Club** (657 Main St., 605/578-3346 or 800/952-9398, www.saloon10.com, daily 11 A.M.–10 P.M., $15–25) is located on the second floor of Saloon No. 10 and features Northern Italian cuisine in a cozy, wood, brick-lined atmosphere. If there is such a thing as Western elegance, the Social Club has mastered it with a rough and tumble version of Victorian style. The restaurant has an extensive wine list (and you can purchase wine to go) and a menu that includes a very wide variety of pasta dishes in addition to steaks. They have a wonderful chicken wellington. This a refreshing change from the standard fare in the hills.

Cozy, elegant, and intimate, ◖ **Jake's** (677

Main St., 605/578-3656, www.themidnightstar.com, Wed.–Sun. 5–9:30 P.M., $25–36), atop the Midnight Star, is famous for fine food and impeccable service. Cajun seafood tortellini is the restaurant's signature dish, and creative presentations of local fare are on the menu, as well. The restaurant serves only hormone-free meats. Braised buffalo shank and wild-caught salmon are two of the regular menu items. The restaurant has an award-winning wine list and won the *Wine Spectator* award of excellence consecutively 2000–2004. In the Black Hills, two restaurants are mentioned as the finest in the state: Jake's is one of them (along with the Corn Exchange in Rapid City).

If you are looking to break away from the flashing lights and ringing bells of the downtown district, head up the hill on U.S. 14A, take a left on Pine Crest Road, and step inside the Lodge at Deadwood. Here you'll find the **Deadwood Grille** (100 Pine Crest Rd., 605/571-2121, dinner nightly 4:30–11 P.M., $18–30). The restaurant is spacious and attractive with faux leather and wood booths, tile floors, brick walls, and nice lighting. The grilled selections include buffalo sirloin, grilled pork chops, Mediterranean sea bass, and scallops. There is a wide selection of soups and salads, and entrées include seafood, pasta, and steak.

When you see the sign "Best Burgers in the Hills," about twenty miles south of Deadwood off U.S. 385, pull into the parking lot of the **Sugar Shack** (22495 U.S. Hwy 385, 605/341-6772, summer daily 7 A.M.–9 P.M., off-season Tues.–Sun. 7 A.M.–8 P.M., $7–9). It may not look like much from the road, but this funky little place can actually back up its claim. Whether or not the burgers are the best in the hills is subjective, but they are really good. The basic burger is a half-pounder topped with cheese, grilled onions, and sweet green peppers. It's the delicious sweet peppers that give the burger its name. There's a small indoor dining area, a wide wooden counter and, in the summer, a shaded patio.

INFORMATION AND SERVICES

The **Deadwood Chamber of Commerce** (605/578-1876 or 800/999-1876, www.deadwood.org) is located at 767 Main Street. Hours of operation are Monday–Friday 8 A.M.–5 P.M.

GETTING THERE AND AROUND

Dakota Taxi (605/920-2020) provides taxi service in the Deadwood area, including shuttle service to any point on the Mickelson Trail and shuttle service to the Rapid City Airport at very reasonable rates. (A ride between Deadwood and Lead costs about $7 for the first person and $2 per person after that.) If you've based your vacation in the Northern Hills, **Discovery Tours** (605/722-5788 or 888/524-5655, www.blackhillsdiscoverytours.com, adult $84, child $54) services the Spearfish, Lead, and Deadwood area. They provide daily tours to Mount Rushmore, Crazy Horse, and Custer State Park, and will pick you up at your hotel. And, for just $40–45 an hour, Discovery Tours will also provide a van and a driver for you to customize any tour or any event that you would like to attend.

THE NORTHERN HILLS

THE BADLANDS

The Badlands are an eerie place. In daylight, the twisted spires and pinnacles look gray and faded, but at early light or at dusk, pale yellow, deep burgundy, and light pinks emerge. A visit to the Badlands is like a visit to another planet, one that is starkly forbidding and strikingly beautiful. Gazing over the plains from the high ridges of the park is not unlike the sense you get while gazing out to sea. Miles and miles of open plain lie before you, with little evidence of humankind. Though the dusty gray guise gives the landscape a barren appearance, the Badlands are filled with life. Host to bison, pronghorn, bighorn sheep, deer, fox, coyotes, prairie dogs, burrowing owls, and other prairie animals, including the rare black-footed ferret, the Badlands are a wildlife wonderland.

The town of Wall serves as the northern gateway to Badlands National Park and is a good choice for overnight stays, since services in the park are limited. Wall is most famous, however, for Wall Drug, the ultimate roadside attraction. Purchased in 1931 by the Hustead family, the drugstore languished until Dorothy Hustead thought to advertise free ice water, in verse, on road signs scattered along the highway. Hot and thirsty travelers began visiting the store the very first day the signs went up. Today, Wall Drug now serves upwards of 20,000 people a day and is a massive complex of shops and photo ops.

HIGHLIGHTS

◖ Badlands Loop Road: This is a 23-mile, 60-minute drive that winds through the Badlands Wall from the eastern edge of Badlands National Park's North Unit to the southeastern corner of the park. With plenty of turnouts and dramatic vistas, it is the perfect route for a day trip to the park (page 188).

◖ Sage Creek Rim Road: This 22-mile-long gravel road winds along the northern edge of the Badlands Wilderness Area and provides some of the best wildlife-viewing in the park. The park's bison herd is in this area, as is the Roberts Prairie Dog Town (page 189).

◖ Ben Reifel Visitor Center: With an award-winning video, exhibits, lots of books, maps, and rangers on hand to answer questions, this is the place to find out about the activities happening in Badlands National Park during your visit (page 189).

◖ Wall Drug: It's hard to believe that a sign advertising free ice water could have created the world that is Wall Drug. This 76,000-square-foot complex is the supreme roadside attraction (page 196).

◖ Minuteman Missile National Historic Site: On a tour of this site's launch facility and missile silo, you'll learn the truth about Minuteman missiles and the "missileers" responsible for their deployment (page 197).

◖ Red Cloud Heritage Center: The Heritage Center includes a beautiful gallery of Native American art, museum, and gift shop. Plan to visit the cemetery, where Chief Red Cloud, one of the great leaders of the Oglala Lakota people, is buried (page 203).

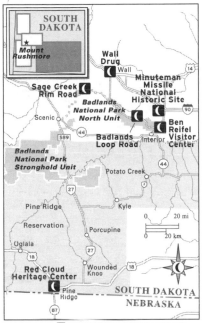

LOOK FOR ◖ TO FIND RECOMMENDED SIGHTS, ACTIVITIES, DINING, AND LODGING.

The White River Visitor Center of the South Unit of Badlands National Park is located on the Pine Ridge Reservation and is operated by the Lakota tribe. Displays at the center include information about the park and about Lakota history and culture. The reservation is vast, encompassing over 3,400 sparsely populated square miles. In addition to the Badlands, the reservation lands include both mixed-grass and short-grass prairie. Visitors interested in Native American history and culture may well want to plan ahead for a visit to the reservation, home to the Oglala Lakota people.

GEOLOGY

The vast area of the Great Plains was beneath an inland sea for almost 500 million years. The sedimentary layers beneath the sea are estimated to have been 5,000–10,000 feet thick, with many of the layers compressed to stone. Between 65–70 million years ago, an uplift in the continent created the Black Hills 70 miles

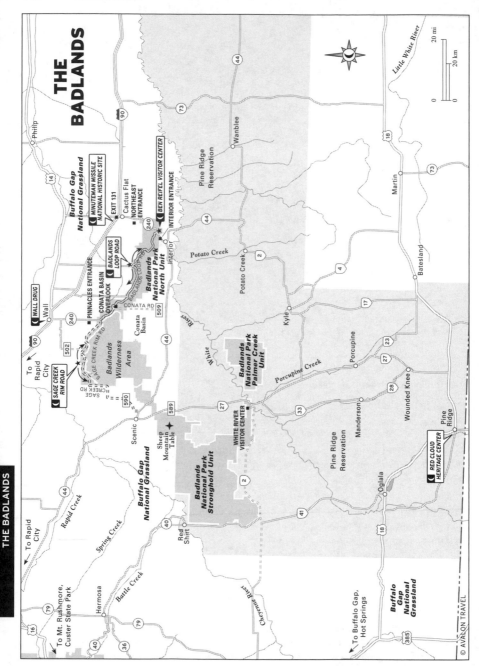

THE BADLANDS

west of the Badlands. The uplift also caused the inland sea to drain, leaving the nearly flat floor of the sea exposed to the surface. The floor of that sea is the oldest formation now visible in the Badlands, called the Pierre Shale. Two geologic processes, deposition and erosion, working on the landscape for 65 million years created the Badlands that we see today. As the wind eroded the sedimentary layers on top of the Black Hills uplift, it deposited those layers across the plains. Streams, sluggishly flowing over the relatively flat surface of the eastern plains, deposited more layers. Volcanic activity deposited yet more layers. As the uplift continued, the streams flowed more quickly and began to carve into the sediments initially deposited by the slower streams, leaving behind the spires, valleys, and fascinating formations we see today. The Badlands Wall, a towering range of spires that runs through the park, was once the northern bank of the White River that carved through the plains. To distinguish the South Dakota Badlands from other Badlands areas in the west, they are frequently referred to as the White River Badlands. The spires of the wall average 800 feet tall and separate the upper prairie flats from the lower grassy prairie of the south and east.

PLANNING YOUR TIME

Badlands National Park is divided into two units: the North Unit and the Stronghold District, or South Unit, which includes the Palmer Creek area.

Getting to the North Unit of Badlands National Park is an easy day trip from Rapid City, or a great detour on the I-90 drive across the state on a trip to the Black Hills. Keep in mind, however, that viewing a sunset or sunrise in the park is one of the peak experiences of a visit. While accommodations are limited, there are primitive campsites and a lodge within the park boundaries. The town of Interior, located at the southern edge of the

North Unit of the park, has limited accommodations. The town of Wall, located eight miles north of the Pinnacles Entrance on the north side of the park, has several accommodations and restaurants. If you are not planning on an overnight stay, try to spend at least 3–4 hours in the park. And for lovers of roadside attractions, Wall Drug, in the town of Wall, deserves at least an hour or two of your time.

The Stronghold District of the park is on the Pine Ridge Reservation and is co-managed by the Park Service and the Oglala Sioux tribe. This area, with the exception of Sheep Mountain Table, is not accessible by road, and there is a lot of private land interspersed with the park lands. The Palmer Creek Unit is accessible for backcountry hiking only and, in order to reach it, visitors must get permission to cross private property. A list of property owners is maintained at the White River Visitor Center, which also has other information about the Southern Unit of the park.

Getting There and Around

There are two routes to Badlands National Park from Rapid City. Highway 44 skirts the southern edge of the North Unit of the park and enters the North Unit through the **Interior Entrance.** It's about a 75-mile drive and should take about an hour and 20 minutes at the posted speed limit (65 mph). The Ben Reifel Visitor Center is located near this entrance. If a night in the park isn't an option, I'd suggest traveling this route to the park. Stop at the visitor center to get oriented and to get a schedule of park-sponsored events for the day of your visit, and then wander north along the Badlands Loop Road. Exit the park via the **Pinnacles Entrance** on the north side of the park. Head toward the town of Wall, where you can visit Wall Drug and take in a late dinner, or just head back to Rapid City along I-90.

The second route to the park is I-90. It is the fastest route between Rapid City and the park:

THE BADLANDS

looking south from the Badlands to the grasslands

© LAURAL BIDWELL

just 63 miles of 75-mph driving. If you are planning on spending the night in or near the park, this is the best route to get there. Visit the town of Wall for breakfast and a peek at Wall Drug, and then head into the park. Get a schedule of events at the park entrance and then travel the Badlands Loop Road headed south. The loop is just 23 miles, but should take some time. There are many scenic overlooks and short walking trails along the way. Stop at the Ben Reifel Visitor Center at the south end of the park, do some hiking on trails near the center, stay at the lodge, and enjoy the evening program sponsored by the park. Get up early enough for the sunrise, exit the park via the **Northeast Entrance** (which will allow a visit to the Minuteman Missile National Historic Site), and then loop back to Rapid City via I-90. Or exit the park and head east on Highway 44, which will also return you to Rapid City. Longer stays allow for a trip through the Sage Creek Wilderness Area via the gravel Sage Creek Rim Road, where some of the oldest layers of the park formations are visible and where much of the wildlife, including the bison herd, is located.

Travelers headed east on I-90 will want to take exit 131 at Cactus Flat and head south on Highway 240 to the Northeast Entrance of the park. It is about 10 miles from the Northeast Entrance to the Ben Reifel Visitor Center. The Minuteman Missile National Historic Site is located off this exit, as well, and is between the interstate and the park entrance.

Visitors who are planning to visit the **Pine Ridge Reservation,** subsequent to their visit to the North Unit of the park, may well want to make a stop at Sheep Mountain Table in the Stronghold District. To do this, take Highway 44 west to the town of Scenic and head south on Bombing Range Road (aka Bureau of Indian Affairs Road 27, or BIA 27/County Road 589). Travel about four miles and look for Sheep Mountain Table Road on your left. This seven-mile gravel road will bring you to the top of the table with spectacular views. Head back to the main road to continue south into the reservation. An alternate route to the reservation: Head south on Highway 44 from Interior and then turn west on Highway 2 to head for Kyle on reservation land.

When to Go

It is worth visiting the Badlands any time of year, but the best time to visit the park is in the spring or early summer. The grasses are still a luscious green early in the year, and the daytime temperatures are milder than the very hot days that occur more frequently in July and August. By the end of summer, the grasses are brown, removing a bit of color from the view, but the spires, buttes, and tables of the area are no less beautiful.

Badlands National Park and Vicinity

In 1872, Yellowstone National Park was created, the first of many land areas set aside for the enjoyment of the people. From that time, a system of National Parks, National Monuments, and other sites have been set aside for scenic, historic, prehistoric, or scientific interest. Peter Norbeck, a United States senator from South Dakota, was the chief instigator for setting aside the Badlands as a National Monument, and that designation was given to the park in 1939. When the park entered into a joint-operating agreement with the Oglala Lakota in 1976 for the South Unit of the Badlands, known as the Stronghold Unit, the managed area grew to over 244,000 acres with 64,000 acres of wilderness. In 1978, it was designated a National Park.

The entrance fee to the park is $15 per car. Bicyclists and pedestrians can enter the park for $7, motorcycles for $10. Passes are good for seven days. The Interagency Annual Pass for designated federal fee areas is valid here. The pass can also be purchased at the gate ($80 annual, $10 lifetime for senior aged 62 and up). The park is open 24 hours a day, seven days a week.

A place of otherworldly beauty, the Badlands are also a paleontologist's dream. Each layer of the Badlands has a story to tell about the plants, animals, and climate of the region at the time of the deposit. The oldest layer, the Pierre Shale, contains the fossilized remains of clams, ammonites, and sea reptiles, proving the existence of the inland sea that once covered the area. As the sea receded, the area became a lush tropical environment, as evidenced by the Chadron Formation. Deposits in this formation are 35–37 million years old and contain evidence of alligators and palm-type plants in the region. Also commonly found in this layer are many ancient mammals, including a rhinoceros-like creature called the titanothere. As the climate cooled and became drier, different kinds of fossils began to appear. Evidences of herd animals, including a sheep-like mammal, have been found.

Paleontologists have been doing research in the park since the first published record of a fossil jaw was found in 1846, and the Park Service intends to continue that tradition into the future. In 1993, two visitors to the Badlands discovered a large backbone protruding from the ground and notified park personnel. For 15 years, the Park Service and the South Dakota School of Mines worked together at "Big Pig Dig," the site where the backbone was found. Over 15,000 bones were recovered from the site, including three-toed horses, tiny deer-like creatures, turtles, and a saber-toothed tiger. (There were no ancient pigs found at the site, which was closed in 2008.) In 2010, a seven-year-old girl participating in the Junior Ranger Program discovered a fossil and reported it.

THE BADLANDS

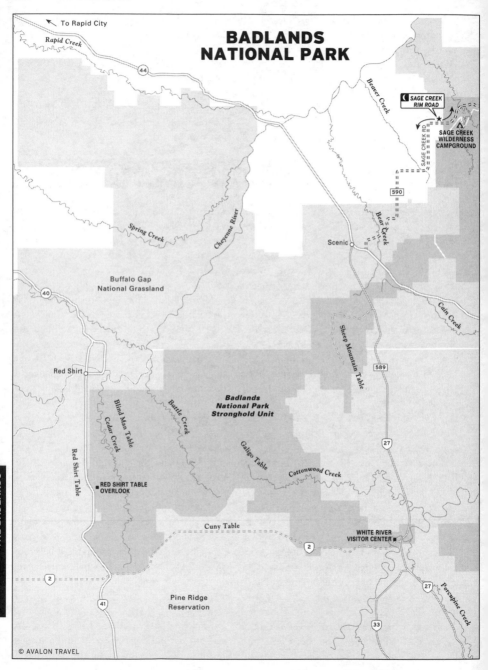

To Rapid City

Rapid Creek

BADLANDS
NATIONAL PARK

44

Beaver Creek

SAGE CREEK
RIM ROAD

SAGE CREEK RD

SAGE CREEK
WILDERNESS
CAMPGROUND

590

Spring Creek

Cheyenne River

Bear Creek

Scenic

Cain Creek

Buffalo Gap
National Grassland

40

Sheep Mountain Table

589

Red Shirt

Blind Man Table

Battle Creek

Badlands
National Park
Stronghold Unit

27

Cedar Creek

Galigo Table

Red Shirt Table

Cottonwood Creek

RED SHIRT TABLE
OVERLOOK

Cuny Table

WHITE RIVER
VISITOR CENTER

2

2

27

Porcupine Creek

41

Pine Ridge
Reservation

33

© AVALON TRAVEL

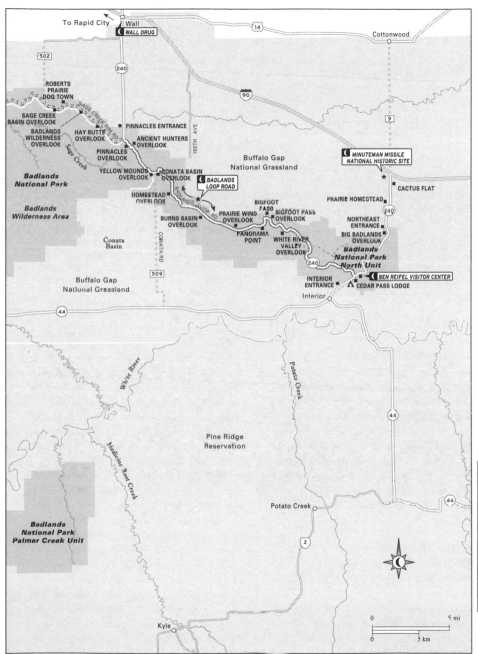

To Rapid City
Wall
WALL DRUG
14
Cottonwood

502

240

90

9

ROBERTS
PRAIRIE
DOG TOWN

SAGE CREEK
BASIN OVERLOOK

SAGE CREEK RIM RD

PINNACLES ENTRANCE

HAY BUTTE
OVERLOOK

BADLANDS
WILDERNESS
OVERLOOK

ANCIENT HUNTERS
OVERLOOK

Sage Creek

195TH AVE

PINNACLES
OVERLOOK

YELLOW MOUNDS
OVERLOOK

CONATA BASIN
OVERLOOK

Buffalo Gap
National Grassland

MINUTEMAN MISSILE
NATIONAL HISTORIC SITE

*Badlands
National Park*

BADLANDS
LOOP ROAD

CACTUS FLAT

BADLANDS LOOP RD

*Badlands
Wilderness Area*

HOMESTEAD
OVERLOOK

PRAIRIE HOMESTEAD

BURNS BASIN
OVERLOOK

BIGFOOT
PASS

PRAIRIE WIND
OVERLOOK

BIGFOOT PASS
OVERLOOK

249

CONATA RD

PANORAMA
POINT

WHITE RIVER
VALLEY
OVERLOOK

NORTHEAST
ENTRANCE

BIG BADLANDS
OVERLOOK

Conata
Basin

509

240

*Badlands
National Park
North Unit*

Buffalo Gap
National Grassland

INTERIOR
ENTRANCE

BEN REIFEL VISITOR CENTER

CEDAR PASS LODGE

Interior

44

White River

Potato Creek

44

Pine Ridge
Reservation

Medicine Root Creek

Potato Creek

44

2

*Badlands
National Park
Palmer Creek Unit*

Kyle

0   5 mi

0   5 km

THE BADLANDS

SAFETY IN BADLANDS NATIONAL PARK

The scenic highways are delightful ways to tour the park, but getting out and hiking the region has its rewards, as well. The region is beautiful but remote, so visitors need to consider safety when thinking about leaving the car behind and walking the wilderness areas of the park. During the summer months, the temperatures in the Badlands can reach over 100°F, and once on the trails, there is no drinkable water available. Be sure to pack in plenty to drink, wear sunglasses, and use sunscreen.

Be aware that bison are free-roaming in the park and are very fast and dangerous. Keep at least 100 yards away from them. You cannot outrun them should they decide to charge. Hikers in the backcountry may find that the bison here are not used to visitors and are somewhat curious. Be sure to keep an eye on their location and drift away from them if they decide to approach. Do not stare at them, as this would be interpreted as aggressive behavior on your part.

Exercise caution when hiking anywhere in the Badlands. The soil can be very loose and cause sliding. The most common injury in the park is a sprained ankle, so be sure to wear good sturdy footgear. The weather in the park can change dramatically on short notice and thunderstorms are common during the summer. At a minimum, a good windbreaker is mandatory gear. For longer hikes, consider carrying rain gear. Remember, also, that cell phone service in this remote area is sporadic at best. If you are planning a long hike, or an overnight stay in a wilderness area, let the park rangers know your plans.

The South Unit of the Badlands was used as a bombing practice range during World War II. It is possible that you could find unexploded ordnance (bullets, etc.) if you hike in that region. Do not pick up any of these items, but please do report your findings to the park service. If you have GPS units, please note the location of the items found.

The skull was determined to be that of a saber-toothed tiger. In June of 2012, the Saber Site and Fossil Prep Lab were opened where the skull had been discovered. Paleontologists are on-site June–August working to uncover additional fossils. The site is open to the public (daily 9 A.M.–4:30 P.M.) and is located near the Ben Reifel Visitor Center. Should you discover any fossils in the park, report them to park personnel. It is illegal to take any of the fossils, plants, or rocks out of a National Park; they are to be left where found.

SIGHTS

Badlands Loop Road

The Badlands Loop Road is the only paved road through the Badlands. It is a 23-mile road that runs between the Pinnacles Entrance in the north to the Ben Reifel Visitor Center in the southeast. The road winds between the ridges of the Badlands Wall, literally a wall of spires and pinnacles that was once the northern bank of the White River. As the river cut into the sediments of the plains, the wall was left behind. There are several scenic turnouts along the road, all of which provide dramatic vistas of the Badlands and of the **Buffalo Gap National Grasslands,** which border the park. Carry your binoculars and keep an eye out for wildlife. From the north, heading to the southeast, stop at the **Pinnacles Overlook,** the **Ancient Hunters Overlook,** and then, if you've packed a lunch, keep an eye out for Conata Road, which is located near Dillon Pass. There are picnic tables about a half-mile south on the road. There are several other turnouts between Dillon Pass and Big Foot Pass, and more picnic tables are at the **Big Foot Pass Overlook.** White park signs along the route announce activities in the area. Be sure to stop at the **Fossil Exhibit Trail.** This trail is marked with interpretive signs and fossil displays and is an

© WWW.TRAVELSD.COM

Bison graze in Badlands National Park.

easy, wheelchair-accessible path that can be traversed in 20 minutes or less. It provides a nice stop for a good stretch. The road ends at the Ben Reifel Visitor Center.

Sage Creek Rim Road

The Sage Creek Rim Road is a gravel road that is located just south of the northern Pinnacles Entrance to the park. The road travels north and west through the park, and then circles the Badlands Wilderness Area. Look for the **Hay Butte Overlook** and the **Badlands Wilderness Overlook.** The formations here are a little softer and less craggy than the spires located along the Badlands Loop Road, but the wildlife is more abundant. The park's bison herd is usually seen in this area. About five miles down the road, look for the **Roberts Prairie Dog Town,** a large colony of black-tailed prairie dogs. They're rodents, but very cute ones, and the barking and social antics of these small animals is fun to watch. At dusk, keep an eye out for the rare

black-footed ferret. Prairie dogs are the ferret's main food source. Just past Roberts Prairie Dog Town is the **Sage Creek Basin Overlook.** This is a great place to head into the park for hiking. It's easy access without the sharp and steep cliffs common off of the Badlands Loop Road. Heading south along this road, you will cross a bridge over Sage Creek. At this point, examine the river bank and you'll be able to see the Pierre Shale—the oldest visible sedimentary layer in the park, dating back over 70 million years. Seven miles past Roberts Prairie Dog Town, a left-hand turn on another gravel road will bring you to the Sage Creek Campground. There are picnic tables and pit toilets here. This is another good starting location for off-trail hiking.

Ben Reifel Visitor Center

The Ben Reifel Visitor Center (25216 Ben Reifel Rd., Hwy. 270, 605/433-5361, www.nps. gov/badl, mid-Apr.–May daily 8 A.M.–5 P.M., June–mid-Aug. daily 7 A.M.–7 P.M., Sept.–late Oct. daily 8 A.M.–5 P.M., Nov.–mid-Apr. daily 8 A.M.–4 P.M., closed Thanksgiving, Christmas, and New Year's) is located at Park Headquarters on the south edge of the Badlands Loop Road. Watch the award-winning video *Land of Stone and Light* in the adjacent theater. The video is a great introduction to the park. It is 20 minutes long and plays every 25 minutes during the day. The video features superb photography of the park, along with a narrative discussion of the wildlife, geology, paleontology, early peoples, and history of the park. Exhibits at the visitor center examine the history, ecology, and paleontology of the Badlands, with murals of the geologic layers of the park, samples of fossils found in the park, and two other videos in the exhibit hall. One of the videos discusses the work of the paleontologist, from the discovery of a fossil in the field to the work that is done back at the laboratory. The second video examines different personal perspectives of the park, with interviews of park rangers, Native

THE BADLANDS

Americans, ranchers, and park visitors. There is also a bookstore on-site, and restrooms.

For the kids aged 7–12, there are Junior Ranger booklets, filled with activities to do in the park. And, during the summer months, there is a 45-minute Junior Ranger Program presented by a park ranger that may include a hike into the prairie, a game, or another activity. A completed activity book, or completion of the ranger-led program, will earn the participant a Junior Ranger badge.

White River Visitor Center

The White River Visitor Center (Hwy. 27, Pine Ridge, 605/455-2878, June–Aug. daily 10 A.M.–4 P.M., closed in off-season) is located 20 miles south of the town of Scenic off of Bombing Range Road (Hwy. 27) on the **Pine Ridge Reservation.** It is a remote location that services people interested in Pine Ridge and in serious backcountry camping and hiking. Exhibits at the center include fossils and Lakota artifacts, as well as some information about historical events in Lakota history. The **South Unit,** or Stronghold District, of the Badlands is not easily accessible, with just one road and no hiking trails. The **Palmer Creek Unit** of the South Unit is surrounded by private property and hikers must get permission to cross private lands to get there. The center has a list of property owners and maps to help hikers plot their routes and gain permissions. The Stronghold District was used as a bombing range during World War II, and there is unexploded ordnance in the area. Hikers are asked to report any finds to the Park Service. Do not touch.

OUTDOOR RECREATION

Vast distances, pastel-colored spires, bright sun, rocks, fossils, fragile flowers, and a fascinating geologic and paleontology history make the park one of the most awe-inspiring sites in South Dakota. Over 64,000 acres in the park are designated wilderness areas. The two wilderness units in the park include the **Sage Creek Wilderness,** accessible from the Sage Creek Rim Road or the Sage Creek Campground, and the **Conata Basin,** which is accessible via Conata Road and the Conata picnic area south of Dillon Pass.

There are no established trails in the wilderness areas, though hiking is encouraged. Feel free to follow the paths carved by the bison or follow personal whimsy as you wander the grasslands and Badlands formations. Enjoy the beauty of the region, but be very careful of drop-offs. Erosion has left a lot of loose, unstable soil, and you could find yourself sliding off the edge of a cliff. If you are planning on spending some time in the park, camping is allowed anywhere that is at least a half-mile away from any road or trail and is not visible from park roads. Keep in mind that prairie grasses grow tall and with hot temperatures and strong winds, fire danger in the park is frequently high. Campfires are not allowed anywhere in the park. Backpacking stoves are allowed. Backpacking this region is best in spring and fall, but those are also times when park usage is pretty low, and there won't be many folks in the vicinity should you run into difficulty. The Badlands are remote and surrounded by high pinnacles that frequently block the use of cell phones. For your safety, stop by the visitor center and let the rangers know your plans.

Ranger-Led Programs

During the summer months, late May–mid-September, there are several ranger-guided programs offered at the park. The time and locations of the talks can be found in the park newspaper, which can be picked up at the Pinnacles Entrance and at the Ben Reifel Visitor Center. All of the programs are free. Programs include a 45-minute **Geology Walk** at the Door/Window trailheads, which are located two miles northeast of the Ben Reifel Visitor Center off of Highway 240. There is a 15–20-minute **Fossil**

Talk at the Fossil Exhibit Trail, located on Badlands Loop Road, about five miles northwest of the Ben Reifel Visitor Center. **Sun Fun** starts at the Ben Reifel Visitor Center and is a program with discussions and activities focused on the sun, including the opportunity to look at the sun through a special telescope. Also held at the Ben Reifel Visitor Center is a program called **Ranger's Choice,** which could be a walk, talk, or an activity. In the evening, plan on attending the very popular 40-minute **Night Sky Program,** which begins at dark, sometime between 8–9 P.M. This program is held at the amphitheater at the Cedar Pass Campground, within walking distance of the Ben Reifel Visitor Center. For children aged 7–12, a daily ranger-led **Junior Ranger Program** includes a hike, game, or other activity; at its conclusion, participants earn a Junior Ranger badge.

In 2012, the park added its first **Annual Astronomy Festival,** held in mid-August. For three days, there are activities focused on the sky. There are special programs on night skies, solar studies, and rocket launching, as well as classes in backyard astronomy and film presentations.

Hiking

Day hiking in the Badlands is a joy. The vistas are grand in all directions and the sharp-edged spires and rounded mounds of the Badlands formations are fun to explore. Remember that hiking is encouraged in the wilderness areas of the park even though there are no specific trails there. Wear good shoes, use sunscreen, carry water, and be aware that fire danger can be very high in the prairie during hot dry summers. Bison roam free in the park and are to be avoided. Admire them from a distance and keep at least 100 yards away from these dangerous and unpredictable animals. Twisted ankles are the most common injury in the park. Watch your footing on the loose sand eroding from spires. That said, for those who prefer some guidance, there are also several marked trails

within the park boundaries, most of which are easy to moderately strenuous.

DOOR TRAIL

- **Distance:** 0.75 mile round-trip
- **Duration:** 30 minutes
- **Elevation Gain:** None
- **Effort:** Easy
- **Trailhead:** Door & Window parking lot
- **Directions:** From the Ben Reifel Visitor Center, travel two miles northeast on Highway 240 to the Door & Window parking lot. The trailhead is on the north end of the parking lot.

The first 150 yards are a boardwalk that is wheelchair accessible. Once the boardwalk ends, the trail slopes upward and travels though a "door" in the Badlands Wall to give great views of the grasslands and the outer wall of the Badlands. On the other side of the door, the trail is not maintained.

WINDOW TRAIL

- **Distance:** 0.25 mile round-trip
- **Duration:** 20 minutes
- **Effort:** Easy (wheelchair accessible)
- **Trailhead:** Center of the Door & Window parking lot

The entire trail is boardwalk. It leads to a window in the Badlands Wall where views of the grasslands, an erosion-carved canyon, and spires of the Badlands Wall are visible.

NOTCH TRAIL

- **Distance:** 1.5 miles round-trip
- **Duration:** 2 hours
- **Effort:** Moderately strenuous
- **Trailhead:** South end of the Door & Window parking lot

The trail starts in a canyon, climbs a rope and log ladder, and follows a narrow ledge to the

THE BADLANDS

climbing the ladder of the Notch Trail

"notch," through which a sweeping view of the White River Valley is revealed. Parts of this trail can be very steep and the narrow ledge can be intimidating for anyone afraid of heights. Do not attempt if there has been recent rainfall.

CASTLE TRAIL

- **Distance:** 10 miles round-trip
- **Duration:** 5 hours
- **Effort:** Moderate
- **Trailhead:** The trailhead for the Castle Trail is across the road from the Fossil Exhibit Trail, five miles northwest of the Ben Reifel Visitor Center.

This is the longest marked trail in the park. On the north end, the trail winds down through some of the park spires and mounds. Most of the trail is level and crosses the grasslands with views of the Badlands formations to the west and to the south. Watch for cactus and for rattlesnakes. The trail ends on Highway 240, on the west side across from the Door & Window parking lot.

Biking

There are no bike rental places in the Badlands, so you have to bring your own, or rent bicycles in Rapid City and haul them to the park. Bikes are not allowed on the hiking trails, or in the backcountry wilderness areas, but they are allowed on the paved and gravel roads in the park. A brochure on loop trips on combined park and county roads is available at the visitor center.

During peak season in the summer, bikers should be cautious on the **Badlands Loop Road,** since it is not a wide road and there can be a lot of traffic. It can be an exhilarating ride, however, and from the Pinnacles Overlook to the visitor center, it is 22 miles of mostly downhill riding.

Slightly off the beaten path is the **Sage Creek Rim Road.** This 22-mile gravel road skirts the northern edge of the wilderness area, runs past Roberts Prairie Dog Town, and passes though the lowest and oldest layers of the Badlands formations.

For the adventurous, a less-traveled and equally beautiful road open to bicyclists can be found in the South Unit of the park. **Sheep Mountain Road** is located about four miles south of the town of Scenic off of BIA 27/County Road 589. It is a seven-mile-long, dead-end dirt road with spectacular views of the South Unit of the park and of the Black Hills, 70 miles to the west. It is a moderately strenuous ride with a total elevation gain of about 400 feet. The most strenuous part of the ride is a 250-foot climb at the end of the road to the top of Sheep Mountain Table. To shorten the ride, it is possible to drive in with a vehicle, pull off the road, and park. The road can be impassable when wet. There are no services here, so bring plenty of water.

Horseback Riding

Horses are allowed in the park, although there are no commercial horse-rental facilities. If you are bringing your horses with you on your trip to the hills, prime horseback riding country can be found in the Sage Creek Wilderness. The **Sage Creek Campground** has a section designated for horse use and a watering hole is located about a half-mile southwest of the campground. This is an easy place to park trailers and ride into the Badlands. Horses are not allowed on marked trails, roads, and highways in the park, but are otherwise allowed. Horse trailers can be parked at any overlook for day use but are not allowed to remain at overlooks and parking lots overnight.

ACCOMMODATIONS AND FOOD

The only lodging, gift store, and restaurant in Badlands National Park is at **Cedar Pass Lodge** (20681 Hwy. 240, 605/433-5460 or 877/386-4383, www.cedarpasslodge.com, mid-Apr.–mid-Oct., closed in off-season, cottages $131, new cabins $137). The facility opened in 1928 and the historic cabins are showing the signs of age. In 2012, the resort company built new cabins. Eventually all of the older cabins will be replaced with the newer versions. The historic cabins are very rustic and small. There are no phones or televisions. They do have air-conditioning and a coffeemaker. The new cabins have televisions, refrigerators, microwaves, and a coffeemaker. The new cabins all have small decks and the furnishings are lodgepole pine. Situated close to the Ben Reifel Visitor Center, neither choice can be beat for location. It's a very short walk to the summer evening astronomy programs put on by the park rangers. If you're looking to experience a park sunrise or sunset, this is a good location to do so.

The **Cedar Pass Lodge Restaurant** (20681 Hwy. 240, 605/433-5460, www.cedarpasslodge.com, Apr.–May daily 8 A.M.–5 P.M., June–Aug. daily 7 A.M.–9 P.M., Sept.–mid-Oct. 8 A.M.–7 P.M., closed in off-season, breakfast $7, lunch $9, dinner $15) has also been nicely renovated. While the classic Indian taco on fry bread has remained on the menu, there are also healthier choices, including a soup and salad bar, some vegetarian selections, and even a gluten-free burger served between two portobello mushroom caps. The dinner menu also has a limited number of entrées, but there is something for everyone, including rib eye steak, Alaskan salmon, Rocky Mountain trout, grilled chicken, chicken fried steak, or even a marinara sauce–topped pasta dish. The featured dessert is ice cream made fresh from cows at the South Dakota State University Dairy Science program.

Adjacent to the restaurant is a lovely gift shop featuring jewelry, books, camping supplies, travel mugs, and souvenirs. The reservation desk for the lodge and the campground is located in the gift shop area.

The campground, lodge, gift shop, and restaurant are all run by concessionaire **Forever Resorts** (877/386-4383, www.foreverresorts.com).

Cedar Pass Campground (20681 Hwy. 240, 605/433-5460 or 877/386-4383, www.cedarpasslodge.com, open year-round, tent sites $16, RV site with electrical hookup $28, winter fees $10 for any site, dump station $1, no water or sewer hookups) is located near the Ben Reifel Visitor Center. In the summer the campground has cold running water, flush toilets, and picnic tables. There are no hot showers. In the winter only picnic tables and trash containers are available. The 96 sites are filled on a first-come, first-served basis. Open Campfires are not allowed.

The **Sage Creek Wilderness Campground** offers primitive camping facilities year-round. There are picnic tables and pit toilets. Pack in water, though, because none is available at this location. The price is definitely right, as camping here is free.

There is limited lodging available in the small town of Interior, South Dakota, which is located just outside of the southern entrance to the North Unit. The ◖ **Circle View Guest**

THE BADLANDS

Ranch (20055 E. Hwy. 44, 605/433-5582, www.circleviewranch.com, open year-round, $105–125) is a working cattle ranch situated on 3,000 acres just six miles west of the Park Headquarters. The ranch is a bed-and-breakfast and provides guests with a full breakfast, wireless Internet, a fully equipped shared kitchen, private baths, and a game room with foosball, table tennis, and a collection of games. The eight rooms are Western in decor, with colorful quilts and wood furniture. The owners of the ranch are happy to set guests up with horseback-riding excursions along the edge of the Badlands. For $50, guests can experience a 1.5-hour private ride arranged by your hosts Philip and Amy Kruse. There are never more than five people on a ride, and frequently it will be just you and a cowboy! In June and again in the fall, the ranch offers guests the opportunity to join in on a cattle drive. This is a working ranch in rural South Dakota; be aware that prairie dog hunting is one of the activities on offer.

The 18-room **Badlands Inn** (20615 Hwy. 377, 605/433-5401 or 877/386-4383, open May–Sept., closed in off-season, $120) is located about 1.5 miles outside of the park boundary in the town of Interior. The inn is run by the same people who run the Cedar Pass Lodge. The rooms are double queens and are very basic. There is television, a coffee pot, and air-conditioning. The room rate includes a continental breakfast. To check in here, it is necessary to go to the Cedar Pass Lodge and then drive back to the inn. The property is considered a backup to the cabins at Cedar Pass Lodge, which are booked first.

The **Badlands Budget Host** (900 Hwy. 377, Interior, 605/433-5335 or 800/283-4678, $75) is another hotel with location, location, location. Within a mile of the southern entrance to the North Unit of Badlands National Park, the hotel is plain, but the rooms are clean and reasonable. The hotel offers free wireless and a continental breakfast, and pets are allowed.

There is an outdoor pool, laundry facilities, and a small grocery store on-site.

INFORMATION AND SERVICES
Information
For information about Badlands National Park, contact Park Headquarters at the **Ben Reifel Visitor Center** (25216 Ben Reifel Rd., Hwy. 270, 605/433-5361, www.nps.gov/badl, mid-Apr.–May daily 8 A.M.–5 P.M., June–mid-Aug. daily 7 A.M.–7 P.M., Sept.–late Oct. daily 8 A.M.–5 P.M., Nov.–mid-Apr. daily 8 A.M.–4 P.M., closed Thanksgiving, Christmas, and New Year's), or the **White River Visitor Center** (Hwy. 27, Pine Ridge, 605/455-2878, open summer season only, daily 10 A.M.–4 P.M.). For more information about exploring the South Unit of the Badlands, contact the Pine Ridge Area Chamber of Commerce at 605/455-2685.

Tour Companies
There are several tour companies that make day trips out to the Badlands from Rapid City and other communities in the Black Hills. Each company has a slightly different offering. **Affordable Adventures** (5542 Meteor St., Rapid City, 605/342-7691 or 888/888-8249, www.affordableadventuresbh.com, $115) is a small-group tour company that provides narrated tours on small vans through the Badlands. The fee includes admission to the park but does not include the price of meals. The Badlands tour includes the Badlands Loop Road, Ben Reifel Visitor Center, and Wall Drug (for shopping and for lunch), and takes about seven hours. Departure time from Rapid City is at 8:30 A.M. This tour is offered year-round.

Black Hills Adventure Tours (201 N. 44th St., Rapid City, 605/209-7817, www.blackhillsadventuretours.com, $119) has narrated driving tours of the Badlands and also provides hiking tours in the park. The hiking tours cater to various levels of fitness, so tour routes

The Badlands offers unusual shopping opportunities.

vary. The hiking tour leaves Rapid City around 9 A.M., returns about 4:30 P.M., and includes around five hours of hiking time. Tours include narration about the history and geology of the park, and the price includes the park admission fee, snacks, and water. Lunch is not included, although they will order sack lunches for participants on request. The company also provides sightseeing tours to the park that include a wildlife tour, the Badlands Loop Road, time to browse the Ben Reifel Visitor Center and have lunch at the Cedar Pass Lodge Restaurant, a stop at the Minuteman Missile National Historic Site, and a visit to Wall Drug. Travel is provided in sport utility vehicles or small vans, depending on the number of participants. Tours are offered year-round.

For an entirely different experience, **Black Hills Aerial Adventures** (I-90, exit 131 at Cactus Flats and look for the helicopter stand just before the park entrance, 605/673-2163, www.coptertours.com, May–Oct., closed in off-season, $49–229) offers five different flying tours over the Badlands. View the spires and buttes from an entirely different perspective. The tours are distinguished by miles covered and flight time. The introductory tour is five miles and takes 5–6 minutes of flight time. Other choices include 8 miles ($89), 12 miles ($109), and 17 miles ($139). The longest tour, at $229, circles about 35 miles of the Badlands and provides about 25 minutes of flight time.

Other Services

Campers and backpackers can find groceries at the **Wall Food Center** (103 W. South Blvd., Wall, 605/279-2331). Remember that there is very little in the way of food available in Badlands National Park at any time—and nothing is available October–early May—so the grocery store might be a good option for creating a picnic lunch. Pick up water while you are there.

The **post office** is located at 529 Main Street in Wall.

THE BADLANDS

Wall

The town of Wall is just eight miles north of the Pinnacles Entrance to Badlands National Park, and it's the largest service provider of food and accommodations for park-goers in the region. The community is even named for one of the park formations, the wall of spires that runs for miles on the north end of the Badlands. Geologically, the Badlands Wall is the ancient northern bank of the White River that carved out the Badlands formations.

Founded in 1907, the town of Wall was, like many of South Dakota's prairie communities, founded on railroad expansion, cattle, and homesteading. In 1931, Wall was a dusty flat-out broke town with a little over 300 residents. Ted Hustead, a fairly recent graduate of pharmacy school at the time, searched the plains looking for a good place to buy or build a pharmacy of his own and settled on the town of Wall. It was not the best choice, or so it seemed. Cars would chug by the little town on their way to Rapid City, 55 miles to the west, but no one stopped in Wall. Ted and his wife Dorothy decided to give it five years. As the end of the fifth year drew near, and success had still not graced the small pharmacy, Dorothy came up with the idea of enticing motorists off the highway with the promise of free ice water. Ted figured it couldn't hurt, and put up signs for miles advertising the free water with jingles that automobile riders could read as they drove. It was an instant hit and Wall Drug has been the driving force of tourism in Wall ever since. Today, Wall Drug is the largest employer in town, followed by Badlands National Park.

SIGHTS
◖ Wall Drug

Wall Drug (510 Main St., 605/279-2175, www.walldrug.com, June–Aug. daily 6:30 A.M.–10 P.M., Sept.–May daily 7 A.M.–5:30 P.M.) is the ultimate roadside attraction. Occupying over 76,000 square feet, Wall Drug sells all the tacky tourist paraphernalia your heart could desire, and the backyard is home to unlimited photo opportunities—including a giant jackalope saddled up and ready to ride; a roaring, smoke-spewing T. rex; and piano-playing, cymbal-clanking stuffed animals galore. But all is not plastic and tack at Wall Drug. The complex is divided into several small shops. A fine art gallery sells paintings, art prints, pottery, and bronze sculptures, and there is a great little bookstore with a fine collection of regional books. Look for Western clothing, leather goods, a rock shop, camping supplies, a jewelry store, donut shop, espresso bar, and a restaurant. And, there is a drugstore. Coffee is still $0.05 and ice water is still free.

Wall Drug still uses highway signs to advertise its offerings. The scope of the sign placement has expanded along with the store's success. Today, you can find signs advertising free ice water at Wall Drug along the highways in many outlying states, including Colorado and Wyoming. Ever visionary, there is even a Wall Drug sign in a London Underground station. And yes, even there, the advertising was successful. Curious Londoners have called the store asking about the signs, and some have come to visit!

National Grasslands Visitor Center

Wall is home to the National Grasslands Visitor Center (708 Main St., 605/279-2125, summer daily 8 A.M.–5 P.M., off-season Mon.–Fri. 8 A.M.–4:30 P.M., closed Sat.–Sun.). The center features over 20 exhibits highlighting the history of the Great Plains, prairie plants, and animals, including the endangered black-footed ferret and its food source, the prairie dog. A 25-minute film called *America's Grasslands* is shown upon request. The center also has

THE BADLANDS

© LAURAL BIDWELL

Ride a jackalope at Wall Drug.

information and maps about recreational opportunities in the grasslands.

Wounded Knee Museum

The Wounded Knee Museum (207 10th Ave., 605/279-2573, www.woundedkneemuseum. org, May–mid-Oct. daily 8:30 A.M.–5:30 P.M., closed in off season, adult $6, senior $5, child under 12 free) is a narrative museum. A path through the museum describes what really happened at Wounded Knee. Learn about Chief Big Foot and his tribe, the Ghost Dance, and the military at Pine Ridge. There are over two dozen exhibits that include historic photographs, as well as information about Lakota culture, the introduction and importance of the horse to the Lakota people, and the Fort Laramie Treaty of 1868, as well as exhibits on the key figures involved in the massacre. There is a small gift shop of Native American–made goods, as well as a small bookstore. The museum sells maps to be used for self-guided tours

of the Wounded Knee Massacre site, located on the Pine Ridge Reservation.

Minuteman Missile National Historic Site

It is ironic that one of the most frivolous of roadside stops, Wall Drug, is just down the street from one of the most ominous and serious. After World War II, relations between the United States and the Soviet Union became hostile as differences in political ideology and the shadow of atomic warfare loomed over both countries. Fear of nuclear attack created an arms race between the two countries that resulted in nuclear weapons stockpiles that could have eliminated life on Earth many times over. The Minuteman missile, named after the Minutemen of the Revolutionary War, was the deterrent weapon of choice for the United States. The missile could be launched in less than six minutes and could reach its target, up to 6,000 miles away, in less than 30 minutes.

Even if the Soviet Union performed a first-strike nuclear attack, the United States could respond quickly enough to "take them down with us." Minuteman missiles were armed with the equivalent of over one million tons of dynamite. This is 60 times more powerful than the bomb that was dropped on Hiroshima, Japan, that killed over 140,000 people. It is a devastating scenario. Minuteman missiles were developed in 1950, though the Minuteman II missiles located in South Dakota were built in 1960. In South Dakota, there were 150 launch silos and 15 launch control centers, all of which were operational by 1963.

In 1991, President George H. W. Bush and Soviet leader Mikhail Gorbachev signed the Strategic Arms Reduction Act Treaty (START) to reduce those stockpiles. All Minuteman II missile sites in South Dakota were deactivated. The START treaty did allow for one launch facility to serve as an interpretive location, and Launch Facility Delta-09 in South Dakota was designated to be the interpretive location.

Three sites, located within miles of each other, comprise the historic site. There is the visitor center, the launch control facility, and the missile launch site. The **Minuteman Missile Visitor Contact Center** (21280 Hwy. 240, 605/433-5552, www.nps.gov/mimi, Apr.–Oct. daily 8 A.M.–4:30 P.M., Nov.–Mar. Mon.–Fri. 8 A.M.–4:30 P.M., Sat.–Sun. 9 A.M.–4 P.M., free) is located off of I-90 at exit 131. The contact station is the Park Headquarters location and is situated next to the Badlands Trading Post (Conoco Station). The contact station should be your first stop for visiting the site. Tour tickets and directions to Launch Center Delta-01, where the tour is conducted, are issued here on a first-come, first-served basis. While at the contact station, view a film that outlines the history of the Cold War and of the Minuteman missile program, and look at the exhibits of Cold War artifacts on display.

During the summer and fall months (May–Oct.), **tours** are scheduled daily 9–11 A.M. and 1–3 P.M. During the rest of the year, tours are scheduled for weekdays only at 10 A.M. and 2 P.M. The ranger-guided tour of Launch Center Delta-01 takes about 40 minutes.

Launch Center Delta-01 is located off of I-90, exit 127, about four miles from Park Headquarters, and is the control facility for the missile launch. It is here that the missileers—those responsible for the firing of the missile, should the need arise—lived and worked (in three-day-on, three-day-off shifts). The upper floors of the site housed the living quarters for the eight personnel required to maintain the site. Basketball courts were installed outdoors, and a television room, library, and weight room were installed inside. The work of the missileers involved hours and hours of boredom, since their only real task was to wait for a signal to launch a nuclear attack. Underneath the living quarters, 31 feet down, was the launch control facility. There were two missileers in the underground facility at all times. Should an emergency war order come through, the missileers would decode it, agree to its authenticity, and then both missileers would open their personal combination safes to retrieve their own keys. It required two keys, turned simultaneously, to launch the missile. The key slots were set more than 12 feet apart so that one person could not launch the missile alone. Debunking the Hollywood myth, there never was a red phone or a red button to push to launch the missile. The formal tour that originates at the contact station at Park Headquarters includes a visit to the underground launch control facility.

Launch Facility Delta-09 is the actual missile silo. The silo is located off of I-90, exit 116. After exiting the highway, head south for about a half-mile and the silo will be visible on the right side of the road. The silo that housed the missile is comprised of an underground launch tube, 12 feet in diameter and 80 feet deep. It was capped by a 90-ton overhead door that would blow off when the missile was launched. Today, the door has been pulled partially off and a glass viewing window has been installed. An unarmed missile sits in the site and the glass window affords a view looking straight down into the silo—and straight at the missile warhead. Rangers are stationed at the facility only intermittently, but a self-guided cell phone tour is available April–October. The site is open year-round, weather permitting.

There are several misconceptions of the missile program that are cleared up on the tour, including the use of dual keys versus a red button. Another misconception was that the missile sites were "top secret." In fact, since the mis siles were intended to be deterrents to nuclear war, their existence was highly publicized and the sites themselves were never hidden. Many, like the silos in South Dakota, were located right next to interstate highways in plain view.

ACCOMMODATIONS

The town of Wall has a population hovering just over 800. On any given evening, though, the town can host over 2,000 visitors. Thanks to Wall Drug and the proximity of Badlands National Park, Wall is full of lodging choices. Best Western, Days Inn, Motel 6, and other chains are available, as are several locally owned establishments.

The **C Frontier Cabins Motel** (1101 S. Glenn St., 605/279-2619 or 888/200-8519, www.frontiercabins.net, open Apr.–Dec., shoulder season cabins Apr.–May and Sept.–Dec. $69–83, summer season cabins $108–131, tipis $60) is located just off of exit 110 on I-90. The motel has 33 rustic cabins with a long list of amenities, including free wireless, microwaves, refrigerators, coffeemakers, air-conditioning, and ceiling fans in every room. There are laundry facilities on-site and the cabins are all smoke free. No pets are allowed. There is a nice sized gift shop on-site, as well as a picnic area, a hot tub, and a playground for the children. The cabins are pine paneled and nicely decorated

in basic hunting lodge/Western style. The tipis are not heated or air-conditioned, but include two cots, two sleeping bags, and a small table. A bath and shower are available to tipi guests.

For basic accommodations, be sure to check out **C Sunshine Inn** (608 Main St., 605/279-2178 or 800/782-2613, sunshineinnatwallsd. com, open Apr.–Oct., Jun.–Aug. $75, Apr.–May $49, Sept.–Oct. $49, closed Nov.–Mar.). Owned by the same family since "sometime in the '70s," the inn offers 26 clean rooms, free Wi-Fi, and a continental breakfast, and allows small pets for a $5 fee. It's the perfect spot for a really reasonable stay near the park.

Another great choice is **Ann's Motel** (114 4th Ave., 605/279-2501, open year-round, summer $75, winter $55), which has free wireless and super friendly service. There are 12 units and six cabins. Pets are allowed in the rooms as long as they aren't left alone or are in kennels.

Campers should check out the **Sleepy Hollow Campground** (118 W. 4th Ave., 605/279-2100, www.sleepyhollowsd.com, Apr. 1–Nov. 1, closed in off-season, tent site $21, RV site $27–31). The campground is located off of I-90, exit 109, and is within easy walking distance of downtown Wall. Facilities include laundry and a small pool.

FOOD

The **Red Rock Restaurant** (506 Glenn St., 605/279-2388, open year-round, daily 11 A.M.–9 P.M., lunch $7–9, dinner $11–20) is a family-style restaurant that serves pies, soups, and salads—all made from scratch. Favorite menu items include the delicious broasted chicken and prime rib dinners, which are served every Friday and Saturday night. Beer and wine are available.

The **Wall Drug Cafe** (510 Main St., 605/279-2175, www.walldrug.com, June–Aug. daily 6:30 A.M.–9:30 P.M., Sept.–May daily 7 A.M.–5 P.M., breakfast $8, lunch $9, dinner $14) offers cafeteria-style dining and seats over

THE BADLANDS

500 people. It's not fancy, but there are some great choices. In the morning, the cake donuts are especially delicious, as are the pecan rolls. The hot roast beef sandwich is as good a sandwich as you'll find anywhere. While you have your meal, take time to enjoy the huge collection of American West–themed art displayed on the walls.

INFORMATION AND SERVICES

Contact the **Wall Chamber of Commerce** (501 Main St., 605/279-2665 or 888/852-9255, www.wall-badlands.com, Mon.–Fri. 8 A.M.–5 P.M.) for additional information about the town of Wall. Campers and backpackers can find groceries at the **Wall Food Center** (103 W. South Blvd., 605/279-2331). Remember that there is very little in the way of food available in Badlands National Park at any time, and nothing is available October–early May, so the grocery store might be a good option for creating a picnic lunch. Pick up water while you are there. The **post office** is located at 529 Main Street.

Pine Ridge Reservation

The Pine Ridge Reservation is located in the southwest corner of South Dakota. The reservation is home to the Oglala Sioux Nation. One of the largest reservations in the United States, it encompasses 3,468 square miles of land. The land of the reservation is varied. In the northwest corner, the multihued peaks, spires, grassy tables, and valleys of the Southern Unit of the Badlands occupy 160,000 acres. The land just south of the Badlands, west and central in the reservation, touches the outer spurs of the Black Hills, with low rolling hills, stands of ponderosa pine, and mixed-grass prairie. The southern and eastern areas of the reservation are prairie grasslands.

Life for the Oglala Sioux (Lakota) has not been easy. Forced to move onto reservation land at the end of the Indian Wars of 1876, stripped of their lands and livelihood, their language, and, in many cases, their culture, the Lakota still have a long road of healing ahead of them. In terms of relative time, the wounds are recent, though the damage is deep. There are signs, however, that out of the poverty and pain a new nation of Oglala Lakota leaders will emerge who will work to bring the community to spiritual and economic health.

Today, the people of Pine Ridge work to share their culture with the world outside the reservation boundaries. Their lands are beautiful, their history important. Visit the Red Cloud Indian School and learn about the history and culture of the Lakota people. Stop at Prairie Wind Casino, one of the first ventures to bring visitors to the reservation, and test your luck. Honor those who were massacred at Wounded Knee. Seek out a powwow. Go horseback riding or hiking near the Badlands and visit the art galleries and shops of the small communities of the Pine Ridge Reservation.

PLANNING YOUR VISIT

With the exception of the South Unit (Stronghold District) of Badlands National Park, the Pine Ridge Reservation is on privately owned land. It is good to plan ahead for a visit to the reservation. The area is vast and the towns are small. A visit to Pine Ridge is more a cultural and historical visit than it is sightseeing. Part of the experience of the reservation is to meet the people there. Some restaurants are in people's homes, and bed-and-breakfasts are in backyards. The powwows are community ceremonies. Many accommodations can set up a personal tour of the reservation, and arrange for horseback-riding trips, gallery tours, and other community events.

There are sights to see without making

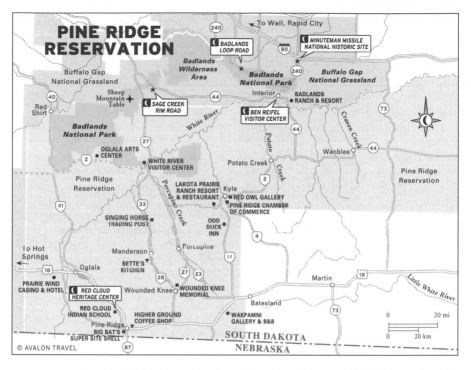

PINE RIDGE RESERVATION

To Wall, Rapid City

BADLANDS LOOP ROAD

MINUTEMAN MISSILE NATIONAL HISTORIC SITE

Badlands Wilderness Area

Buffalo Gap National Grassland

Badlands National Park

Buffalo Gap National Grassland

Sheep Mountain Table

SAGE CREEK RIM ROAD

Red Shirt

White River

Interior

BADLANDS RANCH & RESORT

BEN REIFEL VISITOR CENTER

Badlands National Park

OGLALA ARTS CENTER

WHITE RIVER VISITOR CENTER

Potato Creek

Wanblee

Pine Ridge Reservation

Pine Ridge Reservation

LAKOTA PRAIRIE RANCH RESORT & RESTAURANT

Kyle

RED OWL GALLERY

PINE RIDGE CHAMBER OF COMMERCE

SINGING HORSE TRADING POST

Porcupine Creek

ODD DUCK INN

To Hot Springs

Manderson

Porcupine

Oglala

BETTE'S KITCHEN

Martin

Little White River

PRAIRIE WIND CASINO & HOTEL

RED CLOUD HERITAGE CENTER

Wounded Knee

WOUNDED KNEE MEMORIAL

Batesland

RED CLOUD INDIAN SCHOOL

HIGHER GROUND COFFEE SHOP

WAKPAMNI GALLERY & B&B

0   20 mi

Pine Ridge

BIG BAT'S

SUPER SITE SHELL

SOUTH DAKOTA

0   20 km

© AVALON TRAVEL

NEBRASKA

arrangements through lodgings, but planning ahead is highly recommended. Many of the galleries on the reservation are run by the artists themselves, and they aren't always available on-site. The reservation is large and a long drive should end with more than an empty studio. Call before you leave. And once you get started? Tune your radio to KILI, 90.1 FM, and enjoy listening to the best in community-oriented radio broadcasting.

HISTORY

The Fort Laramie Treaty of 1868 defined the Great Sioux Nation as including all the lands from the Nebraska line to the 46th parallel between the Missouri River and the 104th degree of longitude. The entire Black Hills region was encompassed by this definition. White residents of the Dakota Territory were unhappy with the treaty. It had always been assumed that

there might be a great deal of mineral wealth in the region, and, as early as 1872, the editor of the Sioux City newspaper began publishing stories about the prospects for gold in the hills, as well as openly soliciting recruits for an expedition. The expedition didn't happen, thanks to military commands to abandon the project, but support for an excursion into the hills clearly existed in high levels of government. The secretary of the interior openly proclaimed that the Black Hills were not necessary to the happiness and prosperity of the native peoples.

Not all of the Native Americans in the Black Hills region agreed to sign the 1868 treaty, and so it was decided that an exploratory expedition should head into the hills, ostensibly searching for a good location for a military post. Lieutenant Colonel George A. Custer was assigned to command the enterprise. The Custer Expedition set out for the hills in July 1874.

It was an unusual expedition from the get-go. Over a thousand military troops were part of the group. Native scouts, newspaper correspondents, miners, a scientific corps, a musical band, and many civilian employees were included in the expedition's roster of personnel. The expedition never reported on a good location for a military post, but it did report the discovery of gold in the hills. Dispatches confirming the presence of gold in the Black Hills were sent in early August. By August 12, 1874, the news of gold in the Black Hills was released to the general public.

The first few gold-seeking parties were escorted out of the Black Hills by the military. But the trespassing prospectors came from all directions, and by 1875, at least 800 miners had eluded the government patrols and were in the Black Hills. While the military was trying to keep the prospectors out, local white communities to the east were demanding that the hills be opened to white settlers. The government decided to open negotiations for the cessation of the Black Hills and arranged for a delegation of Native American chiefs to visit the capital in 1875. The chiefs refused to give up the Black Hills and returned home. Despite the native people's refusal to give up their lands, the government held a grand council with the tribes in late 1875 and offered $400,000 annually for mining rights to the hills, or, alternatively, $6 million for the outright purchase of the land. The offer was refused. The government's response was to withdraw the cavalry from the hills, essentially allowing trespassers free access to the hills. Instead of stopping provision trains from carrying food and supplies to the mining camps, the freighters were advised to arm themselves against "hostile natives." The result of that decision was to begin another round of Indian Wars.

In late 1875, continual skirmishes with the native people were occurring in the Big Horn Mountain and Powder River regions of Wyoming, to the north and west of the Black Hills. Military leaders decided that the appropriate action would be a show of force that would bring the tribespeople into the agencies. General Crook initiated a campaign against the tribes in early 1876 from Fort Fetterman in Wyoming, heading for the Powder River country with only 900 troops. After an unsuccessful attack against a band of Cheyenne and a band of Oglalas under the leadership of Lakota warrior Crazy Horse, General Crook and his troops returned to the fort with plans to wait until spring before taking further military action. As spring approached, an attack strategy was designed to overwhelm the native people with three columns of troops: one led by General Crook, heading north from Fort Fetterman; one led by Colonel Gibbon, heading south from Montana, following the Yellowstone River; and one led by General Terry, moving west from the Little Missouri. Serving under General Terry, Lieutenant Colonel George A. Custer was in command of the 7th Cavalry. The plans led to disaster as Custer did not wait for Crook and Gibbon to arrive once he discovered the Native American camp. He divided his small army into three segments, keeping just 223 men by his side. While the other two segments of his command had to retreat from their attack positions and were able to join up, they were not able to go to the aid of Custer, whose forces were completely annihilated. Known as "Custer's Last Stand," it was the last of the major battles to be won by Native American forces.

Offensive attacks against the Sioux resumed in August 1876. At several of the agencies, friendly native people were disarmed and their ponies were removed as a preventative measure. Led by Crazy Horse, two-thirds of the Lakota, who had taken part in the Battle of Little Big Horn, spent the winter of 1876–1877 in the Powder River area. The military alternately skirmished and attempted negotiations. In February 1877, the military went to Spotted Tail, a Native American chief at one of the friendly camps that had not been disarmed, for assistance. Spotted Tail convinced many of the tribespeople to surrender. Some headed into Canada under the leadership of Sitting Bull, but by May 1877, nearly 4,500 Native American people went to the agencies. Crazy Horse and his band were the last to return. They went to the Red Cloud Agency, where Crazy Horse was killed when he resisted being placed in confinement.

The tragic events of the 1876 battles gave Congress the power and popular support to pass an appropriations bill that dictated that the Sioux would not receive any further appropriations unless they gave up the Black Hills. Commissioners, carrying the new agreement, went to several agencies of the Sioux, who, without horses or weapons, gave in. Under the terms, the Sioux sacrificed the Black Hills and all hunting rights in Montana and Wyoming. In lieu of money, the government committed to providing rations for the native people until they could support themselves. The Native American tribes were to be relocated to reservation lands. Many of those that had previously surrendered fled north to join Sitting Bull in Canada. Of those that remained, Spotted Tail's band relocated to Rosebud Creek and the Oglala Lakota picked their site at Pine Ridge, a few miles north of the Nebraska border.

SIGHTS
Wounded Knee Memorial

Located on a dusty hilltop overlooking the grassy plains of the Pine Ridge Reservation, the Wounded Knee Memorial is a small fenced-in cemetery, within which a tall stone stands as quiet testimony, covered with the names of some of the many Lakota people who were killed at the Wounded Knee Massacre of 1890. The memorial has no real address, no telephone number, no hours, and no admission fee. It is located at the junction of BIA 27 and BIA 28 just south of the community of Porcupine.

C Red Cloud Heritage Center

The Red Cloud Heritage Center (100 Mission Dr., Pine Ridge, 605/867-5491, www.redcloudschool.org, Memorial Day–Labor Day Mon.–Fri. 9 A.M.–7 P.M., Sat.–Sun. 11 A.M.–5 P.M., winter Tues.–Sat. 10 A.M.–7 P.M., closed Sun.–Mon., free, donations accepted) is located on the grounds of the Red Cloud School off of U.S. 18, just west of the community of Pine Ridge. The Red Cloud School started its affiliation with the Pine Ridge Reservation as the Jesuit Holy Rosary Mission. The reservation was deemed an Episcopal reservation by the U.S. government, but Chief Red Cloud trusted the Jesuits (the "Black Robes") to provide Native American children with the education they would need to survive in both the white and tribal worlds, and requested that they be allowed on the reservation. The mission was built in 1888. Today, the school teaches over 600 students from kindergarten through high school and has moved out of the old mission into larger classroom buildings on campus.

The Red Cloud Heritage Center opened in 1982, and is housed in the old mission building. The museum's fine arts collection has over 2,000 pieces, including paintings, drawings, and sculptures. The tribal arts collection focuses on Native American artifacts reflecting Oglala culture and history. Every summer late May–mid-August, the Heritage Center hosts the **Red Cloud Indian Art Show,** which brings together the work of artists from Native American tribes across the United States and Canada. There is a **gift shop** adjacent to the museum where the work of local Lakota artists is available for sale. Choose from an extensive collection of porcupine quillwork, beadwork, and a variety of traditional plains art including jewelry, pottery, glassware, star quilts, buffalo hides, and other specialty items.

Be sure to visit the **Holy Rosary Church.** The original church burned to the ground in 1996. The new building, opened in 1998, is a

THE WOUNDED KNEE MASSACRE

In 1877, the Oglala Lakota Sioux surrendered to military forces, and in 1878, in accordance with the treaty, they moved onto the Pine Ridge Reservation. It was a complete departure from their historic and cultural lifestyle. The nomadic life became sedentary. The hunting life ceased to exist, both with the demise of the buffalo and the enforced attempts at agriculture on the reservation. The mission of the government was to force the tribespeople to give up their traditions and culture completely and to assimilate them into white culture. Reservation schools and boarding schools were established and the Lakota language was banned. Traditional dances and ceremonies were also banned. And, just four years after the treaty that forced the people onto reservations, the government wanted to take more land. Justifiably, there was a lot of unrest on the reservation.

In the midst of all of this unrest, a new movement, a new religion, was rising in Nevada. At the center of the religion was a ceremony called the **Ghost Dance.** At the heart of the new religion was the belief that the ceremony would cause white settlers to go away, and that Native American people would be able to return to their former lives. Hearing about this new movement, a delegation from the Cheyenne River Reservation and another from the Rosebud Reservation headed to Nevada to learn more. When they returned, they introduced the Ghost Dance to Pine Ridge and then to the Rosebud and Cheyenne Reservations. The Pine Ridge administrator, newly appointed, panicked and called in the military.

When the soldiers arrived, the Ghost Dancers, fearing that the soldiers were there to kill them, fled into the Badlands. Rumors started that Sitting Bull, who had returned from Canada and was living near Standing Rock, was going to join the dancers in the south and his arrest was ordered. When his band was found, they resisted arrest, and Sitting Bull and several of his warriors were killed on December 15, 1890. A band of dancers, traveling with Big Foot on their way to surrender, heard about the death of Sitting Bull and fled. They were intercepted by units from the 7th Cavalry and escorted to upper Wounded Knee Creek. On the morning of December 29, the cavalry members entered Big Foot's camp to search for weapons and disarm the Native American people. Before they entered the camp, several Hotchkiss machine guns were set up on the ridge, trained on the camp below. In the course of the search, a shot was fired, and the cavalry retaliated with the Hotchkiss guns and other weapons. The number of dead is disputed, but at least 200 men, women, and children, including Big Foot, either died on the battlefield or died later from their wounds or hypothermia. The bodies were found as far as two miles away, as people were killed while they were trying to flee. It was the last major encounter between tribespeople and the military in the West.

The Wounded Knee Massacre was brought to national attention again in 1973 when a group of activists involved in the American Indian Movement (AIM) took over the village of Wounded Knee, laying siege to it for 71 days. Their demands were for hearings to be held on violations by the U.S. government regarding land use and treaty rights, and investigations of other grievances. Their cause elicited a lot of support, but their violent means created conflict not only between white and Native American people, but between tribal factions, as well. Shots were also fired at this Wounded Knee conflict, resulting in two deaths and nearly a dozen other gunshot wounds. Subsequently, charges brought against the AIM members were dismissed when the court judge found the FBI guilty of gross misconduct for its part in the skirmish.

restful spot, with white walls, light wood pews, and beautiful stained-glass windows.

Just to the left of the Heritage Center building, you will see a path that heads up a small hill. It is in this cemetery that Chief Red Cloud lies buried.

Prairie Wind Casino

The Prairie Wind Casino (12 miles east of Oelrichs on U.S. 18, 605/867-6300 or 800/705-9463, www.prairiewindcasino.com, open year-round, 24 hours daily) started as a couple of double-wide trailers, graduated to a tent-like building, and, in 2007, opened its current complex of buildings, which includes the casino, a hotel, and a restaurant. Blackjack, poker, and video and real slot machines are the order of the day. Tournaments are held on a regular basis. Call the casino for information about the schedule. No alcohol is served on reservation land.

For a day trip to the casino, leave your car in Hot Springs and take the bus. The busses travel between Hot Springs and Prairie Wind Casino on the first and third Tuesday of every month. The busses leave Hot Springs at 9 A.M., and leave the casino for the return trip at 3 P.M. Busses fit 37–52 people. Call 605/745-5765 for more information.

RECREATION
Horseback Riding

The **Badlands Ranch and Resort** (20910 Craven Rd., Interior, 605/433-5599 or 877/433-5599, www.badlandsranchandresort.com, May–Oct., closed in off-season, $45) offers 90-minute horseback rides to guests and nonguests alike. Call in advance to make reservations. Rides are offered in the morning (7–9 A.M.) and in the evening (5–8 P.M.) only, to avoid the hot sun of the afternoons. The rides are guided and travel though the Badlands area near the resort.

Horseback riding is also available at the **Singing Horse Trading Post** (BIA 33, 605/455-2143, www.singinghorse.net, open year-round,

$25 for the first hour, $15 for each additional hour). The trading post is located about seven miles north of Manderson on BIA 33, about a half-mile past the intersection with BIA 14, on the right. Please call in advance to arrange your ride.

EVENTS

The **Oglala Nation Pow Wow and Rodeo** is held the first weekend in August at the pow-wow grounds at Pine Ridge. There is a gate fee, set by the Tribal Office early in the year. Call the **Pine Ridge Chamber of Commerce** (605/455-2685) or the **Tribal Office** (605/867-5821, ext. 222 or ext. 227) for directions and more information.

A powwow is a community celebration and dance competition. Be sure to be on time for the grand entry, which is the opening ceremony for the powwow. It is a swirl of color and movement as contestants from each dance category enter the powwow grounds. Watch for the incredibly beautiful beadwork on the deerskin dresses of the traditional women dancers. Listen to the chiming of the hundreds of tiny bell-like jingle cones sewn on each dress of the jingle dancers. Enjoy the sinuous movements of the grass dancers and the flashing swirl of color and movement that announce the arrival of the fancy dancers. The dances are performed to drums, and the dancers are judged on their poise, footwork, demeanor, and showmanship. The pow-wow is held outside and chairs are not provided, so be sure to bring something to sit on.

SHOPPING

The **Singing Horse Trading Post** (BIA 33, 605/455-2143, www.singinghorse.net, June–Labor Day daily 10 A.M.–8 P.M., Labor Day–May Mon.–Sat. 10 A.M.–6 P.M.) started out as a supplier for Lakota arts and crafts, an enterprise it continues to this day. The trading post now also carries finished Lakota-made arts and crafts, as well. They have a wonderful collection of some beautiful beadwork, quillwork,

POWWOWS

The powwow (*wacipi*) is a Native American celebration enjoyed throughout the United States. It is a time to celebrate, to honor, and sometimes to mourn. It is a time to sing and dance, and a time to renew friendships. Powwows are colorful and rhythmic, an art form with historic roots that continues to evolve in contemporary culture.

Powwows are generally two to three days long. Passes can be purchased for a single day or for the weekend. The grand entry is a highlight not to be missed. Several large annual powwows in the Black Hills welcome visitors:

- The **Black Hills State University Lakota Omniciye Wacipi** (1200 University St., Spearfish, 800/255-2478, www.bhsu.edu) is held annually in early April. It is organized through the BHSU Center for Indian Studies and has been held for over 25 years.

- The **Oglala Lakota Vietnam Veterans Contest Pow Wow** (Pine Ridge Reservation, powwow grounds in Pine Ridge, call Pine Ridge Chamber of Commerce for details 605/455-2685, www. pineridgechamber.com) is held in mid-June.

- The **Oglala Lakota College Graduation**

Wacipi (Pine Ridge Reservation, powwow grounds in Kyle, call Oglala Lakota College for details 605/454-6000) is held in mid-to late June.

- The **Oglala Nation Pow Wow and Rodeo** (Pine Ridge Reservation, powwow grounds in Pine Ridge, call Pine Ridge Chamber of Commerce for details 605/455-2685, www. pineridgechamber.com) is held the first full weekend in August.

- The **Black Hills Pow Wow** (Rushmore Plaza Civic Center, 444 N. Mt. Rushmore Rd., Rapid City, 605/394-4111 or 605/341-0925, www.blackhillspowwow. intuitwebsites.com) has been held for over 40 years and is one of the premier gatherings in the country. It is held over the weekend of Native American Day in early October.

In addition to the large celebrations, community powwows are held most weekends at various locations in the hills from early spring to late fall. Check with the local chamber of commerce to see where an open powwow may be held during your visit.

star quilts, and paintings. The trading post is located about seven miles north of Manderson on BIA 33, about a half-mile past the intersection with BIA 14, on the right.

Wakpamni Gallery & Gifts (Hwy. 391, HC64 Box 43, 605/288-1800, www.wakpamni.com, open year-round) is located one mile south of U.S. 18 on Highway 391, then east three miles on a gravel road. It is located on the lovely grounds of the Wakpamni Bed & Breakfast. Call before you stop in as the store is only open when there is demand for it. This beautiful shop features porcupine quillwork, Native American beadwork, wearable art, jewelry, Lakota quilts, and other great items of regional interest. South Dakota–made products include fruit-flavored honeys and chokecherry jam.

Many Lakota artists live and work on the Pine Ridge Reservation and are happy to meet with visitors. They do ask, however, that visitors call ahead to ensure that they will be there. You can meet the artist at the **Red Owl Gallery** (27071 Bombing Range Rd., Kyle, 605/455-2814, www.lakotamall.com/redowl, open year-round, call for appt.) and enjoy original work in acrylics and cast paper. Richard "Codger" Red Owl is a story keeper who incorporates Lakota history, culture, and stories into his work. He also makes handmade drums. Call to meet him at his studio. The studio is located 3.5 miles east of Kyle and six miles north of BIA 2. Watch for his signs.

Randall Blaze, an award-winning potter and sculptor, can be found at his gallery, the **Oglala Arts Center** (off of Hwy. 2, between the White River Visitor Center and Buffalo Gap, 605/441-9790, by appt.). The gallery includes works of other artists, including Don Montileaux and Richard Red Owl.

ACCOMMODATIONS

The **Prairie Wind Casino & Hotel** (U.S. 18, Pine Ridge, 605/867-2683 or 800/705-9463, www.prairiewindcasino.com, $75–85) is located 12 miles east of Oelrichs, or 30 miles west of the town of Pine Ridge on U.S. 18. Amenities include an indoor swimming pool, hot tub, and fitness center. The 78 rooms are decorated in Native American style. The hotel has a dining facility on-site.

The **Wakpamni Bed & Breakfast** (Hwy. 391, HC64 Box 43, 605/288-1800, www.wakpamni.com, $80–100) is a family farm that was renovated in 1995 to serve as a bed-and-breakfast. There are two houses on the property, each with three rooms and two bathrooms available for guests. There is also an impressive gift shop available on the grounds, which features Native American art and craftwork. The three rooms in the main house are decorated with regional themes (the Lakota room, the pioneer room, and the cowboy room). The rooms in the Folks' House are decorated in farmhouse style with lots of antiques and quilts. The property is beautifully landscaped with many flowerbeds around the houses. Two tipis are set up away from the house, facing east in the traditional manner; each can sleep up to three people. A shower house with hot water is available for guests staying in the tipis, as is electricity and primitive bathroom facilities. A full hot breakfast is served to all guests. Your hosts, the Swicks, returned to the family farm more than 25 years ago and are happy to share their knowledge of the area. They can arrange for guided tours of the reservation for you and they can also arrange for horseback-riding excursions. From U.S. 18, go east past the community of Pine Ridge, to the intersection with Highway 391. Head south on Highway 391 for about a mile and look for signs. Go east about three miles on a gravel road to the bed-and-breakfast. From Gordon, Nebraska, go north on Highway 391 for three miles, and turn right (east) on the same gravel road.

The **Odd Duck Inn** (Kyle, 605/455-2972, www.oddduckinn.com, $65 per room per night, plus meals if desired, breakfast $7, lunch $9, dinner $12) is owned and operated by Oglala Lakota tribe member Tilda Long Soldier and her husband, renowned author Mark St. Pierre. Their inn is located north and east of Kyle. Take BIA 2 east from Kyle to the junction of BIA 17. Head south about two miles and watch for the signs. The Odd Duck Inn is about four miles down a gravel road. The inn has two homes available for guests—a total of eight rooms. There are three shared kitchens and four bathrooms available. The homes are equipped with central air, laundry, dishwashers, and wireless Internet. If you are interested in learning about Lakota culture, this is a great place to start. Mark and Tilda are willing to arrange or conduct arts, Lakota culture, Western and Native American, or wildlife tours for guests ($175 base cost, plus $25 per person up to a maximum of four participants, for an eight-hour day).

The **Lakota Prairie and Ranch Resort** (7958 Lakota Prairie Dr., 605/455-2555, www.lakotaprairie.com, open year-round, May 1–Sept. $70, Oct.–Apr. $60) is a clean hotel located six miles southwest of Kyle, across the street from the main campus of the Oglala Lakota College. Each of the 30 rooms comes with free wireless Internet, a microwave, refrigerator, and coffeemaker. The rooms are primarily pine paneled with Native American/Western decor. Laundry facilities are available for guests, and there is a restaurant on-site. There is also a campground on the grounds of the hotel. The cost is $15 for two for a tent site with no hookups, or $28 per night for an RV site with electric and water hookups.

FOOD

Located 12 miles east of Oelrichs, or 30 miles west of Pine Ridge, off of U.S. 18, the **Winds of**

Change Restaurant & Snow's Garden Buffet (U.S. 18, 605/867-2683, www.prairiewindcasino.com, daily 7:30–10 P.M., breakfast buffet Sat.–Sun. only $11.95, lunch buffet $11.95, dinner buffet $16.95–18.95; menu: breakfast $8, lunch $10, dinner $13) is located on the grounds of the Prairie Wind Casino & Hotel. The dining room is large but is warm, with wood floors and muted wall colors highlighted by original paintings of local artists. The breakfast buffet includes eggs, bacon, sausages, hash browns, and biscuits and gravy. The lunch and dinner buffets include soups, salads, and a variety of entrées (such as ham, beef, and chicken) that change daily. The restaurant also has a limited menu available all day, which includes basic sandwiches, hamburgers, and chicken and steak dishes.

Every community needs a great morning meeting place, and Pine Ridge has the **Higher Ground Coffee Shop** (U.S. 18, Pine Ridge, 605/867-5685, Memorial Day–Labor Day Mon.–Fri. 7 A.M.–6 P.M., closed Sat.–Sun., off-season Mon.–Fri. 7 A.M.–5 P.M., breakfast $4, lunch $7). In downtown Pine Ridge, across the street from Pizza Hut on U.S. 18, look for a rose-colored building with coffee beans stenciled on the walls just below the roofline. This is a warm, welcoming place with a fireplace and a wraparound deck that serves pastries and breakfast burritos in the morning and creates a luncheon special every day. The daily special varies from sandwiches to casseroles to whatever the owner is in the mood to create. All the pastries are made from scratch, and homemade pies are served seasonally. And, of course, there is a full menu of hot and cold coffee and other specialty drinks. Look for the friendly and furry store greeters out on the deck. Free wireless Internet is available.

Big Bat's Super-Site Shell (junction of U.S. 18 and Hwy. 407, Pine Ridge, 605/867-5077, Mon.–Sat. 6 A.M.–8 P.M., breakfast $7, lunch and dinner $8) is part museum, part gift shop, part gas station, and part restaurant, all rolled into one. The store is named after Baptiste Gene Pourier (Big Bat), a Frenchman born in 1834 who married a Lakota woman named Jean Richards. With his ability to speak French, English, and Lakota, Big Bat worked as an interpreter for the negotiation of the Fort Laramie Treaty in 1868. The current owners, Bat and Patty Pourier, are Big Bat's great-great-grandchildren. The restaurant serves a full breakfast menu, including egg dishes, waffles, and pancakes. Lunch and dinner include a variety of sandwiches including buffalo burgers, burritos, and subs, as well as a daily lunch special. The ceilings are high and the acoustics are poor so it can be a little loud inside. Look for some special touches. Don Montileaux, a Lakota artist, was hired to do all of the artwork for the building. Montileaux created a 108-foot mural based on Lakota oral history, telling stories related by his grandfather, including "Buffalo Calf Woman" and "The Horse Story." There are historical photos on the wall, and many Lakota symbols and beliefs are displayed and explained throughout the store. After lunch, you can fill your gas tank while there!

Not only will you get home cooking at **Bette's Kitchen** (111 Black Elk Rd., Manderson, 605/867-1739, daily 11:30 A.M.–2 P.M., $6), you'll be served in Bette's home. The kitchen is located one mile south of Manderson, or seven miles north of the Wounded Knee Memorial, off of Highway 28. Look for the signs, as the driveway can be hard to see. Bette's home sits on a ridge on the left as you go up the hill. The specialty of the house is soup made from scratch with homemade bread served daily. Bette is happy to accommodate vegetarians with veggie burgers or vegetarian soup. Relax and enjoy this little center of community activity. Bette is a descendant of Black Elk, and her home is on historic Black Elk land. She is also a former nutritionist and enjoys visiting with the many international visitors to the reservation.

The **Lakota Prairie Ranch Restaurant** (7958 Lakota Prairie Dr., 605/455-2555, www.lakotaprairie.com, daily 8 A.M.–9 P.M., breakfast $7, lunch $8, dinner $12) is located about six miles south of Kyle on Highway 2. It is affiliated with the motel of the same name. The restaurant is a nice, rustic, comfortable, country-style place with lots of windows and booths. A full breakfast menu is served in the morning. Lunch includes sandwiches, buffalo burgers, salads, and soups. Chicken-fried steak is the specialty of the house in the evening. Come here for good solid comfort food in a cozy and friendly environment.

INFORMATION AND SERVICES
Information
The **Pine Ridge Chamber of Commerce** (Lakota Trade Center, Ste. 104, Kyle, 605/455-2685, www.pineridgechamber.com, Mon.–Fri. 8 A.M.–5 P.M.) has information on powwows and other community events, reservation maps, and business directories.

Be sure to listen to **KILI Radio** (605/867-5002, www.kiliradio.org, 90.1 FM) while you are visiting the reservation, and pick up a copy of the *Lakota Country Times* newspaper (605/685-1868, www.lakotacountrytimes.com). The paper is published weekly and can be picked up at convenience stores and grocery stores throughout the reservation.

Tour Companies
Access to the Pine Ridge Reservation is primarily by car. It is possible, however, to arrange a tour with **Affordable Adventures** (5542 Meteor St., Rapid City, 605/342-7691 or 888/888-8249, www.affordableadventuresbh.com, $240 per person), a small-group tour company that provides narrated tours on small vans through the Pine Ridge Reservation. The tours start in Rapid City, travel to the town of Scenic, and then head south to the reservation on BIA 27. The tour varies, depending on the weather, but generally includes visits to the South Unit of the Badlands (Sheep Mountain Table and the White River Visitor Center), Oglala Lakota College Historical Center, Wounded Knee Memorial, Red Cloud Heritage Center, and Red Shirt Table. Tours will sometimes include a step-on narration by Native American guides. Lunch is in Manderson or Kyle.

BACKGROUND

The Land

The Black Hills of South Dakota are frequently referred to as an "Island in the Plains," and the description is an apt one. The Cheyenne River sets the southern border while the Belle Fouche River (pronounced Bell Foosh) defines the northern edge. The Thunder Basin Grasslands of Wyoming to the west and the Buffalo Gap National Grasslands to the east complete the circle around the hills. The hills rise over 3,000 feet above the plains, reaching their pinnacle of 7,242 feet at Harney Peak, the highest point in North America east of the Rocky Mountains. About two-thirds of the hills are located within the confines of the Black Hills National Forest. The southern region is mixed-grass prairie. The north is lush with ponderosa pine, and even the ridges of the rolling hills of the south sport pine silhouettes. Seen from a distance, the deep green trees appear as a dark band on the horizon, giving the area its name. From east to west, about two-thirds of the hills are located in South Dakota, and one-third spills into Wyoming. Several small rivers cut through the hills, most notably Spearfish Creek in the

north, Rapid Creek in the central region, and Fall River in the south, and bring additional recreational and scenic beauty to the area.

GEOLOGY

The Black Hills were formed by an uplift that occurred near the end of the Cretaceous Period or the beginning of the Paleogene Period, 65–70 million years ago. The uplift created an elliptical dome, at the center of which is a crystalline core, comprised of the oldest rocks in the hills. This core is Precambrian, dating back over two billion years. The granite peaks near Mount Rushmore, dominated by the 7,242-foot Harney Peak, are at the center of the uplift. At the time of the uplift, it is estimated that the hills reached an elevation of over 15,000 feet and that the work of wind and water over the last 65 million years has created the hills we see today.

Encircling the Precambrian core of the Black Hills are progressively younger rock layers. Time in the Black Hills looks much like a topographic map, each band a different geological period, marching downward and outward and around the hills, from oldest to youngest through the Precambrian, Paleozoic, Mesozoic, and Cenozoic Eras.

Unlike the Black Hills, in the Badlands, the youngest formations are on the top and time marches straight down. Formed primarily by two geologic processes, deposition and erosion, the oldest exposed (and lowest) layers of the area were created 69–75 million years ago, when the surface area was covered by a warm inland sea. When the hills uplifted, the sea drained away and was replaced by a river floodplain that deposited a new layer every time a flood occurred. A drier period followed, bringing sediments deposited by the wind, the colors varying with time and volcanic activity. As the uplift to the west continued, the water current increased and began to carve into the very

granite spires of the Needles formation

deposits earlier streams had left behind. Some 65 million years later, we have the eroded spires and valleys of the Badlands today.

CLIMATE

The Dakotas have the reputation for harsh winters with frequent blizzards and scorching summers, but weather in the Black Hills is much less dramatic. The hills are semi-arid and residents can expect to see an average of 275 days of sunshine per year. Rainfall is generally less than 17 inches per year, and annual snowfall hovers around 40 inches, most of which is deposited in the upper elevations. There are regional climate differences in the hills, with temperatures a few degrees cooler and snowfall a few inches greater in the higher elevations of the Central and Northern Hills. The southern fringe of the hills, just south of Custer State Park, is frequently referred to as the "banana belt," with weather generally milder than that of the Northern Hills. Open to the southern Chinook winds generated by the Rocky Mountains, and protected by the higher peaks to the north from the cold arctic winds heading south from Canada, Southern Hills weather is not unlike that of Denver, drier and warmer than the regions around it.

The major determinate of climate is latitude, modified by regional variations in topography, elevation, precipitation, and other factors. The Black Hills, roughly situated 43.4–44.5° latitude, share this position with sister cities Corvallis, Oregon; Jackson, Wyoming; Stowe, Vermont; Portland, Maine; and Nice, France.

The climate of the hills varies greatly month by month. January and February are the coldest months of the year. Daytime temperatures average in the 30s, and snowfall averages from five inches in the Rapid City area to 15 inches in the higher elevations. Nights can bring temperatures down to 10–20°F, though single-digit and sub-zero days can occur, particularly in the higher elevations. Frequent sunny days and

Chinook winds from the Rocky Mountains, however, can result in temperatures climbing into the 50s and 60s. March is the snowiest month of the year, and April is not far behind, but temperatures start to warm up (with average daytime temperatures hovering around 40°F in March and 50°F in April, and lows in the 20s and 30s, respectively). In May and June, precipitation changes to rain and then thundershowers, which generally arrive mid-afternoon, move quickly to the plains, and disappear by evening. Temperatures start to rise dramatically, with daytime highs averaging in the 60s in May and 70s by June. Nights remain chilly, still in the 30s and 40s in May, but climb in June to the 40s and 50s. Summers are warm, dry, and sunny, with daytime temperatures reaching into the 70s and 80s and nights averaging in the 50s. Remember that these are averages and actual weather on any given day can be significantly higher or lower than average. Pack those sweaters and keep in mind that at elevations of 4,000–7,000 feet, the sun can be intense. Don't forget the sunscreen and sunglasses, and don't rule out bringing along a brimmed hat for sun protection. September and October traditionally experience mild days, with temperatures in the 60s and 70s in September, and the 50s and 60s in October. At night, temperatures drop to the 30s and 40s in September, and by October, you can subtract another 10°F from the high and low. November and December mark the beginning of winter, with the number of mild versus cool days reversing. Daytime temperatures hover in the 30s, though milder days are frequent. Nights bring readings in the teens, with occasional arctic air from Canada bringing sub-zero temperatures. Sun and warmer temperatures always return quickly, though. Snowfall averages about five inches a month during this period, with early storms generating heavy, wet snows and later storms bringing light and drier snow. The short days of winter cut sharply into the available sunshine and, by the end of this period, everyone is looking forward to spring.

The Badlands, situated in the middle of the plains, have no protection, no shade, and no wind break. As a result, winters there can be very cold, with brisk winds and arctic cold weather arriving undiverted from the north. Summers are hotter than the neighboring region. At a lower elevation and, again, with little shade, temperatures are not infrequently at least 10 degrees higher than the hills to the west.

All of that being said, remember that the difference between climate and weather is a function of time. Climate is the result of years of studies of the averages and patterns of daily weather. Weather is short term. It's what you confront when you wake up in the morning. Be prepared.

Flora and Fauna

The Black Hills occupy an area of approximately 65 by 125 miles; while the area is small, the diversity is great. Located in the middle of the country, surrounded by grasslands and plains, the Black Hills form the ecological junction of many regions. Here can be found wildlife and plant species typical of the Rocky Mountains, the Great Plains, northern forests, and eastern forests.

PLANTS

There are over 1,500 plant species in South Dakota, and of those, over 1,200 species can be found in the Black Hills. The ponderosa pine is the dominant tree found in the Black Hills, and it is found in every region and habitat in the hills. Companion vegetation, however, is dictated by variations in moisture, elevation, temperature, and soil conditions. Species common to prairie grasslands, coniferous forests, deciduous forests, and mountainous forests can all be found in the region. It is estimated that of the 1,200 species of plants found in the Black Hills region, 30 percent originated in the Plains, 25 percent in the Rockies, 5 percent in deciduous forests, and 1 percent in northern forests.

Grasslands

Wind Cave National Park, the Badlands, and the southern area of Custer State Park contain both ponderosa pine forest and mixed-grass prairie environments. In yet another example of how east meets west in the Black Hills, the area west of the Black Hills is short-grass prairie, and east of the Missouri, the prairie lands are tallgrass prairie. Plants that grow in short-grass or in tallgrass prairies can both be found in the mixed-grass prairie of western and central South Dakota. In a rainy year, tallgrass prairie plants will be the most evident. In an arid year, the short-grass prairie plants will thrive. Tallgrass prairie plants require more moisture than short-grass plants and can usually be located, even in dry years, in valleys, where drainage will add moisture to the fields.

Cactus plants thrive in short-grass prairies, and prickly pear and pincushion cactus are common in this region on the drier southern-facing slopes. Other common shortgrasses in this area include bluegrasses, buffalo grass, wheatgrass, and little bluestem. Shrubs include rabbitbrush, sage, mountain mahogany, buffaloberry, dogwood, snowberry, and coralberry, among others.

About 25 percent of Wind Cave National Park is tree-covered; ponderosa pine is the most common tree. There are also scattered groves of elm, aspen, bur oak, box elder, and birch in the park, which are usually found in drainage areas.

Deciduous Forest

A deciduous tree is one that sheds its leaves in the winter, enters a dormancy phase in cold weather, and then, when warmer temperatures return, experiences regrowth. This process allows the tree to withstand extremes of temperature. There are several pockets of deciduous trees in the hills, most of which are migrants from the east. On the eastern side of the hills near streambeds, deciduous trees include the box elder, ash, American elm, eastern cottonwood, dogwood, and willow trees. The northeastern foothills, at lower elevations and with relatively dry slopes, host bur oak trees with an understory (plants that grow in the shade or beneath the canopy of higher trees) of sumac, coralberry, and poison ivy. In the northwest corner of the hills, quaking aspen and paper birch trees can be found. Understory plants include chokecherry, beaked hazelnut, and wild rose.

Coniferous Forest

Ponderosa pine is found everywhere in the Black Hills. There are regional variations in the understory of the forest depending on many factors, including moisture levels, temperature, and elevation. In the Southern Hills, where the environment is generally warmer and drier than the rest of the hills, the understory of the ponderosa pine forest is comprised of little bluestem, yucca, sagebrush, sand lily, and various gramas and needlegrasses. In areas that are at elevations over 7,000 feet, the understory is comprised of juniper, Oregon grape, buffaloberry, and blue wild rye. At the moister elevations of 4,000–5,000 feet, the forest canopy includes both the ponderosa pine and the bur oak, with an understory of chokecherry, Oregon grape, and melic grasses. On the western edge of the hills, skunkbrush and American black currant appear. White spruce is also found in the higher and moisture-rich elevations of the Black Hills. A variant of the white spruce, the Black Hills spruce is the state tree of South Dakota.

Wildflowers

At first glance, the prairie grasslands look to be a sea of soft green or gold, depending on the season. A closer look reveals vibrant color scattered throughout the fields. There are literally hundreds of wildflower species that grow in the prairie grasslands. The pasque flower, a beautiful light-violet flower, is one of the first flowers of early spring and is the state flower. Many species of milk vetches, asters, milkweeds, penstemons, and evening primroses are common.

Beautiful to look at, flowers in the Black Hills were also used for practical and medicinal purposes by many Native American people. The sap of the bright-yellow false dandelion was used to clean teeth, wild blue flax seeds were used to flavor food, purple clover made a flavorful tea, and the purple coneflower (echinacea) was used for headaches, stomachaches, and sore throats.

FAUNA

The mixed habitat of the Black Hills, the rolling plains of the Southern Hills, and the wooded hills and stream valleys of the area all provide homes for a wide variety of wildlife. The South Dakota state bird is the **ring-necked pheasant** and the state animal is the **coyote.**

Mammals

It has been estimated that when Europeans first arrived on New World soil, 40–60 million **bison** roamed the Great Plains. A century after the Lewis and Clark Expedition, less than 1,000 bison were alive in the country. Alarmed, ranchers started private herds, some herds were preserved in zoos, and there were a few small herds left near Yellowstone in Wyoming.

Conservationists and hunters both realized that bison could disappear from the prairie environment forever if action wasn't taken. In 1911, the American Bison Society began searching for places to establish a protected habitat for the bison. Wind Cave National Park was one of the first places where bison were restored to the wild. In 1913, 20 animals

© LAURAL BIDWELL

the hardy prairie dog

were donated to the park; six came from the Yellowstone herd, and 14 were donated by the New York Zoological Society. Today, the herd numbers 375, a quantity just shy of the estimated optimal number of 450 for the bison, and for the available 28,000 acres of range in the park. In recent years, traces of cattle genes have been found in most bison herds. Through testing, however, it has been determined that the Wind Cave National Park herd is pure buffalo, untainted by any trace of cattle genes.

Other animals, including the **pronghorn** and the **elk,** were also reintroduced to Wind Cave National Park in the early 1900s. Today, the pronghorn herd is estimated at 130 animals, and the elk, which drift into and out of the park, have an estimated population of up to 700 animals in summer and 900 animals in winter. The number is higher than optimal, and the park has installed several elk jump gates to encourage them to leave the park. Conservation work continues at the park. The endangered **black-footed ferret** was reintroduced to the park beginning in 2007. That year, 49 animals were released; in 2010, an additional 12 ferrets were released. As of the 2011 animal survey in the park, the black-footed ferret population was estimated to number no less than 46–64 animals, a self-sustaining number.

The bison at Wind Cave National Park are not the only bison in the region. Bison were reintroduced to Custer State Park in 1914, shortly after the Wind Cave herd was established, with the purchase of 36 bison. By 1940, the herd size at Custer State Park had increased to over 2,500 animals. At that size, the herd was overgrazing the rangeland and it was determined that a healthy sustainable herd should number around 1,500 animals, the number that roams through the 73,000 acres of the park today. The annual **Buffalo Roundup,** which occurs in Custer State Park in late September, is open to the public, and is the time when the herd is vaccinated against disease and culled if necessary.

Bison are confined within these large range areas, but most of the wildlife of the Black Hills come and go as they please through the parks and are found throughout the hills. Easily visible animals include **whitetail deer** and their large-eared relatives, the **mule deer**. The beautiful snowy-white **mountain goat** can be seen in the northern corners of Custer State Park and is also frequently spotted around Mount Rushmore National Memorial and Crazy Horse Memorial. The mountain goat is unique to North America but is not a native species in the Black Hills. Stocked in the region in 1924, it has since thrived. The original bighorn sheep species in South Dakota, the Audubon subspecies, became extinct in 1920. A herd of **Rocky Mountain bighorn sheep** were introduced to Custer State Park and can still be seen, generally north of Bluebell Lodge in the park. The **prairie dog** never suffered the threat of extinction and is prolific in Custer State Park and Wind Cave National Park, as well as the prairie regions surrounding the hills. It has been discovered, however, that a virulent strain of plague is threatening colonies in the Badlands, the Conata Basin, and in Wind Cave. Many of these areas have been dusted with insecticide (to kill fleas that carry the disease), though some of the prairie dog acres are still at risk.

Much of the wildlife of the Black Hills is not as easily viewed. Elk are shy animals and are only infrequently viewed without research. The elk is a majestic animal, with heavy, wide antlers. They can stand five feet at the shoulder and weigh over 1,000 pounds. Even in the briefest flash of a headlight, the sheer size of the elk makes its identity unmistakable. The region's only remaining large predator is the **mountain lion,** which has been spotted somewhat more frequently in recent years, likely due to an increase in active hunting, which drives the animal out of its hidden den areas. Other seldom-seen inhabitants of the hills include the flying squirrel, opossum, raccoon, weasel, mink, skunk, badger, fox, coyote, bobcat, and marmot.

Birds

The Black Hills are as far west as most Eastern birds travel, and as far east as most Western birds fly. As a result, you'll want to bring your field guide to North America, or to the Great Plains, and forget packing guides to just Eastern or Western birds. Add to the mix the unique environment near the Nature Conservancy, south of Hot Springs, where a warm water stream and a cold water stream come together. It's an unusual ecological combination that results in an interesting collection of birds, plants, and insects. Bird lists for the region include over 400 different bird species in South Dakota, most of which can be found in the Black Hills.

In the southern mixed-grass habitat, look for the sharp-tailed grouse, long-billed curlew, burrowing owl, and diminishing populations of sage grouse, sage thrasher, and brewer's sparrow. The Badlands region hosts white-throated swifts, and juniper groves are home to long-eared owls and mountain bluebirds. The ponderosa pine forests that dominate the Black Hills provide rich habitat for three-toed woodpeckers, ruby- and golden-crowned kinglets, and swainson's thrushes. Waterside, the western tanager, black-headed grosbeak, lazuli bunting, and bullock's oriole can be found.

The South Dakota Ornithologists Union has identified several birding "hot spots" in the Black Hills, including Sylvan Lake in Custer State Park; the Boles and Redbird Canyons, which are located near Jewel Cave; the Fort Meade Recreation Area; Canyon Lake in Rapid City; Hot Brook Canyon, just outside of Hot Springs; Angostura Recreation Area, south of Hot Springs; Edgemont, with its sage-rich habitat; and Spearfish Canyon and Roughlock Falls in the Northern Hills.

Reptiles and Amphibians

Amphibians fall between fish and reptiles on the evolutionary scale, and many have

LEWIS AND CLARK AND A LUCKY PRAIRIE DOG

Thomas Jefferson was a visionary armchair explorer. In January 1803, even before the Louisiana Purchase had been suggested, before the United States became the official owners of the territories north and west of the Mississippi River, he requested that Congress fund an expedition that would cross the Louisiana Territory regardless of who owned it. It was his wish that the territory become part of the United States, however, and by April 1803, an agreement had been reached (but not yet ratified) for the United States to purchase 875,000 square miles of land for $15 million, doubling the size of the country. By December 1803, the United States took possession of the Louisiana Territory. In 1804, Jefferson's request for a mission to explore the territory became the Lewis and Clark Expedition. The expedition had three missions, one of which was to discover and document new wildlife. The expedition arrived in South Dakota in late 1804. Many of the prairie animals discovered on the trip had never been seen by white explorers before, and in keeping with the expedition's mandate, several live species were sent back to Washington DC. A prairie dog was captured, wintered with the crew in Fort Mandan, and then survived the trip downriver and east to Washington DC. Not all of the live specimens were as lucky. (I'm not sure I'd have wanted to be the one receiving Jefferson's mail at the time.) A sharp-tailed grouse made the trip, but didn't arrive alive. Only one of four magpies survived the trip. Lewis and Clark were also the first to provide detailed scientific descriptions of the pronghorn (which they erroneously called a goat), jackrabbit, mule deer, and coyote. The bounty of the prairies was also revealed. Meriwether Lewis wrote, "Vast herds of Buffaloe deer Elk and Antilopes were seen feeding in every direction as far as the eye of the observer could reach."

changed little from their ancestors that roamed the Earth up to 270 million years ago. Cold-blooded amphibians, at the early stages of their development, live in water and breathe through gills. As they mature, amphibians will usually lose their gills and develop legs, and many become terrestrial. Appropriately, the word "amphibian" means "double life."

South Dakota has a total of 15 species of amphibians. Of these, just about half can be found in the Black Hills region, including two species of true frogs (the **northern leopard frog** and the **bullfrog**), two species of true toads (the **Great Plains toad** and the **Woodhouse's toad**), one tree frog (the **chorus frog**), one spadefoot (the **Plains spadefoot**), and one salamander (the **tiger salamander**). While some amphibians are completely terrestrial, all of South Dakota's amphibians must return to water to lay their eggs.

Reptiles are also cold-blooded, but unlike amphibians, they have never had gills or breathed water in any stage of their development. Reptiles in the Black Hills include turtles, snakes, and lizards. Turtles have been with us since the Triassic period, dating back over 200 million years. In winter, all South Dakota turtles hibernate in burrows or in the mud underwater. There are seven species of turtle in South Dakota, of which four are found in the Black Hills region. These include the **Western painted turtle,** the **snapping turtle,** the **spiny softshell turtle,** and the **smooth softshell turtle.** Both of the softshell turtles are classified as rare. The snapping turtle is the largest, most aggressive, and most common turtle in South Dakota, and it can grow to over 40 pounds. It is not wise to try and pick one of these up. With sharp claws and strong jaws, a snapper can inflict a great deal of damage on ill-placed fingers. The Western painted turtle lives up to its name with a gorgeous red, orange, and yellow plastron (lower shell).

There are 10 different species of snake inhabit the Black Hills. The biggest snake in the region is the **bull snake,** which can range 37–72 inches in length. The **Black Hills redbelly snake,** once thought to be rare, may well be just super shy. A subspecies of the redbelly snake, it prefers high, moist elevations, like the conditions near Mount Rushmore and Harney Peak. The **prairie rattlesnake** is the only venomous snake in the Black Hills. A member of the pit viper family, the prairie rattler has a triangle-shaped head, with a pit on both sides of the head between the eye and nostril. Light brown in color, the snake is marked by dark oval blotches with light borders that become rings near the tail section. They range in length 30–40 inches and have a rattle on the tail. Remember that any snake with a pointed tail is not a rattlesnake. Also remember that snakes are secretive by nature, are not aggressive, and will leave you alone if you leave them alone, unless trapped or endangered in some way.

Insects and Arachnids

The **Western black widow spider** is one of the few venomous arachnids in the state, though it's uncommon for people to be bitten by the spider. A reclusive spider, it is known for the bright-red hourglass shape on its lower abdomen.

In the early spring, the **wood tick** is one of South Dakota's more annoying arachnids. (Ticks are not insects; they are closely related to spiders.) The wood tick can carry Rocky Mountain spotted fever and Colorado tick fever. The deer tick, which carries Lyme disease, is rare in South Dakota.

The insect posing the most problems in South Dakota is not a threat to the human population, but is a threat to the ponderosa pine forest that dominates the flora of the Black Hills. The **mountain pine beetle** has inhabited the Black Hills as long as there has been a pine forest here. The beetle population is cyclical. At times, the beetle is fairly rare, but every 10 years or so, the beetle population increases, and beetles attack healthy as well as stressed trees.

These outbreaks last 5–13 years and then the population declines again. Since 1999, pine beetle infestation in the Black Hills has reached epidemic proportions due to a combination of many factors, including drought, fire suppression, and mild winters. You can see the effects of the beetle in the large number of rust-colored trees in the forest. Pine beetles will die out if subjected to extreme cold for several days in the midst of winter. Measures taken to prevent the spread of the pine beetle include thinning tree stands and prescribed burns. The area around Harney Peak includes the Elk Creek Wilderness and is a place that has high visitation. No logging or burning is allowed in the wilderness. Pine beetle infestation near Harney Peak has prompted the Forest Service to take action. Logging in the area will be noticeable for quite some time.

Fish

South Dakota is home to over 100 fish species, and, of these, nearly 30 species are of interest to anglers. The mountain lakes and fast-moving streams of the Black Hills contain populations of walleye, salmon, bluegill, crappie, perch, bass, pike, trout, and catfish.

ENVIRONMENTAL ISSUES

Several environmental issues confront the various agencies charged with stewardship of the public lands of South Dakota. Employees of the National Forests and the National Grasslands, both under the auspices of the Department of Agriculture, the National Park Service, and the South Dakota Department of Game, Fish and Parks, all have management responsibilities over large tracts of land in the Black Hills. The National Parks and Monuments are recreational in nature. The National Forests and National Grasslands are oriented to mixed-use with decisions to be made regarding issues such as grazing, mining, and logging balanced against recreational use. The South Dakota

High spring vegetation and dry summers bring the threat of fire.

© LAURAL BIDWELL

Department of Game, Fish and Parks regulates hunting and fishing and also manages several large parks, including Angostura Recreation Area and Custer State Park.

Fire

An environmental concern common to every land management agency in the Black Hills is how to respond to fire in the Black Hills. The climate most favorable to ponderosa pine forests includes high spring vegetation followed by conditions favorable to frequent summer fires, including drought and thunderstorms. Fire is important to the ecology of the grasslands and to the ponderosa pine. Fire suppression in the Black Hills was started initially to protect the timber industry. The effect of fire suppression over many years, however, was to ensure a high density of trees, which resulted in far more destructive fires when they occurred. The fires are hotter and more likely to exhibit crowning

behavior. Crowning behavior is just what it sounds like, with fire burning high in the crowns of the trees and traveling quickly from tree to tree, instead of burning slowly and low to the ground. These fires are more difficult to contain once started. As homes are built closer and closer to National Parks, Grasslands, and Forests, fire suppression becomes an important issue for the citizens of the region. All of the agencies involved have tried to balance fire suppression with fire management, frequently with controlled fires, called prescribed burns.

Mountain Lions

Predators have never fared well in South Dakota. Wolves and bears, once active in the region, have been eliminated. Coyote, on the predator/varmint list, can be hunted year-round; there is no daily or possession limit and the cost of a license is just $5. In 2005, the mountain lion, the last big predator remaining in the hills with no history of attacks on humans, was declared a game animal by the state. Since then, the number of allowable kills each season has increased dramatically. The hunting fee for mountain lion is $25, one of the most inexpensive licenses offered.

Hunters and ranchers, both powerful coalitions in South Dakota, are strong supporters of mountain lion hunting. Conservation groups are not as enthusiastic. Many believe that trophy hunting the last small population of lions left in the region is not a reasonable management philosophy. The first hunt limited the kill to a total of 25 animals, with an additional restriction of five breeding-age females. A few short years later, the number of allowable kills increased to 40 animals total, out of which 25 could be breeding females. The State Game Fish & Parks Department set the mountain lion kill for the 2013 season at 100 lions, of which 70 could be female. This is a significant increase; several cougar protection organizations have filed complaints, so far to no avail.

© LAURAL BIDWELL

a National Forest Service display on the mountain lion at Pactola Reservoir

Hunting caused the near demise of the bison, the pronghorn, and the elk in this region, but contemporary hunting organizations are generally inclined to keep populations healthy enough to allow for continued hunting. The mountain lion does not have any such protective organization. The more mountain lions are hunted, the more mountain lions will be visible as they are driven from their dens. The more visible they are, the more they will be hunted. The future of the mountain lion in South Dakota appears grim.

Uranium and Gold

After World War II, uranium became the hot ticket for mining companies. Nuclear power plants were being built and uranium was a crucial element for the power supply of the future. As a result, the price of uranium went up enough to make mining feasible. Mining in the southern Black Hills began near the Fall River County community of Edgemont. Uranium was mined and milled here beginning in 1956 and continuing through 1974, when economic factors caused the mine owners to keep the mines closed. In recent years, due to environmental concerns about global warming caused, in part, by the use of fossil fuels, interest in nuclear energy has rebounded. New nuclear reactors built in China and India have increased the demand for uranium, as well. In 2002, the price of uranium was $9.60 per pound. By September 2008, the price had risen to over $60 per pound. The 2011 earthquake and tsunami in Japan, however, which caused the Fukushima nuclear reactor to fail, caused uranium prices to tumble to around $45 per pound. That price is apparently still high enough to make uranium mining in South Dakota economically feasible.

Exploratory holes are already being drilled near Edgemont, in Fall River County, but not without protest. Three groups, Defenders of the Black Hills, Action for the Environment, and South Dakota Clean Water Alliance, are fighting the reemergence of mining in the area. The major concern regionally is the possible contamination of groundwater. However, the state legislature does not support those concerns. In 2011, a bill that suspended state rules over how uranium is mined was passed. The process has been slow, but it probably won't be long before uranium mining is once again an active industry in the Black Hills.

With the price of gold topping $1,700 per ounce, interest has also been revived in gold mining in the hills. Controversy has erupted over this possibility, since one of the sites selected for new mining permits is along the ridge of scenic Spearfish Canyon. In an area prized for its natural beauty, the specter of mining in the canyon has many in the tourism industry nervous. Lawrence County has already approved a conditional use permit for the mine proposal. Generally speaking, legislation in South Dakota has consistently been for industry over environment. There is no reason to believe that policy will change any time soon.

History

FIRST PEOPLES

It is thought that the first people to make their way into what is now South Dakota came across a land bridge from Asia, through Alaska, and then migrated south. They traveled to North America sometime 15,000–20,000 years ago. Evidence of our first peoples, Paleoindians, here in South Dakota can be traced to around 11,500 years ago. The Clovis peoples were hunters and gatherers of the Old Stone Age. Their weapons were stone and bone and they lived with and hunted giant bison, mammoths, camels, and saber-toothed tigers. Evidence of their life on the plains was uncovered on what is now the Pine Ridge Reservation. The Clovis peoples appeared just as the ice age was coming to a close. As ice age animals became extinct, hunting tools changed and a new era of hunters, called the Folsom hunters, appeared. Folsom spear points, longer and finer than Clovis points, have been found in South Dakota, though no campsites have been located. It was with these spear points that the long-lasting tradition of the bison hunt began.

Archaeological evidence has determined that about 7,000 years ago, the climate of South Dakota began to change. It had been relatively warm and comfortable, but it got much drier, with frequent droughts. Hunting expanded to include smaller game and plant foods were incorporated into the people's diet. Communities were very small. By 3,000 years ago, the weather on the plains was about the same as it is today. Bison hunts, by then, had become fairly sophisticated, with larger bands of Native Americans coming together to use traps and drives to kill larger numbers of animals. It was possible to sustain more people in a single community as the ability to procure food improved. This period, as tribes became larger, was known as the Woodland period. In the west, the woodland hunters are believed to be the predecessors to the Shoshone, Kiowa, Crow, and Cheyenne. Over time, spears gave way to the bow and arrow, pottery came into use, and the first traces of true agricultural practices appeared around A.D. 900. In A.D. 1250–1450, an agricultural people migrated from southern Minnesota. These people, believed to be the predecessors to the Mandan, Arikara, and Hidatsa, were planting corn, beans, squash, and sunflowers.

One of the most successful early tribes of the Dakotas was the Arikara. The Arikara migrated up the Missouri River Basin from Kansas and

Nebraska in the 1500s. They settled in central South Dakota, near the current location of Pierre. The Arikara built earth lodges and lived in small villages. At one time, it is believed that there were as many as 32 villages and as many as 4,000 warriors scattered along the river. The Arikara were non-nomadic and had an advanced system of trade with other tribes. They were responsible for many of the horses that were traded to the Teton Sioux, initially located to the east. Horses were brought up from the southwest by the Kiowa, Arapahoe, Commanche, and Cheyenne, and the Arikara would travel to the Black Hills on their hunting trips and pick them up for trading with other tribes.

The earliest record of the Sioux people, so closely entwined with the history of South Dakota, is from 1640, as recorded by French priests. At the time, the Sioux (so named by the Chippewa, who were French allies) were living near the headwaters of the Mississippi River. They called themselves the Dakota. There were seven different divisions of the Dakota Nation, one of which was the Teton Sioux, or Lakota. The Teton Sioux division, in turn, was comprised of seven tribes, which include the Oglala, Brule, Two Kettle, Sans Arc, Blackfoot, Hunkpapa, and Minneconjou. It is the Oglala Lakota who are recorded as being the first of the Teton Sioux to discover the Black Hills in the late 1700s. At that time, the Black Hills were occupied by the Cheyenne. The Brule were the next to move west, settling south of the Badlands. During 1776–1825, life was good for the tribes in their new location. Guns and horses had been added to their lifestyle; tipis replaced the stationary dwellings they occupied in the east; and game, particularly bison, was plentiful.

THE EUROPEANS

In the late 1600s and early 1700s, the British were developing their trading companies in the Hudson Bay area and the Spanish were active in the southwest. The Upper Missouri Valley was part of the French colonial empire until 1763. Very little attention was paid to the region, however, as the French concentrated their efforts in the Mississippi River Valley.

While the Europeans were developing their holdings elsewhere, their trade goods were making an appearance on the plains near the Black Hills, as intertribal trading brought horses north to the hills and plains, and brought other goods west from Minnesota. Beads, knives, and other iron tools were found in early Native American campsites. There were several French excursions into the Missouri River Valley, but a number of factors kept further development at bay, including run-ins with the Sioux. The first documented European exploration of South Dakota was in 1743, when French explorer Pierre Gaultier de Varennes, Sieur de La Verendrye, may have gotten to within sight of the Black Hills.

In 1763, the French ceded their interests in lands west of the Mississippi to Spain. The Spanish ownership of the lands west of the Mississippi had little impact on the region. In an attempt to oust the British incursions into the area from the north, several excursions were sent upriver from St. Louis to set up a Spanish post near the Mandans in what is now North Dakota. They met with little success. In 1800, Spain ceded the area back to France, and in 1803, France sold it to the United States.

LEWIS AND CLARK

Thomas Jefferson had long wanted to explore the West and to find a water route to the Pacific Ocean. Before the land belonged to the United States, he had asked Meriwether Lewis if he would be interested in leading an exploration expedition to the Missouri River basin with the intent of finding passage to the Pacific. Negotiations with France for the purchase of the Louisiana Territory began early in 1803; by April, an agreement was signed, and by October, this constitutionally questionable purchase was ratified by Congress. The lands purchased were bordered by the Mississippi River on the east and extended west to the Rocky Mountains and north into British North America. Virtually all of South Dakota was included in the purchase. By May 1804, Lewis and Clark were on their way up the Missouri River. They stuck with the Missouri River and didn't head into the Black Hills, but the successful expedition to the Pacific Coast fired the imagination of the American people, affirmed the United States' ownership of the Missouri River Basin, served as the starting point of negotiations with the Native American inhabitants of the West, and opened the country to the fur trade. The American expeditioners now confronted the same issues the Spanish had before them, specifically how to establish friendly relations with the Native American tribes and how to stave off any further invasion by the British into U.S. soil. Unfortunately, the relationship between white explorers and the Teton Sioux was not improved upon by the Lewis and Clark Expedition. Clark wrote in his journal:

> These are the vilest miscreants of the savage race, and must ever remain the pirates of the Missouri, until such measures are pursued, by our government as will make them feel a dependence on its will for their supply of merchandise.

THE FUR TRADE

In the early 1800s, the upper Missouri River Valley was a virtually untapped resource for fur traders. As long as the Mississippi River provided enough bounty for all, there was little motivation to tread deeper into Native American country. But as the pelts became harder to find, traders looked farther west for new resources.

Early fur trading, east of the plains, included very few buffalo hides. Introduced to the market as traders moved west, demand for the hides increased exponentially over the next few years. Safe passage through the area required the cooperation of the Native American tribes that inhabited the region—the Arikara, the Mandans, and the Sioux. When the fur trade was focused on the smaller pelts of the mink, otter, and beaver, the tribes were not particularly interested in trapping. But as demand for buffalo hides increased, the native people, particularly the Teton Sioux, joined the hunt and were active participants in the procurement of buffalo hides. The success of the fur trade was intimately tied to relationships with the Native American tribespeople and to peaceful relationships between their tribes. There were several skirmishes between tribes, however, and between the tribes and the traders, including a war in the 1820s with the Arikara, who the white traders and the Teton Sioux fought together. In 1825, the Atkinson-O'Fallon Commission traveled up the Missouri River charged with the task of negotiating treaties with the upper Missouri tribes. It was a successful expedition. The fur trade initially brought wealth to the Native American people in the form of cooking utensils, guns, and other material goods, but it also eliminated their economic stability and introduced whiskey to a population vulnerable to its abuse. By the 1850s, the heyday of the fur trade was over.

MANIFEST DESTINY

The first time the term "manifest destiny" was seen in print was in 1839, and the idea of American expansion all the way to the West Coast became popular in the 1840s. (In fact, many of the supporters of manifest destiny saw the United States occupying all of North America and Cuba.) By the 1850s, there was a steady stream of white settlers heading west. The constant river of migrants through the central plains caused tension with the Teton Sioux, who hunted from the White River region south to the North Platte. Tension turned to skirmishes, and military outposts started to crop up throughout the West. First Fort Kearney in Nebraska Territory, then Fort Laramie in Wyoming, and finally Fort Pierre in what was to be Dakota Territory were bought from failing fur companies and populated with soldiers. When it was determined that Fort Pierre was not in good enough condition to house a large military contingent, another post, Fort Randall, was established in Nebraska. These were the first military posts established in the region. Once military posts were established, exploration of the region began. Lieutenant G. K. Warren explored the country above the North Platte River and decided that continued military presence in Sioux country was important for the protection of white traders and settlers.

While the military was moving into the region west of the Missouri River, settlers in the east managed to push a bill through Congress establishing Dakota Territory in March 1861. Everything north of the 43rd parallel became part of Dakota Territory, which included the entire Upper Missouri Valley. There was no great rush to the settle the territory, however, as the nation was involved in the Civil War, and trouble with the Native American inhabitants did little to make the lands inviting. The white population of the Dakota Territory in 1860 was estimated to be about 500 people, most of whom were located in the southeastern corner of the state.

In the early 1860s, however, gold camps began to spring up in Montana and Congress authorized three roads through Dakota Territory. One of these roads was planned to cross along the southern base of the Black Hills, and one would pass by the edge of the northern Black Hills. Neither project was successful, but as a result of the gold camps, river traffic up the Missouri increased significantly, and western territories started to clamor for railroads.

In 1863, native tribes were becoming agitated by all the activity of white people in their regions. In 1863–1868, several skirmishes caused increased military activity in Dakota Territory. Beginning with the Minnesota Santee Sioux, who fled west across the Dakota Plains, unrest spread all the way to the Teton Sioux, who roamed between the Missouri River and the Powder River Valley, northwest of the Black Hills. The Cheyenne and Arapahoe tribes moved into the Powder River region, as well. The military was determined to defeat these tribes and to build a wagon road through the region. What ensued was later called Red Cloud's War, for the Oglala chief who led the fight to keep the hunting grounds free of intrusion by white people. While the military did not want peace, the civilians did, and in 1868, the treaty of Fort Laramie was signed. Under the terms of the treaty, the United States abandoned the Powder River country, the military posts were shut down, and the Bozeman Road leading to the Montana mines was closed. It was one of the few success stories for the Native American tribes. But it wasn't to last.

The terms of the treaty also allowed for the construction of a central agency to be built on agency land within the reservation lands. The agency would include a warehouse for Native American goods, a residence for the government-appointed Indian Agent responsible for ensuring that all parties follow the terms of the treaty, and additional residences for a physician, carpenter, miller, blacksmith, farmer, and engineer. The agency would also build a schoolhouse or mission building and a saw mill. Any tribesmember who wished to could select land with the guidance of the agent, if the intent was to farm it. The land would be removed from the common ownership of the tribe and be transferred to the individual, as long as that individual continued to cultivate the land. Clothing, food, and financial payments were also promised to the tribes that signed the treaty.

The treaty of 1868 was not signed by all of the Native American tribes in the regions, and most

THE TETON SIOUX

The tribe that played the biggest part in South Dakota history, particularly in the Black Hills region, was the Teton Sioux. The Teton Sioux tribe has seven subdivisions: the Oglala, Brule, Two Kettle, Sans Arc, Blackfoot, Hunkpapa, and Minnecoujou. All of these tribes played a part in the history of South Dakota. Today, all of the tribes have reservation lands set aside for them in South Dakota.

Famous Teton Sioux leaders include Red Cloud, Crazy Horse, Sitting Bull, Big Foot, and Spotted Tail. Chief **Red Cloud** was an Oglala Lakota chief who was the successful leader of the Native American campaign to close the Bozeman Trail, which passed through the hunting grounds of the Great Sioux Nation. Red Cloud was also one of the negotiators and signers of the Fort Laramie Treaty of 1868. **Crazy Horse,** a great warrior who refused to sign a treaty with the white man, was also an Oglala Lakota chief. The Oglala tribe claims the Pine Ridge Reservation as home. The reservation is located just south of Badlands National Park.

Sitting Bull was a Hunkpapa chief. Leader of the successful battle against Custer in the Battle of the Little Big Horn, also known as "Custer's Last Stand," Sitting Bull and the Hunkpapa tribe eventually settled on the Standing Rock Reservation, located on the Missouri River on the northern border of South Dakota and the southern border of North Dakota. Sitting Bull died when an attempt to arrest him was made during the days of the Ghost Dance, a ceremony that was thought would cause the white settlers to disappear, and would resurrect the traditional lifestyle and culture of the Dakota.

The Cheyenne River Reservation lands are also located along the Missouri River, just south of the Standing Rock Reservation. The Cheyenne River Reservation is home to the Minnecoujou, Two Kettle, Sans Arc, and Blackfoot. Chief **Big Foot** was a Minnecoujou chief who adhered to traditional ways. An early practitioner of the Ghost Dance, Big Foot was the chief of the tribe that was massacred at Wounded Knee in 1890.

The Rosebud Reservation, just east of Pine Ridge, is the home of the Brule tribe. **Spotted Tail** was a controversial chief who believed more in negotiation than in battle. One of the signers of the original Fort Laramie Treaty of 1868, Spotted Tail believed that the westward migration of white people was inevitable. Once the U.S. government violated the Fort Laramie Treaty, the Indian Wars of 1875-1876 resulted. After the Battle of Little Big Horn, the U.S. government was determined to crush the native tribes. Spotted Tail was successful in convincing many native people to surrender and move to reservations and agency lands. When Oglala Lakota warrior Crazy Horse was killed after his surrender at Fort Robinson, many blamed Spotted Tail.

of them did not live on agency lands. Many of the unsigned tribes would come to the agency, however, collect rations, and, on occasion, practice raids on nearby white settlers. In response, the military decided that a military outpost was needed somewhere in the Black Hills.

THE CUSTER EXPEDITION

In response to raids by Native American tribes that had not signed treaties, Lieutenant George A. Custer was placed in charge of an expedition to find a good location for a military post in the Black Hills. Custer took 1,000 men with him and approached the hills from the north. In addition to military members, there were scientists, miners, newspaper journalists, and even musicians along on what must have been one of the best provisioned expeditions in U.S. history. The expedition headed for the hills in July 1874. By July 30, two miners found traces of gold in French Creek. By August 12, the news was released by the military headquarters in St. Paul. By the time Custer returned to headquarters, just 60 days after he left, prospectors were already getting ready to violate the 1868 treaty and invade the tribal lands.

While the military was trying to keep trespassers out, the white settlers were demanding that the hills be opened, and popular sentiment in Washington was with the settlers. Arrangements were made to bring many of the Native American chiefs to Washington to persuade them to part with the hills. The chiefs were noncommittal and returned home. A scientific expedition was then sent to the hills to determine their value for the purpose of negotiation. A Grand Council was held in September 1875. Thousands of Sioux showed up for the council and promptly rejected the $6 million offered for the Black Hills. They also rejected the proposal for an annual rental payment of $400,000 a year for the mining rights to the hills. In addition to the hills, the government asked the Native American tribes to cede the Wyoming Big Horn Country. When the tribes rejected the offer, the government removed the cavalry from the region, opening the hills to the invasion of the prospectors and to a new round of Indian Wars.

THE INDIAN WARS

In late 1875, continual skirmishes with the Native American tribes were occurring in the Big Horn Mountain and Powder River regions of Wyoming, to the north and west of the Black Hills. The "hostile population" was estimated to be about 3,000 strong. Military leaders decided that the appropriate action would be a show of force that would bring the tribespeople into the agencies. General Crook initiated a campaign against the tribes in early 1876 from Fort Fetterman in Wyoming, heading for the Powder River country with only 900 troops. After an unsuccessful attack against a band of Cheyenne and a band of Oglalas under the leadership of Lakota warrior Crazy Horse, General Crook and his troops returned to the fort for the winter. As spring approached, an attack strategy was designed to overwhelm the native people with three columns of troops, one led by General Crook, one led by Colonel Gibbon, and

one led by General Terry. Lieutenant Colonel George A. Custer, serving under General Terry, was in command of the 7th Cavalry.

In May 1876, the three military columns set out from their respective bases. One of the columns, under General Crook, was attacked early on by a group led by Crazy Horse, which prevented Crook from meeting up with Terry and Gibbon. When Gibbon and Terry met, it was decided to divide the troops into two groups and attack the Native American camp from the north and south simultaneously, trapping the tribespeople between the two forces. Gibbon and Terry traveled together to attack from the south. Custer's cavalry headed out on a different path to attack from the north.

Custer arrived at the Little Big Horn River ahead of Terry and Gibbon and did not wait for their arrival, which resulted in disaster. Dividing his cavalry into three segments, Custer began his attack. Two sections of Custer's troops survived the battle, but Custer and the men who stayed with him were wiped out.

Known today as the **Battle of Little Big Horn,** or alternately as "Custer's Last Stand," it was also the last of the major battles to be won by tribal forces. Attacks against the native people resumed in August 1876. At several of the agencies, friendly tribespeople were disarmed and their ponies were taken away from them as a preventative measure. Skirmishes alternated with attempts to negotiate. In early 1877, the military went to Spotted Tail, a chief at one of the friendly Native American camps that had not been disarmed, for assistance. Spotted Tail convinced many of the native people to surrender. Some headed into Canada under the leadership of Sitting Bull, but many went to the agencies. Crazy Horse, reputed to be Spotted Tail's nephew, and his band were the last to return. They went to the Red Cloud Agency, where Crazy Horse was killed when he resisted being placed in confinement.

The Battle of Little Big Horn gave Congress

the power and popular support to pass an appropriations bill that dictated that the Sioux would not receive any further appropriations unless they gave up the Black Hills. Commissioners carried the new agreement to several agencies of the Sioux, where, without horses or weapons, the tribespeople acquiesced. Under the terms, the tribes sacrificed the Black Hills and all hunting rights in Montana and Wyoming. The native people were to be relocated to reservation lands. Many of those who had previously surrendered fled north to join Sitting Bull in Canada. Of those who remained, Spotted Tail's band relocated to Rosebud Creek and the Oglala Lakota picked their site at Pine Ridge, just west of Rosebud.

STATEHOOD

The eastern border of South Dakota was the population, agricultural, and trade center of South Dakota until the discovery of gold. Prospectors flocked to the Black Hills, first to Custer, then north to Deadwood and Lead. For about two years, the rush was on as prospectors filed claims and began a frenzied search for the metal that would make their fortunes. As the search for gold turned into the industry of mining, commerce and government expanded to serve the emerging communities. Freighters brought provisions, timber companies provided building materials, and farmers produced the food. Mining expanded from gold to other minerals including silver, galena, mica, feldspar, tin, lithium, and beryllium. Recognition of the increased population and impact on Dakota Territory came in 1883, when the legislators voted to move the state capital to Bismarck, a central location that could serve both the eastern and western corners of Dakota Territory. By this time, efforts were already underway to admit Dakota Territory to statehood. The selection of Bismarck as the new capital of Dakota Territory, however, caused much resentment in the southern parts of the territory,

and a divisionist movement began, with the desired outcome being the establishment of a separate state of South Dakota. This proposal was rejected in 1883, but voters in southern Dakota Territory approved a state constitution and elected state officers, even choosing senators for the new state. This effort was also rejected at the nation's capital.

The northern sections of Dakota Territory, much less populous than the southern sections, were initially anti-divisionist because they were concerned that separating the territory would result in the southern sections becoming a state and the northern sections being doomed to territorial status. The two sections began to work together, however, with the southern sections willing to share the Dakota name and promising to actively promote the admission of two states to the Union at the same time. This was the winning strategy, and North Dakota and South Dakota became the 39th and 40th states admitted to the Union, respectively, in 1889. The city of Pierre was appointed the temporary new capital of the state of South Dakota until 1890, when its status was finalized, and Bismarck retained its position as the capital of the state of North Dakota.

WOUNDED KNEE

The boom in population and growth of Dakota Territory, particularly the area of what became South Dakota, still had one big deterrent to growth: the separation of the eastern and western sections of the state by large reservations. White settlers pushing ever westward along the Missouri River wanted to press farther into Sioux territory. Three attempts were made to renegotiate the treaties. The first two attempts to negotiate, one in 1882 and another in 1883, clearly ignored the three-fourths signature requirements of the 1878 treaty and were rejected by the U.S. Senate. It wasn't until the Crook Commission of 1889, led by General George Crook, who was trusted by the tribes, that more lands were opened to white settlement. The Sioux agreed to move onto reservation lands that included specific boundaries. To obtain this agreement, Crook promised the tribes many things, including reparations for the horses that had been confiscated from them in earlier years.

The tribes were never paid for the horses and, at the same time that the new treaty went into effect, rations were cut. This contributed to the general unrest on the reservations, particularly among the Sioux tribes at the Pine Ridge and Cheyenne Reservations, who were among the last to be forced onto reservation lands. At the same time, word was reaching the tribes of a new native religion arising in Nevada, a religion punctuated by the Ghost Dance, a ceremony that was supposed to bring back the buffalo and return the plains to the native people. A band of Cheyenne headed to Nevada to meet with Wovoka, the new messiah of the religion, and upon its return, introduced the dance to the Pine Ridge Reservation.

The Ghost Dance frightened white settlers and the Indian Agent in charge at Pine Ridge, who called for military assistance. In 1890, the cavalry, remnants of the 7th Cavalry that was defeated at Custer's Last Stand, entered reservation land to stop the dance. Their first act was the attempted arrest of Sitting Bull, who resisted and was killed. Word of Sitting Bull's death spread quickly, and Chief Big Foot and his band fled south to the Badlands fearing attack. When the cavalry caught up with them, they had already flown the white flag and the cavalry escorted the band to the small village of Wounded Knee. That night, Hotchkiss guns (an early form of machine gun) were set up on the ridge overlooking the valley. In the morning, the cavalry entered the camp with the intent of disarming the band. A shot was fired and, though no one was injured and most of the tribespeople had already surrendered their weapons, the cavalry attacked, killing at least 200 native people, many of whom were women and children.

The Wounded Knee Massacre created much public outcry, and a review was made of many of the policies in place regarding the hiring of agency personnel, the distribution of rations, and other issues. Assimilation of the native people into white culture remained the predominant policy approach. The Dawes Act of 1887 was designed to introduce the concept of private property to the tribes. It was also a way for the government to seize more native lands. Dawes believed that private property, a concept alien to Native American culture, would serve to civilize the native tribes. The act gave the government the power to survey the land and then to allot it to tribe members, essentially eliminating tribal lands and creating private property within the reservation boundaries. The underbelly of the new act was that once the allotments were doled out, the remainder of the reservation land was considered to be surplus land and was available for sale. The end result of the Dawes Act was dramatic. The amount of land held by native people on reservation lands nationwide decreased from 138 million acres in 1887, when it was enacted, to just 48 million acres by the time it was repealed in 1934.

CONTEMPORARY TIMES

The early 20th century saw the state of South Dakota fall in with national trends. When World War I began, South Dakota created a State Council of Defense that encouraged increases in food production and set quotas for fundraising for the war effort, primarily through the sale of war bonds. South Dakota did quite well in both regards, far exceeding food production requests and fundraising quotas.

The 1920s and 1930s brought economic disaster to South Dakota, particularly to the east. In the early 1920s, income from farming decreased significantly and, as a result, farm properties lost value. Farmers were unable to service their debts. Bank failures were not uncommon by 1923, and when the stock market crashed in 1929, South Dakota was already reeling. The Great Depression of the 1930s was not the only disaster to strike the Dakotas at the time. Grasshoppers, drought, severe winter weather, and crop failures added to the already impossible circumstances of farmers. Over 30,000 farm foreclosures occurred in the 1920s and early 1930s. The population of the state declined more than 7 percent as people abandoned their property. Workers in the Black Hills, tied more to mining than agriculture, particularly in Deadwood and Lead, saw shorter hours, but miners were still working and rode through the Great Depression relatively unscathed.

Implemented in the early 1930s, the New Deal farm legislation brought relief in the form of government subsidies and rewards for low production in order to raise prices. It also brought some interesting projects to life. The Works Progress Administration (WPA) put over 3.5 million Americans back to work. One of the projects administered by the WPA was the Federal Writers' Project, which employed over 6,500 people to write about the geography, history, and culture of each state. The WPA guide to South Dakota is still in print today. The Civilian Conservation Corps (CCC), another New Deal project, was also active in South Dakota. There were over 26,000 South Dakotans who worked in the camps at one time or another. The majority were put to work on projects in the Black Hills. Some of the major projects of the camps included the fire towers at the top of Harney Peak and Mount Coolidge, and Dinosaur Park in Rapid City. The buildings used to house the actors and staff of the Black Hills Playhouse in Custer State Park originally comprised a CCC camp. At the end of the Great Depression, the need for the CCC no longer existed, and the program was discontinued in 1942.

World War II had long-term effects on South Dakota. Deadwood and Lead suffered during the war, when the Homestake Mine was ordered to stop producing gold while the war was on. Many of the miners left to work in the copper mines or to join the armed forces, and populations shrunk in these towns. After the war, however, mining techniques were upgraded and gold mining resumed. Several military installations created in the state remained as permanent bases after the war was over. In the Black Hills area, Ellsworth Air Force Base in Rapid City and the Black Hills Ordnance Depot in Igloo, located south of the town of Edgemont, brought increases in population and employment.

National trends in the 1950s and 1960s affected South Dakota and its rural and urban communities. The search for hydroelectric power brought four large dams to the Missouri River in the 1950s, and provided much work for South Dakotans. However, the dams swallowed 500,000 acres of land, about half of which was owned by the Native American tribes located on the Missouri, and once again, reparations were minor. In the 1960s, the heightening Cold War kept Ellsworth Air Force Base in Rapid City fully occupied as over 150 intercontinental missile silos were installed and managed by base personnel. The 1960s also brought two interstate highways to the state, one of which, I-90, was of major import to the Black Hills region, connecting as it did the more populous eastern cities, including those in Nebraska and Minnesota, to the Black Hills. With the increase in automobile travel and truck freighting, however, the importance of the railroad for passenger travel disappeared. By the late 1960s, there were no longer any passenger rail cars traveling to South Dakota.

Lakota Activism

The early 1970s brought an air of discontent and the creation of many social organizations, many of them militant, to the United States. The Students for a Democratic Society, the Black Panthers, and the American Indian

Movement all were known to use violent means to bring awareness to social issues of the day. In 1973, the American Indian Movement (AIM) came to South Dakota. In February 1973, members of AIM took over the community of Wounded Knee, protesting corrupt government. FBI agents were sent to remove the AIM occupiers and a siege ensued. For 71 days, AIM held the community; two people were killed, 12 were wounded, and 1,200 were arrested. The event attracted worldwide attention to the plight of Native Americans in the United States. A subsequent trial of AIM leadership relating to the events at Wounded Knee resulted in the acquittal of all charges of wrongdoing.

For over 100 years, the Sioux argued that the 1877 act ratified by Congress was an illegal act, breaking the 1868 Treaty of Fort Laramie, and that the Black Hills should be returned to the Lakota. The Sioux filed a lawsuit in 1920, the soonest this avenue was open to them, claiming that the Black Hills were taken without just compensation and triggering a legal battle that continues, on the strength of continuous appeals, to this day. In July 1980, however, a small victory was handed to the Oglala Lakota. The Supreme Court of the United States ruled as follows:

> In sum, we conclude that the legal analysis and factual findings of the Court of Claims fully support its conclusion that the terms of the 1877 Act did not effect "a mere change in the form of investment of Indian tribal property."...Rather, the 1877 Act effected a taking of tribal property, property which had been set aside for the exclusive occupation of the Sioux by the Fort Laramie Treaty of 1868. That taking implied an obligation on the part of the Government to make just compensation to the Sioux Nation, and that obligation, including an award of interest, must now, at last, be paid.

The amount due was to be $17.1 million plus interest from 1877. The money has never been collected, as the Sioux believe the Black Hills should be returned to them. This decision has been appealed and the lawsuits continue today.

South Dakota Today

In 1930, the state of South Dakota had a population of about 690,000. The Great Depression, the droughts, and the grasshoppers that attacked the state in 1930–1940 reduced the population of the state by 50,000 people. It wasn't until 1990 that the state population regained its 1930 numbers. Today, the state of South Dakota has a population of approximately 804,000 people, 27 percent of whom live in either Sioux Falls or Rapid City. While the state continues to increase in population, the increase is primarily in the urban areas. Rural counties are getting older, and young people are leaving the state. A conservative state, South Dakota has voted Republican in the last 11 presidential elections. However, this does not make the state predictable on all conservative issues. In the decade ended in 2009, voters twice rejected attempts to make abortion illegal in the state, and passed legislation to ban smoking in all public establishments including casinos and bars. It is a state where conservatives are likely independent and unpredictable. In order to attract more financial institutions to the state, the legislature removed restrictions on interest rates and successfully lured many credit card companies to Sioux Falls, making financial services an important part of the state's gross domestic product. Still, the state's economy remains entwined with the industries of its past: agriculture, ranching, mining, government services, and tourism.

Economy

The Black Hills developed as a natural resource–rich island surrounded by the grasslands of South Dakota and Wyoming. Early industries, including mining, logging, farming, ranching, and tourism, remain major sources of revenue for Black Hills communities to this day. The community of Rapid City, the only major urban area in the region, continues to provide the bulk of the area's services, including health care, retail sales, and financial services. Rapid City is also host to the only commercial airport in the area.

MINING

The early 1900s saw most of the activity related to the mining of gold disappear in the Black Hills. Mining did not disappear entirely, however. In addition to gold, the Black Hills region is rich in other minerals; into the 1950s, the Black Hills led the nation in the production of mica, feldspar, and beryl. Today, there are 43 active mines in the state. Gold remains the leading mineral commodity in the state, in terms of value, even though there is only one active gold mine. In 2008, Wharf Resources, with a mine located near Lead in the Northern Hills, produced 60,665 ounces of gold, with a gross value of $57.9 million. Wharf Resources has been mining in South Dakota since 1982. Today, total mining in the state is estimated to bring in $200 million. The continued escalation of the price of gold may encourage new mining projects in the hills. Currently, new mine permits near the location of Wharf Resources have been filed and are likely to be approved.

TOURISM

In 1875, the Bureau of Indian Affairs sent an expedition into the Black Hills that explored the region south of the areas visited by the Custer Expedition of 1874. Reports of warm water springs in the area of what is now Fall River County began to circulate in the hills. As the gold rush slowed in the Northern Hills, many of the successful individuals in Deadwood began to look for opportunities elsewhere in the hills and the idea of a warm water resort appealed to many of them. By 1881, an investment group dedicated themselves to the development and marketing of the community. As word got out, a steady stream of travelers came to the area to enjoy the mineral waters. At the time, medical tourism—visiting mineral spas—was a popular pastime, and drinking and soaking in the water was said to cure just about every possible ailment. Most of the beautiful sandstone buildings that exist today in Hot Springs were built 1890–1910. The railroad brought travelers to the town by 1891. Hot Springs was the first tourist town in the hills. Today, Evans Plunge, built in 1890, remains one of Hot Springs' major attractions. In the late 1800s, the State Soldiers' Home and the Battle Mountain Sanitarium were built in Hot Springs, due primarily to the healing properties attributed to the mineral water. Today, the Soldiers' Home is the State Veterans' Home and the Battle Mountain Sanitarium is the Veterans' Hospital. Spas, massage therapy, and natural foods are still a part of the Hot Springs economy today.

As miners prospected for gold and other minerals in the Black Hills, a second element for tourism arose: caves. Both Jewel Cave and Wind Cave were not mineral-rich enough to mine, but the caves themselves were interesting and cave tours became the second tourist attraction in the hills.

In 1916, Peter Norbeck was elected governor of South Dakota. Norbeck was a progressive and a conservationist, and during his tenure, he was able to convince the legislature to create

How to attract visitors to South Dakota? Carve a mountain.

© LAURAL BIDWELL

a state park board. As chairman of that board, Norbeck was able to work with the committee to ensure that Custer State Park would be one of the largest state parks in the nation. He also designed scenic highways through the park to make the land accessible to the public.

The crowning achievement of South Dakota tourism was the hiring of Gutzon Borglum to carve a mountain in the state. The idea was instigated by Doane Robinson, state historian, who believed that South Dakota could benefit from the increased use of automobiles if it could come up with a great attraction. Reading about the Stone Mountain carving of Confederate heroes in Georgia, Robinson contacted the carver on that project, Gutzon Borglum, to see if he might be interested in a project in the Black Hills. Initially, Robinson envisioned several carvings in the spires of the Needles formation, honoring both Native American and white heroes. Borglum determined that the spires were too fragile for that kind of work, and selected

Mount Rushmore instead. He also decided that a more national theme was needed to attract people to the area, and picked the presidents who would grace the mountain. The carving started in 1927 and was completed in 1941. Today, over three million visitors a year visit the monument. In addition to the attraction itself, the carving brought new economic life to the defunct mining communities of Hill City and Keystone, which now service visitors with retail shops, dining establishments, and accommodations.

Today, tourism is a growing industry in the state of South Dakota. By 2008, state tourism dollars reached $967 million. In 2010, income from tourism topped 1.059 billion. Today, the travel and tourism industry is the second largest industry in the state and the third largest private sector employer.

CATTLE RANCHING

The relocation of the Oglala and Brule Sioux tribes to reservation land, and the near

open-range ranching

extinction of the bison herds as a result of the fur trade, opened the front range of the Black Hills to cattle. The range cattle industry began in Texas, where huge herds roamed the plains. As rail lines made their way into the Midwest, the cattle were driven north to the rail yards where they were shipped east. Demand for the cattle as provisions in the Black Hills region increased, as well, both for the rations provided to the reservation tribes and for the growing communities. In 1880, the Black Hills Live Stock Association was founded, and by the end of 1882, it was estimated that over 250,000 head of cattle were grazing along the front range of the hills. Farther north, there were still enough bison to halt cattle grazing. In 1880–1886, professional hunters engaged in the slaughter of most of the remaining bison on the plains, allowing the cattle companies to expand into the northern plains. By 1884, the number of cattle grazing the plains that surrounded the Black Hills was estimated at over 700,000 head.

The fortunes of the great cattle companies changed dramatically during the winter of 1886–1887, when early winter storms struck the region. Heavy snows were followed by days of sub-zero weather. The storm caused huge losses, driving many of the cattle companies out of business. Northern companies lost as much as 90 percent of their herds. Custer County and Fall River County, protected by the hills, saw negligible losses.

Another problem facing cattle companies was created by the introduction of homesteaders to South Dakota. While the Homestead Act of 1862 started migration into South Dakota, most homesteaders were initially limited to the eastern corners of the state, and most were coming from neighboring states. With the completion of the railroad to Rapid City from the east in 1883, and from Nebraska in 1886, homesteaders trickled into the Black Hills region, claiming what had previously been public domain lands and putting up fences. Cattle owners frequently found their herds fenced out of watering holes and the land available for open range grazing was diminishing rapidly. At first, the cattle companies leased lands from the reservations, but soon, with the Crook Commission, more lands were open to white settlement and the available range diminished even further. The population of "West River" increased from about 45,000 in 1900 to over 135,000 by 1910. By 1911, the herd law, which held owners of livestock responsible for damages to crops, was applicable everywhere, and the open range period in South Dakota history was over.

While the huge cattle ranches of the past are no longer with us, ranching remains an important industry in western South Dakota. The state's gross domestic product for animal and crop production is over $3.5 billion.

NEW INDUSTRIES

The towns of Deadwood and Lead were long dependent on the mining industry for their survival. By the early 1900s, most of the gold mines in the region were closed or working on limited production schedules. During World War II, all gold mining was shut down temporarily under orders from the U.S. government, and miners left to work in copper mines elsewhere, or enlisted to help in the war effort. Mining resumed after the war, but both production and employment numbers continually declined. Deadwood's population decreased from around 3,000 in 1960 to 1,800 by 1990. As the population shrank, local businesses were shuttered. In 1986, a community group called "Deadwood U Bet" was created, advocating

small stakes gambling in Deadwood. The group was successful and in November 1989, small stakes gambling was legalized. The community, designated a National Historic Landmark in 1961, was determined to use a portion of the revenue earned to save the historic structures in town. As a result of that commitment, most of the historic buildings in the community have been completely renovated. It is estimated that the legalization of gambling in the community created nearly 2,000 new jobs. Approximately 27 percent of the new jobs were held by residents of Lead, but the bulk of the benefit of the gambling initiative has gone to Deadwood. The population decline continues in the county, however, with a decrease of 4.5 percent in the population 2000–2008. However, with the tax revenue generated by the casinos, Deadwood has been able to save its historic buildings and work on establishing the town as a center of tourism. Lead has not yet found the key to economic growth, except as a bedroom services city for Deadwood.

Another new industry coming to the hills is scientific research. After the Homestake Mine, located in Lead, closed in 2002, the National Science Foundation selected the mine as the location for the Deep Underground Science and Engineering Laboratory. Here, experiments in physics (dark matter) will be performed and the site will be a center for mining research, as well as research in geology and biology. The community and many surrounding communities are hoping this facility will pave the way for more science and research facilities in the future.

ESSENTIALS

Getting There and Around

The best way to get around the Black Hills region is by car. For those who don't want to do all the driving, it is possible to arrange for day trips to the Badlands, Deadwood, Custer State Park, and Mount Rushmore through several small tour companies in the region. For visitors planning just 1–3 days in the hills, the tours may be all you need.

BY AIR

There is one commercial airport in the Black Hills region and that is the **Rapid City Regional Airport** (RAP, 605/393-9924 for airport information, 605/393-2850 for flight information, www.rcgov.org/airport). There are several auto rental agencies at the airport (although almost all are divisions of the same company), including **Alamo/National** (605/393-2664), **Hertz** (605/393-0160), **Avis** (605/393-0740), **Budget** (605/393-0488), and **Enterprise** (605/393-4311). Shuttle service is available through **AirportExpress Shuttle** (605/399-9999 or 800/357-9998, www.rapidshuttle.com), which will pick up and drop off at any location in Rapid City or in the Black Hills.

BY CAR

The Black Hills region is relatively small. Major transportation routes include I-90, which enters the hills region at Rapid City; skirts along the Northern Hills past Sturgis, Deadwood, and Spearfish; and then heads off into Wyoming. Highway 79 runs north–south along the eastern edge of the hills and connects Rapid City to the southern community of Hot Springs. U.S. 18 on the south connects Hot Springs and Edgemont, and then continues west into Wyoming and Highway 85. Highway 85 travels up the western and Wyoming section of the Black Hills and cuts into the northwestern corner of the South Dakota Black Hills, joining up with I-90 near Deadwood. All in all, the Black Hills are just 65 miles wide and 125 miles north–south. Any two points within the hills is an easy day trip, though traveling through the hills can take twice as long as traveling around the edges due to the two-lane, winding roads.

one of many rock tunnels in the hills

© LAURAL BIDWELL

Within the boundaries of the Black Hills, major routes include U.S. 16, which is the direct route south from Rapid City into the Central Hills, including Mount Rushmore. U.S. 385 follows the western edge of the developed portion of the hills and runs from Hot Springs, through Custer and Hill City, and winds up halfway between Deadwood and Lead.

While you are never far from a gas station within the confines of the Black Hills, you should keep your tank full when you head out to the Badlands or to the Pine Ridge Reservation. Cell phone service is sporadic, towns are far apart, and a wrong turn can lead you miles and miles from nowhere. It's best to err on the side of caution and fill up whenever the tank is less than half full.

BY BUS AND TOUR

Rapid City has limited city-to-city bus service. **Jefferson Lines** (605/348-3300 or 800/767-5333, www.jeffersonlines.com) has one departure headed east and one departure headed west, daily. The line is the contract carrier in the Midwest for Greyhound and covers the route between Minneapolis and Billings. **Greyhound** (800/231-2222, www.greyhound.com) can get you to Rapid City, but travel times are exceedingly long. There is one bus a day from the Denver area to Rapid City, for instance, and travel time is over 13 hours. The distance from Denver to Rapid City is a little over 350 miles and can be driven in about 6.5 hours.

There are several tour companies that will arrange day trips by bus or van into the hills. Adventure tours that include biking or hiking are offered by **Black Hills Adventure Tours** (605/209-7817, www.blackhillsadventuretours.com). Standard large-bus day-long driving tours to places like the Badlands, Deadwood (for a day of gambling), or Mount Rushmore are offered by **Gray Line of the Black Hills** (800/456-4461, www.blackhillsgrayline.com) and by **Dakota Trailways** (605/642-2353 or 800/499-2652, www.mydakotatrailways.com).

There are also several smaller tour companies willing to customize tours to suit visitors' needs. These companies typically use 7–14 passenger vans as transportation. Two such companies are **Golden Circle Tours** (605/673-4349, www.goldencircletours.com) and **ABS Travel Group** (605/791-2520 or 888/788-6777, www.abstravelgroup.com).

Recreation

The Black Hills of South Dakota are an outdoor enthusiast's paradise. There are plenty of fast-running streams and lakes for fishing and water sports. The national parks and state parks are great for hiking, biking, and horseback riding, and you can also enjoy great rock climbing and exciting spelunking tours.

In particular, there are two special trails for hikers and bikers worth exploring on a visit here. The **George S. Mickelson Trail** winds 108.8 miles along the historic Deadwood–Edgemont Burlington Northern rail line, which was abandoned in 1983. The trail is gravel and, with a grade of less than 3 percent, is accessible to most mobility-impaired users. There is a fee to use the trail of $3 per day or $15 per year. You can download a trail map and obtain other information about the trail at www.mickelsontrail.com, or contact the **Black Hills Trails Office** at 605/584-3896. The Mickelson Trail is maintained by the South Dakota Department of Game, Fish and Parks.

The **Centennial Trail** is a joint project of several governmental agencies. The trail is 111 miles long and winds through much of the scenic beauty of South Dakota. The trail starts in the prairies south of Bear Butte, near Sturgis, and winds through Black Hills National Forest land, the Black Elk Wilderness Area, Custer State Park, and Wind Cave National Park. The trail is open to hiking, biking, and horseback riding (except for portions located in Wind Cave, where only hiking is allowed).

Information about both trails with downloadable maps can be found at www.gfp.sd.gov. You can find information about hunting and fishing licenses at this site, as well.

CAMPGROUNDS

In addition to private campgrounds, the Black Hills National Forest and the South Dakota Department of Game, Fish and Parks offer several campgrounds. Some of the campgrounds are on a first-come, first-served basis and some take reservations. Some are open all year and some are seasonal. For listings and information about all of the Black Hills National Forest Campgrounds, visit www.fs.fed.us/r2/blackhills and select the options recreation/camping. Information includes fees, reservation requirements, whether

© WWW.TRAVELSD.COM

camping in the Black Hills

or not the campground is open all year, and if there is drinking water available; for some, maps are available. For campgrounds that take reservations, reservations can be made by calling 877/444-6777 or going online at www.recreation.gov. Information about South Dakota State Campground facilities, which include Angostura Recreation Area and Custer State Park, can be found by visiting www.gfp.sd.gov and selecting the state parks option. To make reservations at a South Dakota state campground, call 800/710-2267 or go to www.campsd.com.

PARK PASSES

The federal government offers an annual pass, called the America the Beautiful–National Parks and Federal Recreational Lands Pass, to the public that allows entrance to any national park or federal recreation lands with an entrance fee or standard amenities fee. The cost of the pass is $80 per year for adults, and $10 for a lifetime pass for seniors aged 62 and up; the pass is free to active military on an annual basis. Access passes for travelers with disabilities are free and require proof of disability with either a doctor's note or federal disability paperwork. While the Black Hills and the Badlands contain a lot of federal lands—including Jewel Cave, Wind Cave, Mount Rushmore, the Minuteman Missile National Historic Site, and Badlands National Park—standard passes will only be honored at Badlands National Park. There are no entrance fees at any of the other sites, though you will have to pay for parking at Mount Rushmore and for cave tours at the cave sites. If this is the only area in which you are planning to visit national recreation lands in the current year, the cost of the pass may not be cost-effective. The cost to enter Badlands National Park is $15 per car, $7 for an individual hiking or biking in, and $10 for a motorcycle. All of the passes are good for seven days.

Custer State Park is also a fee area. A temporary pass is available for $6 per person or $15 per vehicle, and is good for seven days. The annual pass is $28. The Mickelson Trail, a walking/biking path that runs Edgemont–Deadwood, requires a trail pass, which costs $3 per day or $15 a year.

Tips for Travelers

ATTENDING A POWWOW

A visit to the Pine Ridge Reservation is literally a visit to another country—the reservation is a sovereign nation within the borders of the United States. It is also a place where there are a lot of people willing to share their culture with outsiders.

Attending a powwow is a wonderful way to enjoy Native American culture. It is important to respect the ceremony and the celebration of the tribes and remember that you are a guest. The participants in the dance will be wearing their finest regalia. Honor this and stay away from wearing grungy, torn clothing.

Many powwows, particularly on reservation lands, are held outdoors where there is very little in the way of public seating. Bring lawn chairs or blankets for seating. There are sometimes benches set up around the arena. These benches are reserved for dancers only. Sometimes the areas just behind the benches are reserved for family members, so ask before you set up chairs.

Some of the outfits worn by the dancers are breathtakingly beautiful. Remember to ask permission before you take pictures. Listen to the master of ceremonies for cues. Certain songs and ceremonies require the attendees to stand with heads uncovered while they are played. The Grand Entry Song, Flag Songs, Veteran Songs, and Memorial Songs all require that you stand. Attendees are free to participate in inter-tribal dances whether wearing regalia or not, but should not try to dance at any other time. Blanket dances are held at traditional pow-wows to help defray the costs of the powwows, and to help defray the travel costs of some of the drums. If you see a blanket placed on the grounds and dancers start leaving money on the blanket, feel free to contribute by asking a dancer to place money on the blanket for you. If a dancer drops or loses something off their regalia, particularly an eagle feather, do not pick it up. There are ceremonies for retrieving items that have touched the ground. Ask a dancer or other person in authority for assistance.

It sounds like a lot of rules, but the guiding principle behind attending a powwow is respect. Enjoy the dance, enjoy the food, meet people, and celebrate the beauty of a Native American powwow.

FOREIGN VISITORS

Foreign visitors to the United States must clear U.S. Customs and Border Protection (CBP) to enter the United States. There is valuable information available to foreign travelers on the CBP website at www.cbp.gov/xp/cgov/travel, including what paperwork is required to enter the United States and sample customs declaration forms that will need to be filled out on arrival.

Many banks in South Dakota are not able to exchange foreign currency. In Rapid City, Great Western Bank (14 Saint Joseph St., 605/343-9230, Mon.–Fri. 8:30 A.M.–5 P.M.) is one of the few that can exchange most foreign currencies. If you are traveling on weekends, consider exchanging funds before you leave home or at major airport connections like Denver or Chicago.

The South Dakota Department of Tourism has translated many tourist brochures into other languages, including French, German, Italian, Japanese, and Dutch. To download these brochures, visit the department's website at www.travelsd.com/about-sd/international-information. In addition to the brochures, there are website links and contact information for overseas tourism offices.

TRAVELERS WITH DISABILITIES

South Dakota is an accessible state for travelers with disabilities. Most attractions, hotels, and restaurants are equipped to accommodate visitors in wheelchairs and have set aside parking spaces and provide ramps. All of the federal parks and monuments have provided for some level of access for travelers with disabilities, including wheelchair-accessible trails. Mount Rushmore has a 27-page Braille guide to the monument available upon request from the information desk, and many of the films about the monument are both captioned for the hearing impaired and narrated for the visually impaired. Note that some of the historic buildings in some communities may not be wheelchair accessible. If you have any questions about accessibility, particularly with historic accommodations, be sure to call and ask.

GAY AND LESBIAN TRAVELERS

South Dakota is a conservative and religious state. Overt displays of physical affection are likely to make residents a little uncomfortable. This is true for both straight and gay and lesbian travelers. Be respectful of local reserve. For the most part, as a community deeply involved in hospitality, the people are extremely friendly and welcoming to everyone.

SENIOR TRAVELERS

Most attractions, museums, and many of the restaurants in the Black Hills region offer discounts to seniors, so feel free to ask about discounts even if there are no posted signs. The state also offers a discount on senior fishing licenses if you are planning a fishing outing while in the hills. Many of the hotels in the hills offer discounts to members of AARP

(American Association of Retired Persons, www.aarp.org), as well. For a $10 fee, good for life, all seniors (aged 62 and up) should consider purchasing the senior America the Beautiful—National Parks and Federal Recreation Lands Pass. In the Black Hills, it will allow you to enter Badlands National Park for free and provides a 50 percent discount on cave tours at both Wind Cave and Jewel Cave. Other federal sites in the hills may offer discounts on camping or other facilities for pass holders, as well.

The organization previously known as Elderhostel is now **Road Scholar** (800/454-5768, www.roadscholar.org). This organization has historically offered reasonably priced educational tours to seniors over the age of 55. The organization has lifted most of its age restrictions, but still provides activity-level requirements for the tours, to assist seniors in selecting a tour that will match their individual level of fitness.

TRAVELING WITH CHILDREN

The Black Hills region of South Dakota is geared toward family-style vacations. There are plenty of attractions geared toward children and many of them, like Dinosaur Park and Storybook Island in Rapid City, are free. There are lakes to swim and boat, and trails for hiking, biking, and horseback riding. There are miniature golf courses and trout to feed. It really is a wonderland for kids.

There are a few things to consider if you are traveling with the kids. First, if you are planning on staying at a bed-and-breakfast, check to make sure that children are welcome there, as in some instances, they are not. Second, the environment in the Black Hills region is fairly arid, so make sure that children carry and drink enough water to avoid dehydration and wear sunscreen to avoid sunburn. And finally, keep an eye on the kids when hiking in the higher elevations of the Northern Hills. Very few of the trails have guardrails and some of the drop-offs can be steep and long. This is also true in

the Badlands. The soil is loose and the cliffs are high, so make sure the children are forewarned to stay away from the cliff edges.

TRAVELING WITH PETS

Pets are allowed in many of the public parks in the Black Hills area, but the rules are sometimes very restrictive. In the Badlands, for instance, pets are allowed only in developed areas of the park (that is, on roads and in campgrounds). Pets must always be on a leash and cannot go on hiking trails or enter any of the wilderness areas of the park. At Mount Rushmore, pets, with the exception of service animals, are not allowed anywhere in the memorial. The Black Hills National Forest sites allow pets on the trails, but they must be leashed or under strict voice control. There is an additional $2 charge for animals in campgrounds. Custer State Park allows pets in campgrounds, but pets are not allowed in any of the camping cabins, lodges, or other park buildings.

You are allowed to leave your pet in an unattended vehicle, but this could be very dangerous. Summer temperatures can soar to over 100°F, and even on an 80°F day, the interior of a car can reach temperatures far above those safe for your pet. There are many pet-friendly lodgings in the Black Hills. On a day when you expect to spend a great deal of time at a site that restricts pets, confer with your host to see if you might want to leave your animal for the day, or with a local vet or kennel.

HEALTH AND SAFETY
Wind, Water, and Sun

High altitude, a semi-arid climate, lots of sunshine, and summer thunderstorms can affect your health and safety when visiting the Black Hills. First and foremost, always use sunscreen and wear sunglasses. The high altitudes of the Central and Northern Hills combined with the sunshine can cause **sunburn** in a fairly short period of time. Second, carry water. Hikers,

© LAURAL B DWELL

The Black Hills are pet-friendly, so bring the whole family.

bikers, and others who spend extended periods outdoors need to worry about both **dehydration** and **hyperthermia**. There is no water available on most hiking trails, and where there are streams or lakes, it's not safe to drink the water due to mining chemicals, farm and ranch fertilizers, and pesticides. **Hyperthermia** (overheating) can occur with too much exposure to the sun and can be a medical emergency. Symptoms can include red skin, dizziness, and vomiting. Severe cases may result in confused or even hostile behavior. Mild cases can be treated by getting out of the sun and drinking water. In more severe cases, remove restrictive clothing and splash cool water on the victim. Immersion in cool water, if there are streams or lakes nearby, will also help. Immersion in very cold water is not recommended. The best course of action is prevention. Stay hydrated, monitor your temperature, and rest in the shade frequently on days of high heat.

Conversely, **hypothermia** (overcooling) can also be a problem in the hills, though it's not as common as overheating. Evenings in the hills, especially in the higher elevations, can be relatively cool. If you are out hiking and are caught in a late-afternoon thunderstorm, wet clothing and cool temperatures can bring on hypothermia. Be prepared and carry a windbreaker or light poncho with you when hiking. Symptoms of hypothermia include shivering, slurred speech, and cold pale skin. Older adults, infants, young children, and people who are very lean are at particular risk. If you suspect hypothermia, remove wet clothing and cover up with something warm and dry. Make sure to stay out of the wind and cover the victim's head to maintain body heat. Do not give a victim alcoholic drinks or attempt to massage them into warmth. Hypothermia, like hyperthermia, can be a medical emergency.

Ankle injuries are the most common injuries sustained in the Badlands. The soils are eroding constantly and can cause sliding. Wear good footgear with strong ankle support if you expect to engage in any backcountry hiking. Be especially careful not to get too close to the edges of buttes and spires. The soil is very loose in places and you can find yourself sliding off the side of a cliff.

Insects and Animals

The **West Nile virus** is carried by mosquitoes and there have been several case of the virus diagnosed in the Black Hills. Mosquitoes are found near standing water, and are most active in the morning and at dusk; use insect repellent if planning to hike in marshy areas, or if you are camping near water.

Another disease-carrying pest commonly found in both the Black Hills and the Badlands is the **wood tick**. Ticks in South Dakota can transmit **Rocky Mountain spotted fever** and **Colorado tick fever**. With ticks, the best defense is to be watchful. Repel ticks by tucking your pants into your socks when outdoors in the spring and spray clothing and exposed skin with a tick repellent. Tuck clothing into hiking boots. Wear light colors so that any ticks that may land are easily visible. It takes several hours of feeding before a tick will transmit disease, so check frequently for ticks when you are outdoors. To remove ticks, use tweezers and pull slowly and steadily up and away from your skin. Matches do not encourage ticks to back out, contrary to common mythology. Ticks are most common in the early spring. Remember that ticks like pets, too, so if you are traveling with pets, give them a good going-over and remove any ticks you find. Some pet owners use tick collars or powders on pets and that works well.

There are few toxic creatures in the Black Hills. However, the **prairie rattlesnake** is a local resident. Keep an eye on where you are putting your feet and hands when hiking and scrambling through rock formations.

Rattlesnakes are not aggressive and are as loathe to see you as you are to see them. If you hear any rattling or hissing, back off and head in a different direction. If bitten by a rattlesnake, seek medical attention immediately. In the interim, try to stay calm and minimize physical activity to slow the venom's circulation throughout the body. Do not try to remove the venom with cutting or suction, as both actions could be more dangerous than the bite itself.

The **Western black widow spider** is one of South Dakota's few venomous arachnids. It is uncommon for people to be bitten by the spider. The bite of this spider can cause a wide variety of reactions depending on the age and condition of the person bitten. Symptoms include sharp pain at the time of the bite, which may be followed by muscle cramps, weakness, and tremor. In severe cases, nausea, vomiting, fainting, dizziness, and chest pain may result. Bites are rarely fatal, though they can be dangerous to seniors and to children. The decision to seek emergency care should be made early. If the person who was bitten by a black widow spider has more than minor pain or has whole-body symptoms, seek care at a hospital emergency room.

Problems with predatory animals are near nonexistent in the hills. Mountain lions and coyotes are present, but both are very shy of humans. There are no records of either attacking a human in the state. **Bison,** on the other hand, tend to attract trouble. Bison are free-roaming in Custer State Park, Wind Cave National Park, and Badlands National Park. This majestic animal enthralls visitors, who have a tendency to get too close to them in their quest for better photos. But, as bulky as they are, these animals are remarkably quick and agile. Keep your distance. An aggravated bison can accelerate quickly and reach speeds up to 45 miles per hour. You cannot outrun them. Be especially wary during the rut season, which overlaps tourist season, occurring late July–September.

Medical Care

There are small hospitals and medical clinics in most regions of the Black Hills. Most will provide emergency services and then transfer patients to Rapid City.

- **Central Hills:** Rapid City Regional Hospital, 353 Fairmont Blvd., 605/719-1000
- **Southern Hills:** Custer Regional Hospital, 1039 Montgomery St., Custer, 605/673-2229; Fall River Hospital, 1201 Hwy. 71 S., Hot Springs, 605/745-8910; Pine Ridge Hospital, E. U.S. 18, Pine Ridge, 605/867-3353
- **Northern Hills:** Lead–Deadwood Regional Hospital, 61 Charles St., Deadwood, 605/722-6101; Spearfish Regional Hospital, 1440 N. Main St., Spearfish, 605/644-4000; Sturgis Regional Hospital, 949 Harmon St., Sturgis, 605/720-2400

Crime

Crime rates are low in South Dakota, but keep safety in mind when traveling and follow standard safety procedures. Don't leave valuable items in hotel rooms or in clear sight on the seat of your car. Women and others traveling alone should exercise the same caution that they would on a downtown street in any city. Be alert.

Information and Services

TOURISM INFORMATION

The South Dakota Department of Tourism is a great resource and can be reached at 800/S-DAKOTA (800/732-5682, www.travelsd.com). Free visitor packages can be obtained by calling or making contact through the website. The state of South Dakota is dedicated to increasing tourism to the state and has committed a great deal of resources to accomplish that end.

The South Dakota Department of Game, Fish and Parks (www.gfp.sd.gov) can provide information about parks and recreation facilities (605/773-3391) and hunting and fishing licenses (605/223-7660), and can help make reservations at state campgrounds (800/710-2267).

MAPS

It is easy to become directionally impaired in the hills, particular in the Central Hills, where the roads wind around the peaks. Almost all of the businesses in the Black Hills carry a regional map of the Black Hills created by the Black Hills, Badlands and Lakes Association. This relatively simple map is a great help, so keep one in your glove compartment or travel pack. In addition to the regional map, most of the towns in the hills have street maps available at Chamber of Commerce offices.

For hikers, bikers, and other recreation fans, some of the best trail and recreational information can be downloaded for free from the websites of the National Forest Service (www.fs.fed.us) and National Park Service (www.nps.gov). In addition to hiking and biking guides, the National Forest Service has campground guides, recreation area guides, snowmobile trail guides, and other information about recreation opportunities in the Black Hills National Forest. There are four National Forest offices in the Black Hills: in Spearfish (605/642-4622), in Custer (605/673-4853), in Rapid City (605/343-1567), and at Pactola Reservoir (605/343-8755, Memorial Day–Labor Day). The Forest Supervisor's Office is also in Custer and can be reached at 605/673-9200. Regional hiking and biking maps are also available at the visitors centers in all of the National Recreation spots in the hills, including Jewel Cave,

Mount Rushmore, Wind Cave, Custer State Park, and Badlands National Park.

BUSINESS HOURS

Most restaurants, attractions, and retail shops geared toward tourism are open seven days a week Memorial Day–Labor Day. Closing times vary, but most attractions are open until 8 P.M., retail shops until 6 P.M., and restaurants are generally closed by 9–10 P.M. In some of the smaller towns, however, Sunday can be iffy for retail. If you are planning on a day of shopping, try to fit that in Monday–Saturday to avoid disappointment.

The shoulder of the tourist season—comprising early May, September, and October—generally brings shorter hours for all tourist-related industries and more Sunday closures for retail. Most restaurants, hotels, and attractions remain open through at least October 15. The winter season brings a lot of closures. It is always a good idea to call for information before you head to any particular location October–April. Season's end can vary with weather or traffic patterns.

MONEY

There are still a few locations, particularly in the smaller towns, that do not take credit cards. Glance at an establishment's doors and windows for stickers that identify the kinds of charge cards a store or restaurant will accept; if there is nothing in the window, be sure to ask. Cash works best in those spots, and you'll find that most towns have ATMs. Traveler's checks are accepted everywhere, though in most locations in the Black Hills, only local personal checks will be accepted.

Prices marked on all goods for sale in South Dakota do not reflect sales taxes. The state sales tax is 4 percent, there is a 1.5 percent tourism tax for many industries during the summer months, and there are city sales taxes, as well, which add another 1–2 percent.

There are many categories of personal service workers who receive monetary tips for their services. Restaurant workers and taxi drivers typically receive 15–20 percent of the bill, and bellhops and airport porters expect to receive $1 per bag. If you elect to take a tour, it is appropriate to tip tour guides and/or drivers. For van tours, a nice tip is $5 per person, though don't be afraid to contribute more if the tour was exceptionally fun and informative. For large motorcoach tours, a reasonable tip is in the range of $3 per person.

CELL PHONES

Cell phone reception in the Black Hills is sporadic. While reception is fine in most of the local communities, once you get into some of the more remote locations, like the Badlands and the wilderness areas of the state, signals can frequently be blocked. If you are planning to do any backcountry hiking or camping, remember to notify rangers of your plans. If you run into trouble, you may not be able to call anyone.

ELECTRICITY

Most electrical outlets in the United States use 110–220 volt electricity. Most outlets are three-pronged with two flat and one round grounding prong. Older buildings may have just two-pronged plugs. In those circumstances, most hardware stores will have a converter that will allow you to use a three-pronged appliance in an older outlet.

RESOURCES

Suggested Reading

There are several small presses in the West that publish interesting books about South Dakota and the Plains. Two of the best include the South Dakota Historical Society Press (605/773-6009, www.sdshspress.com) in Pierre and the University of Nebraska Press (402/472-3581, www.nebraskapress.unl.edu).

The Internet has made it possible for just about anyone to find just about any book, even if it is out of print. A few of the books listed here have gone out of print, but are still readily available online, either new or used. If a book is out of print or hard to find, it's noted.

RECREATION
Hiking and Mountain Biking

Gildart, Bert and Jane Gildart. *Best Easy Day Hikes Black Hills Country.* Guilford, CT: Globe Pequot (Falcon), 2006. A pocket-sized, compact guide to some very nice hiking in the hills.

Gildart, Bert. *Hiking the Black Hills Country: A Guide to More Than 50 Hikes in South Dakota and Wyoming (Hiking the Black Hills Country).* Guilford, CT: Globe Pequot (Falcon), 2006. Even more hikes in the Black Hills, for the avid fan.

Knapp, Andy. *Mountain Biking the Great Plains States.* Guilford, CT: Globe Pequot (Falcon), 1996. Included in this guide are 12 Black Hills mountain biking trails with good

maps to the trailheads. The book is currently out of print, but easily obtained online.

Rock Climbing

Junek, Bruce. *Rock Climbing Guide, Spearfish Canyon Limestone.* Boulder, CO: Sharp End Publishing, 2003. This book outlines 308 climbing routes in Spearfish Canyon.

Stephens, Lindsay. *South Dakota Needles: Adventure Climbs of Herb and Jan Conn.* Boulder, CO: Sharp End Publishing, 2008. Herb and Jan Conn were East Coast visitors who fell in love with rock climbing in the Needles. This book includes more than 240 climbing routes in the Needles area. Note that after the Conns conquered the rocks, they headed for the caves, and were instrumental in expanding the known area of Jewel Cave.

NATURAL HISTORY

Jennings, Bob. *Birds of the Great Plains.* Auburn, WA: Lone Pine Publishing, 2005. Though smaller than the *North American Birds Guide,* 325 different birds are listed.

Kirkpatrick, Zoe. *Wildflowers of the Western Plains.* Lincoln, NE: University of Nebraska Press (Bison Books), 2008. A great little guide to wildflowers, organized by color for easy identification.

Larson, Gary and James Johnson. *Plants of the Black Hills and Bear Lodge Mountains.* Brookings, SD: South Dakota State University Publications, 2007. The definitive guide to plants in the Black Hills region, with over 600 listings.

Ode, David. *Dakota Flora: A Seasonal Sampler.* Pierre, SD: South Dakota Historical Society Press, 2006. A beautiful and lyrical look at wildflowers through the seasons of South Dakota, with full-color illustrations and wonderful prose.

Peterson, Roger Tory. *Birds of North America.* Boston, MA: Houghton Mifflin, 2008. The Black Hills region is the western outpost of Eastern birds and the eastern outpost of Western birds. To find them all, you'll need this guide.

Tekiela, Stan. *Birds of the Dakotas.* Cambridge, MN: Adventure Publications, 2003. This is a great compact guide that will fit in a jacket pocket and has good color photos for identifying most of the common birds of the region.

Wassink, Jan. *Watchable Birds of the Black Hills, Badlands, and Northern Great Plains.* Missoula, MT: Mountain Press Publishing Company, 2006. With great pictures and information about some of the more common birds of the Black Hills and surrounding plains, it's a good guide for beginning bird-watchers.

GENERAL HISTORY

Ambrose, Stephen. *Crazy Horse and Custer: The Parallel Lives of Two American Warriors.* New York, NY: Random House, 1996. From boyhood to manhood, Ambrose compares the lives of two military leaders of the Indian Wars of 1876.

Federal Writers Project. *The WPA Guide to South Dakota.* St. Paul, MN: Minnesota Historical Society Press, 2006. Originally published in 1938, this is a fascinating combination of history and road-trip guide, written by out-of-work writers during the Great Depression.

Grafe, Ernest and Paul Horsted. *Exploring with Custer: The 1874 Black Hills Expedition.* Custer, SD: Golden Valley Press, 2005. Follow in the final footsteps of Lieutenant George Armstrong Custer as he explored the Black Hills of South Dakota with 1,000 men, a band, miners, and newspaper correspondents. The book traces the expedition and is illustrated with fascinating then and now photographs. The hills haven't changed that much!

Hasselstrom, Linda. *Roadside History of South Dakota.* Missoula, MT: Mountain Press Publishing Company, 1998. Instead of being organized on a timeline, this history book is geographically oriented and offers a little history and a tale or two about smaller communities frequently overlooked in other history books.

Laskin, David. *Children's Blizzard.* New York, NY: HarperCollins Publishers, 2005. In January 1888, a late-afternoon blizzard struck the eastern plains of South Dakota and Nebraska, catching children headed home. The blizzard killed over 500 settlers. The story is told through interviews and journals of the people who lived through it.

Nester, William. *The Arikara War.* Missoula, MT: Mountain Press Publishing Company, 2001. A detailed history on the first of the Indian Wars, with a lot of information on the culture of Native American tribes of the Missouri River Basin, including the Teton Sioux, who played a major part in the history of the Black Hills.

Schell, Herbert. *History of South Dakota.* Pierre, SD: University of South Dakota Historical Society Press, 2004. A great overview of the history of the state and of the early years of the Black Hills.

NATIVE AMERICAN HISTORY AND CULTURE

Flood, Renee Sansom. *Lost Bird of Wounded Knee*. New York, NY: Perseus Press (Da Capo Press), 1998. This is the story of the only survivor of the massacre at Wounded Knee. Lost Bird was an infant when the massacre occurred and she was found alive underneath the frozen body of her mother.

Lawson, Michael. *Dammed Indians Revisited; The Continuing History of the Pick-Sloan Plan and the Missouri River Sioux*. Pierre, SD: South Dakota State Historical Society Press, 2009. It wasn't enough that the Sioux lost their nomadic lifestyle in the hills and the plains. After they were relegated to reservation land, the Pick-Sloan Plan flooded over two hundred thousand acres of bottomlands, reducing the size of the reservation with no compensation to the tribal communities that had to be relocated.

Lazarus, Edward. *Black Hills, White Justice: The Sioux Nation Versus the United States, 1775 to the Present*. New York, NY: HarperCollins Publishers, 1991. When Native Americans were forced to sign a new treaty after the Indian Wars of 1876, the Black Hills were taken illegally from the Great Sioux Nation. This book traces the history of an event that ended up being one of the longest-running court cases to be heard by the Supreme Court of the United States. You'd think it would be on the dry side? It's not. It's a head-shaking tale of treachery. This books is out of print, but available used.

Marshall III, Joseph. *The Lakota Way: Stories and Lessons for Living*. New York, NY: Penguin Books, 2002. A wonderful book of storytelling and philosophy of the Lakota culture. The book focuses on the 12 core qualities crucial to the Lakota way of living: bravery, fortitude, generosity, wisdom, respect, honor, perseverance, love, humility, sacrifice, truth, and compassion.

Niehardt, John. *Black Elk Speaks: Being the Life Story of a Holy Man of the Oglala Sioux*. Albany, NY: State University of New York Press, 2008. A powerful story of the life of Lakota healer Nicholas Black Elk and the tragic history of his people, as told to John Niehardt.

Pope, Dennis. *Sitting Bull Prisoner of War*. Pierre, SD: South Dakota State Historical Society Press, 2010. For 20 months, Sitting Bull was held at Fort Randall in South Dakota. This book fills in the gaps in his life story and reveals the day-to-day life of Sitting Bull as a captive who maintained his leadership role and his dignity in the worst of circumstances.

Sandoz, Marie. *Crazy Horse: Strange Man of the Oglalas*. Lincoln, NE: University of Nebraska Press, 2008. An in-depth look at one of the Lakota's greatest warriors, who knew that signing a treaty with the white man was an exercise in meaninglessness.

St. Pierre, Mark. *Madonna Swan: A Lakota Woman's Story*. Norman, OK: University of Oklahoma Press, 2003. Written by a current-day resident of the Pine Ridge Reservation of the Oglala Lakota Sioux, the book combines traditional culture with contemporary problems when a Lakota woman is diagnosed with tuberculosis.

Welch, James. *Killing Custer: The Battle of Little Bighorn and the Fate of the Plains Indians*. New York, NY: W. W. Norton & Company, 2007. The Battle of Little Bighorn from the tribal perspective.

RANCHERS AND PIONEERS

Blasingame, Ike. *Dakota Cowboy*. Lincoln, NE: University of Nebraska Press, 1964. Every South Dakota cowboy I've talked to cites this as the best true story of ranchers to be found.

Griffith, Tom. *Outlaw Tales of South Dakota.* Guilford, CT: Globe Pequot, 2008. A fun look at some of the disreputable characters of the Black Hills.

Hasselstron, Linda. *Feels Like Far: A Rancher's Life on the Great Plains.* Boston, MA: Houghton Mifflin, 2001. An insightful look at ranch life on the plains, written by one of South Dakota's best and most prolific writers.

O'Brien, Dan. *Buffalo for the Broken Heart.* New York, NY: Random House, 2002. A self-disclosing and fascinating look at one rancher's attempt to convert his cattle ranch to a buffalo ranch in the Black Hills of South Dakota.

Kohl, Edith Eudora. *Land of the Burnt Thigh* St. Paul, MN: Minnesota Historical Society, 1986 Reprint. Originally published in New York, NY: Funk & Wagnalls, 1938. A lively tale of single women homesteaders in the plains.

OTHER NONFICTION

Norris, Kathleen. *Dakota: A Spiritual Geography.* Boston, MA: Houghton Mifflin Harcourt, 2001. An autobiography with thoughtful reflections on the changes in climate, population, and atmosphere of the state of South Dakota in the author's lifetime.

FICTION OF THE PLAINS AND THE WEST

Looking for the flavor of the West or just looking for a great read? I can't help myself. I own a bookstore, and my specialty is fiction. Here's a list of some absolutely wonderful Western reads.

Adams, Andy. *Log of a Cowboy.* New York, NY: Penguin, 2006. This book, originally published in 1903, is a fictional tale of a cattle drive from Texas to Montana. It is said that this book was the inspiration for Larry McMurtry's *Lonesome Dove.*

Doig, Ivan. *The Whistling Season.* Boston, MA: Houghton Mifflin Harcourt, 2007. A man, assigned the task of deciding whether or not to close Montana one-room schools, thinks back to his student days in a one-room school, taught by two of the most eccentric characters you'd ever hope to meet.

Gloss, Molly. *The Hearts of Horses.* Boston, MA: Houghton Mifflin Harcourt, 2007. An awkward young woman captures the hearts of a small community with her honesty and fortitude as she works to train wild horses.

Haruf, Kent. *Plainsong.* New York, NY: Random House (Vintage), 1999. Written with the rhythm of the plains, this book explores how a place, a region, or a town can affect a life, a relationship, and a family.

Johnson, Craig. *The Cold Dish.* New York, NY: Penguin, 2005. The first in the Sheriff Walt Longmire series, an absolutely wonderful series about a small-town Wyoming sheriff. This flawed, good-hearted, honest man is a character you just have to love.

Meyers, Kent. *The Work of Wolves.* Boston, MA: Houghton Mifflin Harcourt, 2004. I don't think anyone could better depict small-town South Dakota, ranch life, and local humor better than Kent Meyers. Read this one before you visit.

Spragg, Mark. *An Unfinished Life.* New York, NY: Random House (Vintage), 2005. A story of family, friendship, and forgiveness on a Wyoming ranch.

CHILDREN'S BOOKS

Anderson, William. *M Is for Mount Rushmore: A South Dakota Alphabet.* Florence, KY: Gale–Cengage Learning (Sleeping Bear Press), 2005. A cute alphabet book and souvenir for the little ones...or the grandkids left at home.

Bruchac, Joseph. *A Boy Called Slow: The True Story of Sitting Bull.* New York, NY: Penguin (Paperstar Books), 1998. The story of how Sitting Bull got his name, for children aged 4–8.

Horner, Jack. *Digging Up Dinosaurs.* Helena, MT: Farcountry Press, 2007. Written by Montana's state paleontologist, the book is beautifully illustrated and is a fun introduction to fossil finding for kids.

Montileaux, Don. *Tatanka and the Lakota People.* Pierre, SD: South Dakota Historical Society Press, 2009. A beautifully illustrated children's book about the creation story of the Lakota people.

Robson, Gary. *Who Pooped in the Black Hills?: Scats and Tracks for Kids.* Helena, MT: Farcountry Press, 2006. This one is a big hit with the kids.

SCENERY AND PHOTOGRAPHY

Kettlewell, Dick. *Black Hills Impressions.* Helena, MT: Farcountry Press, 2004. This is a book to look for once you arrive. It's a great souvenir book for every visitor.

MAGAZINES AND JOURNALS

There aren't very many magazines published in the Black Hills, but the statewide *South Dakota Magazine* (www.southdakotamagazine.com) contains interesting specialty articles on the towns and people of South Dakota. The magazine is published bimonthly.

Internet Resources

TOURISM

South Dakota
www.travelsd.com

The state of South Dakota is determined to increase tourism, and this website is a great overview of the attractions, history, and culture of the state.

Black Hills and Badlands
www.blackhillsbadlands.com

This website offers a lot of the same information as the South Dakota tourism website (www.travelsd.com), but it also serves as a central reservation service for its members. Just be aware that not all accommodations are listed.

Central Reservations
www.blackhillsvacations.com

Here are listings of special package deals put together by local attractions, accommodations, and restaurants. Several special interest tours include those focused on fly-fishing, Native American culture, and paleontology.

RECREATION

Black Hills National Forest
www.fs.fed.us/r2/blackhills

This is a great source of information about National Forest recreation areas and campgrounds, as well as trail maps, and information about the flora and fauna of the Black Hills.

South Dakota Department of Game, Fish and Parks
www.gfp.sd.gov

Make state campground reservations, find out about hunting and fishing licenses, and learn about South Dakota wildlife here. This is a great website with a lot of free publications, including hunting and fishing handbooks, campground maps, and trail guides.

National Park Service
www.nps.gov

Find a National Park site by state anywhere in the country. A search on South Dakota will allow you to select Jewel Cave, Wind Cave,

Mount Rushmore, the Badlands, and the Minuteman Missile National Historic Site. Choosing any of these selections will bring you to websites with all kinds of information about the history, ecology, and recreational opportunities of the parks.

Great Outdoor Recreation Pages
www.gorp.com
Here is a cornucopia of information about recreation around the world. You can search by state or by activity, find guides, learn about gear, and even make flight reservations from this website.

NATURAL RESOURCES
United States Geological Survey
www.usgs.gov
Look for topographical maps of anywhere in the United States. Buy maps online. Research the natural sciences, including biology, geology, and geography. Download USGS publications. Do an advanced search on publications and input South Dakota. You'll find everything

and more about minerals in the state. Take a look at the social media tab and follow the USGS on Facebook or Twitter. Download USGS wallpapers.

PUBLICATIONS
South Dakota Magazine
www.southdakotamagazine.com
This is a great bimonthly magazine with searchable archives online. If you are interested in a specific topic or community, download the full index of articles and then order back issues. The website is a great resource for researchers and writers.

Rapid City Journal
www.rapidcityjournal.com
The only daily newspaper in the region has a good online calendar of events, some restaurant reviews (check under entertainment), and information on book signings, art galleries, and shows. This website will give you some great ideas for joining in on local cultural events and entertainment.

Index

List of Maps

www.moon.com

DESTINATIONS | ACTIVITIES | BLOGS | MAPS | BOOKS

MOON.COM is ready to help plan your next trip! Filled with fresh trip ideas and strategies, author interviews, informative travel blogs, a detailed map library, and descriptions of all the Moon guidebooks, Moon.com is all you need to get out and explore the world—or even places in your own backyard. While at Moon.com, sign up for our monthly e-newsletter for updates on new releases, travel tips, and expert advice from our on-the-go Moon authors. As always, when you travel with Moon, expect an experience that is uncommon and truly unique.

KEEP UP WITH MOON ON FACEBOOK AND TWITTER
JOIN THE MOON PHOTO GROUP ON FLICKR

MAP SYMBOLS

▦▦▦	Expressway	▐	Highlight	✗	Airfield	⚑	Golf Course
───	Primary Road	○	City/Town	✈	Airport	🅿	Parking Area
▬▬▬	Secondary Road	◉	State Capital	▲	Mountain	⬟	Archaeological Site
─ ─ ─	Unpaved Road	⊛	National Capital	✚	Unique Natural Feature	⛪	Church
- - - -	Trail	★	Point of Interest			⛽	Gas Station
··········	Ferry	•	Accommodation	⇆	Waterfall		Glacier
─▪─▪─	Railroad	▾	Restaurant/Bar	▲	Park		Mangrove
▨▨▨	Pedestrian Walkway	▪	Other Location	⬛	Trailhead		Reef
▥▥▥	Stairs	⋀	Campground	⛷	Skiing Area		Swamp

CONVERSION TABLES

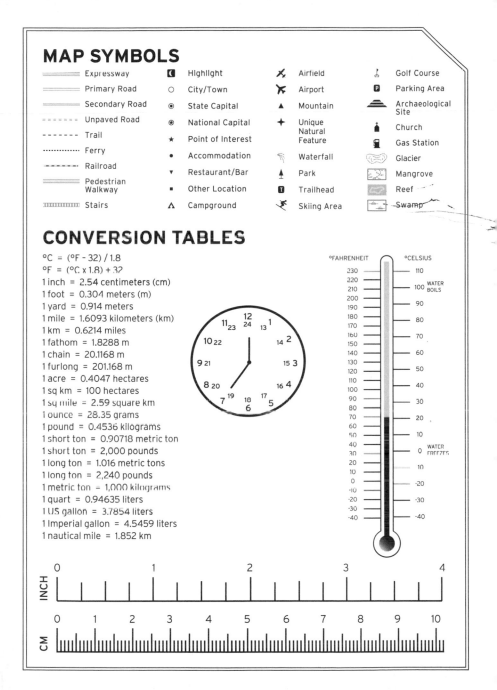

°C = (°F - 32) / 1.8
°F = (°C x 1.8) + 32
1 inch = 2.54 centimeters (cm)
1 foot = 0.304 meters (m)
1 yard = 0.914 meters
1 mile = 1.6093 kilometers (km)
1 km = 0.6214 miles
1 fathom = 1.8288 m
1 chain = 20.1168 m
1 furlong = 201.168 m
1 acre = 0.4047 hectares
1 sq km = 100 hectares
1 sq mile = 2.59 square km
1 ounce = 28.35 grams
1 pound = 0.4536 kilograms
1 short ton = 0.90718 metric ton
1 short ton = 2,000 pounds
1 long ton = 1.016 metric tons
1 long ton = 2,240 pounds
1 metric ton = 1,000 kilograms
1 quart = 0.94635 liters
1 US gallon = 3.7854 liters
1 Imperial gallon = 4.5459 liters
1 nautical mile = 1.852 km

**MOON MOUNT RUSHMORE
& THE BLACK HILLS**
Avalon Travel
a member of the Perseus Books Group
1700 Fourth Street
Berkeley, CA 94710, USA
www.moon.com

Editor: Kevin McLain
Series Manager: Kathryn Ettinger
Copy Editor: Beth Fitzer
Graphics Coordinator: Tabitha Lahr
Production Coordinator: Lucie Ericksen
Cover Designer: Tabitha Lahr
Map Editor: Albert Angulo
Cartographers: Andy Butkovic, Heather Sparks,
  Kat Bennett
Indexer: Rachel Kuhn

ISBN: 978-1-61238-296-8
ISSN: 2154-2295

Printing History
1st Edition – 2010
2nd Edition – May 2013
5 4 3 2 1

Front cover photo: profile of George Washington
  carving at Mount Rushmore National Monument ©
  Fotosearch Premium/Getty Images

Title page photo: Mount Rushmore © www.travelsd.
com
Other color photos: pages 4, 5 bottom, 8, 10, 13, 15,
17 left, 18, 19: © www.travelsd.com; pages 5, 14: ©
shaday365/123rf.com; pages 6, 7 bottom, 11, 12, 16,
17 right, 21 and 22 © Laural Bidwell; page 7 top-
left: © Jim Parkin/123rf.com; page 7 top-right: ©
Ralf Broskvar/123rf.com; pages 23 and 24: © Liane
Harrold/123rf.com

Printed in Canada by Friesens

KEEPING CURRENT

If you have a favorite gem you'd like to see included in the next edition, or see anything
that needs updating, clarification, or correction, please drop us a line. Send your com-
ments via email to feedback@moon.com, or use the address above.